D0169116

Northwestern University
STUDIES IN *Phenomenology &*
Existential Philosophy

Selected Philosophical Essays

Max Scheler

Translated, with an Introduction, by

Selected
Philosophical
Essays

DAVID R. LACHTERMAN

NORTHWESTERN UNIVERSITY PRESS
EVANSTON   1973

David R. Lachterman is lecturer in the Department
of Philosophy at Syracuse University

Contents

Translator's Introduction

No SOONER has a translator laid down the mask of his self-chosen *persona* than tradition insists on his taking up still another, that of a spokesman for the author or the work he has translated. The tropes of this second art are various and venerably familiar. The author in question is an unjustly neglected figure in the development of the subject. Or his work had a seminal influence on his contemporaries or on his successors; his intellectual career mirrors the political and cultural tensions and predilections of his own age. Or his philosophical positions seem remarkably to prefigure those taken by contemporary thinkers. The list can, of course, be extended.

The translator of Max Scheler (1874–1928) could, in reasonably good conscience, tailor any or all of these to fit his subject. And yet, if he chooses to move out of this twilight world of historical influences and adumbrations, if he is, to some extent, concerned to readmit Scheler into the "living speech" of present-day philosophizing, then the obstacles in his path cannot be overlooked. Thus it seems prudent to begin on what might strike some as a queer and ill-chosen note and ask: is it any longer worthwhile to read Scheler as a philosopher?

Let me begin by trying to say why this question seems unavoidable.

The problems of philosophical appropriation, of making a philosophical work or idea one's own, match in complexity those of interpretation. Indeed, one is tempted to suggest that the two sets of problems interpenetrate: it is, at least in part, at the urging of one's own philosophical concerns that a body of past philosophical work begins to open itself to interpretation. To say this is to say only that one's own questions offer an initial *entrée* to the texts. It is not to say that the consequent interpretations are complete or binding, nor is it to commit one, straightaway, to any version of historicism. Most important, this suggestion is not intended to depreciate the role played by one's sense of the strangeness of certain texts of the past (or, for that matter, of the present) in encouraging a more penetrating interpretation and, as a result, in reshaping, perhaps completely, the questions asked of those texts. Furthermore, the dangers latent in this way of approaching a philosophical work should be evident. As Scheler says in another context, if, *as soon as* I hear another person speaking to me of his own experiences, I think "The same thing happened to me!" I may no longer be really listening to what he is saying. Still, the possibility of philosophically appropriating the text turns on the reader's eventual identification of what is said in it as within the compass of his most generous intellectual sympathies. The more remote this eventuality appears, the more closed the work must seem not only to interpretation but to appropriation as well.

One circumstance in which a philosophical work may be more readily accessible is the existence of an ongoing "tradition" of discussion and commentary. By virtue of such a tradition, the ways in which a work of the past is germane to the philosophical inquiries of the present are more immediately manifest. There is, needless to say, no guarantee that the essential thought of the work is captured or exhausted in this historical tradition. And it is certainly not the case that the philosophical significance of the work in question *is* the tradition which has issued from it. Nonetheless, when a work has become a part of a continuing tradition, the distance between it and "contemporary" thinking is, at least initially, reduced. Thus, Scheler's opaque position in the history of twentieth-century philosophy makes it even more likely that his work may remain an utterly "closed book" for many readers.

To many of his contemporaries Scheler seemed the outstanding philosophical talent of the age. He commanded the attention and respect not only of Husserl and Heidegger but also of Martin Buber, Ortega y Gasset, Nicolai Hartmann, Ernst Cassirer, H.-G. Gadamer, Alexander Koyré, and Karl Löwith. The theoretical program of phenomenology first articulated by Husserl in his *Logical Investigations* (1899–1901) seemed to have come to its most productive fruition in Scheler's variegated works. When he spoke, at the end of the essay, "Versuche einer Philosophie des Lebens," [1] of the "faint beginnings of the reformation of Europe's *Weltanschauung* and thus of its concept of the world," there is no question but that Scheler saw himself as one of those who would bring this movement to completion.

Today, it is impossible to speak of a Schelerian school or tradition in European philosophy, at least not in the way one can speak of a Husserlian and a Heideggerian tradition. Scheler's works and ideas are not the focal point of ongoing discussion and analysis,[2] nor have they been so much absorbed

1. "Versuche einer Philosophie des Lebens," *Die Weissen Blätter*, I (November, 1913), 203–33. Reprinted in *Vom Umsturz der Werte*, 4th ed. rev., *Gesammelte Werke* III (Bern: Francke, 1955), 311–41.

2. This is not to say that there have not been some excellent works written on Scheler's philosophy. Of works which cover it as a whole, the three most helpful are Gerhard Kraenzlin, *Max Schelers phänomenologische Systematik* (Leipzig: Hirzel, 1934); Maurice Dupuy, *La Philosophie de Max Scheler: Son évolution et son unité* (Paris: Presses Universitaires de France, 1959); and Manfred S. Frings, *Max Scheler: A Concise Introduction into the World of a Great Thinker* (Pittsburgh, Pa.: Duquesne University Press, 1965). Other valuable studies are Alfred Schutz, "Max Scheler's Epistemology and Ethics," in Schutz, *Collected Papers*, Vol. III (The Hague: Nijhoff, 1966); Manfred S. Frings, *Person und Dasein*, Phaenomenologica XXXII (The Hague: Nijhoff, 1969); Frings, *Zur Phänomenologie der Lebensgemeinschaft: Ein Versuch mit Max Scheler* (Meisenheim am Glan: Hain, 1971) (Supplement to *Zeitschrift für philosophische Forschung*, no. 24); Frings, "Max Scheler: Rarely Seen Complexities of Phenomenology," in *Phenomenology in Perspective*, ed. F. J. Smith (The Hague: Nijhoff, 1970); and Eiichi Shimomissé, *Die Phänomenologie und das Problem der Grundlegung der Ethik: An Hand des Versuchs des Max Scheler* (The Hague: Nijhoff, 1971). Herbert Spiegelberg, *The Phenomenological Movement* (The Hague: Nijhoff, 1960), has a good section on Scheler, as does Wolfgang Stegmüller, *Main Currents in Contemporary German, British and American Philosophy* (Bloomington: Indiana University Press, 1970). More critical studies include John Findlay, *Axiological Ethics* (London: Macmillan, 1970); Roman Ingarden, "Was wir über die Werte nicht wissen," in *Erlebnis, Kunstwerk und Wert, Vorträge zur Ästhetik, 1937–1967* (Tübingen: Niemeyer, 1969); and Michel Henry, *L'Essence de la manifestation* (Paris: Presses Universitaires de France, 1963), II, 715–35. A full bibliography of works by and about Scheler can be found in Wilfred Hartmann, *Max Scheler—Bibliographie* (Stuttgart: Frommann, 1965). A supplement to the work is given in Frings, *Zur Phänomenologie der Lebensgemeinschaft*.

into general philosophical awareness as to be recognizable despite their anonymity. Common opinion seems to regard Scheler only as a historically important transitional figure between the phenomenologists (of the Munich school) and the Heidegger of *Being and Time*.

In the English-speaking countries Scheler is still very close to being an unknown quantity.[3] It is only in Latin America, owing, no doubt, to Ortega's influence, that Scheler's ideas have wide currency.[4]

This state of affairs does not simply register the contingencies of intellectual history but seems to me to reflect difficulties inherent in Scheler's work itself. To bring these to light may seem unencouraging, especially in an introduction to newly translated works by him. Nonetheless, the question of the accessibility (and possible appropriation) of Scheler's philosophy cannot, I believe, be answered unless these difficulties are candidly discussed.

These difficulties can be conveniently exposed under three headings: the present state of the Schelerian *corpus;* Scheler and foundational thinking (Husserl and Heidegger); Scheler and "analytical" philosophy.

1. A survey of the body of Scheler's extant writings undoubtedly leaves the present-day reader with an impression of "chaos." There is, I believe, much external and some internal justification for this impression.

At the time of his rather sudden death in 1928, Scheler had published eleven books and a considerable number of essays and articles. He also left behind a large quantity of unpublished manuscripts, notebooks, and loose pages. His widow, Maria Scheler, with the support of an editorial committee originally headed by Martin Heidegger, undertook the task of producing a complete and uniform edition of his published and unpublished writings, to comprise thirteen volumes in all.

Cooperative work on this project was ended by the political

3. My point is perhaps well illustrated by the fact that John Passmore's *A Hundred Years of Philosophy* (London: Duckworth, 1957) contains only two minor footnote references to Scheler.

4. Thus, Hector D. Mandrioni, in his book *Max Scheler: Un estudio sobre el concepto de "espirito" en el Formalismus de Max Scheler* (Buenos Aires: Itinerarium, 1965), can speak without irony of "la ubicación de Scheler en el conjunto del pensiamento filosófico contemporáneo" ("the ubiquity of Scheler in the context of contemporary philosophy") (p. 21).

upheavals that began in 1933; Maria Scheler continued to work on it by herself until her death late in 1969. By that time, six volumes had been published. The editorship has now been assumed by Professor Manfred Frings, of DePaul University, who brought to completion Volume One, which contains Scheler's early writings (1899–1914). The remaining unpublished manuscripts, as well as the definitive texts of Scheler's last published writings, await publication.[5]

These extrinsic circumstances mean that a comprehensive view of Scheler's thinking is not yet possible. However, even the texts now available raise the question of what one might call the internal architectonic of Scheler's philosophy. Let me try to make this a bit clearer.

At the center of Scheler's work stands his book, *Der Formalismus in der Ethik und die materiale Wertethik*[6] (*Formalism in Ethics and Nonformal Ethics of Values*, to be published in an English translation by Manfred Frings and Roger L. Funk, by Northwestern University Press). It is for this work that he is primarily known, in Europe and elsewhere; in all likelihood future discussion of Scheler will continue to have his ethical theory in central focus. Nonetheless one must keep in mind that Scheler intended to publish major, systematic works on the theory of cognition (*Erkenntnistheorie*), philosophical anthropology, and metaphysics,[7] in addition to several volumes in which he planned to take up and develop specialized themes briefly discussed or alluded to in *Formalismus*.[8] Moreover,

---

5. A full report on the history and present state of this edition is in Manfred Frings, "Bericht über der Sachlage am philosophischen Nachlass Max Schelers," *Zeitschrift für philosophische Forschung*, Vol. XXV, no. 2 (1971).

6. This was first published in two parts in Husserl's *Jahrbuch für Philosophie und phänomenologische Forschung* (Halle: Niemeyer, 1913 and 1916). A separate edition was published in 1916. Two other editions appeared during Scheler's lifetime (1921 and 1927). All references in this volume are to the fifth edition, edited by Maria Scheler (Bern: Francke, 1966). I shall cite this work hereafter as *Formalismus*.

7. See Scheler's remarks in his Preface to the second edition of *Formalismus*, reprinted in the fifth edition, pp. 13–14. "Erkenntnis und Arbeit," in *Die Wissensformen und Die Gesellschaft*, 2d ed. rev., *Gesammelte Werke* VIII (Bern: Francke, 1960), contains several references to the author's *Metaphysics* and his *Philosophical Anthropology*, both of which "will appear shortly."

8. The subjects Scheler had plans to treat include "Die Sinngesetze des emotionalen Lebens" (The Laws Governing the Sense of Emotional Life), a specimen of which is published under the title "Über Scham und

Scheler produced during his lifetime a major work on the philosophy of religion [9] and his extensive *Die Wissensformen und die Gesellschaft*, containing an essay on the sociology of knowledge ("Probleme einer Soziologie des Wissen") and a long study entitled "Erkenntnis und Arbeit: Eine Studie über Wert und Grenzen des pragmatischen Motivs in der Erkenntnis der Welt." Scheler says in the preface to this volume, "People will only understand the author's metaphysics if they have read this book." [10]

Now there can be no question that Scheler in fact *aimed at* producing a philosophical *system*. In the Preface to the first edition of *Formalismus* (1916) he turns the tables on Nietzsche, declaring that "the will to system" is so far from being a "will to falsehood" that, on the contrary, "the unwillingness to take note of the systematic character present in the things themselves must be looked upon as the result of a groundless will to anarchy" (5th ed., pp. 10–11). In the light both of the preceding survey of Scheler's literary production and projects and of his expressly systematic aims, a number of interrelated questions seem unavoidable: How, in fact, is this system to be articulated? What is to be its pivotal or foundational part? Is ethics to remain the central element, subordinating all other philosophical disciplines to itself? Or will metaphysics play the leading role? [11] What relationship will

Schamgefühl" (On Shame and the Feeling of Shame), in Maria Scheler, ed., *Schriften aus dem Nachlass: I, Zur Ethik und Erkenntnislehre*, 2d ed. rev. (Bern: Francke, 1957), and "Solidarismus als Grundlage der Sozial- und Geschichtsphilosophie" (Solidarity as the Basis of the Philosophy of Society and History).

9. *Vom Ewigen im Menschen, Religiöse Erneuerung*, 4th ed. rev., *Gesammelte Werke* V (Bern: Francke, 1955), English translation by Bernard Noble, *On the Eternal in Man* (London: Student Christian Movement Press, 1960).

10. I have omitted from this survey the numerous essays and articles Scheler wrote on contemporary social, political, economic, and educational issues (including the feminist movement, capitalism, militarism, and adult education). Most of these can be found in *Vom Umsturz der Werte* and *Schriften zur Soziologie und Weltanschauungslehre*, 2d ed. rev., *Gesammelte Werke* VI (Bern: Francke, 1963). It is important to emphasize that these were not merely *pièces d'occasions*. On the connections between Scheler's philosophical and political activity, see the excellent biography by John Raphael Staude, *Max Scheler: An Intellectual Portrait* (New York: Free Press, 1967).

11. Scheler's conception of metaphysics (and its relation to other philosophical discipline) is extremely difficult to pin down, especially since it appears to have undergone considerable change in the course of his

obtain between the projected metaphysics and the projected philosophical anthropology? [12] What is the status of the theory of cognition vis-à-vis these other disciplines? Of the philosophy of religion? [13]

---

career. The following brief indications will have to suffice. In the Preface to the second edition of *Wesen und Formen der Sympathie* (Bonn: Cohen, 1923), English translation by Peter Heath, *The Nature of Sympathy* (New Haven: Yale University Press, 1954), Scheler refers to metaphysics as "the most central philosophical descriptive" which is concerned with the "ground of all things" (5th ed. [Frankfurt am Main: Schulte-Bulmke, 1948], p. xiv). Equally, in "Erkenntnis und Arbeit," Scheler writes that "The movement of metaphysical thought has its goal in the first place in the question how the ground and cause of the world as a whole must be constituted if the essential structure the world does have is to be possible" (p. 208). What is problematic is the *cognitive status* or truth of metaphysical descriptions. As early as 1915–16 Scheler denied the possibility of a "scientific metaphysics" and suggested instead what he calls a "relative metaphysics" (see "Absolutsphäre und Realsetzung der Gottesidee," *Schriften aus dem Nachlass*, I, 207–17). "Relative metaphysics" has an essentially hypothetical character; its possible results can claim only "conjectural evidence" (*Vermutungsevidenz*). In "Probleme einer Soziologie des Wissens," *Versuche zu einer Soziologie des Wissens* (Munich: Duncker & Humblot, 1924), Scheler again says that metaphysical results are "permanently hypothetical" and "only probable," but, at the same time, he ascribes to metaphysics "a spontaneous, evident cognition [*Erkenntnis*] of the absolute being which must be carried out by each person" (p. 87), and asserts that it shares with science "a strictly rational method and a basic orientation toward the world in general" (*ibid.*). (Compare "Metaphysik und Kunst," *Deutsche Beiträge*, I, no. 2 [1947], 107, 114.) Three further comments are in order here. In *Wesen und Formen der Sympathie*, Scheler points to the "unity of logical style" of metaphysics and the theory of cognition in the treatment of the existence of the alter ego (p. 204). Furthermore, in the Preface to the third edition of *Formalismus* Scheler acknowledges the considerable changes in his views on metaphysics and philosophy of religion since the appearance of the second edition (1921), and then goes on to say, "Ethics seems to the author, as much today as it did previously, important to any metaphysics of absolute being, but metaphysics is not important to the foundation of ethics" (p. 17). In the last stage of his thinking, Scheler subordinated metaphysics as the knowledge of essences (*Bildungswissen—prima philosophia*) to knowledge for the sake of salvation or redemption (*Heilswissen, Erlösungswissen*) (see "Erkenntnis und Arbeit," pp. 200, 59; and "Philosophische Weltanschauung," in *Philosophische Weltanschauung* [Bonn: Cohen, 1929]).

12. See *Man's Place in Nature*, trans. Hans Meyerhoff (Boston: Beacon Press, 1961), p. 3: "The questions 'What is Man?' and 'What is man's place in the nature of things?' have occupied me more deeply than any other philosophical question since the first awakening of my philosophical consciousness." Compare Karl Löwith, "Max Scheler und das Problem einer philosophischen Anthropologie," *Theologische Rundschau*, Vol. VII (1935).

13. Scheler's philosophy of religion was subject to greater change or oscillation than any other sphere of his thought. He wrote in 1926 that he

A reader already familiar with some of Scheler's work might have wanted to interrupt this line of questioning almost as soon as it was begun, not without a certain justice. He might have pointed to two relevant considerations which would tend to make my inquiry into the character of Scheler's philosophical "system" seem premature, if not altogether inappropriate.

First, the incompleteness of the textual record, especially since the surviving manuscripts of the planned works on metaphysics and philosophical anthropology are not yet available, surely precludes any positive "conclusions" as to Scheler's definitive intentions.

Second, the characterization of Scheler's work hitherto provided is much too *static;* Scheler was above all, as it has become something of a commonplace to say, a *dynamic* thinker, and this means that his philosophical conceptions were always evolving, his plans for a synoptic ordering of these always *in fieri.* Accordingly, it is to mistake the inner spirit of Scheler's way of proceeding to ask for the kind of programmatic blueprint my questions conjure up.

I readily acknowledge these two objections and add to them a plausible third. To a reader coming to any one of Scheler's works for the first time, this whole debate must seem abstract and unavailing. Programmatic and diachronic questions alike really have little to do, this reader might say, with helping someone to get his bearings in relation to the arguments and preoccupations of the text he is now starting to read. In short, there are no genuinely intrinsic problems here, merely documentary or editorial ones.

2. Stated in this last way, the third objection should start to lose its plausibility, at least for one group of readers, namely, those who come to Scheler already familiar to some extent with the works and intentions of Husserl and Heidegger. It is probably not going too far to say that a member of this group will come to Scheler's texts with an implicit orientation shaped in large part by his sense of these two authors. Thus, "getting one's bearings," for the reader with this kind of preparation, does involve something more than hearing about Scheler's creative versatility and dynamic manner of thinking; perhaps

---

could no longer call himself a "theist" in the usual sense of the term. See Maurice Dupuy, *La Philosophie de la religion chez Max Scheler* (Paris: Presses Universitaires de France, 1959).

it even requires some provisory sense of the guiding intentions of Scheler's thinking in relation to those of Husserl and Heidegger respectively.

To draw out only the main lines of these relationships with anything approaching the required precision would consume more space than I have at my disposal. I shall nonetheless try to bring what I take to be the distinguishing features of these relations into contrasting relief. In doing so, I shall be attempting less to describe Scheler's intentions in a positive manner than to specify what is likely to seem strikingly absent from his work to the reader versed in Husserl and Heidegger.

Let me begin by offering a quite general observation, knowing only too well the risks I run of being irremediably superficial. What links Husserl and Heidegger and separates them from Scheler is their *explicit* preoccupation with foundations, with the most radical or original sources of possibility, including the possibility of the philosophical enterprise itself.

First, a few lines about Husserl and Scheler. It is important to bear in mind that Scheler was not Husserl's student in any formal sense. When the two men met for the first time, in Halle, in 1901, Scheler had already marked out the territory he was going to explore a decade later in *Formalismus:* the realm of objective values and the correspondingly objective feelings of value.[14] The Sixth Investigation in Husserl's *Logical Investigations* (1901) and, more precisely, the notion of categorial intuition (as distinct from sensuous intuition) provided Scheler with the means of establishing, through what he calls phe-

14. See "Beiträge zur Feststellung der Beziehungen zwischen den logischen und ethischen Prinzipien," *Frühe Schriften, Gesammelte Werke* I (Bern: Francke, 1971), pp. 61–112. (This is Scheler's Jena dissertation, written under Rudolf Eucken.) See also Scheler's remarks concerning Husserl in the Preface to the second edition (1922) of his Jena Habilitationschrift, *Die transzendentale und die psychologische Methode: Eine grundsätzliche Erörterung zur philosophischen Methodik, Frühe Schriften,* pp. 201–3. Scheler's potential receptiveness to Husserl's *Logical Investigations* could be detected in the latter work in his attempt to refute psychologism. See page 321, on the "indissoluble unity of actuality and validity" characteristic of what he calls here "the life-form of spirit" (*die Lebensform des Geistes*). Manfred Frings, *Zur Phänomenologie der Lebensgemeinschaft,* p. 68, n. 16, reports that in a letter to Adolf Grimme dated May 4, 1917, Scheler asserted that he had already worked out his basic phenomenological conceptions *before* reading any text of Husserl's. See, too, Scheler's account of his relationship to phenomenology in "Die deutsche Philosophie der Gegenwart," in *Deutsches Leben der Gegenwart,* ed. Philipp Witkop (Berlin: Bücherfreunde, 1922), pp. 127–224.

nomenological intuition or phenomenological experience, the a priori nonformal essences and essential connections obtaining in this and other realms.[15]

It is against this background that Scheler's "application" of phenomenology to concrete domains must be viewed. To put matters crudely, the chief task of Husserlian phenomenology is to discover the ultimate sources of the validity of whatever is *experienced* as objectively binding despite the vicissitudes of its subjective apprehension. This means that the project of phenomenology stands in the closest connection with the claims of the sciences (e.g., pure logic and pure mathematics). The phenomenological question is not *whether* these claims are valid, but "what sense and scope this validity can have." [16] Moreover, if it is only in *experience* that these claims to objective validity come to light, the question becomes: In what modality of conscious experience does their validity secure both its possible sense and its absolute or apodictic evidence? [17] If Husserl's intention is considered in this way, one can say that his works trace out a single trajectory from the first edition of *Logical Investigations* (1898–1901)—if not the earlier *Philosophie der Arithmetik*—which take their start from the problem of the foundations of logic and pure mathe-

15. See *Formalismus*, pp. 67–99, esp. 67–73. On Husserl's ethical theories, see Alois Roth, *E. Husserls ethische Untersuchungen* (The Hague: Nijhoff, 1960). Note that Husserl, in the *Idee der Phänomenologie*, ed. W. Biemel (The Hague: Nijhoff, 1958), says: "Naturally the universal phenomenology of reason also has to solve the parallel problems of the correlation of valuing [*Wertung*] and value [*Wert*], etc." (p. 14).

16. See Husserl, *Phänomenologische Psychologie, Husserliana* IX (The Hague: Nijhoff, 1962), p. 265, on the distinction between the "natural question of right" and the "transcendental question of right."

17. I have obviously had to disregard in this brief sketch all of the nuances, complications, and modifications Husserl's thinking evinces not only over the course of time but even in single works. In particular, I have said nothing about the role played by the concept of the life-world in the later writings. On this subject, see the text from Husserl MS BI 5 ix, p. 31, cited in Gerd Brand, *Wert, Ich und Zeit* (The Hague: Nijhoff, 1955), English translation, "Intentionality, Reduction and Intentional Analysis in Husserl's Later Manuscripts," in Joseph Kockelmans, ed., *Phenomenology* (Garden City, N.Y.: Doubleday, 1967), p. 209. An excellent critical study of the project of discovering apodictic foundations may be found in David Levin, *Reason and Evidence in Husserl's Phenomenology* (Evanston, Ill.: Northwestern University Press, 1970). On the centrality of "evidence" in Husserl's phenomenological program, see Eugen Fink, "Das Problem der Phänomenologie Edmund Husserls," in *Studien zur Phänomenologie* (*1930–1939*) (The Hague: Nijhoff, 1966), esp. p. 202.

matics, to *Formal and Transcendental Logic* (1929) and *The Crisis of European Sciences* (1935–36). His primary and enduring emphasis is on the *possibility* of phenomenology itself as the ultimate, foundational science.[18] "Philosophy can take root only in radical reflexion upon the meaning and possibility of its own scheme." [19]

More important in this context than any specific criticisms Scheler advances against Husserl,[20] or against the alleged changes in Husserl's conception of phenomenology,[21] is the fact that for Scheler, although scientific concepts together with the concepts of natural or naïve experience receive their

18. See, *inter alia,* Husserl, *Formale und Transzendentale Logik, Jahrbuch für Philosophie und phänomenologische Forschung,* Vol. X (1929), pt. 2, chap. 7, p. 236, English translation by Dorion Cairns, *Formal and Transcendental Logic* (The Hague: Nijhoff, 1969), p. 268.

19. See Husserl, *Ideen III* (The Hague: Nijhoff, 1952), *Nachwort,* p. 160, English translation by W. R. Boyce Gibson, *Ideas* (New York: Humanities Press, 1931), Author's Preface to the English Edition, p. 27.

20. The best known of Scheler's criticisms is his objection to Husserl's phenomenological reduction. Scheler's main arguments can be read in "Idealism and Realism," translated below. See also his comments on the reduction in "Erkenntnis und Arbeit," pp. 281–82. See Aron Gurwitsch's attempt to expose Scheler's misunderstanding of the transcendental-phenomenological reduction, "Critical Study of Husserl's *Nachwort,*" in *Studies in Phenomenology and Psychology* (Evanston, Ill.: Northwestern University Press, 1966), pp. 110–11. Scheler also criticizes, among other things, Husserl's thesis that in the mental sphere there is no distinction between appearance and reality (see "The Idols of Self-Knowledge," translated below) and the status assigned to "categorial intuition" as "founded" on sensuous intuition (see "The Theory of the Three Facts," translated below, and "Erkenntnis und Arbeit," pp. 310–11).

It is worth noting that Scheler planned to write a two-volume work on logic, a long fragment of which is extant and will be published by Manfred Frings. This material (dating from ca. 1906) will make it possible to arrive at more precise and detailed judgments of the relation between the early Husserl and Scheler.

21. Scheler takes issue chiefly with the "idealistic" inflection Husserl allegedly gave to phenomenology in the period after *Logical Investigations.* See *Frühe Schriften,* p. 201. It cannot yet be settled whether any of Scheler's ideas influenced Husserl's later thinking. (The correspondence between Scheler and Husserl would be particularly valuable in this context.) Nonetheless, one may want to explore the "parallel" between Scheler's analysis of the "natural world-view" (see below, "Phenomenology and the Theory of Cognition" and "The Theory of the Three Facts") together with his emphasis on "taking interest in" (see below, "*Ordo Amoris*") and Husserl's notions of passive pre-constitution, the typification of natural experience, and thematic interest (see *Erfahrung und Urteil,* ed. Ludwig Landgrebe [Hamburg: Claassen, 1964], pp. 381–403, esp. p. 386; an English translation by James S. Churchill and Karl Ameriks, *Experience and Judgment,* is forthcoming from Northwestern University Press).

foundations in phenomenology, phenomenology itself is not principally concerned with laying those foundations or with clarifying the *sense* the objectivities or generalities science and natural experience display. According to Scheler, there are facts (i.e., essences and essential connections) peculiar to phenomenology itself; and it is with investigating these facts, in whatever concrete domain they may be instantiated, that phenomenology is chiefly concerned. Put in a different way, Husserl shows his deep affinity with Kant when he takes over the rubric "critique of reason" and applies it to phenomenology;[22] Scheler persists in setting himself apart from the Kantian program when he declares that "the great and important problem of the origin [*Ursprung*] of cognition (of any kind) is itself only one part of the total problem of a priori relations between essences."[23]

Both these ways of putting this contrast stand crucially in need of detailed qualifications which I cannot provide here. The core of each would, I think, remain intact even after the qualifications had been added. It is not so much that Scheler unquestioningly *applied* phenomenology as that for him "phenomenological experience" can be (and is) pursued for its own sake, independently of any part it might play in furnishing apodictic foundations for nonphenomenological experience.[24]

3. Partisans of Husserl's extreme methodological self-consciousness may find sufficient reason for uncertainty in the foregoing remarks. Readers who have become convinced of the "epochal" character of Heidegger's initiative in *Being and Time* will, perhaps, find Scheler's contrasting position even more disconcerting.

22. The subtitle of *Formal and Transcendental Logic* is "Search for a Critique of Logical Reason" (*Versuch einer Kritik der logischen Vernunft*). On Husserl's relation to Kant, see Iso Kern, *Husserl und Kant* (The Hague: Nijhoff, 1964), esp. pp. 179 ff. ("Husserl und Kants Forderung einer Kritik der reinen Vernunft als der Bedingung der Möglichkeit einer wissenschaftlichen Metaphysik").

23. *Formalismus*, p. 91.

24. This independence goes hand in hand with Scheler's interpretation of phenomenology as "the most intensely vital and most immediate contact with the world itself" ("Phenomenology and the Theory of Cognition," translated below). A good account of the differences between Husserl and Scheler may be found in Shimomissé, *Die Phänomenologie*, pp. 67–73. See also M. Schümmer, "Die Wahrnehmungs- und Erkenntnismetaphysik Max Schelers in der Studien ihrer Entwicklung unter besonderer Berücksichtigung der Beziehungen Schelers zu Husserl" (diss., Bonn, 1964).

Once again, *in this context,* neither the abundant parallels between Scheler and Heidegger nor Scheler's documentable anticipations of Heideggerian positions [25] are as crucial as *what appears to be* the radical difference in the *self-understanding* within which each thinker undertook and pursued his philosophical work.

For Heidegger as for Scheler, Husserl's theory of categorial intuition in the Sixth Logical Investigation helped to open the path to his own questioning.[26] Heidegger's *question* is familiar to most under the title "The Question of Being." What connection holds together the theory of categorial intuition and the question of Being?

Heidegger has more than once written that Franz Brentano's dissertation, "Von der mannigfachen Bedeutung des Seienden nach Aristotles" (1862), was the point of departure of his first independent attempt to enter into philosophy.[27] Husserl, in sections 43 and 44 of chapter 6 of the Sixth Logical Investigation, expounds the theory that the "concept of Being" (along with other categories) has its true source neither in reflection upon judgments (such as, e.g., "Gold is yellow"), nor in reflection upon fulfillments of judgments, but in the fulfillment of judgments themselves (e.g., in the state of affairs "gold-being-yellow").[28]

25. Manfred Frings deals with some of these parallels and anticipations in *Person und Dasein.* One "parallel" might plausibly be said to hold between Scheler's description of *Person* and Heidegger's analysis of *Dasein.* To be more specific, Scheler maintained that "the person carries out [*vollzieht*] its existence [*Existenz*] only in the lived-experiencing [*Erleben*] of its possible lived-experiences [*Erlebnisse*]" (*Formalismus,* p. 385), while Heidegger writes in *Being and Time* that "Dasein in every case determines itself as an entity in the light of a possibility which it itself *is* and which, in its own Being, it somehow understands" (*Sein und Zeit* [Halle: Niemeyer, 1927], p. 43, English translation by John Macquarrie and Edward Robinson [New York: Harper & Row, 1962], p. 69; translation slightly modified). This parallel becomes especially worthy of reflection in the light of Heidegger's charge that Scheler defined the Being of *Person* as *Vorhandensein* (see below). Other suggestive similarities to Heidegger's thinking may be detected in Scheler's thesis that "the *world* is the objective correlate [*Sachkorrelat*] of the person" (*Formalismus,* pp. 392 ff.) and that this analysis of knowledge is an "ontological relationship" [*Seinsverhältnis*] ("Idealism and Realism," below).

26. See Heidegger, "Mein Weg in die Phänomenologie," *Zur Sache des Denkens* (Tübingen: Niemeyer, 1969), p. 86.

27. *Ibid.,* p. 81.

28. See Husserl, *Logische Untersuchungen* (Halle: Niemeyer, 1900), II/2, 141, English translation by J. N. Findlay, *Logical Investigations*

Aristotle and Brentano speak of the diverse or manifold meanings of "Being." Husserl speaks of the concept of Being. Is there a bridge between these two? In this speculative reconstruction of the genesis of Heidegger's questioning, another key Husserlian notion, that of the variety of ways or modes in which an object or state of affairs can be given to acts of intentional consciousness, apparently provided the sought-for link. In his first Marburg lectures in 1923–24, Heidegger declared that "with Husserl's discovery of intentionality, in the sense that the investigation of intentionality is simultaneously the thematization of the entity in the mode in which it encounters us at any one time [*Seienden im Wie des jeweiligen Begegnens*], for the first time in the history of philosophy the basis was expressly and clearly found for a radical ontological investigation." [29]

This variety in the modes of possible givenness can be said to account for the *diversity* of the meanings of "Being." However, Heidegger has continually insisted that the question which has determined the entire course of his thinking is "What is the simple and unitary determination of Being which prevails through all the manifold meanings?" [30] To bring this question into view requires that one's focus be shifted from the variety of the modes of an object's possible givenness to the fact of givenness itself: What allows for the possibility of something's being given at all (in whatever mode), for its being encountered by someone?

Husserl had emphasized the correlativity of intentional act and the givenness intended or "meant" in this act. Against this background, it should be clear that the question of the possibility of givenness as such cannot be answered until the character of the entity to whom anything can be given or disclose itself has been adequately specified. It is at this point that Heidegger's critique of Husserl's theory of transcendental sub-

---

(New York: Humanities Press, 1970), II, 783. It is important to point out that Husserl does not single out Being in this passage as in any way unique vis-à-vis the other "categories" such as unity, plurality, totality, etc. On Husserl's concept of Being, see Kern, *Husserl und Kant*, pp. 188–91.

29. Cited in Ernst Tugendhat, *Der Wahrheitsbegriff bei Husserl und Heidegger* (Berlin: de Gruyter, 1967), p. 262.

30. See Heidegger's "Letter to Father Richardson," in William J. Richardson, *Heidegger: Through Phenomenology to Thought* (The Hague: Nijhoff, 1963), p. xi.

jectivity shows its importance.[31] Avoiding all detail, let me say only that, for Heidegger, human *Dasein*, in virtue of the kind, or, better, style of Being peculiar to it, appears to ground not only the possibility of givenness *tout court*, but also that of the intelligibility or understandability of the mode of what is given. Accordingly, "fundamental ontology," which is to address itself to the question of the meaning or sense of Being *as such*, "must be sought in the existential analysis of *Dasein*," for it is a feature of the Being *of Dasein* that *Dasein* "*is* in the manner of an understanding of Being," and this understanding is instanced in *Dasein*'s relations both to entities with different styles of Being and to itself.[32]

The inadequacies of this sketch of Heidegger's program in *Being and Time* are as obvious to me as they are to any reader versed in that work.[33] Nevertheless, what I have said does, I hope, furnish a context within which Heidegger's criticisms of Scheler can be made to yield at least an initial sense. If philosophy is obliged to engage in radical, ontological questioning, then no concept or notion can be admitted into a philosophical account of any subject-matter until it has been ontologically clarified, that is, until its possible sense has been traced back to the understanding *Dasein* has of some one or some ensemble of its own possibilities. For Heidegger, central notions in Scheler's ethics (e.g., value, person) and philosophical anthropology fail to meet this demand. Scheler, in Heidegger's judgment, does not inquire into the peculiar style

31. See Heidegger's comments on Husserl's draft for the *Encyclopaedia Britannica* article, "Phenomenology," in Husserl, *Phänomenologische Psychologie*, pp. 601–2. See also Walter Biemel, "Husserls *Encyclopaedia Britannica* Artikel und Heideggers Anmerkungen dazu," *Tijdschrift voor Philosophie*, Vol. XII, no. 2 (1950). The link between fundamental ontology and the analysis of Dasein appears in *Sein und Zeit*, p. 13 (*Being and Time*, p. 34).

32. See Heidegger, *Kant und das Problem der Metaphysik*, 2d ed. (Frankfurt am Main: Klostermann, 1951), pp. 206 ff., English translation by James S. Churchill, *Kant and the Problem of Metaphysics* (Bloomington: Indiana University Press, 1962), pp. 235 ff.

33. Among other things, I have made no reference to the notorious "turning" in Heidegger's thought which has led some commentators to speak of an early and a later Heidegger. I must content myself here with the suggestion that a route can be seen to lead, however sinuously, from the notion of "encountering" (*Begegnen*) in the Marburg text cited above, through the theme of "disclosure" (*Erschlossenheit*) in *Being and Time*, to the motif of Alētheia which figures so prominently in Heidegger's later writings (e.g., "Zeit und Sein" in *Zur Sache des Denkens*).

of Being which is man's, and thus he presupposes the traditional (and inadequate) ontological account of man's being
as "presence-at-hand." [34] This means that, *on Heidegger's reading,* Scheler's results, however true they may be in a factual or
ontic sense, are ontologically inadequate.[35]

4. To readers nurtured on so-called analytical philosophy,
the virtues Scheler has just been said to lack might seem
something less than splendid vices. "Analytical philosophy" (or
"conceptual analysis") is nowadays a rubric broad enough to
accommodate thinkers as diverse as Quine and Sellars, Ans-
combe and Chisholm. It is, I think, prudent to distinguish what
one might call the "analytical attitude" from an analytical
ideology. The former rests, minimally, on the conviction that
patient discursive argumentation is the proper medium in

34. See *Sein und Zeit,* pp. 47–49 (*Being and Time,* pp. 172–75).
35. It could probably go without saying that the metaphysical concepts
Scheler was elaborating in his "Geist and Drang" period, concepts such as
that of the universal life (*Allleben*) and the ground of the world (*Welt-
grund*) (see "Erkenntnis und Arbeit," pp. 359–61; also *Wesen und Formen
der Sympathie,* pp. 79–84, and "Idealism and Realism," below), would
strike Heidegger as intransigently, that is, traditionally, "onto-theological":
the world-ground remains a being among beings, albeit an absolute one.
On the other hand, the idea of a "transcendental inference," which
Scheler articulated in connection with his philosophical anthropology, presents a more complex problem if looked at from a "Heideggerian" standpoint. Scheler claims that we can move in thought from the "essential
images of man . . . to conclusions about the true attributes of the Supreme principle of all things" (see *Philosophische Weltanschauung,* pp.
11–12). One's critical expectation that an idea of this sort would be condemned out of hand as anthropomorphic or subjectivistic will be at least
temporarily frustrated if one reads Heidegger's recently published comments on a similar issue in Schelling. See Martin Heidegger, *Schellings
Abhandlung über das Wesen der Menschlichen Freiheit* (*1829*) (Tübingen: Niemeyer, 1971), pp. 196–98.
Whether Scheler himself planned to work out an ontology, in either
the traditional or the Heideggerian sense, is a question I cannot settle here.
Manfred Frings (*Max Scheler,* p. 203) refers to a note by Scheler in
Formalismus (p. 538, n. 3) and asserts that its content shows that Scheler
quite clearly intended to investigate "the relation of foundation between
values and being." Yet Scheler says in this passage only that "the *Dasein*
of an *object* [*Objekts*] is founded on its being-a-value [*Wertsein*]" (and
this, by the way, in the context of a discussion of the different structural
forms of cultural unity or community). Furthermore, Scheler's sporadic
uses of the terms *Ontologie* and *ontologisch* do not permit any unambiguous inferences to the sense he assigned them. (Compare, *inter alia,* "Erkenntnis und Arbeit," pp. 295–96, 329; "Phenomenology and the Theory
of Cognition," below, pp. 136–201; "The Theory of the Three Facts," below,
pp. 202–87.)

which to deal with philosophical questions; partisans of the latter are persuaded that *only certain kinds* of philosophical questions are at home in the analytical medium (e.g., questions having to do with prephilosophical behavior of concepts in a particular natural language).[36] Scheler (like Husserl and Heidegger) undoubtedly offers problems to such partisans, but that, I would say, is neither surprising nor especially consequential. On the other hand, those who enter into the analytical attitude can more legitimately show uneasiness in the face of the discursive texture of Scheler's thinking, quite apart from any challenge they may raise to specific conclusions.

There is something queer in this. Scheler had no truck with what he calls "literary philosophizing"; I mentioned earlier the systematic intention of Scheler's thinking. Furthermore, Scheler is continually promising his readers a "rigorous proof" of this point or reminding them of his "rigorous refutation" of that one. His thinking, in his own judgment, is not woven from a fabric of isolated *aperçus:* these, one is tempted to say, have both their attractions *and* their place—which is not philosophy as Scheler conceived it. Nonetheless, the first impression almost any of Scheler's works is bound to make on a reader sensible of the claims of clear and rigorous argument is that of an artless mélange of unargued assertions and incomplete arguments. Scheler will seem to be rhetorical when he should be dialectical, edifying when he could have been more carefully persuasive, self-contradictory when he ought to have aimed at coherence.[37]

Moreover, Scheler's claim to be uncovering pure essences or pure essential connections scarcely squares with his frequent reliance on the experimental findings of contemporary physiologists, psychologists, and other empirical scientists. It seems as though Scheler's work is in some danger of falling

36. Some of the contrasts between phenomenology (in its Husserlian form) and linguistic analysis are brought out clearly by Robert G. Turnbull, "Linguistic Analysis, Phenomenology and the Problems of Philosophy: An Essay in Metaphilosophy," *The Monist,* Vol. XLIX (January, 1965). Scheler's views on language are presented in "Phenomenology and the Theory of Cognition," "The Theory of the Three Facts" (both translated below), and "Zur Idee des Menschen," in *Vom Umsturz der Werte,* pp. 177–83.

37. It is only fair to mention that such criticisms would not be novel. See the various estimates of Scheler's work made by his contemporaries in Dupuy, *La Philosophie de Max Scheler,* II, note II, 732–36.

victim to the same reproach he addressed to the neo-Kantians of the Marburg school, namely, that their "transcendental results" are all too quickly set aside by the progress of the sciences.[38]

Some of these features can be partially explained by the character of Scheler's philosophical working style. He comes through the texts as an impatient, even precipitous, thinker, a thinker who took more joy in beginning, in getting under way, than in bringing to completion, not to say logical perfection, what he had begun.

One consequence is that the questions Scheler raises may seem more fruitful for contemporary philosophizing than any of his conclusions.[39] Even here, however, thinkers who share in the analytical persuasion will find that simply to make precise what these questions are indeed asking demands more than the ordinary share of the reader's own work. If this means that the appropriation of Scheler's work in this quarter will inevitably be piecemeal and not wholesale, perhaps this is only as it should be.

Having canvassed some of the difficulties Scheler's readers are likely to encounter, I might seem under obligation to state the virtues they can anticipate. Here I am inclined to reply, as I think a translator should: "To the texts themselves!" In the case of the five essays translated below, some purely bibliographical information will prove useful;[40] beyond providing this I shall try to bring into focus the principal themes in each. Finally, the temptation to draw some general "morals" from Scheler's philosophizing is irresistible, and so I shall end this introduction with some brief reflections on this topic.

Let me begin by saying a word or two about my rationale in selecting just these five essays.

All five are closely connected, if not in time, then in content, with Scheler's master work, *Formalism in Ethics and the Non-*

38. See *Frühe Schriften*, p. 202. See also Nicolai Hartmann's obituary tribute, "Max Scheler," in *Kant-Studien*, Vol. XXXIII (1928). (It is worth observing that Scheler's relation to the natural sciences of his day reminds one of the early work of Merleau-Ponty.)

39. Compare Dietrich von Hildebrand, "Max Scheler als Persönlichkeit," *Hochland*, XXVI (1928–29), 71.

40. My information about the origin and state of the manuscripts comes from Maria Scheler's "Bemerkungen zu den Manuskripten" in Volumes III and X of the *Gesammelte Werke*.

formal Ethics of Value. Thus, if read in conjunction with that work, this volume will permit one to see how Scheler arrived at certain positions, how he elaborated certain themes treated tangentially in the *Ethics,* and how he continued to work on problems posed there but not discussed.[41]

Second, these essays furnish the materials for a broader and more detailed view of Scheler's theoretical work in (phenomenological) psychology, epistemology, and metaphysics than has hitherto been possible for readers without access to the original texts. Since I have already alluded to the "systematic" dimension of Scheler's intentions, it seems unnecessary to add further comment on the desirability of having these new works available.

Finally, four of the five essays are fragments and three were not published in his lifetime.[42] (I shall give detailed information on the origin of each one below.) Ordinarily I would think it inadvisable to present works of such an incomplete character, especially when their author is comparatively little known to most readers. However, in Scheler's case not only are these fragments almost all that he wrote on some of these topics, but their form seems to me to be to some extent faithful to the manner in which he wrote and thought. Scheler, as his contemporaries have written and as I have asserted, gave the sense of being interested above all in making a beginning; the fragments translated in this volume will perhaps allow a glimpse of the manifold commencements of his thought.

"The Idols of Self-Knowledge," the first essay translated here, was originally published under the title "Über Selbsttäuschungen" ("On Self-Deceptions"), in 1911 in the first issue of the journal *Zeitschrift für Psychopathologie.* Scheler expanded this original version for inclusion under the present title in his two-volume collection of essays, *Abhandlungen und Aufsätze* (Leipzig: Verlag der Weissen Bücher, 1915), the second edition of which (Leipzig: Neue Geist Verlag, 1919) appeared

41. This group of essays will also show that too much has sometimes been made of the alleged discontinuity in Scheler's thinking over the course of his career. While it is true that his religious views were quite volatile, his earlier work in the phenomenology of the mental, in the theory of cognition, etc., remained the foundation for later speculations.

42. To be absolutely precise, all five are fragments, since "The Idols of Self-Knowledge" was meant to have a second part, "Special Forms of Self-Deception." No manuscripts for this second part have been found.

under the name *Vom Umsturz der Werte* (*The Overturning of Values*).

Scheler continued to cite this comparatively early essay during every phase of his subsequent career. Perhaps his own estimate of its importance is best illustrated in the fact that he chose a chapter from it to represent his work in an anthology of characteristic selections from the outstanding philosophers of all time, prepared in 1925 by Josef Feldmann.[43]

The main critical thrust of the essay is to refute the prevalent assumption that mental phenomena are evidentially superior to physical phenomena, or, put more strongly, that one *cannot* be deceived or mistaken about one's own internal mental experiences. Scheler's attempt to refute certain versions of this thesis of incorrigibility (especially Brentano's) leads him to work out the difference between illusion and (judgmental) errors and then to analyze the distinction between the mental and the physical. The starting point of his analysis is not any mark or feature allegedly present in physical phenomena and absent from mental phenomena (e.g., extension) but rather the essential difference in *orientation* or *directedness* between the acts of what he calls internal perception and those of external perception. In other words, both the "mental" and the physical take their distinctive identity from the manner of their being given or perceived.[44]

The various notions that come into play in the course of this analysis (e.g., inner sense, the lived-body, the forms of multiplicity characteristic of mental and physical phenomena) [45]

43. Josef Feldmann, *Schule der Philosophie* (Paderborn, 1925), pp. 409–14.

44. The best account of these matters is in Barnhard Lorsched, *Max Scheler's Phänomenologische des Psychischen*, Abhandlungen zu Philosophie, Psychologie und Pädagogik, Vol. XI (Bonn: Bouvier, 1957). See also Paul A. Schilpp, "The Doctrine of Illusion and Error in Scheler's Phenomenology," *Journal of Philosophy*, Vol. XXIV (1927). Brentano's doctrine is set forth in "The Distinction between Mental and Physical Phenomena," in *Realism and the Background of Phenomenology*, ed. Roderick Chisholm (Glencoe, Ill.: Free Press, 1960).

45. Scheler constructs two terms to designate these different forms of multiplicity or manifold (*Mannigfaltigkeit*). The form characteristic of mental phenomena is *Ineinandersein*, literally, "being-into-one-another." According to Scheler the data of inner perception interpenetrate one another within the ego (*Ich*) in such a way that, for example, past, present, and future mental contents or lived-experiences are equally and immediately "present" in the "completely undivided ego." Scheler also uses the phrase "togetherness in the ego" (*Zusammen im Ich*). I have

reappear in *Formalismus*, especially in connection with the question of the relation of ego and lived-body. The ethically fundamental notion of Person, Scheler argues, can only be clarified and given its full meaning once this relationship has been understood and false theories of the unity of the Person have been refuted.

With the second essay, *"Ordo Amoris"* ("The Order of Love"), we shift into a different key. The two manuscripts from which the editor assembled this date from 1914–15 and 1916. In 1923 Scheler announced in a publisher's advertisement that this essay, together with another work, "Liebe und Erkenntnis" ("Love and Cognition"), would appear in print as the planned second volume of *Vom Ewigen im Menschen*. This volume never appeared. The editor shortened Scheler's title from "On *Ordo Amoris* and Its Confusions" to *"Ordo Amoris,"* since no pages were found among the author's papers that were to deal with the basic types of these confusions and their origins.[46]

It would not be a complete exaggeration to say that the subject of *"Ordo Amoris"* was always the leitmotiv of Scheler's thinking. The Pascalian phrase "la logique du coeur" which he appropriates epitomizes the theses Scheler had already expounded in his Jena dissertation, "Beiträge zur Feststellung der Beziehungen zwischen den logischen und ethischen Prinzipien" (Contributions to the Establishment of the Relations between Logical and Ethical Principles), in 1899.[47] The heterogeneity of

---

translated *Ineinandersein* as "mutual interpenetration." (This *Ineinandersein* is rarely perceived as such: see Scheler's remarks on the phenomenon of *Sammlung*—"intense concentration on oneself"—in *Formalismus*, pp. 417–18.) The second form of multiplicity is designated by the terms *Auseinandersein* and *Aussereinandersein*, both of which present difficulty to the translator. Literally, the terms mean "being-separate-from-one-another" and "being-exterior-to-one-another." These are clearly relational terms; Scheler's thought is that physical phenomena (and phenomena of the lived-body), corresponding to external perception, "stand apart from one another" whether in space or in time or in both ways. The form *Auseinander* is said to be (ontologically) prior to both spatial extension and temporal succession. I have generally translated these terms as "mutual apartness" or "mutual externality." Alfred Schutz gave "disconnectedness," while Maurice Dupuy suggests "extériorité mutuelle." On this whole subject, see Frings, *Zur Phänomenologie des Lebensgemeinschaft*, pp. 28–47.

46. See "Bemerkungen zu den Manuskripten," *Schriften zur Soziologie und Weltanschauungslehre*, p. 516.

47. This is printed in *Frühe Schriften*, pp. 11–159.

the evaluative and the logical judgmental orders *does not entail* the irrationality or nonobjectivity of acts of preference and aversion, of love and hate. If it is the case that an objective hierarchy of values and disvalues subsists, then the ordering of an individual's subjective preferences can conform or not conform to this objective ordering insofar as there is a form of intentionality proper to the act of feeling (*Fühlen*), a value or disvalue. The intentionality of acts of feeling is not that of acts of thinking; but acts of feeling are not, for that reason, any less in an immediate relationship to the objects of their proper domain.

One further point should be noted. When Scheler maintains the primacy of acts of love and hate over acts of willing and cognition, when he says that love is what first awakens both willing and cognition, he is careful not to confuse the thesis he is advancing with the quite different claim that the properties of the objects of cognition are determined by the particular kinds of values ingredient in an individual's *ordo amoris*. In other words, a particular constellation of essential values (*Wertwesenswelt*) in which *ordo amoris* is manifested determines *which* objects are accessible to an individual's cognitive apprehension, not *what* those objects themselves are. Cognition does not lose its own specific character or proprietary domain.[48]

The next two essays, "Phenomenology and the Theory of Cognition" and "The Theory of the Three Facts," stand in the closest alliance with each other. In *Formalismus* Scheler refers more than once to his "still unpublished views on the theory of cognition" or to his work "Phenomenology and the Theory of Cognition" "which will soon appear." The manuscripts of the two essays translated here represent portions of this work which Scheler mentions but never in fact published.

The first essay was prepared as an invited contribution to the new periodical, *Die Geisteswissenschaften,* which began appearing in October, 1913. The outbreak of World War I prevented further publication and thus Scheler's essay never ap-

---

48. See *Formalismus,* p. 149, n. 1: "All 'perceptual,' 'representational,' and generally cognitive consciousness of the world is first of all independent of this 'practical world.' We certainly do not want here to subscribe to Fichte's principle: 'What kind of philosophy one has depends on what kind of man he is.'"

peared in print. The manuscript dates from around 1913–14.

The second essay comes from manuscripts written at a slightly earlier date, around 1911–12, and is not expressly connected by the author with the first.[49] However, their substantive connection can be seen from a "table of contents" Scheler sketched in 1913 or 1914. His planned work was to have three major sections: a formal part, a material part, and a critical part. In the sketch for the formal part there are five subsections:

1. The Essence of Phenomenology:
   a. Lived-experience;
   b. Insight into Essence;
   c. Essential Connections.
2. Phenomenology and Psychology (Experimental Phenomenology, Metaphysics, Theory of Cognition, Phenomenology, and the Theory of Evolution).
3. Truth (Criterion), Cognition, Illusion, Error, Pure Logic, Being; Object; Division of Objects, Perception, and Judgment.
4. Levels of Existence (*Daseinsstufen*). Against "Idealism."
5. The Three Kinds of Facts. The Real (Oswald Külpe).

The contents of the first essay partially coincide with the first four subsections, while the second essay answers to the fifth subsection.

It is difficult to specify one main purpose of these two works, because of their incompleteness and because of the variety of themes they explore. It is, however, clear that Scheler wanted to use the invitation mentioned as an occasion to articulate his understanding of the "phenomenological attitude" and to repudiate any attempts to identify phenomenology with (or subordinate it to) either psychology or epistemology.

It is within this context that he works out a richly suggestive theory of the standards or measures of cognition

___

49. The main manuscript of "Three Facts" breaks off before the end of section II. The appendixes have been added by the editor from additional manuscript material, each one dealing with questions or themes announced in the main text.

(*Massstäbe der Erkenntnis*) [50] and sets about distinguishing properly phenomenological facts from "facts" peculiar to science and to natural experience. Scheler's theory of a domain of nonformal, a priori essences and essential connections is of central importance to his critique of Kantian ethics and to the nonformal ethics of value he wished to substitute for Kantian formalism. Thus the account of so-called phenomenological experience and of the self-givenness [51] of phenomenological facts developed in these two essays is an indispensable complement to *Formalismus*. Equally relevant are the notions of existential relativity (*Daseinsrelativität*) [52] and of the order of foundation (*Ordnung der Fundierung*), both of which play important roles in Scheler's ethics and, it is fair to conjecture, in his metaphysics.[53]

"Idealism and Realism" is perhaps the most tantalizing of the essays translated in this volume. It appeared in the periodical *Philosophischer Anzeiger*, Vol. II, in 1927, a year before Scheler's death. As the reader will see, only two of the five

50. I have translated *Erkenntnis* as "cognition," and *Erkenntnistheorie* as "the theory of cognition," in order to preserve the distinction Scheler draws between *Wissen* (translated as "knowledge") and *Erkenntnis*. To put things as simply as possible, *Wissen* is used to designate a simple or immediate "participation by one being" (i.e., the knower) in the nature (*Sosein*) of another being (see "Idealism and Realism," below). *Erkenntnis*, on the other hand, is more complex and always involves a knowledge of something *under* some description, concept, idea, etc. Thus, in adequate cognition there must be a "coincidence" between some intended meaning or sense and an intuitive datum which answers to or fulfills this intended meaning.

51. The translation of *Selbstgegebenheit* as "self-givenness" can be a bit misleading. It does *not* imply that the *datum gives itself*, but rather that the datum is itself fully or completely present to awareness, and not merely, for example, symbolically designated. The French phrase *en personne* captures this sense nicely, but the English "in person" suggests a restriction to human beings that is not a feature of Scheler's theory.

52. "Existential" in the phrase "existential relativity" does not have anything to do with so-called existentialism. Data are existentially relative when their givenness essentially depends on the particular organization of the bearer(s) of those acts in which they are given (see "Phenomenology and the Theory of Cognition," p. 136). Scheler is especially interested in objects that are existentially relative to "living creatures generally" (and not only to man); he sometimes calls these *vital-daseinsrelative*. However, he also writes, "Philosophy can be designated as the attempt to achieve a knowledge of objects which are no longer existentially relative to life and to the possible values of life" ("Erkenntnis und Arbeit," p. 209).

53. See, for example, "Erkenntnis und Arbeit," pp. 295–98, and "Idealism and Realism," below.

parts Scheler planned to include in the work were published in this format. The fifth, unpublished part was announced as a confrontation with Heidegger's *Being and Time,* which had appeared earlier the same year in Husserl's *Jahrbuch.* Heidegger, in a letter to Frings dated August 6, 1964, stated that "Scheler was one of the very few, if not the only one, who at that time immediately recognized the question posed in *Being and Time.*" [54] When Scheler invited Heidegger to Cologne to give a lecture on Kant, the two thinkers spent three days together "in extended discussion about the relation of the question formulated in *Being and Time* to metaphysics and to Scheler's conception of phenomenology." [55] One can only await with great eagerness the publication of the manuscript for the fifth part of "Idealism and Realism" under Frings's editorship.[56]

However, the absence of this part does not diminish the value and interest of the two parts that were published. Scheler prefaces his exposition of "The Genuine Question of Reality" (part III) with a critical diagnosis of what he calls the *prōton pseudos* or "primary error" committed by Idealism and Realism alike, namely, the presupposition that whatever status the "nature" (*Sosein*) of any object has vis-à-vis the mind, the status of its existence (*Dasein*) vis-à-vis the mind must be the same. If this presupposition is overturned and *what* an object is, is allowed its independence from the fact *that* this object really exists, then the ground is cleared for the possibility of knowledge of essences (phenomenological *Wesensschau*) as well as for a philosophical examination of the nature of reality and the consciousness of reality.

In *Formalismus* Scheler had brought out the importance of the phenomenon of resistance (*Widerstand*) for the understanding of the realization of values. It is only by way of this phenomenon that consciousness of what he calls "practical reality" is given. And in a footnote to this passage he remarks,

54. See *Person und Dasein,* p. xii.
55. *Ibid.*
56. At the present time one can consult the Appendix, *ibid.* (pp. 112–15), which contains Scheler's marginal notes in his copy of *Sein und Zeit.* It would be interesting to know if Heidegger, in turn, took note of "Idealism and Realism," especially Scheler's theory of space, time, and prespatial, pretemporal "apartness" (*Auseinandersein*). See Heidegger's remark in the 1962 lecture "Zeit und Sein": "The attempt in *Being and Time,* Section 70, to reduce the spatiality of Dasein to temporality cannot be sustained" (*Zur Sache des Denkens,* p. 24).

"We leave undecided here the question whether phenomenal consciousness of reality and actuality *in general* rests on an experienced resistance." [57] "Idealism and Realism" can be read as Scheler's attempt to decide this question in favor of the view adumbrated in this note. (Those specimens of his metaphysical and anthropological thinking to which English-speaking readers have had access [e.g., *Man's Place in Nature* and *Philosophical Perspectives*] must have seemed arbitrary in the absence of the theoretical foundations they receive in this essay.)

It may be worth stating that the theory of resistance sketched in this essay is the essential complement to the analysis of the "striving" (*Streben*) which was so central to Scheler's account of ethical action and evaluation and to his critique of Kantian "rationalism" in *Formalismus*. In the constellation of these and related notions one can begin to get a glimpse of how Scheler's "systematic intention" might have been fulfilled.

These brief indications of the origins and content of the five works translated here will, I hope, suffice to give the reader an initial orientation. I have no doubt that most readers, coming to Scheler's writings from a phenomenological, an analytical, or some other background, will on more than one occasion experience that intellectual disquietude which, as Heidegger once wrote, comes over the philosopher "when he studies the historical expressions of that which corresponds to his own world of questions." But, over and above the particular and possibly more sporadic discoveries one can make, there are, I think, some more general "lessons" to be learned from Scheler's philosophizing, especially as it receives expression in the texts translated here. I shall try to make three of these lessons explicit, even at the risk of sounding "edifying."

First, there is Scheler's critical resistance to any form of "reductionism." When Scheler employs the notion of an "order of foundation" (*Fundierungsordnung*) between facts or phenomena, he does so *not* to elicit a privileged class of phenomena *in terms of which* all others may be reductively explained, but to articulate the manner in which some one item or kind of item makes possible the *intelligible givenness* of some other items or kinds of items. Hence, to say that acts of preference

57. *Formalismus*, p. 150, n. 1.

or aversion *found* acts of cognition is *not* to say that acts of cognition are *identical* with acts of preference or that the former can be constructed out of the latter. There is, after all, something suspiciously "inbred" about reductionistic patterns of explanation, since the privileged phenomena sit as both judge and jury, so to speak, of the logical culpability or intractability of the phenomena subject to reduction. Scheler's explanatory practice ordinarily consists in trying to give each class of phenomena its due; "we ought to respect," he once wrote, "the plenitude of the world and the fineness of the web of existence." [58] If this practice results, as it undoubtedly does, in explanations that are more complex and less "regimented" than those of reductionistically motivated explanations, one must at least pause to wonder whether or not such complexity is in fact ingredient in both pre-reflective and theoretical experience.

The second lesson is of a piece with the first. From the perspective of Heidegger's initiatives in *Being and Time,* it appeared that Scheler was helplessly caught in the "toils of onticity," unable to bring to sight the radical ontological basis of the matters-of-fact he establishes. This critique needs to be balanced by a "home truth": insofar as ontological truth remains germane to those experiences, facts, or beings for which it is, *qua* truth, foundational, the effort to disclose ontological truth cannot be divorced from the task of distinguishing and clarifying the phenomena at an ontic level.[59] This is especially the case where the "human things" are at issue, for the particular weight or primacy assigned to certain "extreme possibilities" (e.g., anxiety) [60] among the complete repertory of man's possibilities predetermines, one suspects, the course of subsequent ontological inquiry. It is against this background that Scheler's investigations of "values," of ethical comportment, of loving and hating, of what he calls the life-community

58. See *Die Ursachen des Deutschenhasses: Eine nationalpädagogische Erörterung* (Leipzig: Wolff, 1917), p. 125.

59. I leave unconsidered here Heidegger's move to a "thinking of Being without (or apart from) being(s)" ("Zeit und Sein," p. 25). The view of ontic and ontological truth presented is based closely on Heidegger's *The Essence of Reasons*, trans. Terrence Malick (Evanston, Ill.: Northwestern University Press, 1969), pp. 21–25, a bilingual edition incorporating the German text of *Vom Wesen des Grundes*.

60. See Heidegger's comments on *Angst* reported in Z. Adamciewski, "On the Way to Being," in *Heidegger and the Path of Thinking*, ed. John Sallis (Pittsburgh, Pa.: Duquesne University Press, 1970), p. 13.

(*Lebensgemeinschaft*), take on crucial importance. To take a single instance, if the claim he makes in *"Ordo Amoris"* that man is first and foremost an *ens amans* (a loving being) were to be sustained, then foundational or ontological thinking would have to begin by addressing itself to *this* possibility of human experience and human self-understanding.[61]

The last lesson is more elusive and less likely, I think, to win the spontaneous endorsement of most contemporary students of philosophy. Nevertheless, it would be unfair to suppress all mention of it, since it does figure centrally in Scheler's understanding of what it is to be pursuing philosophical insight.

Scheler is well aware that, in his conception of love and of its connection with knowledge, he joins company with Plato (as well as with St. Augustine and others). Despite their innumerable disagreements, Plato and Scheler seem to argue that a kind of pre-understanding of what would constitute the fulfillment of philosophical inquiry is accessible not in any act of theoretical cognition but in and by virtue of eros itself. Saying this is to do no more than raise the question of whether eros, understood as the "tendency to go outside of oneself in order to participate in another being,"[62] is indeed the precondition for the disclosure of the intelligibility of the world.

I have tried in this Introduction to prepare the way to the translated texts by making plain the obstructions readers might confront as they come to Scheler from various antecedent perspectives or traditions. I have also tried to suggest, with insufficient detail, what attractions these works might hold. Perhaps, as he makes his way into and among these texts, the reader will come to share a sense of Scheler articulated some time ago by Alexandre Kojève: "He was, in spite of everything, a true philosopher."

61. See Frings, *Person und Dasein,* pp. 47–87, and Otto Bollnow, *Das Wesen der Stimmungen* (Frankfurt am Main: Klostermann, 1941; 3d expanded ed., 1956).
62. See "Erkenntnis und Arbeit," p. 204.

Notes on the Translation

SCHELER'S WRITINGS present some unusually frustrating difficulties to the translator. It is not only that his work in large measure bears the stamp of a Kantian and Husserlian vocabulary in which terms like *Anschauung, Vorstellung, Wesenheit,* and *Gegebenheit* have long been the bane of would-be translators. Custom has sanctioned some makeshift equivalents for these. It is not only that he shares with many other German philosophical authors certain syntactic proclivities which will necessarily remain alien to the English eye and ear. These can be suppressed. In the end, one has to face up to the problem of Scheler's "style."

Scheler himself confessed to his problems with writing style. "I have the word," he said, "but not the sentence." Anyone confronting the German text might well feel surprise, for it is *sentences* he seems to have in abundance. His sentences are long; a single one can easily run the length of a standard English paragraph. They are frequently forbiddingly complex, syntactically and semantically, without an internal architecture to guide the reader through the maze. In combination, they often compound the reader's dismay instead of easing it. There are times when one looks in vain for an "on the other hand" to answer to an initial "on the one hand," and, in general, the logical "progression" of his writings can be unhelpfully obscure.

It is as though something of his speaking manner, as reported by his contemporaries, had made its way onto the printed page. Having begun on one topic, he quickly thinks of another that must be accommodated within the sentence already under way. Qualifications and amplifications are added as they occur, with little regard to grammatical fluency. (His favored mark of punctuation seems to be the dash—*Gedankenstrich*, in German.) The fact that four of the five essays translated here are fragments, three of them unpublished, of course does nothing to ameliorate this state of affairs. In short, Scheler's style can be strikingly "non-sequacious," as De Quincey said of Hazlitt's.

All this puts the translator under a rather heavy burden. He will not succeed in giving the lie to the time-proven adage: "Traduttori sono traditori"; he is free only to choose the manner of his treachery.

Mine has ranged all the way from the simple conversion of passives into actives, through the repossession of verb phrases from compound abstract nouns and the shifting of clauses in an effort to relieve the top-heaviness of a sentence, to the redistribution of sentences within a particularly recalcitrant paragraph. Infrequently, and as a last resort, I have dropped inconveniently intrusive material from the main text to the footnotes. Perhaps more often, I have added particles and other connectives to give a passage some necessary coherence. In matters of vocabulary, I have tried to avoid what might be called the "neologistic fallacy," that is, the belief that a newly minted, exotic coinage in one's own language is bound to help the reader understand the sense of the original.

It would have been naïvely generous, or so I think, to have wanted to reproduce Scheler's style intact. When literalness and lucidity are at odds with each other in a philosophical work, the translator must assure victory to the latter. Even so, the reader of these essays will sometimes have to concentrate in order to get past some inevitable residual roughness.

I have frequently inserted German words and phrases in square brackets in the text. This serves to keep the reader aware of Scheler's technical terminology as well as the translator's stratagems.

In addition, when Scheler merely alludes to an author or title I have tried to trace the exact bibliographical reference he is likely to have had in mind. Further information about less well-known figures is furnished when their names are first mentioned.

Finally, I have taken over and adapted most of Maria Scheler's notes to the first four essays. (The fifth has not yet been published in the *Gesammelte Werke*.) These notes provide helpful cross-references to other of Scheler's works, especially to *Formalismus*. I have added a few such cross-references of my own. All material not by Scheler himself is enclosed in square brackets and labeled the work of the translator (Trans.) or the editor (Ed.).

Somewhat surprisingly, there are no translations of the material included in this volume into French or Spanish, both languages in which Scheler is otherwise well represented. However, I have profited from looking at Maurice de Gandillac's French translation of *Formalismus* and at Maurice Dupuy's versions of numerous passages from the present essays in his two-volume work, *La Philosophie de Max Scheler* (Paris: Presses Universitaires de France, 1959). Moreover, I found Professor Peter Heath's translation of *The Nature of Sympathy* and Professor Manfred Frings's books and articles on Scheler extremely useful in preparing my translation.

I would like to thank Professor James Edie, of Northwestern University, and Professor Frings, of De Paul University, for their enthusiastic response when I first suggested this project. An anonymous referee for Northwestern University Press gave me much-appreciated advice on one of the essays, while the editors of the press displayed exemplary patience. Professors Henry Groen and Gerd K. Schneider, of the German Department at Syracuse University, helped me through some eleventh-hour quandaries. I was also fortunate to be able to consult Professor Hans-Georg Gadamer on certain difficult points of terminology. I want to express my gratitude to Mrs. Helen Hause for her skillful and friendly help with the final preparation of this manuscript. Finally, I want to thank my wife, Judith, for her unfailingly generous assistance and encouragement.

Selected
Philosophical
Essays

The Idols of Self-Knowledge

PREFACE

IN THE *Novum Organum* Francis Bacon placed his critical theory of the Idols as the preface to his positive methodology for the investigation of external nature. We should, he thinks, purify the "turbid mirror" of our understanding by recognizing and resolutely fighting against our natural inclinations to illusion and error. In what follows, I shall attempt to do for the sphere of inner and self-perception exactly what Bacon undertook for the sphere of external perception.

There is perhaps no more fundamental obstacle to any kind of knowledge of the psychic world [*der seelischen Welt*] than the position of many scientists and philosophers, both now and in the most recent past, that inner perception, as opposed to the external perception of nature, can never deceive, that here the lived experiences themselves coincide with self-evident and adequate knowledge of lived experiences. This theory, stemming from Descartes, of the superior self-evidence of inner over external perception is one of the foundations of every form of subjective idealism and egocentrism. It is one of the foundations of that false kind of confident self-certainty which has grown up in the course of the development of our culture. Protestantism, in particular, has tried to turn this self-certainty into a legitimate human attitude. For many people it has become

Translated from the German "Die Idole der Selbsterkenntnis," in *Vom Umsturz der Werte*, 4th ed. rev., *Gesammelte Werke* III (Bern: Francke Verlag, 1955), pp. 215–92.

[3]

the mainstay of an immoderate negativism and criticism directed against all forms of being other than the self, namely, God, nature, and objective culture. In the following this theory will be deprived of its presumed support.

A philosophy based on the procedure of phenomenological insight into essence [*Wesensschau*] ought to assert, against all forms of so-called phenomenalism and agnosticism, that absolute being, in every sphere of the external and the inner world alike, can be known with self-evident and adequate knowledge. Furthermore, it should assert that any actual separation and detachment of our spirit from this absolute being rests not on something inalterable in the constitution of the knowing subject, but only on weaknesses and inclinations which we can, in principle, overcome. However, if phenomenological philosophy claims the ability to prove this fundamental thesis, one which restores metaphysics and a way of life and being turned toward all forms of absolute givenness to their ancient privileges, then it is doubly obligated to investigate with thoroughness and precision the various forms of the seclusion of man from being (the man of our times, in particular). Similarly, it must investigate the causes and motives of every possible illusion concerning God, external objects, and man himself. At present, however, no form of seclusion cutting man off from things has taken possession of him more profoundly and more intensely than that which cuts him off from *his soul*. Those who believe in the theory of the nondeceptiveness of inner perception with a "clear conscience" stamp the character of a permanent condition upon the misery this confinement produces. This theory is thus the greatest obstacle to man's insight into his true depths.

However, the following study may also be understood as a contribution to the general theory of illusion. The concept of illusion must play a central role in a philosophy which would like to owe its final results not to rational construction but to an intuitive procedure in which one is turned toward the pure "What" (*Essence*) of the world. Its role must be similar to the role played by the concept of error in rationalistic systems. Indeed, where rationalistic philosophy tried to reduce all illusions to errors of judgment and inference, and even tried, finally, to reduce the essence of illusion to that of error, intuitive philosophy will show that all errors are based on illusions. Indeed, it will prove that error itself (in its essence) is a limiting case of a certain kind of illusion, namely, an illusion of reflection, which occurs when we consider the results of our mental acts. Moreover, a sensationalistic empiricism can no more understand the essence of illusion than philosophic rationalism. No form of illusion has anything to do with the pure material of sensation, on which the object of illusion, the phantasm [*das Phantom*], is based. These two points may be briefly illustrated for the case of perceptual illusion.

The entire field of perceptual illusion (including both inner and external perception) is "located," so to speak, between *thinking* in the proper sense, the sphere of judgment and inference, and pure *sensations*, which in every case can only be present or not be present, in a normal or abnormal manner. To be sure, sensations can give rise to an illusion; however, the illusion and its phantasm can never consist in sensations as such. If Aristotle's well-known assertion that, strictly speaking, there are no "illusions of sense" meant only what I have just said or something similar—for instance, that the senses as such can neither deceive nor err—we would have to agree. However, the falsity of Aristotle's assertion is shown by the fact that he draws from it the conclusion that all illusions are only erroneous judgments, which are distinguished from all other errors (for example, those which result from false inferences) by their immediacy. The essence of illusion consists in the fact that something is "given" in intuition (and thus also given for all possible inferences and judgments, even for mere "suppositions") which "is not itself present" (does not exist). For this reason, illusion has nothing to do with "the true" and "the false," which belong entirely within the sphere of propositions and judgments. For if the judgment conforms to what is given, it is "true," and it is "false" if it conflicts with the given.

"The moon (as a visual object) is a golden disk in the night sky" is, on a certain level of the existential relativity of the object [*für eine gewisse Stufe der Daseinsrelativität des Gegenstandes*], an indubitably true proposition. It is true regardless of whether A and B see it (from their respective positions), whether C is blind and does not see it at all, or whether D, because of color-blindness or a constriction of his visual field, sees it differently than someone with normal vision. That a normal person sees it as such a disk is simply the result of its *being* such a disk. Thus, it is not the case that *only* the statement "I see the moon as a golden disk" is true, while the statement "The moon is a golden disk" is not.[1] Similarly, it is possible to judge correctly or incorrectly about a hallucinatory or illusory object, and the proposition in which it is expressed can be "true" or "false" according to its conformity to the phantasm.

The distinction between illusory and self-evident perception does indeed involve the cognitive value found in knowing, discerning, and cognizing [*Wissen, Kennen, Erkennen*]. Nevertheless, it has so little to do with the distinction between truth and falsehood that a person who has never been perceptually deceived could at the same time still be involved in making patently false judgments. Conversely, a person who passed his life in patent illusions could make both true and false judgments about all the phantasms he introduces.[2]

Illusion must be no less sharply distinguished from another standard [*Massstab*] of simple knowing, discerning, and cognizing that has just as little to do with "true" and "false" or with error and correct thinking—the standard of the adequacy or inadequacy of perception. The distinction between true and false can no more be reduced to the degrees of the adequacy of an intuitive cognition (as Spinoza, for example, wanted to do) than can that between illusion and its opposite, self-givenness. "*Adequation*" means the fullness of what is given to us in an act of perceiving an object (or representing an object, etc.). Adequacy is distinguished from the mere completeness [*Vollständigkeit*] of knowledge about a thing which results from perception. Completeness concerns only the set of possible aspects, characteristics, and properties which could figure in

1. The perception of the golden moon disk first becomes an illusion when this object is given in perception as existing absolutely vis-à-vis the observer. [See below, note 2.—ED.]

2. Judgments are correct when the proposition which they express is "true"; "to be true," however, means that the proposition conforms to the state of affairs about which the judgment is made. [On existential relativity, illusion, and error, see the chapter on the standards of cognition in "Phenomenology and the Theory of Cognition," below. See, further, chap. V, secs. 3–5, in *Der Formalismus in der Ethik und die materiale Wertethik: Neuer Versuch der Grundlegung eines ethischen Personalismus*, 5th ed. rev., *Gesammelte Werke* II (Bern: Francke, 1966), on relativity and subjectivity; and in the author's later works, "Erkenntnis und Arbeit," in *Die Wissensformen und die Gesellschaft* 2d ed. rev., *Gesammelte Werke* VIII (Bern: Francke, 1960); and "Idealism and Realism" (1927), below.—ED.]

several possible perceptions of the same thing. The presence of an illusion in no way entails either that *fewer* characteristics of the perceived thing are given in it than in a perception which "gets" the thing in full, or that the individual act of perception involved is less adequate than in the latter case. The person who takes a wax figure for a real woman can still have grasped all (or any number of) the characteristics of the wax figure; what is important is only that they count for him as characteristics of a real woman. He can also possess any of its characteristics as adequately as one likes. Illusion is also sharply distinguished from the degree of adequacy because its occurrence is always sudden and abrupt, in contrast to the *continuous* increase or diminution of the latter (although an illusion, too, can be more or less intense).

If these differences give the upper limit of the possibility of perceptual illusion (where it meets the sphere of thinking), its lower limit is fixed by the fact that a perceptual illusion can indeed be built on illusions of seeing and hearing, but it is never a visual or auditory illusion as such. (On the other hand, visual and auditory illusions are genuine illusions; thus, they are totally distinct both from the material of sensation and from its normal or anomalous origin.)

We distinguish genuine perceptual illusions from mere (although genuine) illusions of sense in the following way. The stick lying halfway in the water looks "broken." However, this is not a genuine perceptual illusion but a (normal) illusion of sense, dependent on physical conditions, for the stick appears broken only as an object of sight, not as an object of touch. Thus, the material of sensation is completely normal in the case of the stick *qua* visual object as well as in the case of the stick one can touch, for the illusion is physically determined by the refraction of light. Likewise, it is an optical illusion that the vertical sides of a rhombus (drawn or constructed out of thin rods) appear to be longer than the horizontal, an illusion which in this case depends on physiological conditions. For when the rhombus is rotated ninety degrees, the sides that looked longer appear shorter and vice versa. A genuine perceptual illusion, however, exists whenever different sense-functions, simultaneously or in succession, furnish the same sense-contents that we are led to expect by the illusory object, namely, by the phantasm with its particular character. This occurs, for example, when I receive the impression of the form and feeling of the back or foot of a real chair even while I am touching the back or foot of a hallucinated chair. In this case we do not perceive something objectively nonexistent because we experience a primarily visual or primarily tactile illusion; rather, we experience this visual or tactile illusion *because* we think that we have before us in perception a nonexistent object such as a chair. Within the range of normal cases, the well-known Burmester illusions [3] are, in a certain sense, perceptual illusions, although here the illusory objects are not [4] permanently present for the sense of touch, as they are in the previous case.[5]

Thus, all anomalous sensations, such as sensations of color when one's eyes are closed, so-called secondary sensations, and the various kinds of after-images and the like have no claim to the title "perceptual illusion," which is exhibited in genuine hallucination. Such sensations can certainly serve as the material of illusions, especially when they lie outside the normal range. In principle, however, this is the same for all sensations, even normal ones. Sensory material of some kind usually exists for even the most genuine hallucinations, not only for illusions, however difficult it may be in particular cases to discover what it is. There is no hallucination which depends exclusively on conditions of the central nervous system. There is always some centrifugal stimulation coming from the external senses, however indirect this may be.

In the following I shall develop the theory of illusion only for illusions concerning psychic experiences and only for the principal illusions of inner perception.[6]

There are many reasons why one may be interested in illusions concerning "psychic processes." (This is how we shall

3. [Scheler refers to the so-called palisade phenomenon investigated by Ludwig Burmester in the early part of the century. In this optical illusion an observer watching the rapid rotary motion of a wheel through the palisades of an iron fence sees the rigid spokes of the wheel curved upward toward the vertical diameter.—TRANS.]

4. [Reading "nicht," from the 1915 edition of the text, which has apparently dropped out of the 1955 version.—TRANS.]

5. For it is the varying perception of structure which governs and determines the order of the components of the visual object.

6. H. Leyendecker has recently extended this investigation to cover the sphere of illusions in general. See his work which links up with our discussions, "Zur Phänomenologie der Täuschungen" (diss., Halle, 1913).

principally understand the ambiguous term "self-deceptions" [*Selbsttäuschungen*].) First, there is the phenomenologist or epistemologist who must define an illusion in contrast to an error. He must exhibit the immediately given facts of psychic being and the way in which these facts are known [*ihre Erkenntnisart*]. He must also exhibit the stages in which these facts are intuited, perceived, noticed, observed, and, finally, conceptually determined in judgments. This task does not belong to psychology, but to the theory of the cognition of mental phenomena, which is prior to any psychology, just as the theory of the cognition of nature is prior to natural science. Second, there is the psychologist who tries to *explain* illusions by presenting the mechanism responsible for their realization. Third, there is the psychopathologist who must know which psychic functions become disturbed or defective in abnormal self-deceptions. That is, he must know whether that which is disturbed in the various kinds of hallucination and illusion is the pure material of sensation or the function of perception and its components; the elements of sensory memory which are mixed in with the content of perception or the additional representations which are reproduced in perception; or, finally, the function of assertion and belief which is situated in the faculty of judgment. Furthermore, the psychopathologist must be interested in knowing the steps involved in imagining a pain. That is, he is interested in knowing how a pain with no objective basis is given to a hysterical patient. Controversies over what is or is not a case of shamming (for instance, the controversy over legislation concerning accidents connected with traumatic neuroses) [7] can be settled only by a more securely established morphology of self-deceptions, even though a morphology of this sort in no way coincides with the explanation of self-deceptions. The removal of pathological self-deceptions through medicine or education is intimately connected with the knowledge of *which* functions through which a psychic process is apprehended are disturbed when an illusion persists.

The psychotherapist has an even deeper and more fundamental interest in the present question. In present-day psycho-

7. See the following essay, "Die Psychologie der sogennanten Rentenhysterie und der rechte Kampf gegen das Übel," in *Vom Umsturz der Werte*, 4th ed. rev., *Gesammelte Werke* III (Bern: Francke, 1955).

therapy two conceptions of the goal of any form of psychotherapeutic aid contend with one another. The first of these might be called that of the psychic surgeon. According to this conception, to use psychotherapy means to interfere (in any way one can) with the patient's psychic experiences, in order to bring about a certain result. The ultimate aim of this interference is to force these experiences back onto the track of normalcy. All the methods of suggestion, for example, rest on this conception. A mechanistic version of associationism usually forms the theoretical background of this view of the goal of psychotherapy.

We can call the second the psychoanalytic or, preferably, the "Socratic" conception, since, in the school which goes by the former name, both conceptions of the goal are thoroughly confused with one another. According to this conception, the ultimate aim of psychotherapy is to lead the patient to *insight* into himself, especially into his actual past experiences, or, equally, to free him from self-deceptions. If the therapeutic technique requires interference with the course of the patient's psychic life—if, for example, hypnosis and suggestion are applied—these procedures are always serving the goal of furnishing the patient with the insight he lacks. In this case causal interference with the phenomena is not meant to alter the phenomena, to suppress some and introduce new ones. Its goal is analogous to that of a scientific experiment which occasionally interferes with nature in order to make what already exists more distinctly and discretely visible and thus to make its relations with various things intelligible. The theoretical background of this therapeutic ideal is the idea that one kind of "mental illness" is rooted not in the content and course of the mental processes the patient actually experiences, but only in the way these are grasped, suppressed, or given meaning, interpreted and judged in the functions of inner and self-perception. In other words, this form of mental illness is rooted in our *attitude* toward these processes and in the way we are cognizant of them. According to this theory, "mental illness" rests on disturbances of the functions of the "consciousness-of" mental experiences. It is only in this context that the concept of self-deception acquires its full and preeminent meaning. For, in the final analysis, at least one part of psychotherapy is oriented toward putting an end to self-deceptions.

Two things are left unchanged by this distinction between psychotherapeutic ideals: the unambiguous causal determination of a psychic disturbance, and its relation to disturbances in the nervous system and brain. The concept of self-deception and the view that there are various functions and acts through which we grasp, organize, and interpret mental processes do not imply that there is an element of arbitrariness in self-deception, or, consequently, in the anomalous operation of these functions. Rather, according to this second point of view, everything can take place in a strictly determined way, although the law governing the functions must be *distinguished* from that governing the mental contents. Even a self-deception can be necessarily and unambiguously determined. Here, too, we must be on our guard against equating being governed by law with being governed by mechanistic laws (i.e., by laws of association).[8] Moreover, the second point of view allows us to see, among other things, that in every psychic disturbance resting on a functional disturbance of this kind, there is a sign of a disturbance in the nervous system and brain. It is not a matter here of a theoretical conflict between a *materialistic* and a *spiritualistic* conception of mental and emotional disorders, but of the conflict between a *theoretical conception* based on functions and one based on contents, a conflict which has equally dominated both psychology and physiology until today. For this reason, this conflict must be settled independently in both of these fields. Of course, this cannot be shown here in any detail.

A single suggestion might be made. Whoever thinks through the second conception will be forced, in the end, to break with that view of the relationship of the body and the soul that holds that the content of mental experiences is unambiguously determined by conditions in the nervous system and brain (whether causally or in the manner of so-called parallelism). The brain and nervous system have an unambiguous causal relation, not to the content, but to what we perceive of it, to the way in which we perceive it, in short, to the coming-into-play of the functions through which we grasp the facts of our mental life. External perception is no different in this respect.

8. [On the forms of mechanical associative law, and their common existential relativity, see *Formalismus*, VI, A, 3, g.—ED.]

There, too, it is not the content "red," or "green," or "sour," and so on, but the act of sensing, of seeing or tasting, the different steps involved in perceiving this content through processes in the retina or tongue, that gets unambiguously determined in the optic or gustatory nerves and in their termini in the brain and its parts.

For this reason, the Socratic psychotherapist neither can nor will ever criticize the content of his patient's life, morally or in any other way. He will not try to change it like the obtrusive and cynical spiritual physician or preacher, nor will he try to give it any other direction than that which issues from itself. His unique goal is to get the patient to see and survey the content of his life as completely as possible. What the patient then does with his life is his own affair (or a matter of ethics), not the doctor's. Psychotherapy cannot change the content or the value of his life. It can change only what and how much the patient takes in and comprehends and the way in which he does so.

This second therapeutic ideal is considerably more modest than the ideal of the psychic surgeon. It is characterized by Socratic *reserve,* instead of the "surgeon's" cynical intrusion into the way other men manage their lives.

[I] THE ESSENCE OF ILLUSION IN CONTRAST TO ERROR

THERE ARE TWO POSSIBLE SOURCES for the falsehood of a proposition concerning an actual object, sources which ordinary language has already divided into "error" and "illusion." According to this distinction, illusion always has its proper sphere in immediate cognition; error, in indirect or mediated cognition, especially in inferences. If, on the basis of some moisture which I see on the way to my house, I judge that "it has been raining," and if I find afterward that farther along the street is not wet, and if, finally, I learn that a street-cleaning truck has passed by my house, I know that my judgment is in error. The rain was in no way given to me in the moisture which I saw; however, I *inferred* that it had rained or I associated the idea of rain with the moisture and then brought it into logical connection with the latter. The case is entirely different if I find that "in its cloak of mist the oak has grown into a towering giant." This is an illusion. Similarly, if the stick lying halfway in the water looks broken to me, this, too, is an illusion.

In illusion there is, first of all, a certain content, namely, that which I think that I see, sense, or feel. It makes no difference whether I make this or that judgment about this content. If I do judge, a proposition results which is false as regards the actual case, but can be true as regards the illusory phantasm; but I need not make any judgment at all. However, there is still another element in illusion apart from this content. The mere appearance of the broken stick is certainly not yet an illusion. Illusion consists rather in my taking the state of affairs of the stick's being broken, which is there before me in the appearance, for a real property of the actual stick. Although I do not have in my intuition the actual stick as it is actually constituted (otherwise, illusion would be impossible), nonetheless, at the first glance the sphere of being of "solid things" [*die Seinssphäre "fester Dinge"*] is present to me. I look past the appearance into this sphere of being and mistakenly assign the phenomenal state of affairs to it. There are those who might think, "What good are these complicated distinctions?" The broken stick and the straight stick are, they would say, two completely equivalent appearances and the only distinction between them consists in the fact that the first appearance belongs to the sense of sight, the other to the sense of touch. Our habit of expecting that the stick will also feel broken to the sense of touch leads to illusion. If I run my hand along the stick this expectation will be disappointed. Our then calling the stick which is present to the sense of touch the "real" or "actual" stick is unjustified and arbitrary. This is the result of our instinctive inclination to prefer the data of touch over those of sight as witnesses to what we call "real." [9] If this account were correct, an inference (or equivalent proceeding) of the following form must have been made on this occasion: "If I handle the stick, it will also be broken." The expectation built upon this inference would be disappointed. Illusion, then, would be reduced to a case of error. Nonetheless, the distinction between illusion and error retains its force despite this attempted reduction. This conception of illusion cannot explain how it is

9. So, for example, Ernst Mach in *Die Analyse der Empfindungen* (Jena, 1908). [English translation by C. M. Williams and S. Waterlow, *The Analysis of Sensations* (Chicago, 1914).—TRANS.]

that we refer both appearances to the *same* real thing. Why don't we say, "There are *two* sticks, one for the sense of touch and one for the sense of sight"? Then there would be no illusion. Moreover, the preferred position of the datum of touch explains nothing. This preferred position of one appearance over another still fails to render that identical reference to the same "stick" intelligible. Besides, it is not correct that we give preference to the data of touch as signs of the real over those of sight.[10] (For not even the advocates of this theory will dare to assert seriously that the sense of the word "real" was discovered through a sensation of touch.)

If, when I cross my fingers, two balls are "given" to me, while, in fact only one is there and I see only one, then I don't say: "There are actually two." In this case the datum of sight has priority. In addition, the illusion is not diminished when we feel along the length of the stick; we merely avoid making a false statement on the basis of the illusion. Not only does the pure content of the appearance remain, but also I still "think" that I "see" the stick as broken. Illusion, therefore, cannot last only as long as that unfulfilled expectation lasts, for at this moment the expectation no longer exists and yet the illusion is still there.

Thus we must admit that in both appearances we immediately perceive the *same* real thing. Only in this way is a contradiction possible between the *propositions* built upon these appearances, namely, "The stick is broken," "The stick is straight." However, a contradiction of this sort cannot be considered an instrument with which we construct the real thing.[11] The presupposition of this theory, that we first of all perceive visual and tactile appearances and then construct the real bodily thing out of them, is totally wrong. We perceive *things-*

---

10. [On the problem of reality, see "Erkenntnis und Arbeit," chap. VI.—ED.]

11. Just as little can the assumption of the existence of a continuous, objective magnitude, of weight, for example, be understood on the basis of the contradictions which come about in conformity with our sensibility; as if the contradiction, weights $A = B$, $B = C$, $A < C$, first led to the assumption of a continuous, objective magnitude of weight. For it is the apprehension of the contents of sensation as "signs" of an already *assumed* continuous, objective weight that first introduces the contradiction. In opposition to this view, compare H. Poincaré, *La Science et l'hypothèse* (Paris, 1902). [English translation by W. Greenstreet, *Science and Hypothesis* (London, 1905).—TRANS.]

themselves and as such, however incompletely and one-sidedly; it is through subsequent acts of reflection that we first find out what parts of the given were given to us in mere seeing or touching. In the visual appearance of the "broken" stick I look at once at the stick as a thing. There is no need for me to expect that, under certain conditions, I shall get a sensation of touch, for example, in the course of the muscular sensations connected with grasping, etc. And the illusion consists now in this: Without any hesitation, I apprehend the brokenness of the stick, which is given in the visual appearance, as a real property of the physical stick. That is to say, I mistakenly assign this state of affairs (which, to be sure, as a visual content and state of affairs, is incontestable, and can be physically explained) to a level of being [*Seinsschicht*] on which it does not belong: to the level of really existent *things* [*dinglich realen Daseins*]. Therefore, more than one state of affairs and more than one level of being are always involved in an illusion. Accordingly, an illusion occurs whenever (1) I do not apprehend the state of affairs *b* on the deep level of being *B*—here, for example, the level of real things—but do apprehend the level *B* itself, in which the state of affairs is found; and (2) I apprehend another state of affairs *a* in immediate intuition and perceive it, not on the level *A* in which it is found and which I also apprehend (here the level of the visual object), but on the level *B* (thus, within the sphere of real things). Consequently illusion is wholly independent of the sphere of judgment, the sphere of "believing," "asserting," and "supposing." Illusion takes place in the prelogical sphere of states of affairs [12] and consists in an incongruous relation [*unangemessenen Verhältnis*] between at least two states of affairs and the levels of being to which they belong.[13]

Error is quite different, for it consists in a relation between the state of affairs signified in the judgment and the state of affairs existing in intuition. It consists, therefore, in a contradiction between what I signify in a judgment, or, better, what is signified in the meanings and combinations of meanings in-

12. For a more precise account of the subject, see A. Reinach, "Zur Theorie des negativen Urteils," in *Festschrift für Th. Lipps* (Leipzig: Münchener Philosophische Abhandlungen, 1911).

13. [See the later distinction between metaphysical, epistemological, and common illusion in "Phenomenology and the Theory of Cognition," below.—ED.]

volved in the judgment, and the state of affairs given and existing in intuition. Here, too, we have two states of affairs, one
signified, the other existing; one merely thought, the other given
in intuition. However, there is no question here of levels of
being. While illusion remains wholly within the sphere of the
intuitive, error consists in a relationship between what is
thought and what is intuited. The false statements which a
victim of hallucination, for example, makes about the reality
around him are not errors and need not be. He can describe the
color, form, size, and position of a hallucinatory object—a bear,
for instance—in such a way that the state of affairs signified
by the judgment corresponds completely to what is given in
intuition. In this case he commits no error at all. He can successively take note of this and that feature of the hallucinatory
object and subsume it under meanings; he can draw correct
inferences from what he sees before him. Naturally, he can still
make an error if he asserts the existence of states of affairs
which are not given to him in intuition or which are given to
him differently than he asserts.

Nonetheless, one distinction clearly emerges. The pure phenomenon which is given in an intuition is always a *fact*
[*Tatsache*] and as such is incontestable and unassailable.
Naturally, illusion does not consist in the content of this fact
but only in my assignment of this actual content to a level of
being other than its own. In the case of error, I can assert a
state of affairs which in no sense exists or subsists. This is
impossible in the case of illusion, in which that which is "meant"
or "intended" [*das Gemeinte*] always "subsists" in some way or
another. Illusion concerns only the "mode" of existence, not
existence itself. In the case of error I can posit a content which
contradicts every content in the sphere of intuitive states of
affairs. This, too, is impossible in the case of illusion, for what
makes up the *content* of the illusion is always an actually
intuited content, and there can be no illusion about this. Illusion occurs when this factual content is perceived on a level
of being to which it does not belong. Thus, every illusion can
(in principle) be removed and disillusionment can be brought
about, if one can learn to see a content on its rightful level of
being without forcing the content itself to vanish or change.
For example, there is no longer an illusion if I assign the

brokenness of the stick to the visual object. There is also no illusion any longer if I retrace a feeling of hatred whose original object has been suppressed so that it has thereby become an attitude which can extend to all possible objects, back to its original object. Illusion is brought about only by my perceiving the actual thing, the stick, as broken. Similarly, only the fact that I hate things which were not originally given to me as "hostile" constitutes illusion.

Furthermore, we may call attention to one phenomenological distinction between error and illusion. In illusion, what leads to a false statement does not proceed from "me." I do not feel myself active in the illusion. Rather, "an appearance passes itself off as something" which it is not. In error, on the contrary, I am the one who gives the meaning, who interprets, etc., and error is the result of these conscious activities. Thus I arrive at a false proposition through my conscious activity. In illusion, on the other hand, an appearance claims to be something which it is not. It is like a "lie," but a lie which has its origin in the object, not in me. Even if we could explain this situation by bringing in involuntary and unconscious activities of the self (in quite the same way people explain the phenomenon in our volitional life of "being attracted" or "being repulsed" by things, whatever they may be, by bringing in certain involuntary intentions to move the limbs), the appearance itself is irrefutable. Illusion, therefore, is far less individual, far less subjective, than error. The mechanism which brings it into being operates independently of that self which is consciously acting, deliberating, or judging, and which knows how to distribute its attention arbitrarily.

[II] ILLUSION AND INTERNAL PERCEPTION

WE CANNOT DEFINE the concept of illusion concerning mental processes more precisely without first having settled a few things about the mode in which the mental content of cognition generally becomes *accessible*. If we disregard the sphere of judgment and inference—the seat of error alone, not of illusion—we can confine ourselves to those functions and acts through which we get access to the *material* for acts of thought, and those in which we expand, in thought, the immediately given mental content into the idea of a real mental being entering into causal relations.

The sum total of these acts and functions is commonly called "inner perception," "inner intuition," "inner observation," "notice," "reflection," and, by a few philosophers, simply "inner sense." It is obvious that these words denote very different things and that the corresponding concepts must be more precisely distinguished.

Before we set to work on (1) the existence of a special "inner perception," (2) the distinction between this and "external perception," and (3) the kind of evidence belonging to "inner perception," let us be on guard, first of all, against some very common "equivocations." We often find self-perception, self-observation, or even self-consciousness, used as synonyms of inner perception. But this is clearly without any justification. For if "self" [Selbst] is to mean here the individual object of perception, then we could say that inner perception could coincide with self-perception only if there were no mental states of affairs which could be given without having an immediate intuitive relation to the individual "self" of the perceiver. However, mental processes do exist which are indifferent to the ego [Ich], that is, those which become perceptible without any positive or negative relation to a *particular* "ego," as well as processes alien to the ego, those which enter into the experienced individual "ego" with an obtrusiveness and compulsiveness similar to that of an external reality, e.g., compulsive motives or ideas. For example, we can think a thought without knowing whether it is our own or only the fruit of reading. We can have a feeling without knowing whether it is our own feeling or one which came into us only through psychic contagion [Ansteckung]. Thus, self-perception can be absent not only in, for example, the external perception of a color, which *always* runs its course without conscious relation to the self and without being accompanied by an awareness that I am the one who is performing this function. Inner perception or perception of a mental content is not necessarily connected with self-perception either. Only someone who wants to base the whole of psychology on individual consciousness of the "ego," as Theodor Lipps does, could dispute this. Thus the "ego" or the mental self [das psychische Selbst] is only one object among others of inner perception, although one of a special sort.

However, this equation is misleading in still another sense. One's own self is not at all given to one *only* through inner perception. If I gaze at my arms, legs, and hands, then I perceive myself in all these just as much as I do when I look, through experiences or feelings, to my self which is experiencing them. *Self*-perception is opposed not to external perception but to the perception of *another*. It is in no way obvious that the latter necessarily coincides with "external perception." This is deduced, for the most part, only by those with the peculiar idea that the soul of another can never be perceived but can only be "inferred" from his bodily behavior (which is allegedly the only thing accessible to "perception"), or "emphatically projected" into the image of his corporeal existence, out of the store of what I myself have experienced.[14]

The question of the existence of an inner perception is not concerned with the merely contingent use of the term, when we ask whether it is "I myself" or "another" who perceives the mental; it is concerned with whether there is a particular class of acts and act-orientations which deserves to be called "inner" perception, as distinguished from "external perception" or "perception pure and simple." Mental facts would appear and be cognized in these acts alone.

The existence of a special act-orientation called "inner perception" has been disputed on many sides; those who affirm its existence have done so in different senses.

14. It is not true that we must first comprehend the expressive manifestations of another's experiences, laughing, crying, blushing, entreating, etc., or better, the color, form, shape, and movement of these as properties and activities of *physical bodies*, before they can be grasped as symbols of psychic experiences. The other's physical body is no more "given," in the sense of intuitively "self-given," than the other's soul is. It, too, is supposed [*vermeint*] and thought to stand behind the appearances. It is precisely in this way, however, that shame or entreaty can be imagined [*vermeint*] and "perceived" in the appearances, without my having to *start* by grasping the phenomenon of blushing as a flow of blood to the head and cheeks. I perceive the "shame" in this, I perceive the "joy" in the laughter, and I have no need of an inference. This is not the place to go into this difficult problem with greater precision. A detailed theory of the perception of another's soul can be found in the appendix to my book *Zur Phänomenologie und Theorie der Sympathiegefühle und von Liebe und Hass: Mit einem Anhang über den Grund zur Annahme der Existenz des fremden Ich* (Halle: Niemeyer, 1913). [English translation by Peter Heath, *The Nature of Sympathy* (London: Routledge & Kegan Paul, 1958).—TRANS.]

At one time people asserted that the physical and the mental are only generically *different objects,* like trees and houses, which are given or perceived *in the same way.* These generically different unities would then have to be definable, that is, we would have to be able to specify which features distinguish mental from physical objects. I want to start by considering somewhat more closely these attempted definitions, especially the Cartesian, which equates the physical with the extended, the mental with the nonextended, and then the definition of Franz Brentano, for whom hearing, seeing, judging, believing, or everything actlike, etc., is mental, while the content in these, e.g., color or tone, is physical.

After the ancient concept of *Psyche* = power of life had fallen into ruin,[15] only one attempt that I know of was made to give a definition purely in accordance with the characteristic contents of the objects. This is the classification, current since Descartes, of physical and mental objects into extended and nonextended, or, positively, into "extended" and "thinking." However, this distinction is, first, a pure metaphysical construction without *any* antecedent investigation of the phenomena. At bottom, no search was made for anything common in the appearances themselves, in the individual facts; two kinds of real substances were simply set up, with *physical* becoming the mode of the first kind, and *mental,* the mode of the other. Second, this distinction has no basis in the phenomena. How could the mental *not* be extended, especially in the broad sense in which Descartes uses the term, so that all qualities—color, tone, even solidity, time, and force, etc.—fall on the mental side? Is an odor not extended? How is a color or a tone, for example, going to be a mode of a nonextended thing? Isn't a sensible pain extended? Isn't hunger extended, since it is felt to be filling the epigastric region? I picture a red wall to myself. If I picture and "see" a certain existent red wall as existing, then it encounters me in *its* extension as well, although without the bodily character of a perceived object. Here the extension of the wall is given in the act of picturing and the content of this picture is extended, however little the

15. For Aristotle, biology coincides with the psychology of the nutritive soul (*to threptikon*), which he ascribes to plants, and the sensitive (*to aisthētikon*) and locomotive (*to kinētikon kata topon*) soul, which he ascribes to animals and men in addition to the first.

wall given as real enters into it. In another case I merely imagine a red wall (without seeing it before me inwardly), or merely remember seeing a particular red wall, when I succeed in recalling the act of seeing itself. There is a distinction between these and the first case, in which I see the wall *itself* inwardly. In the last two cases the red wall itself is not phenomenally face-to-face with me. I no longer picture it in the same space of the actual things around me. I know that the given is dependent on me and, so to speak, held up by me. The given has only a symbolic relation to the wall itself. But what is represented or pictured is no less extended than before. If someone says, Yes, but the "picturing" is not extended, then I deny that psychology has anything to do with this act. It is concerned with "representations," that is, with things, and these *are* extended. Certainly, it never has to do with things in space! Nonetheless, with extended things! Extension is far from being spatial extension. What then is the distinction between the thought of extension and the representation of extension, if not that the representation (as content) is *itself* extended? To be sure, "representing" the red wall is, in a philosophical-phenomenological sense, an intentional relation. This act is undoubtedly not extended; but neither is this act the thing "representation of a red wall." And empirical psychology is concerned with this, with this something given as a real thing in internal perception. The real object, "red wall," and the real object, "representation of the red wall," arise from the same phenomenal *content,* which is given "in person" when the red wall is represented.

The sensory feelings, too, are undoubtedly extended. The Cartesian doctrine, that a pain and a feeling of the sweetness of sugar owe their extension and their phenomenal location to a process of so-called projection from the center to the peripheral areas of the body, is a completely groundless assumption. It is just as groundless as the theory, already refuted by Hering,[16] Mach, Avenarius,[17] and others, that the

---

16. [Ewald Hering (1834–1918), a German physiologist with special interests in the theory of color vision.—TRANS.]

17. [Richard Avenarius (1843–96), a "positivist" philosopher who tried to develop a "naïve realism" free of the elements introduced ("introjected") into reality in the act of knowing. His principal work was the *Kritik der reinen Erfahrung,* 2 vols. (Leipzig, 1888–90).—TRANS.]

content of sensation is first *projected* into space. This is the result of a metaphysical construction which starts with a pointlike soul located in the brain, a soul whose mode of existence certainly would have to be "primarily" nonextended.

However, as little as everything mental is unextended, so little, on the other hand, is everything physical extended. The intensive magnitudes (e.g., velocity, magnitude of tension, etc.) remain an irreducible datum, despite Descartes's attempt to exclude them from what is given in nature and to *reduce* them completely to extensive magnitudes, in whatever way they could be measured in terms of their proportionality to extensive magnitudes. All the various attempts to reduce the concept of force or the datum of intuition which fulfills it to a so-called empathetic projection [*Einfühlung*] of the soul's experiences of activity or the sensations of muscular tension onto natural objects have proved a total failure. The fact that we refer certain passive sensations in the muscles to sensations of muscular tension presupposes the physical givenness of "tension." The concept of movement, which Descartes wants to reduce to the concept of mere change of place, finds its fulfillment only in the static or dynamic *tendency* of that which is capable of moving from point to point. This tendency is always given along with the continual change of place of an identical something, and it is through this tendency that simple change of place first gets the quality "moving," that is, first becomes a *movement*. Quality, however, a category which Descartes wanted to deny to everything physical and to assign to the mental alone, retains an extramental significance in mathematics (e.g., qualitative geometry of *analysis situs*) as well as in physics. Since this question cannot be discussed in detail here, permit me to refer to the excellent treatment of this last point by Duhem.[18]

Furthermore, the Cartesian construction is completely shattered against the fact that the totality of the manifestations of *life* and the givenness of the "body" (which is sharply distinguished from the sum of organic sensations and all merely corporeal unities) find *no place at all* in the classification of merely "extended" and unextended "thinking" substances and

18. See P. Duhem's works on the foundation and history of mechanics and physics. [E.g., *Etudes sur Léonard de Vinci*, Series I–III (Paris, 1906–13).—TRANS.]

their modes. The givenness of "life" and "living body" cannot be reduced to the empathetic projection of a primarily psychic feeling onto external objects of perception, or to a mere grouping of physical appearances which are also found in what is (phenomenally) dead, or, finally, to a mere "combination" of physical and mental phenomena. They represent an ultimate, elementary class of phenomena.[19]

Wherever we look we will find no features which mental facts possess and physical facts do not. Meumann once remarked in his critique of W. Wundt (who also rightly denied [20] that the distinction between mental and physical is a distinction between definable genera of objects such as, for example, the distinction, between trees and houses) that it is certainly clear that "feelings, activities, relations" are present only within the mental, while atoms, e.g., exist only in the world of physical objects. Now, in the first place, that is no definition; and regardless of that, Meumann's notion is mistaken. What does he understand by feelings? One can understand by this term a quality or an aggregate of qualities, e.g., those which are identically the same in my experience of pleasure or displeasure *and* in the pleasant or unpleasant features of a thing [*Sache*], identical in *my* felt serenity and repose and in the serenity of the blue sky *and* in the repose of a forest. If by "feeling" one understands *this* quality, then one has no right to say that *feelings* are mental. What is pleasant and unpleasant, serene and tranquil, can be found just as originally in the object of *external* perception and thus in physical objects. If we understand by "feeling," as Lipps, for example, does, a "determination of the self," a feature of self-experience, then these are indeed mental facts, but then we are not defining feelings according to their content, but according to their mode of being and givenness, which *eo ipso* cannot be further defined. Analogously, there is something common to any feeling I have of "soaring effort" and the force of resistance which I sense in the

19. I have treated this question with more precision in the appendix to my book on the feelings of sympathy and intend to continue my investigation of those aspects of the question which are important for laying the foundations of biology, in a work on the foundations of biology which will appear shortly. [This work never appeared.—ED.]

20. W. Wundt, *Grundriss der Psychologie,* 10th ed. (Leipzig, 1896, 1911), p. 3. [See E. Meumann, "Wilhelm Wundt zu seinem achtzigsten Geburtstage," *Deutsche Rundschau,* Vol. XXXVIII (1913).—TRANS.]

flying stone I want to stop, or the tension in a thread which I am tugging, an identical content of something "dynamic." My own activity and the activity in the "leaping" or "rushing" river and the "activity" which is, as I said, a component as a "tendency" in every external phenomenon of movement, contain something common, an identical material of pure intuition, which *can* be mental as well as physical, but for just this reason is originally neither one nor the other. It makes still less sense to call relations "mental." Is the distance between two material bodies, for example, the sun and the earth, not a physical fact? Here, too, we must draw some distinctions. We distinguish (1) the essence of relations themselves from the essence of the consciousness of relations, that is, the essence of the consciousness of the difference between two weights, say, which are physical objects, *or* between two objects of sensation which are mental facts. We distinguish (2) factually existing relations, for example, the distance between two bodies, or the differences between two colors, from relations between states of consciousness; in other words, we distinguish relations of physical objects from relations of mental states, such as the differences between sensations. Only the relations of lived-experience (in the latter sense) are "mental facts"— *not* the experiences of relations and *not* the relations between physical objects. "Atoms," however, do not belong here. It is a question here of the *phenomenal points of departure* for all mental construction, and not of any of the products of that construction themselves.

Precisely because there is *no* such definition of "mental" and "physical," it emerges quite clearly that "mental" is a genuine essence; not a particular existent content, but a form of existence, associated with a correspondingly particular form of intuition, in keeping with the essential connection between the form of an act and the form of existence. Thus, the concept of "the mental" is not abstracted from individual mental facts as something "common" in them. Nevertheless, the "mental" is still a matter of being in general, and the intuition associated with it is still a matter of a pure and formless intuition. This thesis in no way implies the so-called theory of ordering and the doctrine of viewpoint. Only because the mental is a form of existence and givenness does it make sense to speak of the distinction between external and inner intuition (and percep-

tion) as a distinction in the direction and form of intuition.[21] If mental objects were distinguished from physical objects by common features specifiable in their definition, or distinguished from physical objects only by a different arrangement of the *same* elements, then this way of talking would make no sense. We would then have to say that the mental and the physical are not one thing perceived in two different *ways,* but one thing perceived in one and the same way. Just as there is no special perception for plants and animals, an inner and an external perception could not exist as kinds and modes of perceiving. The distinction between forms of perception first emerges just because it is *not* a distinction between empirical objects.

The theory of Franz Brentano,[22] Samuel Alexander, and Carl Stumpf is on the border between that type of theory which holds that mental and physical facts can be differently defined and those theories of order which reduce the difference to one in the method of observation. It asserts (in Brentano's version) that *acts and functions* are mental, e.g., judging, observing, synthesizing, comprehending, willing, hearing, seeing, feeling, remembering; and that the "appearances" which are "intentionally" given in these acts or functions are physical. Stumpf defines the theory more clearly and thereby modifies it: (*a*) Appearances and acts [23] are immediately distinct in experience [*Erleben*]. No predicate of functions is ascribed to appearances (and conversely). Furthermore, appearances and acts vary independently of one another. *The same tone* can be heard, represented, judged, observed, contemplated, etc. Moreover, acts do not first provide appearances with their "relations" and "aggregations"; rather, these relations and aggregations are already met with [*vorgefunden*] in particular functions. (*b*) Stumpf, unlike Brentano, does not identify appearances with the physical but assigns appearances to

21. [See *Formalismus,* VI, A, on the distinctions among the qualities, directions, and forms of intuition.—ED.]

22. [See Franz Brentano, "The Distinction between Mental and Physical Phenomena," in *Realism and the Background of Phenomenology,* ed. Roderick Chisholm (Glencoe, Ill.: Free Press, 1960), pp. 39–61.—TRANS.]

23. [See Carl Stumpf, "Erscheinungen und psychische Funktionen," *Abhandlungen der Königlichen Preussischen Akademie der Wissenschaften* (Berlin, 1907). In this article Stumpf groups together acts, states, and experiences under the concept of "mental functions."—ED.]

"phenomenology," which does not pose any questions of reality. Appearances are, first, the contents of sensations [*Sinnesemp-findungen*] (and their spatial and temporal properties), and, second, the images of these in memory (appearances of the second order). These three immediate givens (functions, appearances, relations) are not the objects of inquiry; rather they furnish the material for the concept-construction which first leads to objects. "Objects" alone, not appearances, are "physical"; objects which "are inferred from appearances and are the subjects [*Träger*] of changes, arranged in spatio-temporal relations."

Brentano, however, also holds that the acts and functions are perceived by inner perception and that this perception is "evident," while, on the contrary, the "contents," for example, colors or tones, perceived in the acts are never perceived with evidence and hence can always exist or not exist. ("Evidential superiority of inner perception.")

This division is equally misleading for phenomenology and for psychology. Is what is called "act" the same in psychology and phenomenology? Certainly not! If in "inner perception" I look at myself and what is given as something belonging to me, I carry out an act of inner perception, perhaps encompassing an act of noticing, or of observation (e.g., observing a fantasy-image present at this moment or a sensory feeling, etc.), and I do so in exactly the same way that I perform an act of observation in external perception when I observe the sun through a telescope, for instance. In this sense of the word "act," an act can *never* become the object of any sort of perception; it can never turn into an object at all, never become an "entity" [*Dasein*]. The being of a genuine act consists rather in its performance [*Vollzug*] and therefore is *absolutely,* not relatively, distinct from the concept of an object. This performance can come about straightforwardly or with "reflection." Still, this "reflection" is no "objectification," no "perception," and hence no "inner perception," which is itself only a particular kind of act. Reflection is only a hovering, completely unqualified "consciousness-of," accompanying the act as it is being performed; reflection is possible only when the person is not totally absorbed in carrying out the act. "Reflection" is distinct from all representational [*vorstellig*] conduct in general. Even the performance of an act of external perception can be given in this way in reflection.[24] Pure intuition, furthermore, can be "given"; the quality of an act and the equality, difference, and identity of the quality in several acts can be objectively [*gegenständlich*] given. But none of this is by any means the act itself. Thus, I can in a second act verify "that I just now remembered yesterday's fine weather." Then the act of remembering just performed is not given to me *qua* act in act number two; only its quality, namely, that it is an act of remembering, is given. I know only, on the basis of an essential interconnection, that an act "belongs" to it, something of the same nature as what I am now performing. Psychology is never in any way concerned with acts in this sense, acts whose essential content is "intentionality" or "consciousness-of" and whose mode of being is "performance." For psychology is entirely concerned with existent objects [*daseienden Gegenstände*]. (1) There is no activity which could be increased or intensified (as in all attention). (2) There is no phenomenal time-duration [*Zeitdauer*] in it; an act in this sense is something that cuts through all phenomenal time-duration and never spreads itself over a duration of time. (3) An "act" furthermore is absolutely distinct from an object. I can still say, in this (phenomenological) way of looking at things, that this act performed just now is an act of remembering, of willing, etc.; but I can never say that "this act of remembering is constituted in such and such a way." For I can be certain of one thing: that at which I am looking here is never the act itself, the act of remembering, but is always something that belongs to its (fully reduced) *content*.

What Stumpf calls "functions" are something totally different from an "act," which is performed and can "be" only in its performance. Functions are not performed but "perform themselves." This is the case with, for instance, seeing, hearing, even noticing, observing, comprehending, and judging. I am thus not denying that there are "functions," but I agree with Stumpf when he distinguishes the functions from what appears in the function of seeing or of hearing, etc., that is, from color or tone. Functions themselves, looked at from the perspective of the genuine act and the inner distinctions in the act's inner quality, form, and direction, still belong among the

24. [See *Formalismus*, VI, A, 3, a, b, on act, performance, and reflection.—ED.]

"total materials" of acts. These materials are divided, in turn, into functions and appearances. The distinction between functions and acts consists, then, in their manner of being and of being given. (1) Acts are performed (by persons); functions perform themselves, they run their course (as mental). (2) Functions become objective in inner perception, at least in immediate memory; acts do not. (3) Mental functions are changing modes of behaving and operating that presuppose some kind of act-performance and something given in it. Functions have no constitutive meaning for the essence of "consciousness-of" and its species, and therefore none for the essence of the mental. Whatever belongs to acts and to their different qualities, forms, directions, and basic species is part of the constitution of every finite "consciousness of something," during each instant of its existence. This is completely independent of the stage of development this consciousness has reached (for instance, perception, immediate expectation, immediate recollection; striving, feeling, having a representation, inner perception, external perception, consciousness of the body). Thus, these qualities, etc., are contained in all conscious experiences (however simple these may be). This is not so for the operation of functions; attention can be missing, seeing or hearing can be in play or not, and so on. It can be difficult to distinguish that which is a function and that which is an act. Whoever thinks he can reduce memory and expectation to reproduction and judgment [25] must deny that they belong to the sphere of acts. The question of judgment is especially difficult; for my part, I do not count judgment as belonging to the sphere of acts, although it does belong to "thinking," in the sense of grasping the meaning of anything in general.

Regardless of this, I must contest Brentano's thesis that there are only physical appearances, or that *all* "appearances" as such are "physical," and Stumpf's theses that (1) "appearances" of the first and second order are not objects of psychology; (2) there are no physical appearances, since only the objects which are inferred and thought and thus cannot "appear" can be "physical"; (3) the object is equivalent to what is "thought," what is "grasped in a concept"; and (4) functions

---

25. [See the criticism of the reproduction theory of memory and expectation in *Formalismus*, VI, A, 3, g.—ED.]

are always "mental." Instead there are not only physical but also *mental appearances*. I am not acquainted with any psychology which does not concern itself with memory images, fantasy images, and states of feeling, and with the natural course of all these. Any consistent psychological associationism which in general did not recognize functions would be condemned from the start as total nonsense. And yet, such an associationism still has a demonstrable justification.[26] However, it is not possible to distinguish functions from appearances to such an extent that the two are assigned to completely different sciences. Even Stumpf does not follow his distinction in practice. To say that tones and colors are not necessarily mental appearances is indeed quite correct; but to say that they cannot be appearances is incorrect. For, as part of the content of a particular self-consciousness, they are appearances; they are appearances to the extent they are experienced in relation to the self. The tone we hear is not, necessarily, a mental fact. "Hearing" is indeed a function; but, insofar as it comes into play in external perception and is trained on, for example, corporeal things, it is not necessarily a mental function. It is a function of the body or a vital function, which does not need to be given in either inner or external perception, but nonetheless *can* be given. But the tone which is experienced as sensed [*empfunden*] by me, which has an experienced reference to the self, is a "mental appearance." This is then all the more true of the tone which I "hear inwardly," of the landscape "inwardly before me," when I am conscious that I am "supporting" them in representation. Everything which is given in an imaginative-space, an inner visual space which diverges from real space (e.g., Kandinsky's "pseudo-hallucinations"), is also a "mental appearance." In contrast, the Starnberg Sea itself, which I am now apprehending when I remember seeing it, just as it is, there in the real landscape of Germany, is not a mental but a physical appearance, even though I have it only in my memory. I can remember physical events, a thunderstorm, for instance, as well as mental events, such as a personal experience with a man. Does the mental experience now become a "physical appearance" (as Brentano has it) because it is an "appearance" and not a function like "remembering"?

26. [On the relative justification of the theory of association, see *Formalismus*, VI, A, 3, g.—ED.]

Or an "appearance of the second order," with which phenomenology would have to do? Here the impossibility of this
definition is obvious. In what way, moreover, would the represented Apollo or a centaur be a physical appearance? Certainly this object is distinct from the "act of representing it"
[*Vorstellen*]. But this "representing" is an act in the phenomenological sense. It has nothing at all to do with the "representation" of the psychologist. Yet this concept of "representation" has its justification, which is demonstrated as soon as I
state that for Greek believers Apollo was not only an intentional
object distinct from the representation of Apollo, which is
what he always is for phenomenologists, but was also intended
to be a *religious* object as well, an object of devotion, perhaps.
For me it is not a religious object, but only the "representation"
of one. Here it is clear that "representing" as an act is as necessary for the Greeks who represented Apollo *as* it is for me; for
I must again in this sense "represent" the representation of a
religious object. " 'Representation' of a 'representation' " makes
sense as a verbal combination only if the first word "representation" designates the *act* of representing; the second, the representation as a *thing* [*Vorstellungsding*], which is what the psychologist understands by the term. A "representation" in this
sense is a *thing* in exactly the way a stone is a thing. The representation thus falls entirely within the range of objects and
appearances. Consequently, there are physical as well as mental
appearances.

We saw that none of these attempted definitions withstands
criticism.[27] An investigation of the question shows that we cannot conceive the unity of the "mental" except by looking at the
particular way in which we perceive it, which was just now
called "inner perception." Inner perception, therefore, is not

27. The sphere of the mental is certainly wider than that of intentional
acts. It embraces sensations and states of feeling as well. Also, one cannot
deny that the content of a fantasy is mental, whatever may be imagined
in it, whether a physical or a mental thing. On the other hand, the acts in
which something mental is given—thus the act of inner perception itself
with all its characteristics—should not be called mental, if we want to
avoid an infinite regress. The three concepts of consciousness are: (1)
Consciousness = a "consciousness-of," any intentional "meaning" and
being trained upon; (2) Consciousness = the sum of the phenomena of
inner perception; and (3) Consciousness = the sum of an individual's real
experiences. The second is a species of the first, and the third is derived
from the second.

the perception of the "mental," which has already been established independently of this mode of perception and defined as a generic unity of objects. "Mental" is a meaning which is fulfilled *when* we strike out in the particular direction which the act of an "inner perception" takes and, so to speak, follow it up. "Mental" is that which comes to light through inner perception. As I said, we would have no right to speak of an external and an inner perception if the mental and the physical were definable and generic distinctions between objects. We do not speak of a distinct perception of trees and a distinct perception of houses.

The essence of the mental thus becomes visible in every act of inner perception, just as the essence of the physical does in every act of external perception. No comparison of several objects is necessary for this. On the other hand, the physical can appear *only* in external perception; the mental, *only* in inner perception.

The many attempts made to reduce the distinction between mental and physical to a *distinction in the way the same content is ordered,* or, in other words, to substitute, for these two species of perception, distinctions merely in the way thought relates their content, cannot succeed.[28] The distinction of physical and mental may be open to doubt in concrete cases, that is, it may be doubtful whether a particular appearance is mental or physical; in no case is the essential distinction first *created* by thought and judgment. It is a distinction in the *essence of phenomena* and in the mode of perception corresponding to them. If one says, with Mach, Avenarius, and others, that the "mental" is the environment [*Umwelt*] which is relative to an organism, or that it is the appearances of this environment so far as they prove to be dependent on a central nervous system, then, in fact, one makes the "mental" merely a *relation* between the physical phenomena of which the "organism" or the "nervous system" consists. What one defines here is the domain of facts belonging to the physiology of the senses.[29] We must already be of the opinion that everything mental can be reduced to the contents of sensation, desire, and feeling, to organic sensations, to memory and to the faint

28. [See *Formalismus*, VI, A, 3, e.—ED.]
29. As W. Wundt has already done, quite correctly, in his critique of "immanent philosophy."

reappearance of perceptual contents, if we are to take this classification into serious consideration.

Every theory of ordering breaks down because of the simple fact that the distinction between physical and mental is not first *created* by thought but is something we *encounter*. The theory of ordering is correct only in what it denies, namely, that what is in question is a definable distinction between genera; it is not correct in what it asserts.

We must regard every attempt to reduce the two species of perception to one as a failure.

For example, Berkeley and his idealistic followers tried to prove that sensation is a limiting case of "reflection." Berkeley thought that he had shown that there is no primitive [*ursprüngliche*] perception of matter. He reached this conclusion after he had identified "external" perception with "sensory" perception and let the distinction between this and memory and representation be solely a distinction in degree. Thus he adhered to memory as the primary phenomenon and construed external perception merely as a vivid memory and "representation." Second, he took what Locke called "secondary qualities" (which, for Locke, were facts not of reflection but of sensation, even though relative to man) to be facts of reflection. Furthermore, he tried to show that the primary qualities are inseparably linked to the secondary. (For instance, a tactile sensation can be gradually turned into a pain and extension is only a dependent moment in a color, separable from it only in words, as his nominalism would have it.) This is not the place to show the unsoundness of the reasons Berkeley advances on behalf of his theory that the content of outer perception is only the most peripheral layer of what he ambiguously calls "the content of consciousness," the outermost limit, as it were, of the contents grouped around the self, whose absolute existence he *presupposes*. At least he did seek to advance positive reasons for his principle *esse est percipi* and did not content himself, like most so-called modern idealists, with the ambiguous expression that everything perceived and thought is a "content of consciousness" just because it is perceived and thought. If we call everything that can in general be grasped in an intentional act and can be "meant" a "content of consciousness," then the sun, the moon, and the stars are surely "contents of consciousness." Only, this is a nonsensical way of talking. We mean something entirely different if "appearance in consciousness" [*Bewusstseinserscheinung*] is to mean an appearance given in inner perception—in short, a *mental appearance.* Then, however, the assertion that all appearances are appearances in consciousness contains a *radical error,* for it implies that everything intuitively and immediately given, everything not resting on inference and judgment, is a mental appearance in inner perception. Consequently, "external perception" would simply not exist. However, we must deny this peculiar notion and maintain that there are also "physical appearances," appearances which were never originally the "content of consciousness" or "mental," contents which can in no sense be derived from the mental or based on the mental. Whatever appears in the mutual externality [*Aussereinander*] of space and time is a physical appearance; whatever appears in an immediate relation to the ego in general, in a "togetherness" [*in einem "Zusammen"*] which is foreign to this spatiotemporal externality and fills a manifold irreducible to the latter,[30] is a mental appearance. Both kinds of appearance are given with *equal* immediacy. Furthermore, the very same degrees of mediacy are present in the composition of the "objects" which cognition and thought identify, directly or indirectly, in both these domains of knowledge. Therefore, it is a fundamental mistake to equate the domain of the phenomenal, or, in general, the immediately and intuitively given appearance, with the domain of "appearance in consciousness" or "mental" appearance. It is equally a mistake to regard the physical as resting on acts of thought (whether it is simply an identifying act or an inference from mental perceptions or from sensation to an "external world"). It is a fundamental mistake to identify the physical with what is given "mediately" or "indirectly," as Wundt, for example, does. The physical in general, taken as an essence, is given to us in every act of external perception, whatever its "reality" may be and whatever the outcome of the further division of the whole class of physical phenomena into what has physical and what has physiological conditions. Thus the appearance of a broken stick in the water is physically

30. See, on this, section IV of the present essay. [On the form of the manifold of the mental and the physical and the corresponding forms of perception, see also *Formalismus*, IV, A, 3, e, f, g, and the index of subjects in the 5th ed.—ED.]

determined, the perspectival image of a body is a geometrically and physiologically conditioned physical appearance.[31] That an appearance in external perception depends on the body of the perceiver does not turn this appearance into a mental content, but only into a more or less *existentially relative* object (in proportion to the kind of dependence). But not all existentially relative objects are for this reason "mental" or "subjective." [32]

Just as little as the content of external perception can be regarded as originally part of the content of inner perception, so little, *conversely*, can the content of inner perception be regarded as given by external perception, as though the content of inner perception were only the product of the genetic development of "elements" which we first encounter in the content of external perception. The error of thinking that the content is such a product, which is the antithesis of "idealism," underlies the sensationalistic theory that all mental facts, including feelings, efforts, etc., must rest on complicated combinations of so-called sensations (including the organic and visceral sensations which, according to this theory, lie at the innermost limits of external perception and, prior to analysis, create the illusion of a particular "mental" state of affairs and a particular kind of perception, namely, "inner perception"). A representation is here identified with a faded sense-content of decreased intensity.[33] Feelings, yearnings, even the self should be analyzable into complexes of organic and visceral sensations and the particular "tones" of these elements. Afterward, it doesn't make the slightest difference whether we stop with these elements of external phenomena and regard any mechanistic reduction of these into physics as simply an expedient symbolic representation of their relations and dependencies or look upon the mechanistic reduction as the way to get hold of the "real." In either case, one turns the "psychic" [*seelischen*] facts into mere complexes of elementary physical phenomena and the "psychic" [*seelische*] becomes a category which properly designates only a future, *unsolved problem of*

31. All mirror images, virtual images, rainbows, etc., although not physically *real*, are nonetheless *physical phenomena*.

32. [See *Formalismus*, V, 3, on subjectivity and relativity (existential relativity).—ED.]

33. How much this contradicts all the facts has been shown too often to need repeating here.

natural science. The "psychic" is then only the residue of fact which has not yet been fully analyzed and explained by natural science. With each step in the progress of science the ground is cut from under the "psychic," and in a complete natural science this category would disappear.

If, nonetheless, the distinction between inner and external perception is indisputable and irreducible, then the question is, What does distinguish them, apart from the difference in the orientation of these two acts of perception? [34] (It is only this difference which we can experience.)

For our purposes it is above all important that we not regard the distinction between these two orientations as in any way relative to the body, or, accordingly, to the functions and organs of the senses. This distinction exists even if we imagine that the body no longer exists.[35] Thus "external perception," as the orientation of an act, has nothing at all to do with "sensory perception." If its concrete actualization is tied to the cooperation of sensory functions, its *essence* is completely independent of them. What reaches us through this or that sensory function, seeing, hearing, smelling, etc., out of the abundant stock of what is given in an act of external perception, is a separate question. And still another question is which organs and which changes in them and in their cerebral appendages must cooperate if the content is to reach us.[36]

The grouping of appearances given to us in external perception into the physically and the physiologically conditioned (or the distinction of these two moments in any one appearance) is irrelevant here. This division takes place only *within* the domain of "appearances of external perception" or of "physical phenomena." That which has only or predominately physiological conditions may well be called "human," even "subjective" (e.g., all physiologically conditioned illusions of sense); it does not thereby become mental. The course Descartes inaugurated was in principle misleading. This course consisted in demanding first a *physicalistic* explanation of *all* external

34. See section IV of the present essay. A completely satisfactory examination of this question cannot be given here.

35. It goes without saying that "inner perception" has nothing to do with perception of what is localized "in" the lived-body.

36. We determine this only by reflecting on seeing, hearing, tasting, etc., and by looking to what is emphasized in the perceived whole by the function.

appearances and then bringing in the occurrence of physiological processes only so far as they can be considered the effects of the stimulation of physical realities assumed to underlie the appearances. In the field of the physiology of the senses, Hering (by presupposing that color *phenomena* and not their physical definitions are well ordered) was the first to make a fundamental break with this mistaken course. He was followed by Pavlov, who made an even wider break when he extended the scope of physiology.[37]

It is also wrong to regard all appearances as primarily "mental," thinking to make one's way into the physical domain only through an "inference" or an "interpretation." In every act of external perception the existence of the physical, of "nature," is immediately evident. Any further question can only concern the level of *existential relativity* of the object within this appearance which we must grasp in thought; that is, the question concerns the degree and type of its dependence on the properties of the being who comprehends it (e.g., general and individual, normal and abnormal, properties). This is often summarily called "the question of the reality of the external world." However, the external world is not a previously assumed reality "beyond consciousness" (as the obscure expression has it); rather, the further question of what is "real" in that world and in what sense it is real must be based on the evidentially given existence of the external world as a "phenomenon."[38] We need no "lawful conjunction" of the contents of several acts, no special "ordering," to lead us to something "physical." Rather, "nature" is given to us as an indeterminate *whole* in every act of external perception; it provides the background against which the sensory contents of the present moment stand out more sharply. It is not the case that the contents of different sense-functions are first given to us in separate little parcels—for example, red, hard, sour, loud—

37. A brief and instructive account of Pavlov's expanded physiology is given in his lecture before the Königsberg Society of Natural Scientists. See my remarks in the study *Der Formalismus in der Ethik und die materiale Wertethik*. [See *Formalismus,* chap. III. Pavlov's lecture, entitled "Naturwissenschaft und Gehirn," was first published in German in "Ergebnisse der Physiologie," Vol. XI (1911), and is included in his *Sämtliche Werke* (Berlin, 1953–54).—TRANS.]

38. I cannot go into the question of the essence of reality here. [See the later work, "Erkenntnis und Arbeit," above all, chap. VI, and likewise, "Idealism and Realism," below.—ED.]

which must first be "bound together" by an additional activity of conjunction and ordering; instead, it is immediately this same material unity which we touch *and* see when we touch and see a red hard surface, for example.[39] Even the existence of the matter or the unity of the thing in the sphere of external perception is self-evidently given to us in every act of external perception. The only thing that might involve hypothesis or interpretation is the question of its inner constitution (continuous or discrete) or the problem of what properties we ascribe to its ultimate elements in the present state of science. The unity *itself* is not a "hypothesis." Analogously, in inner perception a self is always given, indeed the "totality" of a self, as the background against which this or that content stands out in relief. Its existence is also immediately evident and we have no need of any "hypothesis" or "inference," or of any metaphysical assumption of a "substance," etc. There is no need of a "combination" and "synthesis" of a multiplicity of moments of consciousness by means of memory or reproduction. The act of inner perception has the right and the ability to pursue *every* experience of the self; it encompasses all the levels of consciousness and all the temporal moments of life, however widely separated they may be. Only the selection of what in fact appears in this act as a part of the present moment is determined by bodily processes [*Leibvorgänge*] and secondarily by mental causality.

The error of making external and inner perception relative to the lived-body [*Leib*] is best shown by the incontestable fact that the "lived-body" (to be sharply distinguished from the "corporeal body")[40] is given to us in inner as well as in external perception and is given to us as the "same," immediately, and not through any coordination. It is "the same hand" which I *see* here and in which I *feel this pain*.[41] Illusions in this context hold only for the coordination of particular contents with

39. All "development" and all "learning" concern only the coordination of given contents with definite, real things; but that identity itself is not a matter of learning or of development.

40. [On the "lived-body" and the "corporeal body," see *Formalismus*, VI, A, 3, e.—ED.]

41. The assertion that pain is unextended or is first projected out of the center is a totally arbitrary assertion, which also belongs among those errors (which I shall discuss in section III of this essay) in which the normal case is made intelligible by analogy with anomalous illusions (e.g., pain in an amputated limb).

the *real* sphere of actual experiences and actual bodily parts. However, these illusions presuppose this immediate identification. Any medical "inner diagnosis" rests on this basic principle. The same body is given to us in external perception as the "corporeal body" [*Körperleib*] and in inner perceptions as the "personal body" [*Leibseele*], a unified totality, a constant element in the content of our consciousness, within which the different sensations in the individual organs and the vital parts are first distinguished.

External perception is carried out *via* the sensory functions. The uniform and basic function of these, running through all their various modes, is the phenomenal production of pure "sensation." External perception comes about through *external sensibility,* which is first a general function and only afterward gets particularized by the sense organs in animals of different species.[42] The sense-function insinuates itself, so to speak, between the *act* of external perception and its possible *content;* it merely selects, from the total domain (of such contents), the elements of importance to the animal's current actions. Thus the sense-function has an *analytical* role which is important to the animal; it has no role in producing the content of external perception.[43]

Now it is fundamentally important for psychology, if it is going to progress, to recognize that inner perception, too, does not proceed directly to the self and its experiences, but is likewise *mediated by an "inner sense."* It is a great mistake to think that only that which is encountered in consciousness at some present moment has a psychic existence, while every past experience is present only in physiological dispositions or in the

42. The laws governing the functions of "seeing" and "hearing" can therefore be defined independently of the particular excitation and constitution of the sense organs and are the same in so-called inner seeing or inner hearing (of, say, a fact given in memory) as in actual seeing and hearing. (Examples of such laws are those governing the range of so-called sensory attention bound up with certain functions, or the perspectival alterations of contents as they are localized near one or at a distance, etc.) These functional laws are the same despite the different apparatus of the sense organs in different animals and must be investigated in their proper form of lawfulness [*Eigengesetzmässigkeit*].

43. The recent researches of Bergson and Pavlov show an interesting agreement with this idea. See H. Bergson, *Matière et mémoire* (Paris, 1908). [English translation, *Matter and Memory* (New York: Humanities Press, 1962), and Pavlov's lecture mentioned in note 37.—TRANS.]

dispositions of a metaphysical soul-substance or the like.[44] It is equally mistaken to think that psychic existence belongs only to what the individual can experience with the consciousness *that* this is what he is experiencing and with the consciousness of *what* this is. Just as it would be senseless to regard only the "slice" [*Ausschnitt*] of nature present to us in sense-perception as "actual" and to place everything else in "dispositions" or "possibilities of perception,"[45] so this idea of psychic reality makes no sense. It is not the experience itself, but only its appearance for inner sense, which is given to us in what is momentarily present to us (quite apart from any special attention, notice, or observation). The mental experience depends as little on the "brain" and the "senses" as the sun, moon, and stars do. In both cases, however, the external and internal phenomenon of sense is dependent on the *lived-body* [*Leibe*] and primarily on the nervous system.

To think that the mental is in some way more dependent on the body than the physical is also an error in principle of which biology, physics, and psychology are equally guilty. Rather, in both objective domains there are some appearances and elements of appearances dependent on the body and some which are independent of it. In both domains there is a definite order among the objects which are existentially relative to the body and its particular qualities. In both, however, there is also a level of *absolute existence* independent of the body. It would be senseless for a man to think he is doing physics, when he is merely ascertaining external, sensible appearances and inquiring into their dependence on the body (for then he is doing physiology of the senses); it is equally senseless to equate the facts and phenomena of "inner sense" with psychic reality. There is, certainly, a "physiology of the inner sense," just as there is one of the external sense. The chief contents of so-called physiological psychology belong to this discipline. But this science is fundamentally distinct from psychology, since the latter treats the *real psychic experience* and not what the individual apprehends of it in his "inner sense."

44. [See the critique of the theories of mental and physical dispositions in *Formalismus*, VI, A, 3.—ED.]

45. John Stuart Mill and others have asserted just this. In his examination of Hamilton's philosophy, Mill reduces even matter to a "constant group of possibilities of perception."

What is dependent on the body is not the real psychic experience, but the manner of comprehending it through inner sense. This alone can be "disturbed" or perturbed; psychopathology does not treat mental disturbances, but disturbances of comprehension through "inner sense." By the way, it is not our opinion that the mental, in its reality and independence of the phenomenon of inner sense, is "transcendent" in the sense of a "thing-in-itself" (which is implied by Kant's doctrine of inner sense, which has a completely different orientation).[46] We distinguish inner perception from "inner sense." The inner sense is, like the external sense, only an *analyzer* of perception, not something which positively furnishes the content of intuition. Inner perception alone does this. From the content of inner perception, inner sense picks out and brightly illuminates only what has, in the mental experience, a corresponding degree of importance for the body's activity and interest. However, just as, with regard to the external world, we can free ourselves by intuition and thought from the momentary phenomenon of sense, we can achieve this freedom in the sphere of inner perception, that is, in psychology. We can achieve every conceivable degree of this freedom, including, in principle, an intuition of the absolute object, if this is the name we give to the object which is conditioned only by the act of external and inner perception and by nothing else.

The inner sense, as we conceive it, is no hypothesis, much less a metaphysical hypothesis. It is a real fact [*Tatbestand*]. It contains nothing beyond the recognition that every mental experience which a living creature can actually have in his inner perception has to bring about some kind of characteristic *variation* in his bodily condition exhibiting a lawlike relation to the body's motor impulses [*Bewegungsimpulsen*].[47] While it is

46. In general, our concept of "inner sense" is in no way similar to Kant's. Kant equates inner perception and inner sense, which is just what we refuse to do. His theory that time is the form of "inner sense" will not stand up to examination. Time is an essential feature [*Moment*] of the content of external intuition and is not first mediated by a temporal ordering of acts of comprehension, e.g., acts of comprehending a series of the phases of some movement, which are then transferred to these phases themselves.

47. A more precise proof of this thesis will be given in an independent work dedicated to the theory of "inner sense." [This work did not appear. See *Formalismus*, VI, A, 3, e, f, g, and the index of subjects.—ED.] The restoration of the concept of "inner sense" was recently stimulated by

true that mental experiences cannot be reduced to bodily states, complexes of sensations, etc., it is equally true that a characteristic bodily state, along with a particular motor intention, is connected with every perception of a mental experience. Otherwise the experience cannot cross the threshold of inner sense. To this extent every experience, in our view, insofar as it is perceived, remains in some measure dependent on the states of the body, both the personal and the corporeal body. However, the experience itself and its pure intuitive content are never dependent on such a state, contrary to what psychophysiological parallelism thinks.

That there are things like "illusions of inner perception" rests on the fact that an inner sense, an *analyzer* of what is important to life, is interposed between experiences and the perception of them. This explains why here, too, there is "semblance" [*Schein*] and "reality." In addition it explains why there is a whole *series* of *levels* of the mental objectivity of one and the same experience, dependent in different degrees on the constitution of "inner sense" and thus "existentially relative," in different degrees, to the individual who apprehends it. Unfortunately it has become the favorite doctrine of today's fashionable philosophy that "appearance" and "reality" do not exist in the mental world, that here everything is simply present or not, that the mental is exactly as it appears, hence that it is a true "thing-in-itself." If this were correct, then indeed there would be no illusion of inner perception.[48]

O. Külpe in his works on the psychology of abstraction (see also *Einleitung in die Philosophie der Gegenwart*), and (rather abstrusely) by Freud (see *The Interpretation of Dreams* [1913]). See also Bergson, *Matière et mémoire*. [Oswald Külpe (1862–1916) was an influential philosopher and the leader of the so-called Würzburg school of theoretical psychology. He developed his version of critical realism in *Erkenntnistheorie und Naturwissenschaft* (Leipzig, 1910). The title Scheler probably meant to cite should read *Die Philosophie der Gegenwart in Deutschland* (Leipzig, 1902; 5th ed., 1911).—TRANS.]

48. Recently Husserl, to whose works I feel profoundly indebted, has also sided with this theory. He says: "Mental being, being as 'phenomenon' is, in principle, not a unity which could be experienced as individually identical in several separate perceptions, not even in the perceptions of one and the same subject. In the mental sphere there is, in other words, no distinction between appearance and being, etc." ("Philosophie als strenge Wissenschaft," *Logos*, I [1910], 312 ff. [English translation by Quentin Lauer, "Philosophy as a Rigorous Science," in *Edmund Husserl: Phenomenology and the Crisis of Philosophy* (New York: Harper & Row, 1965), p. 106; translation slightly modified].) In the first place, we do not

However, ordinary language already distinguishes between the advent [*Neuhinzutreten*] of new experiences and a new or different conception [*Auffassung*] of experiences which emerges when they are relived or remembered. It makes a differ-

---

see how this assertion is to be reconciled with the penetrating remarks in *Logische Untersuchungen* (Halle: Niemeyer, 1900) [English translation by J. N. Findlay, *Logical Investigations* (New York: Humanities Press, 1970), II, 852 ff.] on "inner and external perception" in which Husserl contests not only the evidential superiority of inner over external perception (contrary to what Descartes and Brentano taught him), but says expressly: "As against that it appears to me that inner and external perception . . . are of a completely equivalent epistemological character, etc." [p. 859]. Husserl here has changed his opinion.

In fact, however, Husserl seems to me to confuse here the essence of "phenomenon" with that of the "mental," to confuse phenomenology and psychology, although in another place ["Philosophy as a Rigorous Science," p. 91], the "phenomenology of consciousness," which has to do with "pure consciousness," is sharply distinguished from "psychology," which has to do with "empirical consciousness" or with consciousness as "nature."

Naturally Husserl is right when he says: "A phenomenon is no substantial unity, it has no 'real properties,' it knows no real parts and no causality. . . . It makes no sense to attribute a nature to phenomena, to investigate their real component parts, their causal connections" ["Philosophy as a Rigorous Science," p. 106, slightly modified].

Certainly a "phenomenon" is not "observable" but only "intuitable" [*erschaubar*]. But from this certain fact I conclude that psychology, even descriptive psychology (which still rests on "observation"), has nothing to do with phenomena, since every sentence in a textbook of psychology treats a "sensation" or a "representation," for example, as a substantial unity; every sentence assigns "real properties" to it (which it has, whether or not they are given to the one experiencing it) and assumes "real parts" and causal relations between the objects treated. The phenomenology of the mental, the theory of the essential constituents of the mental and its modes of givenness, has on its part as little to do with psychology as the phenomenology of number has to do with arithmetic. On the other hand, everything Husserl says about "phenomenon" holds true, including what he says about the mental phenomenon. "Phenomenon" means only what is immediately given in living acts; what stands before me "in person"; that which *is* in the same way it is *meant*. I can seek out this givenness, however, in any object I please, in the non-mental as well as in the mental, and, once again, in "thingness" and in "reality."

Husserl is entirely right that the scientific concepts of thing, process, and cause cannot be transferred to the sphere of mental facts and that the "unity" of the mental has forms quite peculiar to it. But we cannot conclude from this that these concepts have no sense at all in the mental sphere; we can conclude only that they are to be freed of the specific modalities which they assume in the sphere of external perception and the particular manifold of national being: spatial externality. There is a sharp distinction between "thing," "matter," and "physical body," and just as certainly as the real self or the "character" is not a piece of matter or a physical body, so certainly is it a thing. A "representation" which evokes

ence whether love or hate for a person ceases or whether the man in question *deceived* [*getäuscht*] himself and took something for love or hate which was not love or hate at all.[49] It makes a difference whether love is not present at all or whether a man cannot feel it for a time or does not acknowledge it. In such cases, we are prevented from saying that all emotions [*Gemütsbewegungen*] (that is, all which have this particular quality) are *equally* real, or that one man did love or hate the other five minutes or three weeks ago and his saying that he "deceived himself" only expresses the fact that his expectation that his emotion would last longer or have particular effects has not, as things turned out, been fulfilled. Rather we make a sharp distinction in life between *this* state of affairs and a *genuine illusion.* Likewise, we distinguish between the mistaken subsumption of an experience under an inappropriate concept and the *intuitive* presumption that the experience is really present. Thus, in "sentimental moods" we take merely imagined feelings to be actual and real, or we take the feelings of the characters in a novel we are reading to be real and our own. In such cases there is not only a "mistake," e.g., a false subsumption, but an "illusion," in the sense defined earlier. It is not true that the anger, the sorrow, or even the pain of a hysterical patient is, *qua* experience, identical with the anger, sorrow, or pain of a normal person and that only the objective causes and effects (e.g., the expressive movements) are different. The sick person still *sees* quite clearly that deeper *level* of his psychic person where a certain serenity abides, even when his alleged anger is being most violently expressed.

---

another, because in part it shares identical elements with the latter, is a "thing" and has "real parts." A motive for an act of will is a real occurrence and can subsist even when the agent does not know it or imagines he has an entirely different motive; it is the cause of this act of will. Indeed, a fact of observation and a causal theory of psychology can never contradict the phenomenology of the mental, nor can it ever prove its statements, since the theory of the essences of the mental and of their essential interconnections—as Husserl so strikingly urges—is the presupposition of all psychology. Husserl does *not* seem to have shown that this holds less true of natural science, or even of mathematics.

49. Instead, it was, for example, a solidarity of interest, which hides behind the word "love," or an attraction caused by an external impression reminiscent of someone loved before, or a flight from oneself, or custom or a community of similar persuasion, etc.

It is just that he does not see this serenity itself, and for that reason he transfers his merely imagined anger onto this deeper ontological level of his self.

But there is even more. It is an error to say that the distinction between a thing or a process and the modes of its appearance is not applicable in the psychic domain. The psychologist, who talks of an "idea" [Vorstellung], who allows this idea to cause this or that or lets it fade away or reproduce itself, cannot avoid bringing it under the category of a real thing or process and ascribing to it determinations, modes of action, and relations which *are present* whether or not they appear to the person having the idea. Admittedly the idea is not a "physical body" [Körper]; but we distinguish sharply between the idea of a thing [Dingidee] which is indifferent to external and inner perception and the idea of a physical body [Körperidee]. The concepts "character," "soul," and "real self" are also concepts of a thing [Dingbegriffe]; their correlative objects are genuine things, without needing to be transcendent substances. One and the same real experience—for example, a feeling of grief—can be now more, now less exactly perceived. We can so "lose" ourselves in the outermost levels of our life that this grief wholly disappears from view or is present only as completely "general impression," while we are laughing and joking and feeling this sense of "joy" even at that outermost level. Nonetheless, it is a well-defined grief with a full complement of predicable characters [aussagbare Merkmale]. An experience can present to us different sides in turn, where by *side* we must understand not only spatial sides such as a corporeal thing or a physical process has. However, this variety of its sides is not the same thing as an alteration of the experience itself. One and the same pain has different aspects when we experience it in different modes, e.g., with suffering, with patience, with enjoyment, with surrender to it, with resistance to it, etc. In the process, it is always presenting new "appearances."

Thus real experiences and their causal nexus are no more present in the phenomenon of inner sense-perception than the real nexus of nature is present in the phenomenon of external sense-perception. There are as many levels of consciousness in the former as there are levels of existence [*Daseinsstufen*] in external nature, all characterized by the degree to which the perceived object depends on the apprehending subject and his general and individual properties. A feeling of sickness, for example, can be present but removed from the sphere of inner sense, or only from the sphere of noticing [*Bemerkens*]. It can be present in the latter but removed from the sphere of attention [*Beachtens*]; it can be present there without being brought under observation [*beobachtet*]; and it can be observed without our judging or establishing under what concept it should be subsumed. What a distance separates what anyone experiences from what he experiences with such knowledge that he can *say* what it is he is experiencing!

We can call that context of experience which is beyond the reach of inner sense—even, at times, in appearances functioning as symbols for it—the "*subconscious* part" of the ego. But it must be clear that this subconscious part has absolutely nothing to do with the so-called unconscious, which is merely a construction for the causal explanation of psychic life and is taken to be, for example, the locus of "mental dispositions." These have nothing to do with one another because the subconscious experience is not simply absent from inner intuition or something which can only be inferred; rather, its presence or absence, its having this nature or some other, *modifies* the *total* content of inner intuition at any one time, even though the person experiencing it cannot straightforwardly specify in words the particular form [*Inhalt*] this modification takes. Thus the subconscious is still something *conscious*, just as much so as the "supraconscious," while the so-called unconscious can never be present for consciousness in any sense but is only inferred. Hence, the subconscious experience is in principle accessible to inner perception, and what makes it subconscious is only that it does not, at a given time, make an impression upon the inner sense. It is when inner sense is excited that experiences first acquire that degree of liveliness through which they are actually perceived as present occurrences [*gegenwärtige Vorkommnisse*]. The subconscious, however, is no less distinct from what goes unnoticed, which must already belong to the sphere of the supraconscious.

[III] A General Error in the Conception
and Explanation of Illusion

THE PREVAILING CONCEPTION and explanation of (inner and outer) illusions in general rest, I find, on a mistaken methodological assumption. It seems worthwhile, not only to expose this mistake over again in each case, but by taking some examples, to stop it once and for all from adding to the confusion here. The mistake is that, in explaining illusion, we do not *presuppose* the case of "correct" insight which serves as the correlate of every illusion; on the contrary, we *start from illusion* and explain the case of correct insight in exactly the way we believe illusion must be explained. Briefly, one tries to reach the normal case from the abnormal case, taking the normal to be a special instance of the same law [*Gesetzmässigkeit*] that holds sway in the abnormal, simply noting that something objectively real corresponds to the normal case.

This same mistake is made when normal sense-perception is conceived as a "true hallucination" (*Taine*), as a formation which is in no way phenomenally distinguished from hallucinations except that an actual thing corresponds to it and, accordingly, that an existential judgment based upon it is "true," while nothing corresponds to the hallucination. Or we assume that an objective excitation explains the normal case, while for hallucination we assume either a purely central excitation or a centrifugal excitation of the peripheral surfaces of the senses. According to this theory, there should not be any phenomenologically distinctive feature of natural perception. We are meant to conclude that, since the total content of natural perception is dependent on the intactness of certain cells and fibers of the cerebral cortex *and* on the excitation and stimulation of these, while hallucination depends only on this stimulation (disregarding here centrifugal stimulation), then the immediate cause of these two phenomena is in no way distinguished. Hence one can imagine that the content of experience is not altered even if the more remote causes, namely, the links in the causal chains which end in this immediate cause, are destroyed or varied as widely as possible, so long as they still terminate in this last link, the immediate cause. Such a proof or one similar to it is wholly unjustified. We are not justified in judging natural perception by analogy with hallucination. Only if we asume that natural perception gives us something actually existent whose content is not determined by our body and, thus, not by our "brain," do we have the right to speak of phenomena which, although they are similar in other respects, are determined by the brain and therefore belong to the sphere of hallucinatory illusions. Even what we say about the body, the brain, stimulation, etc., can be expressed only if we assume that natural perception is competent to give us something actual with a content which is independent of our body. And only because we have learned from natural perception what "actuality" is, what the "external world" is, and what it is for a content of reality to be independent of us, can contents which in fact are not real and independent of us, like those of natural perception, but are only centrally conditioned, nonetheless be combined with features such as "consciousness" of reality, the external world, and independence of our brain, as happens in the case of hallucinations. More briefly, it is only for this reason that this content makes its appearance, charged with the character and the essential elements of the act of "perceiving." If we wish to carry out this proof in accordance with the principle of the "economy of causes," then we must rather say: since the abolition of the causal links leading up to the immediate cause in the cerebrum could not alter the contents of experience, then, given the indubitable difference between natural perception, which gives us a real and independent content, and hallucination, the sense of this "causal condition" must be entirely different in these two cases. In natural perception only the perceiving of *this particular real content, as distinct* from other contents, is conditioned by the brain. In other words, the brain determines the selection of this content out of the abundance of contents which might exist at other times. Thus the brain conditions, first, only the "perceiving" as a real act with just *this* nature *as opposed to* representing, judging, etc., and then the *choice* of just this real content over other equally real contents to be that which the individual who has this brain is going to perceive. In the case of hallucination, on the contrary, the brain conditions, first, the *content itself* (and not its selection from among other possible contents), and, second, the reproduction of that quality of appearance which is essentially connected with a natural perception. That is, hallucination is an illusion in which we merely think we perceive without in fact perceiving, and its content is relative to the brain of the hallucinator, while the content of natural perception is relative to the things which are present and actual.

The theory that illusion and perception are the same makes the same mistake. According to this theory, illusion ought to come about when memory-elements are much more numerous than pure elements of sensation in the combinations of the two formed through simultaneous association or assimilation. However, according to this theory, every natural perception already contains a more or less rich mixture of these memory-elements—all the more rich, clearly, the richer and more developed the spiritual life of the perceiver is. Accordingly, not only is there no essential difference between perception and illusion, only one of degree, but the theory also has the remarkable consequence that, the *richer* our experience becomes, the less does perception agree with the existent facts and the more it comes to stand on the same footing as the illusions of a sick person. When a scientist makes a simple observation, say, of the color of a line in the spectrum of the sun, he is quickly filled with an abundance of "memory-elements" so that he might convert the simple datum of observation into an element in a richer and intuitive [*anschaulichen*] context, that of a particular property of the sun.[50] According to this theory, he would be most like someone under the mistaken illusion that he sees every possible grotesque face in the shimmering post of his bedstead. It will not do to say, in conformity with this theory, that the difference is that, in illusion, memory-elements are added on which are not reproductions of features of "the same thing" which is now being experienced [*empfunden*] and which earlier gave rise to other sensations [*Empfindungen*], while, on the other hand, the memory-elements in perception *are* of this sort. For, on this theory, the content of perception, insofar as it furnishes a particular thing and for this reason goes beyond the content of sensation (which can be the same in perceptions of other things, e.g., the whiteness of snow is the same as the whiteness of a powder), should be composed only of the added memory-elements. Con-

50. One thinks of the course of events leading to Kirchoff's discovery of spectrographic analysis.

sequently, it no longer makes sense to say that in perception, but not in illusion, reproductions of earlier sensations of "the same thing" are present. For this "same thing" can be found and verified in consciousness only when these reproductive elements are added. This addition, however, could also take place in illusion. So long as assimilation and association are in play, not between finished products of perception and representation but between their elements, we have no criterion for distinguishing whether or not it *is* a matter of reproducing elements of "the same thing." For the elements of the sensation of *A* can be as similar as one likes to the memory-elements of *B* which are dispositionally present; or *A* and *B* can have common parts which reinforce one another. Conversely, elements of the representation of *A* can be dispositionally present that are not at all equivalent to the elements of the sensation of *A*, and then *A* and *B* must weaken one another. Only when we have finished products of perception and memory (which are given also *as* memories) can we talk of checking whether what is reproduced traces back to the perception of "the same thing." There is no question of this in the present case.

The following examples are analogous to such defective explanations. Some think they have "explained" the intuition of a bas-relief when they have referred to the distribution of light and shadow on a surface (e.g., a painted surface), which can in fact produce the illusion of a relief. However, is it not obvious to everyone that one must already have the original *phenomenon* of a relief in order to see it [*hineinsehen*] in such a distribution of light and shadow? This case does not differ in principle from the case where we suddenly see a cat in the picture puzzle. The activity of synthesizing the lines, colors, and shapes of the given, which we must also carry out in the perception of a real cat, is not sufficient if we want to understand this sudden seeing. For if these activities are to take place in such a way as to lead to the picture of a cat, then the unity of meaning "cat" must in some way already prescribe which elements of the given the synthesizing activity should take and which it should leave alone. Consequently, we would not want to "explain" the element of meaning which is present in the perception of a cat in the same way we explain the apprehension of the cat in the picture puzzle.

Or, to take another case: We deceive ourselves about *what*

is going on in the soul of a man. The basic form of this illusion is that we "empathetically project" the effect his expressive movement has on us and on our psychic life into the other person's feelings. And for this it makes no difference whether it is the direct effect it has on our feelings or is a reproduction of those experiences which normally led to such an expression in us, evoked when the tendency to imitate the movement we see is aroused. To the extent that something of this sort happens, we deceive ourselves about what goes on in the other's soul when we take our own experiences to be his.[51] This occurs in all cases of the contagious spread of feeling through laughing together, weeping together, threatening together (as in, e.g., mass agitations). This is clearly the opposite of appreciative and understanding fellow feeling, in which one's own grief, self-enjoyment, etc., are based on the intentional "feeling" of the other's grief, etc., or on the sensitive "understanding" of this feeling in the other. It is precisely the *other's* feeling which does not come to sight in the case of a contagion of feeling based on imitation. How perverse is the attempt of Lipps and others to explain genuine fellow suffering [*Mitleid*] on the analogy of the contagion of feeling! What we explain in that way is only the illusion that we suffer "with" the other. Certainly, many people do consider the contagion of weeping and tears, or even the momentary weakness of their nerves, or a shock which comes from aesthetic aversion, to be "genuine" fellow suffering. The motive here may be the vanity which would gladly let an event which is similar to one of positive value be taken for one which is itself positive. But this is an illusion. And it presupposes that we recognize the real fact of *genuine* fellow suffering, etc.; otherwise, how should we be able to "see" it in the case of contagious feeling? This is analogously true of other illusions, e.g., the illusion that a person feels remorse over a deed, when in fact he is only dragging into his memory of the deed the unpleasant consequences it can cause—anxiety, perhaps, and fear of the social consequences that public knowledge of this deed can have. "Genuine" remorse cannot be explained in terms of this illusion of remorse. The illusion of remorse presupposes the phenomenon of genuine remorse. This is equally true when,

---

51. See the appendix to my *Nature of Sympathy.*

e.g., someone takes the effect of an originally morbid tendency to torment oneself, to hurt oneself, or to flog oneself, for "remorse," "consciousness of sin," or "bad conscience." For we can never explain these genuine phenomena by such means.[52]

The desire to explain the understanding of processes in the soul of another, e.g., historical psychic facts, by means of "empathy" [*Einfühlung*], is also fundamentally mistaken. The crucial *source of illusion* concerning the psychic life of another is displayed by showing that *A* has imported his own experiences into *B*, that "the masters hold their own spirit to be the spirit of the ages." However, I have not yet shown how our perception of another's mental life normally comes about. Any understanding of another rests on the fact that I hold in check my own experiences, which occur to me, for example, when another is recounting his experience, in order to hear *only* [*rein*] what belongs to the other. Therefore the introduction of the analogous customs and concepts of our own epoch for the sake of historical understanding never produces clarification; it leads only to illusions about the historically given, however "ingenious" [*geistreich*] such a procedure appears. In the same way men immediately succumb to illusion about the experience another man is recounting when they start off with the words: "Yes, something similar has happened to me, too," and from then on can only take in the other's experience and transform it into the schemata of what they have experienced themselves.[53]

There are widely circulated theories of the same type which would explain the consciousness of "force" in external nature, of "animate" beings, and of "values," by importing feelings, desires, etc., into the sensibly perceived content. All these theories end by making the special motives which can lead to *illusions* about the objective existence of these facts, e.g., the mythological desire to revivify the dead, into the basis of our understanding of the normal perception of these things, e.g., living organisms.

52. See Nietzsche's explanation of "bad conscience." [*The Genealogy of Morals*, trans. F. Golffing (Garden City, N. Y.: Doubleday, Anchor Books, 1956), Second Essay.—TRANS.]

53. [See pt. 1, chap. III ("Genetic Theories of Fellow-Feeling"), in Scheler's *The Nature of Sympathy*, on the subject of the "self-experienced" and the understanding of another.—ED.]

[IV] GENERAL SOURCES OF ILLUSIONS
OF INNER PERCEPTION

FRANCIS BACON TRIED, as we saw, to establish a theory of idols for the sake of specifying the most important sources of illusion in external perception and observation. It seems to me that at the present time it would be very useful for psychology to make an analogous attempt in the domain of inner perception. There is nothing better qualified to reduce *ad absurdum* the false theory of the evidential superiority of inner over external perception, the main prop of all "idealistic" and "psychological" theories of knowledge. At the same time, the *genuine evidence belonging to inner perception* and observation would come more sharply into view. Moreover, in making this attempt we would make clear the supreme difficulty of all genuine inner perception and the abundance of possible levels on which a psychic product [*Gebilde*] can be given.

Without pretending to completeness, I would like to concentrate here on some of the main sources of the ordinary illusions of inner perception.

Nothing has harmed psychology as much as the thesis that it must be pursued by way of analogy with natural science. If this means only that it must proceed as "exactly" as possible, in the sense of "precisely," that it should rest on observation, experiment, the inductive method, then naturally we have nothing in the least to object to. But this demand leads to error if one transfers the basic categories of the being of nature [*Naturseins*], whether consciously or unconsciously, to *psychic* facts, or if one proceeds, consciously or unconsciously, according to the principle that the division of the psychic manifold into individual structures should occur by means of the relation these structures have to objects of nature (the physical objects and events in the external world or the corporeal substrata of mental events). Such a procedure nearly causes the disappearance of the idea of a "pure psychology," one which sets itself the opposite task, namely, to separate, from psychic states of affairs and their description, all the distinctions, characteristics, etc., which come from considering the external world—even those which are given along with *natural* inner perception—and only then to attempt an explanation of this purified material. Clearly, the specification of a sensation, e.g., as a sensation in the limbs, as a muscular sensation, as a sensation of motor-tension, etc., is no *psychological* specification. We have said only that this sensation is the very one which I have when this or that organ (muscle or limb) is activated; such determinations are *extra*-psychological. Nor is it a psychological specification if the concept of sensation is divided into its species only by means of its felt contents, like color and tone, or if we can define sensation in general only in terms of the concept of stimulation. If what I know about a representation is only that it is the representation of a house, then psychologically I know *nothing* about it! I say only that it is the X of the psychic manifold which stands in a symbolic and representative relation to a house, e.g., a particular physical thing. There is no species of representations which we can call "representation of a house," any more than sensations of muscle and limb can be called different species of sensation. Moreover, from the standpoint of the critique of knowledge, it was extremely naïve of this "scientific" psychology to presuppose that the concepts of magnitude, of number, of causality in the style of natural causality, of "laws" in the style of "laws of nature," are all applicable to the mental and are to be encountered there. Whether this is the case or not, the very question whether the concept of number, or the concept of magnitude, can be applied to the mental and to the form of its multiplicity, must be considered a completely open one.[54]

In one respect we must consider that progress has been made when some more recent philosophers refuse to measure or to count the mental itself, indeed deny the possibility of doing such things; however, they also make it a principle that everything mental must be determined only *indirectly*, i.e., according to its relation to the physical, to what has physical magnitude and is numerically determined.[55] This is progress insofar as it avoids the illusion of thinking that one measures or counts the mental itself, an illusion on which one school of

54. See Bergson, *Essai sur les données immédiates de la conscience* (Paris: Alcan, 1938). [English translation by R. L. Pogson, *Time and Free Will* (New York: Macmillan, 1910).] We in no way share Bergson's results.
55. See Hans Münsterberg, *Grundzüge der Psychologie* (Leipzig, 1900).

scientific psychology is based and without which its origin is unthinkable. However, insofar as these philosophers at the same time make it a conscious principle that psychic facts are "given" and "definable" only indirectly and after we have passed through the physical; insofar as some of them claim that the mental is in each case simply the residue left after the original data have been logically treated and adapted to the explanation of external nature, or that the mental is what is "at any one time given only to one person" and, accordingly, can be only indirectly defined and described in terms of physiological connections; insofar as they say all this, their school breaks even more radically with the idea of a *pure* psychology and must appear to be an even greater error to those who still consider a pure psychology a possibility.

As it is, these questions of principle can be decided only by an extensive attempt to eliminate all naturalistic categories from the description, definition, and explanation of psychic fact [*seelischen Tatbestandes*]. At the same time, we must separate those forms of thought and intuition which can be meaningfully applied to *all* objects from those which are restricted to the material region of the "external being of nature," and then, finally, produce a positive theory of psychological categories and intuition. I cannot try to furnish such a theory here. What follows is said only in the conviction that a "pure psychology" is possible and that it is the task of psychology to eliminate all the forms of thought and intuition which are specifically necessary and useful in the knowledge of the physical world.

Theories hitherto have for the most part emphasized only one of the two fundamental sources of illusions, namely, man's inclination to impute or "project" facts of his inner perception, in short, his psychic experiences, into the physical objects of nature. Far more rarely has it been noted and acknowledged that he also has the tendency *to transfer to the psychic world* facts, relations, and forms which belong to material *existence* [*Dasein*]. Not only is our language in the first place a language concerning the external world; man's interest is predominantly focused on the external world. The world, even "in the first instance," is so far from being merely his "idea," as it is in "idealism's" prattle, that he is scarcely aware of the transitory form of his idea, its oscillation, and the incessant metamorphosis going on behind the firm and solid things which it symbolizes.

Although both worlds are equally "real," or "actual," these words nonetheless signify primarily the reality of the *external world,* to which the psychic is opposed as "only an idea," "only a feeling," etc., just as though it were "scarcely actual." Although from the standpoint of pure cognition psychic facts "exist" no less originally, and are no less real, there is an attitude, easily understood on biological grounds, which sees to it that, in a possible content of intuition, the physical reality is the first to be grasped and observed. This is in keeping with the order of importance that the consequences of cognition have for the organism. It is only when obstacles beset the elaboration and formation of this physical reality, only when it is distorted in some way, that our gaze reverts to the mental facts which are there at the same time. Külpe has shown, in his splendid investigations into the objectification and subjectification [*Subjektivierung*] of sense-impressions, e.g., of a smell or of a flash of light, that in cases where the "immediate criteria" he introduces for the objectification and subjectification of contents are uncertain, what results is *not* a subjectification but a *false objectification* in accordance with indirect criteria.[56] This does not prove that external perception is epistemologically superior to inner perception or that the latter is epistemologically based on the former. Nonetheless, it does show that in our normal, natural view of the world, the *predominant* tendency of illusion is to presume that what is really mental is physical, not to take what is really physical to be mental.

We should, I think, consider it *pathological* when the opposite tendency appears to predominate in individuals or entire generations. Up till now no attempts have been made to demonstrate this. It would be of great interest if such a demonstration were made. It seems to me that the predominant direction of illusion is reversed in all the psychoses involving an increased excitability, mostly when the sick person continues to focus on the conditions of the body-self [*Leibich*]. The entire environment, together with the events in it, is "given" here only as the sum of changing stimulants of the feelings, espe-

56. See the "Festschrift für W. Wundt," in *Philosophische Studien,* Vol. XIX (1902).

cially the sensory, bodily feelings of the sick person. The "world" is here actually, not in the perverted, epistemological sense of a *soi-disant* "idealistic philosophy" given to him as his "idea." This is true not only of the domain of representation but also of the activity of the will. *Normal* willing looks directly to the realization of the willed content, for example, leaving the room. Any willing of the requisite means, like "crossing to the door," "lowering the latch," the execution of the necessary movements, etc., is subordinated to the content of this goal and takes place, so far as there are no particular obstacles, almost by automatic impulse. If the willing meets with an obstacle, that is, if the willed content does not realize itself according to expectation, then a phenomenon of resistance is "given." This resistance can be given in such a way that it is not referred either to external objects offering resistance (physical or social facts) or to obstacles posed by the body and the mechanisms which serve to carry out movement, or to inner mental resistances. In this case the resistance is just undifferentiatedly and simply there. However, the *normal* direction of striving is characterized by the fact that, when we are in doubt concerning the cause of the obstruction, we always place the blame on the relatively *external* side. It is only when the apprehended obstacles cannot be put aside that we revert to the bodily or mental sphere as the possible seat of the obstruction. In the *anomalous* life of the will things are different. Here the contents of indirect effort, e.g., the effort to move one's arm in order to take down an object from a chest, interpose themselves as *separate,* more or less vivid contents before the genuine goals and themselves become the object of a conscious effort. The phenomena of "hesitation" and pathological indecisiveness occur in this way. The sick man who "wants" to leave the room, lingers with the content "go to the door," and then "push back the bolt," etc.[57] Certain mentally conditioned forms of stuttering belong here—cases which are based on the fact that the sufferer is thinking about what he wants to say *right now* and is not, like the normal man, mentally trained on the thoughts to be expressed *in the future*. Instead of letting the thought translate itself automatically

57. [See *Formalismus,* chap. III, on the normal course of voluntary actions and the experience of resistance and on the pathology of the activity of the will.—ED.]

into expression, he is intent on the expression itself as a separate content of activity. Certainly it is biologically useful to place the blame on external things in doubtful cases of experienced resistance and not on "us," whether our bodily or mental resistances. A man on the point of crashing the car he is driving into a tree will have less of a chance of changing course at the last instant if he concentrates on the movements of arm and hand he must execute, instead of on avoiding the tree. Thus an inversion of the order of our intentions, which results in our first looking for the cause of an experienced obstacle in ourselves, is the product of an abnormal attitude. As a result, the question "Can I?" pathologically crowds out the questions, "Do I want to?" and "Should I?" And pathological indecisiveness is the outcome.

There is, it seems to me, a whole series of cases in which certain theories of *normal* psychology show their falsehood just because what they assert takes place only in *pathological and exceptional cases,* but in no way in normal life. Among these I count the view of thinking held by associationistic psychology. The normal person, when he replies to a question, takes his bearings from a unity of meaning reproduced in the contents of his answer (the "supra-representation," as Liepmann says) [58] and "associates," in the strict sense, only his fleeting ideas. This means that a constitutive factor of meaning [59] must "drop out" if an approximately pure case of association is to occur. However, we do *not* get the "meaning," as nominalism holds, through a complicated process of associating contents which are dispositionally stimulated by the nucleus of the sound complex. Analogously we dwell on the so-called memory image only when memory is disturbed or is hindered by present stimuli, while in normal memory a present "image" is not given at all. In spite of this, the prevailing theory of memory makes this "image" its starting point! Even when the "image" is present, its properties—for example, the richness or meagerness of its features, its vagueness or definiteness, its vividness or dullness—have no unambiguous functional relationship to objective fidelity. Nor do they have any such relation to the evidence of memory or to the fullness of what is remembered. On the other hand, when the "image" presses

58. [See Hans Liepmann, *Über Ideenflucht* (Halle, 1904).—TRANS.]
59. Or a relational structure in thought.

forward this leads to those *illusions* of memory in which the patient's fantasy-experiences have the significance of memories.[60]

Analogously, the pathological *omission* of the consciousness of reality can show that a special phenomenon is present in the "reality" [*Wirklichsein*] of the objects "intended" in the sense-contents which is not given along with these sense-contents themselves or with *their* fullness, intensity, and vividness (contrary to what sensationalism held). The phenomenon "there is something real here" can be present without our having a particular *image*, a definite "what" before our eyes.[61] The theory that consciousness of reality is a matter of judgment, that the concept "actual" should find its fulfillment in a reflection on the affirmative judgment, is contradicted by cases in which actuality is denied in the *judgment* but is present in the *phenomenon*, as in a certain class of genuine hallucinations. This holds similarly for theories that the consciousness of reality should be based on a relation to the will, on the phenomenon of something's "obtruding itself upon our will." The pseudo-hallucinations described by Vasily Kandinsky[62] show that this phenomenon can be present *without* a consciousness of reality. Analogously, those cases in which the patient's perception is in fact confined to that content of a thing which he is seeing (the surface and the side facing him), while the other contents (that the thing has an inside, that it has properties and sides which are not given at the moment) are given to him only in the form of an "expectation" which he could fulfill by walking around it, opening it (or "looking around to see if the world is still there behind it," as the author observed in the case of a hysterical child), demonstrate the mistakenness of those theories that the normal perception of a thing rests on a "context of expectation."[63] In normal perception we expect to see the other sides *because*

60. See G. Störring, *Vorlesungen über Psychopathologie* (Leipzig, 1900), p. 268.

61. See also William James, *The Varieties of Religious Experience* (New York, 1902), chap. 2, "The Reality of the Invisible."

62. See also Störring, *Vorlesungen*, p. 262.

63. Thus, Cornelius in his *Versuch einer Theorie der Existentialurteile* (Munich, 1894). [Hans Cornelius (1863–1947) was a philosopher of positivist persuasion, whose main works are *Psychologie als Erfahrungswissenschaft* (Leipzig, 1897), and *Transzendentale Systematik* (Munich, 1916).—TRANS.]

we think we are seeing a "real thing" and not conversely. We "expect" this because we already have "that it has another side, has an inside" in the content of immediate intuition. Analogously, cases of the "estrangement of the perceptual world" show that in normal perception there is a quality of "familiarity" and "certainty," which has nothing to do with the intactness either of memory or recognition (both of these can be undisturbed when this estrangement occurs), and which is probably connected with a factor of intentional feeling which enters into every normal perception. Analogously, cases in which psychic blindness [*Seelenblindheit*] is not bound up with a disturbance of the activity of association show that such blindness occurs when the "moment of meaning," which is an ingredient in normal perception (without any judgment or subsumption of what is perceived under a concept), drops out.

The abundance of the non-sensory factors contained in normal perception and the poverty of most philosophical theories of perception are seen in the proper light by means of the *method* of *psychopathology* applied here. Its abstract expression is the basic principle that *everything is to be considered "given" in the content of normal perception whose pathological omission, increase, or diminution alters the perceptual content in any discoverable direction. Accordingly, the task of the phenomenology of perception is to make this "something" the object of a special intention and thus to bring it to an intuition which is as discrete as possible.*

If this principle is systematically applied we can, for the first time, hope for the final disappearance of the mistaken assumption that everything which is not sensory or is not derived from a sensory content (like the associative elements) must be logical, that is, that it must lie in the sphere of judgment. We can hope that the components of perception will be taken as what they are, in their fullness, and not as what they "could" or "should" be for the sake of some arbitrary theory of their genesis.

The theory that in order to carry out the voluntary movement of an organ, for example, of the hand, we must first have a representation of movement, a reproduction of an equivalent movement performed earlier, belongs to the same class of cases. Self-observation shows that in normal life this is not at all the case. A normal child, for example, can simply copy the form of a letter his teacher has written on the board. When he sees the form, the sequence of motor-intentions through which such a form was produced is somehow given to him, independently of the sequence of the so-called sensations of movement unambiguously connected with particular organs and their initial situations. The child first comes to know these *through* and *in* the execution of those motor-intentions, in the movement of his first attempts at writing.[64] In contrast, idiot children must have their hands guided by the teacher in order to learn to copy what they see. Only when the natural liaison of the motor-intentions with the visual form drops away does the "representation of movement" contain that meaning which many psychologists, Ziehen, for example, ascribe to it even in the case of normal movement. I said that a tendency to look for an experienced resistance in oneself first of all is an abnormality. This is also confirmed by genuine cases of "aboulia" [namely, willessness]. Here not only is the enforcement of the will against reproductive or perseverative tendencies [65] in psychic life obstructed, not only is the translation or volition or decision into movement obstructed (which, again, can rest on an inner disturbance of the motor-intentions, e.g., in the case of false movements, seizure, etc., or on a defective coordination of the reproduced motor-sensations felt in the organs, or, finally, on simple objective paralysis), but even *the act of willing itself* is obstructed. The tendency to shift the resistance onto the self reaches its utmost limits, and willing itself becomes the goal of striving. Thus, the sick man can no longer "will," because he strives after "willing" itself, because he is constantly "willing to will," is constantly and with lively emotion training his attention on willing. He can be freed from this condition, as I have often seen, by becoming liberated from

64. Cases in which the ability to speak and to walk is suddenly acquired, without any preceding attempts at learning, also belong to this context. See Bastian, *Über Aphasie und andere Sprachstörungen*, pp. 8 ff. [Scheler is referring to the German translation, by M. Urstein (Leipzig, 1902), of H. C. Bastian, *A Treatise on Aphasia and other Speech Defects* (London, 1898).—TRANS.]

65. One especially intense obstruction the act of will encounters through perseverative tendencies is represented by the so-called hysterical counterwill which, it appears, completely frustrates decision, without any reason.

his fixation with willing and by training his attention on the "contents" to be realized, contents lying in the direction of his predominant interests. Analogously, the religious "will to believe," so often mistaken by "modern" individuals for belief itself, positively excludes any genuine belief.[66]

Finally, illusion in the domain of *values*, their relations to feelings, and their correlative objects shows a similar natural direction. A man's feeling is absolutely directed upon the values which adhere to things [*Sachen*], so much so that, in the presence of the values which he feels in things, he is inclined to overlook his own emotional reaction to the values, his "joy" over something or his "grief." He is inclined to impress on his own reaction the quality of that very value which has caused him to react. Thus the primary direction of illusion is not the projection of one's own feelings into things and their values. Its primary direction is the exact opposite, namely, a displacement-from-the-*outside*-to-the-*inside* [*von-aussen-nach-innen verlegen*] of the felt value-qualities [67] of *things* and situations into the sphere of the feelings of the states of one's own self. Thus we often think we are joyous because an expensive meal is offered us or because a valuable ring is sent to us. We think we are sorrowful because we walk in a funeral procession, although a glance behind the periphery of our consciousness would show us that we are not sorrowful. This does not mean that we only judge that we are sorrowful or joyful. We do indeed have the feeling itself, but "only in a spurious" way; the feeling is like a "shadow" of the genuine feeling. In this fashion the brightness, the sublimity, or the gloominess of a landscape often seems to overflow onto us. These are all qualities adhering to the landscape itself, fixed characteristics which do not vary with our states of feeling (for a sad or gloomy landscape does not become cheerful and bright because a cheerful man is passing through, not even for this man himself).

In principle we can apprehend such characteristics without having already experienced the feelings, that is, the states of the self associated with this quality. Thus, "we feel ourselves honored" when we enter a house where fame and

---

66. The analogue of this holds also for the will to love. [On "wanting to love" and "wanting to believe," see *Formalismus*, IV, 3.—ED.]

67. That is, value-qualities perceived in the mode of feeling.

splendor are in the air. Here, too, the facts are turned upside down by the subjectivistic and idealistic theory that "values" are "above all" only the effects of things on our emotional state, that is, they are only the associative reproductions of feelings for which the "constant dispositions" lie in things, but which are only emotionally projected into these things.[68] "Projection of feeling," when it actually occurs, represents the rare, abnormal direction illusion takes. When our gaze strays from the value felt in things to the feeling we have when we actually possess this value, or even to the feeling of the value [*das Fühlen des Wertes*] as a special function of the reception of value [*Wertaufnahme*], a phenomenon begins which, if only quantitatively increased, leads to abnormality and disease. The Epicurean who strives not for wealth, honor, friends, women, and the values immanent in these objects, but for the "pleasure in them"—the Epicurean who calls other men "fools" because they seek these values of things [*Sachwerte*] instead of pleasure—is in fact sick in his soul and uses his theory to justify only his own sick attitude. So, too, the gaze of the sick autoerotic is forever straying from the loved object and its value to his own sensation, until this and the sensuous feelings adhering to it crowd in front of the value-objects and obscure these from him, to such an extent that, in the end, he is completely shut up in his own sensation and its analysis as though in a prison.[69] It seems to me that

68. [See *Formalismus*, I, i, and VI, on the critique of this and the following theories of value.—ED.]

69. Autoeroticism, where sexual pleasure is concerned, should not be *objectively* defined, e.g., as self-satisfaction, but must, like all such perversions, be *intentionally* defined. Self-satisfaction, where it is not a feeble search for the sensation of pleasure but is connected with love, is not necessarily autoerotic, e.g., it is not so if it is practiced only because the beloved object is absent, although one's fantasies remain directed upon it. Autoeroticism, naturally, must be distinguished from everything which language calls "egoism." The "egoist" does not strive for pleasure as "his pleasure," for the pleasure he, as an isolated individual, can get, without looking to others at all. But this is what the autoerotic does. He seeks pleasure "without regard" to the other or in indifference to the other's benefit. Thus, he does look at the other, but does not "take him into consideration." Even in the case where this pleasure is sensual pleasure, where egoism occurs in the sexual sphere, the two phenomena remain utterly distinct. Autoeroticism is, on the other hand, present even in normal sexual intercourse, when one's intention is trained upon one's own person, upon one's sensation, as much as upon one's erotically important values, like beauty, life-force, etc., and the other person is grasped

in cases of this kind it is not the pure material of feeling, the quality of the feeling, its strength, and its conjunction with particular contents which have changed in relation to normal life; rather, the function of feeling has lost its primary directedness to values, to those above all which are external and not one's own. It has acquired in place of this a preference for being trained "upon itself" and its own states. Nonetheless, this kind of disturbance lies much deeper than a mere disturbance in the focus of attention to which even diseases of the heart have been traced, as in the case of paying continual attention to the sensation of heart palpitation. Feeling and attention are distinct functions and the former submits to voluntary guidance even less than drive-based [*triebhafte*] attention itself. It is not because we pay more attention to our states of feeling that we feel them more; on the contrary, attention results in the dissolution of feelings. It is because feeling turns onesidedly in their direction and turns away from values that we can attend to feelings more closely. Attention as such does not make feelings, as it does the contents of representation, richer and more vivid; rather it destroys them.[70] For this reason, an increased emotional excitability in hysterical states, for example, cannot rest on increased attention to one's own feelings.

Certain disturbances of the *feeling of sympathy* and of *love and hate* furnish a special case of this reversal of the direction of illusion in emotional life. If, for example, one finds that a melancholy man gives up all the "altruistic" activities he practiced prior to his illness, or that a mother who previously loved her child ardently and took complete care of him, can appear indifferent when her child is screaming himself blue in the face with hunger, then it is a mistake to say, in these and analogous cases, that the act of love itself or its translation into willing and acting has suffered an injury. Instead, the functions of clear and distinct comprehension of the states of the other's soul, e.g., his hunger and pain, have disappeared here. The activation of the act of love can be based only on the emotional perception of the other's expres-

---

only as the "servant" of one's own beauty, or as the cause of what happens in the individual in question.

70. [On the role of attention on the different levels of feeling, see *Formalismus*, V, 8.—ED.]

sions. This mother sees, as it were, only a screaming child turning blue in the face, but not his hunger and his suffering. These might well be given to her by association or through judgment and inference, but they are not given in the manner of immediate feeling. Loving as such, together with its capacity to be activated if only the mother could see the child's condition, might well be present.[71] Thus, her defect is not an *ethical defect,* which could only concern behavior toward an already given state of another's mind. Here, too, the reception of the other's condition and intentions is obstructed because feeling is trained predominantly on itself. One can almost speak of an emotional blindness to the other's states of mind, which naturally influences one's consciousness of their reality as well.[72] Here, too, that which is present is a disturbance of psychic function, not necessarily an alteration of the material of feeling.

As the example shows, it is not at all normal for us to come to understand another's states of mind by reproducing our own similar states of mind, which are bound up with analogous expressions, and then by projecting what is reproduced into the other. Rather, this furtive glancing at "what we ourselves experienced," when the other is expressing his feeling or recounting his states of mind, is the beginning of a disturbance in the direction of feeling which in the extreme

71. That the feeling of another's suffering and another's joy is not fellow feeling [*Mitfühlen*] is shown by the fact that these components are present even in the case of wickedness, or, what is worse, in the case of sensual pleasure in cruelty. Sharing in another's joy or in another's pain is *not* built upon that. This holds true even more of loving and hating, which are more original than mere fellow feeling. See also my remarks in *The Nature of Sympathy* [pp. 133–34].

72. The ability to feel another's states of feeling has naturally been subject, in the course of history, to a rich development. In the form of an ability to suffer or to feel delight or take joy in something, it has kept step with the development of the ability to suffer or to take joy in one's own pains and feelings of sensory well-being. The capacity for feeling is entirely independent of sensibility to pain and pleasure and the laws of their intensification, since the former concerns the suffering or enjoyment of those sensations and these can vary independently of the states of pain and pleasure. We must always take this factor into account when we pass ethical judgments on undeveloped mores, usages, and modes of behavior, in order to avoid taking the narrower scope and differentiation of this capacity for feeling for a lack of sympathetic feeling, commiseration, and rejoicing with another, or even for a lack of love. This would only mislead us into making a totally unjustified judgment.

instance leads to emotional blindness. The natural direction of illusion is not that of taking one's own for the other's or of "emotionally projecting" oneself into other persons, but the opposite, namely, *taking the other's for one's own*. We live "first and foremost" in the modes of feeling typical of our environment, our parents, family, and teachers, *before* we gain awareness of our own modes of feeling which perhaps diverge from theirs. Among our own feelings we are first aware only of those which correspond to the direction of feeling typical of our narrower or wider society and its tradition. A long and critical confrontation is always necessary before we can make our *own* feelings clear behind these feelings we vicariously reproduce, before we can begin to raise our own spiritual head, so to speak, out of the stream of the emotional tradition of society. We are more ready to take our own feeling to be mere imagination (a mere representation of a feeling), because it does not "fit in" with the feelings society feels, than to question the feelings of our neighbors [*Nebensmenschen*] because we cannot make them coincide with analogous experiences of our own. This is the normal direction of illusion, the one it takes even with regard to the emotions we can feel in the personae of art and religion. The young girl in love does not project her experiences into Isolde or Juliet; she projects the feelings of these poetic figures into her own small experiences. Only later does a genuine feeling of one's own perhaps break through the web of this fantasy of feeling. It is then that illusion first takes the opposite direction, the direction of genuine empathy [*Einfühlung*].[73]

73. One cannot speak of a "representation of feeling" if one takes "representation" to mean the content of an image. In this sense one cannot represent to himself feelings themselves, but only their causes and effects. But it would be quite wrong to say, on this basis, that feelings are always equally actual, that they are connected with representations only by means of reproduction (to yield representation of feelings). On the contrary, there is, in the sphere of feeling, a distinction which corresponds to that of perception and representation (so far as these words mean "direct possession" and "indirect possession," that is, a mere symbolic "intending" via something else). This distinction has nothing to do with the reproduction of a feeling. I am able not only to know a past experience of feeling and judge it as something I have had, but I can also "feel it again," even though my state of feeling at the moment does not have the same quality as the past feeling. I can remember great pains and deep sorrow with a cheerful spirit, when I experience these feelings "imaginatively" [*vorstellig*]. This recollective experience of a feeling [*dieses*

I shall now introduce a second and no less important general source of illusion in inner perception. The first consisted generally in shifting facts derived from external perception to inner perception, in shifting facts which derive from the perception of another to self-perception. The second rests on the fact that we transfer to *psychic facts* themselves forms of multiplicity which are proper only to the *physical* world, together with certain *temporal and causal* relations between the physical causes and effects of psychic facts, and, finally, the *simplicity* and *complexity* of the physical causes of *psychic* facts.

The kind of *unity and multiplicity* belonging to what is given in inner perception is *sui generis* and incomparable with any other. In the first place, it must be completely distinguished from that unity which exists between the intentional acts insofar as their objects are reciprocally identifiable. If one calls this latter unity the "unity of consciousness," then by "consciousness" one means each and every "consciousness of," not only consciousness of the "phenomena of consciousness" in the narrower sense, that is, consciousness of those facts which are the concern of psychology, as distinguished from arithmetic, physics, etc., but also that "consciousness of" in which, for example, numbers or physical appearances are given to us. The unity and multiplicity we are speaking of *here* are, on the contrary, the unity and multiplicity of *the given in inner perception.* They are not contained in that most general unity mentioned above and do not belong to all acts of intentional apprehension [*Erfassen*] but belong only to what is given in the acts of "inner perception." Second, the unity and multiplicity are totally distinct from, and opposed to, those of the being of Nature. The multiplicity of the latter exhibits an "apartness" [*ein Auseinander*] [74] which inheres identically in the forms of space and time; the differences of

---

erinnernde Fühlen eines Gefühls] is not its recurrence in weaker form. Accordingly, there is also a fantasy of feeling itself which does not first arise from the fantasy of imaginative life, as a way of living in "images," but is primitive and often guides the latter. This is given, e.g., when we playfully "feel out" and combine feelings we have never in fact experienced.

74. The datum of "mutual apartness," a phenomenon which is identically contained in the spatial and temporal manifold, is quite distinct from the idea of "extension," which also belongs to much that is mental.

space and time are determined through the particular order-ing of this apartness. The original psychic multiplicity, en-countered in every act of inner perception whatever and es-sentially connected with the essence of this act, exhibits a multiplicity in which there is no longer any "apartness." Here there is only a "togetherness" [*Zusammen*] in the "ego" which cannot be further defined (where "ego" means only the form of unity appropriate to this multiplicity).

Thus, the manner in which feelings, thoughts, or images are together in the "ego" (in greater abundance, perhaps, in a particular act of inner perception) is neither temporal nor spatial, but intuitive [*anschauliche*], although intuitive *sui generis*. This manner becomes clearer the more we turn away from the peripheral strata of phenomena of consciousness, the stratum of sense-images, and the body-self [*Leibichs*], where the distinction between mental and physical is espe-cially difficult, and apply ourselves to the deeper strata, those of spiritual [*geistige*] feeling and striving and the sphere of thoughts. Even the semblance of an "apartness" continually diminishes the more we make our way toward the center, toward that element whose mental character brooks no doubt. This must be the starting point for the knowledge of the *es-sence* of the mental in general. On the periphery of such a unity of consciousness we still find an extension and a streamlike succession of facts with one distinguished point, that which is given "as present" [*als gegenwärtig*]. Over against this, and given along with it, stand what is given "as past" and what is given "as future." The acts of "remembering" and "expecting" correspond to these latter modes. Thus, a pain in the legs, for example, has a certain *original* extension and a localization, however senseless it would be to call it "spatial," or to want to measure its extension or determine its position in space and nature. "Fatigue," too, still has these determina-tions, although more vaguely, while a "feeling of languor" no longer exhibits them. This streamlike succession exists all the more clearly and distinctly when we hold to the periphery of consciousness, while it clearly diminishes when we turn to the deeper world of feeling and striving.[75] In *no* case, however,

75. There are two fundamentally different phenomena of this "se-quence" which make their appearance according to whether our interest is forced onto the more peripheral or the more central level. If we focus

are this extension and succession an *apartness* of elements, a form which is in no way given along with extension and succession. Thus I apprehend, for example, the "succession" of tones in a melody; I apprehend them not as simultaneous but as "succeeding one another." No mere order among the qualitative characters of tones which were "in the first place" given as simultaneous could give me the phenomenon of "succeeding one another," unless the latter lay in the phenomenon itself. However, this "succession" is equally found in the unity of *one* form which I apprehend as a whole in *one* act. This succession has nothing to do with the objective sequence of tone-phenomena, to say nothing of the sequence of stimuli and nervous shocks which correspond to these physically and physiologically. The succession is no more measurable than the extension of a pain. It is based on the whole of the melodious "form" and the whole of the unity of "rhythm." Its particular character, its "quickness" or "slowness"—qualities which have no meaning for objectively measurable time— [76] depends on and changes with these forms.

Even in the intuitive content of an act of memory and an act of expectation, I *immediately* encounter this succession once again, under the right circumstances. And I do so without having to return to the objective time-sequence of events in the external world and without being forced to perform inductive operations. In *every* act of inner perception something is given to me as "present," something as "past," and something as "future," and all in an immediate fashion: however, the total stock [*Gesamtfülle*] of what is so given can increase and diminish. What is given to me in this way appears against the indistinct background of the *completely undivided*

essentially on the body-self [*Leibich*], then this appears to be the constant thing by which our desires and thoughts, to speak metaphorically, "flow past" as "fleeting forms." If, on the contrary, we live with complete "collectedness" in the sphere of the central self, its content appears "lasting" and "stable," and the content of the body-self (which we do not grasp only as the sum of so-called organic sensations, but as a vaguely articulated whole, in which so-called organic sensations can afterward be found through analysis) takes on that character of "flowing-past." I would like this to be understood correctly. It is not a matter here of "theories," but of experienced phenomena which formed the historical starting points of all possible fine "theories." [See below, note 76.—ED.]

76. For the objective time of mechanics there is no being-present, being-in-the-future, and being-past. These are essentially bound up with a lived-body. [See *Formalismus*, VI, A, 3, f, g.—ED.]

"ego." Thus, the ego appearing in inner perception is always present as a co-intended totality [*als Totalität mitgemeint*].[77] The ego of the present stands out only as a particularly bright and luminous summit. There is thus no question of my having to construct the unity of the whole ego piecemeal by joining together the perception of the present ego with the "egos" remembered from the past, as I would assemble a physical body out of its parts. Whatever element of the "whole" ego with its stock of experience is not given to me as a separate content can still be "given" as something which is well defined and characterized by its perceived relationship to a given. These phenomena of relation point, so to speak, to *all* the points of my life. I have an immediate consciousness that these "threads" which I apprehend, along with every act of inner perception, come to an end here and there in my past, although the end-points are not intuitively given to me as contents of awareness.

Unities of consciousness, which I come upon in acts of inner perception, can be variously rich in content. But every one of these diverse totalities unified through one act belongs again to a totality of the same *nature and multiplicity*, although one of a higher order. There is no more justification for letting them succeed one another in objectively measurable time than there is for thinking of them as spread out in space.

We have shown that the world of consciousness, in keeping with its constitutive form, is a completely different world than the world of external perception. We have also shown how we must wrestle, as it were, with the language we use to describe the external world in order to describe even the simplest structures of the world of consciousness. One absolutely essential source of illusion consists in transferring this ultimately underivable form of multiplicity more or less "pictorially" into the forms of space and time familiar to us from the external world. We do this primarily by replacing the psychic facts *themselves* with the functions they perform as mere symbols for physical objects and their spatiotemporal order. Or, we replace them with the order of bodily processes

---

77. See also Dilthey, "Der Aufbau der geschichtlichen Welt in den Geisteswissenschaften," *Sitzungsbericht der Berliner Akademie,* 1910. [Now in *Gesammelte Schriften*, 5th ed., Vol. VII (Stuttgart, 1968).— TRANS.]

and the parts of the lived-body to which they still have a specifiable relation. Or, finally, we replace these psychic facts with the expressive manifestations and movements of the body which they evoke.

This process of replacement is manifested, first, in the manifold "images" taken from the external world that are always threatening to conceal the peculiar form of the unity and multiplicity of consciousness. It is in evidence, for example, when one speaks of "consciousness" as a stage or box where "ideas," like identical material things, are entering and departing, impeding and disturbing one another, as happens in the whole "picture book" of Herbartian and English psychology. Nonetheless, the English associationistic psychology as a whole is merely an unwitting attempt to analyze the form of mental multiplicity in such a way (and to acknowledge as "given" in it only so much) that when it has been analyzed it *still* can be coordinated with spatiotemporal events in the body, particularly those in the nervous system.[78] However, in the strict sense this is the case only when symbols, thought of as "atoms" (Hume's "ideas" and impressions, for example), insinuate themselves in place of mental facts themselves, and when only *one* original mode of conjunction between them is accepted, that of association by way of contiguity.[79] Whatever does not fit this schema is not acknowledged as a psychic fact. This whole idol, the production of a "mechanics of the mind" in which the basic concepts of genuine mechanics, such as mass, force, energy, etc., find a vague application, is only the tendency, already present in a natural intuition but here pushed to its extreme by science, to transpose the psychic manifold into the forms of space and time. Associated with this tendency is the natural, vague idea that the soul is "in" the body and that thought is "in" the head, and the familiar primitive theories of localization which let ideas take up residence in the cells of the ganglia. Furthermore, the question of the "seat" of the soul-substance, which occupied philosophy for so long a time, belongs here. People pictured the soul

78. See the essay "Versuche einer Philosophie des Lebens." [In *Vom Umsturz der Werte*, 4th ed. rev. *Gesammelte Werke* III.—TRANS.]

79. Association based on similarity is already incapable of such coordination. See my study, *Formalismus* [VI, A, 3, g, and the critique of the theories of the mental as an ordering, as a substance, and as a stream, secs. e, f, g.—ED.]

"raised" above the "flux" of psychic occurrences and exercising its power on this flux or "combining" the "events" which were initially separated in time. Moreover, a picture recently presented as superior to these more static images is equally connected with this tendency. In this, the "psychic" is a "stream of experiences" flowing past in objective time. A direct causality and conformity to law ought to obtain between these experiences as they succeed one another in time, as Wundt, for example, asserts. Finally, there is the assertion that "consciousness" is only a "generic concept" in relation to individual contents of consciousness, or that it is merely a different "arrangement of the same contents" than the arrangement of physical phenomena—possibly, the order which they acquire "in relation to an organism." [80]

All these assertions and pictures push illusory motifs already present *in natural intuition* to their extreme consequences. They arrest research at the most peripheral stratum of consciousness, that of sensation, and lead to the absurd claim that everything psychic can be reduced to so-called sensations and complexes of sensations or be "reworked" into such. If the originally psychic manifold is subsumed under objective time, for example, a vast number of insoluble problems must immediately arise. I mention here only that it immediately becomes impossible to comprehend the fact of memory (and of expectation). What makes memory a real fact is not that at one moment of time a representation *B* is present which is identical with or similar to a representation or an experience *A* which occurred at some previous moment, *plus* a "symbolic function" directed upon the earlier experience. How would we come to know of that experience *A* whose existence in a previous moment in time is presupposed by this conception? If perception of the psychic were restricted to the self of the present moment, then *A* would be eternally transcendent, a thing-in-itself which we could strike out without altering the experiential given in the least. It is a totally mistaken idea that *A*, which on this view is found at another position in objective time, one which no longer "is" and thus cannot prove itself effectively present [*wirksam*], is to be brought once again into temporal contact with the soul's

80. E. Mach and Avenarius, for instance, assert this.

present life through the substitution of a so-called disposition, whether psychic or merely physiological. Such a disposition inferred from the present state of the soul explains nothing, since it is a completely unknown X. To assume a disposition for A presupposes that I know something about A itself, whatever it may be, if A is not to be a completely empty sign. If, however, we leave out the totally obscure mental "dispositions" and omit the assumption of a so-called unconscious, then the classification of the psychic manifold under objective time drives us to epiphenomenalism, that is, to the denial of any continuous connectedness of psychic facts in general. This is not a lesser illusion, since it rests on the assumption that nature is only effectively real [wirklich] so far as it is perceived. In fact, however, A is a real experience in the unity of the relevant consciousness, an experience which, in principle, can have effect on *every* subsequent moment of consciousness, without being previously reproduced in a special representation. It appears in its rightful context in the background of memory as immediately as the so-called present content of consciousness does, without "first" needing to be vicariously represented [vertreten] in the present content of consciousness by some special element, e.g., a so-called memory-image. The same applies to the effective reality of that which is expected or the "real influence" exercised on the present course of events by the "tasks" posed from without or within (instinctually or by a voluntary decision). This real influence is exercised without a new representation of the expected contents or the tasks.[81] If we make the contrary assumption, we have no solutions to the problem of the successive comparison of items, the problem of time-consciousness, or, finally, the problem of mental causality in general. We can only hint at this here.

Another general and closely connected idol of inner perception (indeed, of the intuition of phenomenal givenness in general) is the idea that the given is grasped, identified, distinguished, and captured in concepts only so far as it can

81. The anticipatory effect of a task set by posthypnotic suggestion, an effect consisting in a peculiar agitation felt shortly before the time comes to perform the proposed deed, belongs in this context, as does the interesting problem of the influence of a man's "future" (good or bad) on his present state of mind. See "Die Psychologie der sogennanten Rentenhysterie," *Vom Umsturz der Werte*.

function as *a sign for the sphere of physical reality*. We know that the "natural" intuition of the world is already opposed, so to speak, to physical science, because it is receptive to the full range of observable qualities only so far as they and their conjunction contain *signs* for things, for "solid things" and their differences first of all, or for things as elements of relationships, primarily those having some *practical* importance. To be sure, colors and tones, which in physics are only so many "signs" for the motion of hard particles, do appear in "natural intuition," but *only so far* as they assume the role of symbols for our perceptions of things which represent the true intention of natural intuition, and for certain perceptions of relationships and structures. We first see "cherries" and hear a "wagon going past"; color and tone enter secondarily into what is "given" here only insofar as they mediate these "unities of perception." Thus there is in natural intuition itself a kind of "crypto-mechanism" which we *must first destroy* if we are to get to phenomenal being. One of the profound motives of science is to destroy this crypto-mechanism.[82] A whole series of basic formal properties of elementary sensory-appearances, properties which permit these appearances to be arranged formally and ordered in certain ways, were overlooked for so long, or treated as mere complexes, only because they have no strict analogue in the physical dimensions within which a stimulus can vary. For example, the specific brightness of colors and the basic qualities of vocal tones were overlooked,[83] as though the possible arrangements of these qualities could not, in principle, be more numerous than the physical possibilities of the variation of the stimuli associated with them, or as though one could distinguish the directions of phenomenal variation only after discovering the univocal dependence of these on some physical variation. From the start, it is only a *practical, biological focus* that causes us to give heed, first of all to the spatiotemporal system of solid things and their movements, and then to their qualities, forms, structures, and possible variations, only to the extent that they

82. [On the "crypto-mechanism" of natural intuition in regard to psychic being (association), see *Formalismus*, VI, A, 3, g, and the later investigation "Erkenntnis und Arbeit," III, C.—ED.]

83. See the pertinent general remarks of W. Köhler on this subject, in "Akustische Untersuchungen," pt. 1, *Zeitschrift für Psychologie*, LIV (1910), 241 ff.

can be signs and symbols for variations in this mobile world of solid things. We do not do this at the command of any sort of "logic" or of an "a priori understanding." This same focus is also in effect with regard to qualities with a more pronounced subjective character and even more to the more central "facts" of inner perception. It is only in the course of experience that these are either connected with external things through the mediation of the body-self [*Leibich*] *or*, if this is lacking, are immediately present in the self, as in the case of "spiritual" [*geistige*] feelings. The qualitative abundance of the smells and tastes of food and drink remains unknown just to the extent that hunger and thirst long for and seize upon these *things*. The hungry person loses the taste-quality of food and the connected sensuous feeling of well-being in the pleasant sensation of "filling the stomach" and the satisfaction attached to it. As the immediate need *retreats*, the qualitative fullness expands.

This holds true of all "qualities," especially of "value-qualities." It is not the nature of value-qualities to be "subjective," "human," etc., because in natural behavior they are, in fact, mostly apprehended as *signals* for certain actions and are distinguished, conceptualized, and given names only so far as they are signals for different actions unified by certain goals. Their "human" and "subjective" character consists rather in the fact that we apprehend them only insofar as they possess this meaning of a "signal given by the environment for our practical measures." There is a precise analogy here between value-qualities and the qualities of sensory phenomena. We tend, in natural intuition, to comprehend the intuitive content of the latter only so far as it can bring out the distinctions in the spatial and temporal relations of solid things, their forms and sizes, and their *significance*—as "church" or "chair." Analogously, all value-qualities in natural intuition primarily function as a means for distinguishing the "bearers" of values and are especially concerned with a particular class of values, namely, the economically important goods which, at the artificial [*künstlichen*] stage of "society," find their purest expression in prices, that is, in the amount of money they can command. The society of money tends to empty values of their qualities [*dequalifizieren*] as thoroughly as the mechanistic view of nature "dequalifies" intuitive sense-qualities.[84] The "commodity character" of things, which does not rest on an intrinsic property of these things but only in their exchangeability with a view to increasing wealth, becomes, as it were, a *substance* to which other qualities, the aesthetic, for example, are first attributed. And this is not merely an accidental analogy, as some have thought; both facts have *the same* root. Both phenomena follow the same law, that all phenomenal contents of the world as a whole (felt-values as well as perceived contents) tend to become *bare symbols for,* and *means for distinguishing among,* those contents upon which the *most elementary, most general, and most forceful drives* of an animal are directed. In *both* cases the artificial forms of the society of money and the mechanistic view of nature only make absolute tendencies which already inhere in man's natural behavior and which diminish the concrete qualitative fullness of the world. A purely *cognitive* focus on the world must break altogether with these tendencies.

What I have said is doubly true of the *central* strata of inner perception. What "first of all" come under our perception within the flowing stream of our psychic life are those unities of value which are objectively "universal" (although they are not given to us "as" universal) and are qualified to symbolize the variations of our bodily condition. That they *are* unities of value is shown by the obvious fact that it is so much easier for us to assess and judge our own and another's experience than to comprehend and understand it "psychologically." It is especially difficult and requires special effort to eliminate consideration of "good" and "bad." The value of an experience is not an "addition" to the given resulting from an act of assessment and from reflection on this (as Herbart and F. Brentano, for example, assumed). On the contrary, it is the *primarily* given fact from which we must first artificially *abstract* the value-free [*wertindifferent*] state of affairs.[85] This primary givenness of value is also demonstrated by the fact that, when memory and expectation are hampered, the value-

---

84. See G. Simmel, *Philosophie des Geldes* (Leipzig, 1900), and W. Sombart, *Der moderne Kapitalismus,* Vol. II (Leipzig, 1902). See also my essay on the "Bourgeois." [In *Vom Umsturz der Werte,* pp. 341–61.— TRANS.]

85. [See the critique of the judgmental theory of values in *Formalismus,* IV, i.—ED.]

quality of the pertinent content is what *first* comes to light. We know that it was something "pleasant" or "painful," something "important" or "indifferent," "sordid" or "noble," that "happened to us yesterday" or "is going to happen tomorrow," but we still do not know *what* it is. Thus the values of experiences are always brightly on display within the compass of our consciousness, while the bearers of these values are not themselves present to us. We feel an emotion to be "bad," even though we have not yet grasped some definite content at which it is aimed. Therefore we can suppress it before it comes to fruition. The manifold of consciousness which is articulated into experiences by unities of value appears in inner perception only to the extent that these experiences are *signs of bodily conditions* and that their changes are signs of *changed* bodily conditions. Every experience, for example the unity of an emotion, a feeling of sadness, perhaps, or of joy, or one of strong compassion, or an act of will, is accompanied by a change in the total state of bodily sensations and the sensuous feelings connected with these.

There is a source of illusion in ordinary inner perception which consists in *overlooking* all the qualitative differences between those emotions and strivings which have *the same kind* of effect on the condition of the body. We are "born" psychologists of organic sensations, and only if we "overcome" our original inclination to be aware of the whole of psychic life only so far as it serves to satisfy bodily needs, only so far as it is an index of the changed conditions of the body or provokes certain bodily movements, are genuine, "pure" psychic facts disclosed to us. All those transitory experiences which do not determine simultaneous changes of the bodily state, together with different externally directed actions, are comprehended only vaguely and indistinctly, if at all; they are a "nothing." Only a difficult and fundamental turning aside from bodily conditions and from the sphere of external action lets the genuine psychic phenomena, their differences as well as the law to which they conform, emerge from the mysterious obscurity of the self. The form of law based upon the body and its processes does not "explain" or univocally define those phenomena and their laws; on the contrary, it "distorts" them, in the sense in which friction distorts the pure "enforcement" of the law of free fall. Thus we have to grasp the concrete event by *superimposing both* forms of law on one another.[86] The states of the body and their objective correlates do not determine the *content* of what is given in inner perception, any more than they determine what is given in the sphere of outer perception; they determine only the *selection* made from among whatever we in fact grasp at any one time in inner perception. Thus, whoever allows body-states to correspond in one-to-one fashion to psychic processes and contents, in the manner of psycho-physiological parallelism, confuses a condition of the *perception* of the mental with a condition of the *mental itself*. He behaves just like a physiologist of the senses who imagines he is doing physics.

Accordingly, a psychology unwilling to convert a general inclination to self-deception into the *principle* of its research must not strive to "reduce" psychic facts as far as possible to elements of the state of the body, organic sensations, and sensory feelings. On the contrary, it must strive to peel these away from the concrete fact and investigate the nature and the special legitimacy of *what remains*. It is thus merely a consequence of that source of illusion in inner perception when someone wants to reduce the abundant qualities of the *feelings* to pleasure and displeasure, together with their objective correlates. Certainly what all of us first pay attention to in feelings is not their radically different qualities but only the terminal point at which they flow into the *sensory* feelings of pleasure and displeasure (the sphere of the sensuously pleasant) and into the body-self, thereby indicating what promotes or hinders the inner life-processes of the organism. But the "feeling of life" is *not* a sum of sensory feeling. Its modifications, such as "healthy" and "sick," "languid" and "vigorous," "rising" and "falling" (ascent and descent), etc., cannot be represented by the subtraction and addition of sensory feelings. The law governing the changes and rhythm of the feeling of life *cannot* be understood in terms of the law governing sensory feelings. The feeling of life can be understood still less in terms of the law of *spiritual* feelings, like melancholy and sadness, bliss, etc.[87] The so-called James-Lange

---

86. See the further development of this point in the second part of *Formalismus*, VI, A, 3, g.

87. [See *Formalismus*, V, 8, on the mutual irreducibility of the different levels of feeling.—ED.]

theory of affects [88] is a clear example of this illusion. It is unquestionably important to bring to light the significance of the sensations involved in the discharge of an affect in expressive movements, and, still more, the inner visceral sensations which are even more intense when the external expression of the affect is suppressed. Nevertheless, the qualitative abundance of the affects and the intention governing them, for example "being-angry-about-something," together with the focus of this intention which is subject to such far-reaching individual variations, remain completely unexplained. Those cases in which the theory fits the facts are not cases of the normal manifestation and discharge of the affect, but *pathological* cases. It seems to me that the fact emphasized by all who are acquainted with hysteria, namely, that the intensity of the expression of the affects is not in proportion to the inner state (for instance, the individual appears much angrier than he really is, or much sadder, to judge from his moans and effusive tears, so that the uninitiated will always be deceived), indicates that the inner quality of feeling and intention on which those expressions are normally based is not present or has been added only afterward as a representation of feeling. But just this reveals the mistake this theory of affects makes in the *normal* case. The hysterical patient is actually "pleased *because* he laughs and sad *because* he cries," as someone has paradoxically expressed this theory. The normal man behaves *in the opposite way.* The patient's concern for the impression he makes on a spectator, for example the doctor, or for the "social image" he presents, immediately and, as it were, automatically, induces the discharge of the affect; the patient's own feeling and intention are introduced only afterward. Thus the deception of the observer is always a result of an antecedent self-deception, and this fact distinguishes hysterical behavior from any comedy or simulation which begins in the conscious sphere of will and judgment and aims directly at the observer.

A more indirect source of illusion is allied with the source previously discussed and, in the last analysis, rests on it. This consists in our inclination to grasp, in the psychic content of

88. [Briefly, the James-Lange theory holds that an emotion is the feeling accompanying bodily changes as they occur in the muscles and viscera (James), or in the circulatory system (Lange).—TRANS.]

inner perception (or the perception which is achieved in memory), only that which *can lead to useful or harmful actions*. I do not mean the subsequent "assessment" of a perceived emotion, a state of feeling, a striving or longing, as useful or harmful. I mean that the useful and harmful are so influential that these ideas act as *forms of comprehension* or, in other words, forms through which a selection is made of what experiences in general come into the field of inner perception. A young girl who is "well brought up" in the eyes of a petit bourgeois society does not, on the whole, perceive any excitations of feeling in the presence of young men who cannot "marry" her, who "cannot provide for" her; she "does not confess these feelings to herself." Now psychic processes which lead to the very same actions can naturally be widely distinguished in themselves; however, since our general tendency is to take hold of them in inner perception only as determining grounds for the possible *actions,* the individuals concerned remain ignorant of such differences.

A whole class of self-deceptions belongs here, that is, deceptions concerning the motives of one's own conduct. These illusions go in two directions. On one hand, we are inclined to impute to ourselves and to others considerations which have been added as "causes" and "motives" only after an action has been performed and its aftereffects have become obvious. That which happened because of primitive motives without any reflection, and had a useful effect, allegedly happened *because* this useful effect was willed. This is the well-known illusion of intellectualistic, popular psychology.[89] When an action could have taken place as a result of motives with *different* values, even when the less worthy motive has moved us, we are inclined to assume the motive which has the *higher* value. Contrary to what ethical utilitarianism thinks, it is not because the good is truly useful that we give names expressing ethical commendation to acts of volition and action which either proceed from considerations of usefulness or owe their existence to impulses which have objectively useful effects (this is the only thing that explains the origin and preservation of these impulses). It is rather because it is itself useful for a person to *seem* (to himself and others) to have acted

89. See also W. Wundt's *Ethik* (Stuttgart, 1886), which is inclined to call this illusion that of the "popular psychology of reflection."

from ethical motives. When a person has acted in fact from the motive of usefulness, this interpretation of action is falsified. Love, for instance, is certainly something totally different from "solidarity of interest"; but we often fancy we are in love when nothing but a solidarity of interest is present. It is not ethical actions that are in any way determined by usefulness and harmfulness, but the act of *social praise and blame.*[90] Political demands which are in fact dictated by group interests would not always be issued as a demand "for the general good" if this concealment of the motive of interest did not make the demand more persistent and its fulfillment something expected of everyone. The utilitarian explanation of ethical phenomena is thus in reality an explanation of *social illusions* concerning ethical phenomena that are expressed in social praise and blame.

As I have already mentioned, a further general source of illusion of inner perception is the introduction of facts and relations which obtain among the *physical causes and effects* of psychic facts into these psychic facts themselves, thereby falsifying the real state of affairs.

If I am listening to another person recount something to me, naturally the sound waves must first strike my ears and then be conducted into the brain by the sensitive elements. However, does this make it true that in consciousness as well *first* mere acoustical complexes, *then* memories of hearing, and *then* meanings must be given? In fact, this is not so. What I find here in the *first* place is rather the meaning-content of his speech; acoustical complexes intrude themselves only to the extent that my understanding of his meaning is obstructed. When the acoustical complex itself becomes an independent phenomenon, it is for the most part given only in immediate recollection, whereas its meaning has already been previously grasped. How erroneous it is, then, to read the sequence of physical causes into the sequence of phenomena of consciousness! Certainly, if I am to understand another's experience, his bodily gestures or his voice must first be objectively there

90. I have given a more precise proof of this thesis in Part II of *Formalismus.* [See the critique of the ethical utilitarianism in *Formalismus*, IV, 1.—ED.] I have applied the principle above in my attempt at a description and explanation of English "cant"; see the appendix to my book *Der Genius des Krieges und der Deutsche Krieg* (Leipzig: Verlag der Weissen Bücher, 1915).

and stimulate my eyes and ears, etc. But it is again an illusion to think that for this reason I must first have seen a corporeal motion or "another's body" generally in order to be able to understand another's joy, for example, on the basis of this perception of his face drawn up in laughter. Only when I am expecting a *simulation* or when I am face to face with a completely alien mode of expression, for example, when I am among strange people or exotic animals, do I grasp the bodily gestures as such *before* interpreting their meaning. Ordinarily the qualities, lines, and forms which come into view are not first given to me as symbols of a body in motion (e.g., the raised hands folded together in entreaty). I immediately see in them and through them the "joy" or the "entreaty," just as immediately as a doctor examining a patient sees the *very same* qualities, forms, and lines as symbols of the bodily parts in motion. Once again the objective, causal derivation [*Hergang*] of the case deceives us about the facts of consciousness. Analogously, the illusion often arises that since, in order to carry out a willed action, I must first execute this and that movement, this movement itself must have been willed and must have been present in a "representation of consciousness."

The schema which still dominates the textbooks of psychology has fundamental importance for the theory of the sources of illusion of inner perception. This is the schema according to which there is, in every individual's life, a "stage of development" at which only "sensations" are given, then one where "perceptions" are formed, with which "reproductions," "memories," and, finally, "meanings" and "judgments" are then allied. In fact there is nothing of the sort in consciousness; it is an essential law that there *cannot* be. An *ideal* construction of the content of consciousness, on the model of the analysis of its physical causes which has decomposed this content into moments corresponding to *these* physical causes, is here made into an *actual* derivation, a "history." *Constitutive* elements of every perception, the simplest as well as the most complicated, are seen as *genetic* formations which follow one another in sequence. In actuality, the development of consciousness is carried out simultaneously with the formation of sensory representations; the two reciprocally influence one another. The same is true of perception and memory. If we are looking for the bodily processes corresponding to a given perception, then we should let only the *whole* of the centripetal process correspond to the *whole* of the perception; not single components of this process to components of the perception. Only the two different directions of possible variation, one taken by such and such a nerve process in its unity, the other taken by such and such a perception, may lead to knowledge of additional and more specialized dependencies among the elements of these two series.[91]

What holds true of the temporal sequence of the causes and effects of the mental also holds true of the *simplicity and complexity* of the causes and effects of psychic states of affairs. Thus, the appearances of the bright colors are simple (although they have manifold, immediately evident relations of dependence), however complicated the physical causes of color-vision might be. There are no yellow and red "components" in *orange*. To take an example from a completely different sphere: the organization of a *thought* which I express in words and sentences in no way corresponds to the combination of the parts of the relevant *sentences*. The thought stands before me as a simultaneous *unity*, whereas the words succeed one another. The thought finds its "expression" in the sentence, but not in such a way that a particular "part" of the thought must correspond to every part of the sentence, e.g., to every word. This "scholastic principle," that the sentence is a "picture" and not merely a means of expressing the thought, misled not only medieval grammar and logic, but also the entire medieval hermeneutic and art of textual interpretation. And the illusion, in which we import into thoughts themselves the structure of their expression, recurs again and again even today. This is especially so in the case of the theoretical conception of the understanding of spoken sentences, a conception which has so long misled the thinkers working on the theory of aphasia. Normal understanding does *not* come about in the following way: first we hear the sounds of the words and a particular meaning allies itself word by word with each sound complex we hear, then the successive combination of these meanings gives us the "thought." Rather, from a few words

91. The physiological theory of the perception of structure also follows this line of thought, which Wertheimer has briefly developed in his study, "Experimentelle Studien über das Sehen von Bewegung," *Zeitschrift für Psychologie,* Vol. LXI (1912).

whose meaning is given to us to begin with (I mean the meaning of the words themselves, not the thoughts which the speaker "intends" with them), we grasp the speaker's whole "theme" in these meanings. Starting with this, we think along with him, sketching in, so to speak, the parts of the thought in vague and still indefinite unities of meaning which are then "filled in" and more sharply defined in the words we go on to hear. In every act of understanding there is an attitude which has the conceptual sense: I already know what you want to say. It is only because of this that we can decide how far the other has succeeded in *adequately* expressing his thought and can distinguish between what he intended to say and what he *actually* said. Thus, as we see in cases where at first we do not understand but hesitate between possibilities, the "act of understanding" a thought, that is, mastering the unitary intention which holds sway in the ongoing act of speaking, is not a long, incremental process, as the understanding of the individual words would be; at a certain point it suddenly occurs, like a light which suddenly illuminates the darkness. Analogously, we suddenly come to "understand" a melodic unity, or the aesthetic "sense" of a complex of colors and forms.

The phenomenon of "repression" is another general source of illusions in inner perception. This phenomenon has recently been given strong emphasis by the school of Sigmund Freud, although it is entangled in such a net of questionable theories that one would do well at the start not to keep to the theory and language of his school. We understand by "repression" not a causal hypothesis, but an actual *phenomenon* which frequently appears in acts of inner perception. It consists in an instinctual looking away from the stirrings of imagination, of feeling and longing, of loving and hating, from such stirrings as would result in a negative value judgment if fully perceived (a judgment coming from one's own "conscience," or a social judgment based on a code of rules we acknowledge). It would be very wrong to limit this phenomenon to the memory of earlier experiences. Memory only offers it a particularly rich field. However, it is also at hand in the inner perception of present experiences. Someone will ask: How, then, is "repression" possible in that case? For "repression" is strictly distinguished from "ethical self-control," that is, a conscious and voluntary obstruction and suppression of *fully seen* experiences.

What distinguishes them is both the fact that (in repression) the experiences are indeed there but are not *seen,* and the fact that they are not altered by conscious acts of the will but are simply placed out of sight by an instinctive drive. Is it not necessary that the experience already be inwardly perceived if it is to be "repressed"? Let me recall what was said earlier. The aroma of *value [das Wertparfüm],* so to speak, of an experience, of a stirring of feeling, or striving, is already present to inner perception, even if the experience itself, especially the *content* to which the striving or feeling, the hate or love, is directed, is *not* yet present.[92] The drive reacts to this initial *value* of the stirring and keeps the experience from crossing the threshold of inner perception. In this way, the experience remains barred not only from the sphere of *judgment* (for it is often the case that no judgment is made concerning completely perceived experiences) but also from the sphere of inner perception itself. It is an entirely different matter when an experience *is* perceived and pride, or shame, or motives of duty come into conflict with its inherent tendency and obstruct its translation into expressive movements or into actions. Those obstructions are real mental processes; they have nothing to do with inner illusions. In the case of repression *no* such real conflict of motives occurs, since shame, pride, disgust, fear, anxiety, or whatever else is the ground of repression, does not constrict the experience or obstruct its further unfolding but only obstruct the *perception* of the experience.[93] It is just for this reason that the experience can *really* unfold without being obstructed by such involuntary counterforces—or by ethical self-control. Thus, a clear dividing line runs between ethical self-control, or a real conflict of motives, and that looking-away and closing one's eyes which is called "repression." Ethical self-control sees the enemy face to face, while in a real conflict the forces countering the experience remain victorious.

Repression of the memory of previous experiences is no less sharply distinguished from any ordinary "forgetting," as well as from positive *illusions* of memory. While common defects of memory do not occur in accordance with any rules, here

92. [On the priority of the value-components over the components of images and meanings, see *Formalismus,* especially IV, i.—ED.]
93. In Freud and his school, these two fundamentally different things are continually confused with each other.

the defects contain a certain meaningful *tendency* which corresponds to a quite definite "interest," a "striving" or "counterstriving" of the individual. This is why we correctly hold the individual responsible for this sort of "forgetting." Also, what has been repressed can be far more easily restored to the full light of memory than what cannot be remembered only because the mechanism of reproduction is disturbed. In repressed memory the mechanism of reproduction is not disturbed, any more than the mechanisms of the external visual organ and the sensibility responding to its stimuli are disturbed in the case of hysterical blindness or the constriction of the visual field owing to hysteria. Indeed, the experience which is repressed is very frequently "reproduced." It is not "dead," but "alive" in the highest degree, and it continuously works its way into what is given to inner perception. However, it is not "seen in memory." Even this must be understood *cum grano salis*. The individual is well aware that "there, in a certain direction, something is still present" characterized by values like base, common, hateful, evil; but he does not see *what* it is.[94]

We must equally distinguish repression from positive *illusions of memory* in which an experience is not only not seen but another is given in its place. However, even the positive illusions of memory must be completely distinguished from incorrect judgments about what is remembered and from defective reproduction.

One of the most prolific sources of illusion in inner perception, and especially in inner *self*-perception, is the impor-

---

94. The experience has a mode of givenness, analogous to that of an object in the field of vision of a man constricted by hysteria. This object lies outside his constricted field but, unlike an instance of constriction owing to organic damage (through the destruction of nerve elements in the lateral portions of the retina), it can still meaningfully guide the movement of the eyes in its direction. In this way the object comes to lie within the constricted field, or on the retina. The object is seen but is not grasped in one act of vision together with what lies within the constricted field. In organic constriction of the same magnitude, it is only a mechanical accident if the eye movement follows in the direction of the object. See E. Jaensch, "Zur Analyse der Gesichtswahrnehmungen," sec. V, *Zeitschrift für Psychologie*, Vol. IV (Supplement) (1909). [Ernst R. Jaensch (1883–1940) was the leader of the Marburg school of psychology. Scheler cites him with great frequency. His work on "eidetic images" was translated into English by Oscar Oeser as *Eidetic Imagery* (London, 1924). See also *Über den Aufbau der Wahrnehmungswelt und ihre Struktur im Jugendalter* (Leipzig, 1923).—TRANS.]

tance attached to the *communicability* of experiences and the possible *consequences* of this communication for the comprehension and perception of these experiences.

It would be a great mistake to think that language, the tool of communication, has simply the meaning and function of communicating experiences which have already been perceived. In fact, the influence of language reaches much further. The traditional words referring to psychic states have a wide-reaching impact on what we *generally perceive* in our own and in other's experiences. An experience for which there is no special word, or a particular quality of an experience for which there is only a quite general undifferentiated term, is for the most part not perceived by the individual who goes through the experience or is perceived only to the extent that it corresponds to this term. Thus, it is not the case at all that in order to "understand" and to use a word which refers to something mental, we ourselves must have already gone through and inwardly perceived the experience in question. A child knows the meaning of the words "jealousy," "compassion," "mortal agony," etc., long *before* he has met with these experiences himself. From the first his relation to his experiences is such that he grasps more clearly only those which are suited to fulfilling these meanings. Whatever escapes the broad mesh and coarse boundaries of these meanings remains at least unnoticed; or, if one of these meanings is applied to it, it takes on (for consciousness) a cast other than its own. To inspect these experiences themselves, beneath the layer of experiences which function only as "fulfillments" of the current meanings of words, to examine their particular nuances which disappear in these word meanings, presupposes a rare freedom of self-observation. The few who have been capable of such can rightly be called "discoverers of feeling" (not "inventors," as Ribot [95] says). Such "enlargers of the empire" of the microcosmos, like St. Francis of Assisi, Rousseau, and Goethe, are distinguished not by their extraordinary experiences or by a greater number of these, but, above all, by their ability to comprehend their experience *in its purity*. This means to comprehend it independently of the power of linguistic tradition and the "natural psychology" embedded in every lan-

95. [Théodule Ribot, nineteenth-century French psychologist, best known for his work *La Psychologie des sentiments* (Paris, 1896).—TRANS.]

guage. The first things we observe in our psychic life are not the phenomena of experience themselves, but rather the *interpretation* put on these by the linguistic tradition of society. For example, there can be no doubt that the expression "conscience," which first received its present meaning in Christian times, is not a constituent of consciousness like the experience of "ought" or of "ethical evidence" in general, but is a metaphysical-religious interpretation of certain acts of feeling and judgment like a "call," "warning," etc., delivered by the "voice of God." The features of "conscience"—that it is "one" for all men, that it says the same thing in the same circumstances, that it cannot deceive, that it is a unitary organ for the knowledge of what is ethically right, etc.—make sense only if we presuppose that a *God* speaks in these emotions. This must be the case even if a man who uses the word has cut himself loose from theological ideas. Yet there can be no doubt that the *experience* underlying his use of this word is first "given" to the individual in this interpretation as an element in a context of metaphysical-theological meaning, before it is before him as it is in itself apart from this interpretation.

This holds true, in the first place, of *individual* experiences, of the individual factor in all experiences, which, because it is individual, is "proper" to us.[96] This individual aspect, far from being what is primarily given in inner perception while everything else is given through an emotional projection [*Einfühlung*] of what each one experiences for himself, is rather the latest and last thing which can be given. Inner perception first shows us only that aspect of experiences which corresponds to the *traditional* forms and modes of experience current in the family, in the people, and in the other forms of society of which we are members. Only an ongoing *emancipation* from the traditional focus of inner perception, from the *historical system of categories* within which inner perception takes place, enables us to grasp the psychic experiences of the individual. Medieval zoologists, even when they had the animals they were describing before their eyes, gave them exactly the descriptions they found in the books of Aristotle, Dioscorides, and others. If tradition has this power over external perception, its power

96. The individual should not be *defined* by what is proper to each one of us or by what distinguishes us from one another.

over inner perception is all the greater.[97] A tradition is *not* formed through the communication of another's experiences which would allow us to grasp them *as* the other's experiences, together with the memory of what was communicated brought on through association with presently given contents. The basic processes are, first, the "psychic infection" spread by the other's experiences which we contract by sharing in his action and in the experience he has in performing it. The result of this sharing is that the other's experience, which objectively determines ours, is also given to us "as our own." Second, we continue to let what reaches us in this way determine our experience without reflecting on an *act* of memory. That is, it belongs to the essence of experiences determined by tradition for them to be given to us "as our own" and "as" present experiences. Only a slow process of coming to know ourselves as individual essences, a process accompanied by hindrances of every kind, allows us to separate what we ourselves experience from what is only forced upon us by this sort of infection and does not belong to "us." Generally speaking, only a systematic *historical critique* is capable of breaking the power of tradition and freeing the authentic life of the epoch concealed behind the "sham life" of tradition [*dem traditionellen "Scheinleben"*].

The assertions that, in the other's experiences, "we can understand only what we ourselves have first experienced" and that all understanding presupposes a reproduction of one's own experiences, come from a mistaken epistemology. What is essential is only that an experience be given in a relation-to-the-self [*Ichbeziehung*]. This relation is what first gives the experience the mode of being of a "conscious experience." How-

97. C. Stumpf has already shown that sensation "can be overcome" through memory and that Helmholtz's definition, "Sensation is what cannot be overcome through memory, judgment, or will," is unsatisfactory. (*Über den psychologischen Ursprung der Raumvorstellung* [Leipzig, 1873]). He makes reference to the fact that even when our eyes stay still, we see a uniformly blue surface as uniformly blue, although its sensory components would force it to grow dimmer toward the borders. This is also shown by the colors seen and intuited in memory [*Gedächtnisfarbe*] as described by Hering—an elementary phenomenon, so to speak, of the "tradition"—in which no trace of association, assimilation, or judgment can be found. This is shown even more strikingly by the pathological cases in which, instead of the objects actually present at some spot, others, which previously stood there and have frequently been seen, are given as what we perceive.

ever, the relation-to-the-self expressed in "I am now thinking this thought" naturally does not determine whether a thought given in this way is "my" thought, in the sense of being something I have thought out for myself, or whether it is a thought which is handed down to me by language, or one which I have read, etc. It is an entirely new question what aspects of the thoughts, feelings, and strivings which I (as an objective individual) have, and which exhibit this most general relation-to-the-self in the midst of experience, are uniquely "mine." And this is not decided by these two relations. This is not the sense of "one's own experience" which allows us to say that we understand in others only what we have experienced ourselves. In fact, the opposite is true. One's own experiences are, at first, *completely veiled* from inner perception by the alien experiences which rest on shared action, vicarious sensation, and vicarious feeling, by experiences which are given to us, through an illusion, "as our own."

In this context a line by Friedrich Nietzsche is altogether true: "Each man is furthest from himself." This line appears paradoxical only because it reminds us of the saying, "Each man is closest to himself." Nietzsche, however, is thinking of *knowledge;* the proverb has interest and practice in mind.

Consequently, the reasons one frequently hears advanced in behalf of the superiority of a psychology resting on "self-observation" over all objective methods, such as experimental psychology and historical ethnopsychology, are mere fictions. Among the reasons advanced are that all these objective methods presuppose a psychological knowledge resting on self-observation, and that an entirely new source of possible deception about another's psychic life slips in here, e.g., deceptions brought about by the verbal description the experimental subject gives of his experiences. As a matter of fact, each and *every* observational and inductive psychology presupposes a *phenomenology* of the mental which exhibits the constitution of the mental and its essential interconnections. But this holds as true of the psychology resting on *self-*observation as it does of the psychology resting on observation of *others.* Phenomenology, however, has as little to do with self-*observation* as it does with the *observation* of others. In phenomenology things are "brought to sight" [*erschaut*], not observed. It makes no difference whether the mental essences and essential connections with which phenomenology is concerned are brought to sight in our own or another's experience, nor does it matter whether this is done experimentally or not.[98]

Knowledge of psychic processes in others does *not* presuppose our having observed the same or similar processes *in ourselves*. We can construct in imagination, from the constituent elements common to all mental being and events, combinations we have never experienced ourselves. In this way we can *extend* our knowledge of the psychic world far beyond our own experiences. If this were not the case, if we could know in the other only what we had already "experienced ourselves," we could not imagine what use any *historical* knowledge or observation of men would be to us. Then we would only be turning on our own heels.[99]

The objection, that the understanding of the words in which the experimental subject describes his experiences insinuates itself into the heart of experimental methods, is valid only so far as the subject's speech does not "express" or "make known" his experiences but tries to adjust itself to what the subject inwardly observes and to communicate the result of his observations. If he "expresses" his experiences, then I grasp them *in* his words (just as I grasp his joy *in* his expressions, e.g., in his laughter), or in any other "reactions" in which an experience becomes graspable. However, in the other case we should not forget that, as we saw, even in self-observation, language and its verbal meanings interpose themselves between observation and the observed fact and frequently lead observation astray.

All things considered, the sources of illusion in self-observation are not fewer, but *more numerous* than in obser-

98. Not all experiments have an inductive sense or need to have one; e.g., Galileo's experiments to prove the principle of inertia. Precisely in this way, even a physiological experiment can be put in the service of phenomenological illumination. It has a function analogous to that of so-called illustrative experiments in mathematics.

99. If the word "experienced" in the sentence "one understands only what one has experienced" means as much as "experienced oneself and really experienced," then the sentence is false. If it means every function of consciousness, then the understanding of another's experiences is also a subspecies of "experiencing," and we experience something new when we understand another.

vation of others. The immediate closeness of the facts in the case of self-observation is not the same as cognitive proximity. Where it is a question of facts which strongly affect our interests, practically and ethically relevant facts, observation of others enjoys the advantage of that *objective* attitude which we can find so difficult to apply to ourselves. Moreover, the observation of others can give us directly what is being experienced at present, where self-observation can give these experiences only in immediate recollection.[100] Indeed, it seems to me a question whether this special attitude of "self-observation," which is utterly distinct from self-perception, is not itself a mere imitation of the observation of others, a way of looking at our own experiences "as though through another's eyes." This would entail that self-observation could bring to givenness only what, in principle, can be seen by another. We would then have to think of self-observation as *derived* from observation of others, and thus as a form of behavior which already presupposes *social life*.

Just as we are inclined to take the *interpretations* of experience given to us by tradition for *facts* of experience, and to take others' experiences which we merely imitate for our own, so, too, the *total picture* which we form of ourselves is not determined by unbiased perceptions of our living, individual self but depends completely on the pictures, judgments, and opinions which the surrounding *society* has of us. Whatever corresponds in us and in those members who are most important to us to the positive and negative value-categories of this society occupies, from the start, a *privileged position* in the range of our attention. All this taken together presents a singular object, our "*social self*." What I am calling here the "*social self*" is not merely the sum of the ideas, images, and judgments which the single members of our society have of us and which can be communicated to us or not. Rather, my social self is an *independent object* which I can regard no differently than the members of society do.[101] It is the object

---

100. It won't do to identify "inner perception" with immediate recollection, as Lipps wants to do. See the recent and excellent remarks of G. F. Müller, "Zur Analyse der Gedächtnistätigkeit," in *Zeitschrift für Psychologie*, V (1911), 68 ff.

101. Compare the appendix to my *Der Genius des Krieges* and what is said there about the "gentlemen."

which is built up from what is "socially relevant," that is, from what comes under *social value-categories* in all my experiences. Each person forms his own particular "picture" of this and can judge it differently than anyone else. No individual (including ourselves as individual in relation to ourselves) is given to natural intuition "as" an individual pure and simple. What is given is a *starting point and terminus of social relations,* of actions, rights, and duties (which are his as an example of a class, a vocation, an office, etc.), and this *is* given "as an individual." The illusion consists precisely in this! We take the "role" we play in society, the "so and so" with whom society reckons, to be our individual self. In the same way that this self was formerly covered up completely by the "body-self," it is also covered up by the social self and must be found, with difficulty, *behind* that self. The content of the social self changes in the same individuals when the system of social value-categories in which we live changes, or when the nature of the "ruling powers" under whom the individual lives changes, together with the conditions of their favor and disfavor, their praise and blame. A courtier in the court of Ludwig XV who sees himself, so to speak, through the king's eyes, perceives himself in one way; the English burgher of the seventeenth century, who sees himself in the light of bourgeois "public opinion," in another way. A modern industrial worker, whose self-consciousness and feeling of self are first based on his membership in the "struggling proletariat," in his trade union, etc., perceives himself differently than a monk, who sees himself through the eyes of his superior, or than a genuine saint, who views himself through "God's eyes." [102] When we become aware of a "man," the first thing we see is his social self. "We speak" with this, we question and we negotiate with this. We remain at this level of acquaintance with by far the greatest number of men and only with a very few do we break through the masks. Even in our memory of a man what appears to us is, for the most part, the *society* in which we previously saw him, and he appears only as an element of this. In the case of so-called great men, a more or less *mythical figure* takes the place of the social self, and it is this figure which has

102. G. Misch has shown, in his *Geschichte der Autobiographie* (Leipzig and Berlin, 1907), how slowly the focus on the social self has been displaced in favor of a focus on the individual self.

genuine historical effectiveness; the individual soul almost completely disappears behind it.[103]

The degree to which one lives in the social self naturally
varies widely among individuals, peoples, and professions. The
Frenchman, for example, is used to living much more intensely in it than the German; the German more intensely than
the Russian. Living in the social self is pathologically intensified by highly intensified suggestibility. So, too, is living in
terms of the picture a beloved person has of an individual, or
the picture a physician has of a hysterical individual. This explains the extreme dependence of all affects and actions on the
presence or absence of the "onlooker" or of a particular onlooker in such cases. It is equally the origin of the mania for
drawing attention to oneself or for suspending all one's tendencies toward self-preservation for the sake of making the
onlooker feel pain or pleasure by one's own actions, in accordance with the formula: "It serves my father right! . . .
Why doesn't he buy me any gloves?" It is also the source of the
illusion in which one speaks about the capacity for ethical
sacrifice when life, health, and honor are given up in behalf of
goals of the onlooker which are valuable in themselves while,
in reality, no sacrifice is made. For sacrifice presupposes that
one's own self and one's goods and values are *seen*, which is just
what does *not* happen here. In cases of this kind, it seems to
me, there is absolutely no deliberation of the form: "What will
the other do, say, think, judge, feel, when he *sees* that I do
this?" Rather, the individual sees himself, inwardly and outwardly, through the eyes of the onlooker, and everything he
experiences, feels, judges, and wills is only a *consequence* of,
a reaction to, the alleged "picture" which he offers to the onlooker. His own life and experience immediately become a
dependent function of the image the other has of him, and
they vary with the content of this image. The individual *feels* a
value in himself only when he is envied for it; he feels a pain
only when he sees himself pitied; and so on. He seeks out pain
in order to make himself be pitied or to annoy or injure the
onlooker.

It makes no difference to this phenomenon of "being subjected to another's image of oneself" whether one's actions

103. [On the social self and the intimate self, see *Formalismus*, VI,
B, 4.—ED.]

accord with or go against the trend of the other's intentions, goals, and opinions. Concordance and discord depend on the ethical qualities of the individual, which are quite independent of this pathological disturbance. Nonetheless, we can frequently observe that an aggravation of this behavior easily turns into hatred, even when the result of the phenomenon is that one feels, wills, and acts in accordance with the other's intentions; for example, when one's own joy or one's own suffering tends to be based on the joy or suffering felt in another, and not, as in the opposite case, where one's own suffering is based on the joy one sees in another. When one begins to suffer from one's slavish and hateful dependence on the changes in the other's state of mind, the suffering and the hatred easily slide over onto the object, the other. The result is that frequent alternation of hate and love which is so characteristic of some neuroses.

Thus there are utterly different ways in which we can go about getting *knowledge of a man.* In one case, his character is for us only an X, from which we explain and make intelligible to ourselves all his individual actions, utterances, and expressions. We proceed *externally* and *inductively.* We must be prepared to change our assumptions about his character with every new action, utterance, or expression we observe, if these appear unintelligible in light of our hypothetical assumptions. His "character" is for us, then, only the sum total of all his permanent "dispositions" to actions and activities. Thus differential psychology need only refine this method in order to test individual intellectual, volitional, and emotional capacities, the sharpness, scope, and type of memory-performance [*Gedächtnisleistung*], etc. However, it is certain that, even if the knowledge of a man achieved by this method reached an ideal perfection, we might *never* obtain a total picture in which we have evidence (in accordance and in comparison with our intuitive knowledge of the individual) that *only this man* and no other fits this picture. Instead, we would always be aware that we could substitute other men for this one.

If we compare the procedure and the results of this method with the *evidence* with which this individual is *uniquely* and *unmistakably* given to us, often in gestures of secondary importance (for example, when we hear a man clear his throat as he comes to our door, when we glimpse a certain way of walking from a distance, hear a seemingly meaningless conversation, or feel the sense of a laugh without being even remotely capable of telling someone else what the cause of it really is), then it becomes clear to us that the former method is not the only one in which the individuality of another person is cognitively [*erkenntnismässig*] given to us. If we compare the quantity of material the first method requires for the construction of this person's character (and this quantity can be arbitrarily increased, if there is need), in addition to the great uncertainty of the evidence that the person in question is actually grasped "as an individual," with the extreme poverty of material in the second method and the greater certainty of the evidence that the individual himself is given to us, their differences are sufficient proof that two fundamentally different *kinds* of knowledge are present here.

However, this teaches us something else. Often we interpret what is reported to us about a man, or interpret an expressive movement or an action we observe, in the light of an image of his individuality which is certainly *not* based on this kind of inductive material. Rather, any inductive material makes sense only if we have presupposed this image, which is so much richer in content. We grasp an individual ego in his intentions; we evaluate him, we judge him, and we compare his actions and expressions with this ego only when we see in these more or less complete "presentations" of that *individual essence*. Indeed, any more profound ethical judgment does *not* place the actions of a man under a general, basic principle of right and wrong, but compares his actions with an ideal, although individual, self. This is something quite different from a sum total of "dispositions" which would be obtained from his concrete actions; completely different, too, from what Kant, for example, calls "intelligible character," which is unknowable in general and is the same for every individual. In a way as yet unexplained, intuition gets hold of this "ideal self" when, so to speak, it *draws out and extends* the lines of the individual's basic tendencies which have been recognized in a few actions and expressions. And just as we know from a small section of a curve the law of its curvature as a whole, so here we *bring to sight* the totality of the individual essence.

I shall mention still a third form of everyday behavior which points to this mode of knowledge. Someone tells us that this or that thought has been expressed, that someone has had this and that experience of pity or joy, whatever it may be. In a case like this we are aware that our knowledge is incomplete, that we still have no notion of the concrete incident. So we ask *"Who* said this?" *"Who* has had this experience?" And if we recognize the individual in question from our own experience, then the content of the tale is immediately augmented by a knowledge which could not have been obtained from any more detailed description of the experience. "Indeed, if it was so-and-so, *then* I understand it, then I know what was involved."

In fact, the "individual self" is so far from being a "sum of experiences," some sort of "combination" or "totality" of dispositions for such experiences, or an object merely constructed to fit these, that in the last analysis *all* experiences and *all* motives are incomplete and *abstract* unities so long as I do not know and see *whose* experiences they are, of what *individual self* they are the experiences.[104]

Thus, the first of these methods presupposes the second, which goes back to an immediate intuition [*Intuition*] of the individual self, an intuition which is essentially possible in any experience, even the simplest.

The reason why we so often overlook this is, first, our dominant focus on the social self. This focus is based on the natural intuition of the psychic and on the sources of illusion imbedded in it, and is made absolute by science. In this way, however, the individual self finally disappears completely and becomes a mere relationship and ordering of "single experiences," just as the individual was first regarded as a mere *point of intersection of social circles* and social relations, as the starting point of socially relevant expressions and actions. The ultimate foundation of "associationistic psychology," which turns our soul into a democratic society of ultimate elements, is that it allows *only* the social self of man to become the object of knowledge. In fact, however, the individual self is an *indivisible unity* which experiences itself along with every experience. What we call "experiences" are not *parts* [*Teile*] of the self, but *abstract symbols* for it, from which we reconstruct

---

104. [On the abstract and the concrete essences of acts, see *Formalismus*, VI, A, 3, a.—ED.]

once again this unified totality in the interest of social understanding and agreement [*Verständigung*].[105]

However, the course of our conceptual reconstruction should never be made into a history of the *things-themselves* if we do not want to succumb to the *most primary* of all self-deceptions, a deception concerning the *essence* of our self.

105. See also the remarks of H. Bergson in his *Introduction à la métaphysique* (Paris, 1903) [English translation by T. E. Hulme, *An Introduction to Metaphysics* (New York: Liberal Arts Press, 1955)], which are, in part, quite good.

Ordo Amoris

THE NORMATIVE AND DESCRIPTIVE MEANING OF ORDO AMORIS

I FIND MYSELF in an immeasurably vast world of sensible and spiritual objects which set my heart and passions in constant motion. I know that the objects I can recognize through perception and thought, as well as all that I will, choose, do, perform, and accomplish, depend on the play of this movement of my heart. It follows that any sort of rightness or falseness and perversity in my life and activity are determined by whether there is an objectively correct order of these stirrings of my love and hate, my inclination and disinclination, my many-sided interest in the things of this world. It depends further on whether I can impress this *ordo amoris* [1] on my inner moral tenor [*Gemüt*].

Whether I am investigating the innermost essence of an individual, a historical era, a family, a people, a nation, or any other sociohistorical group, I will know and understand it most profoundly when I have discerned the system of its concrete value-assessments and value-preference, whatever organization

Translated from "Ordo Amoris," *Schriften aus dem Nachlass:* I, *Zur Ethik und Erkenntnislehre,* 2d ed. rev., ed. Maria Scheler (Bern: Francke Verlag, 1957), pp. 347–76.

1. [I have kept Scheler's Latin phrase *ordo amoris* ("the order or ordering of love") throughout the translation.—TRANS.]

this system has. I call this system the ethos of any such subject.[2] The fundamental root of this ethos is, first, the *order of love and hate,* the organization of these two dominant and predominating passions, within a social class which has become exemplary for the others. This system always has a hand in directing the way the subject sees his world as well as his deeds and activities.

Thus the concept of an *ordo amoris* has two meanings, one normative and one purely factual and descriptive. The meaning is not normative in the sense that this order is itself a sum of norms, for in that case it could be laid down only by some will, whether the will of a man or of God, but not known in an evidential way. We can have just this knowledge of the ranking of everything which is possibly worthy of love in things, in accordance with their inner values. Such knowledge is the central problem of all ethics. However, the highest thing of which a man is capable is to love things as much as possible as God loves them [3] and in one's own act of love to experience with insight the coincidence and intersection of the divine and the human act at one and the same point of the world of values. The objectively correct *ordo amoris* becomes a norm only when it is seen as related to the will of man and as commanded to him by a will.[4]

However, the concept of *ordo amoris* also has a fundamental descriptive value. For it is the means whereby we can discover, behind the initially confusing facts of man's morally relevant actions, behind his expressions, his wishes, customs, needs, and spiritual achievements, the simplest structure of the most fundamental goals of the goal-directed core of the person, the basic ethical formula, so to speak, by which he exists and lives morally. Thus, everything we recognize as morally im-

2. [On ethos, see *Der Formalismus in der Ethik und die materiale Wertethik: Neuer Versuch der Grundlegung eines ethischen Personalismus,* 5th ed. rev., *Gesammelte Werke* II (Bern: Francke Verlag, 1965), chap. V, sec. 6; on ethos and exemplar, VI, B, 4, and 6, a, and the essay, "Vorbilder und Führer," *Schriften aus dem Nachlass,* chap. II.—ED.]

3. The idea of the objective *ordo amoris* does not depend on the thesis that God exists. [See the end of *Formalismus,* p. 579, on "the independence of the validity of all the fundamental doctrines of ethics from any philosophical investigation of religion and the religious ethos."—ED.]

4. [See *Formalismus,* IV, 2, on value and norm.—ED.]

portant to man (or to a group) must be reduced, however many steps it may take, to the particular structure of his acts of loving and hating and his capacities for love and hate; it must be reduced, in other words, to the *ordo amoris* which governs these acts and expresses all of man's stirrings and emotions.

[I] ENVIRONMENT, FATE, "INDIVIDUAL DESTINY," AND THE ORDO AMORIS

Whoever has the ordo amoris *of a man has the man himself.* He has for the man as a moral subject what the crystallization formula is for a crystal. He sees through him as far as one possibly can. He sees before him the constantly simple and basic lines of his heart [*Gemüt*] running beneath all his empirical many-sidedness and complexity. And heart deserves to be called the core of man as a spiritual being much more than knowing and willing do. He has a spiritual model of the primary source which secretly nourishes everything emanating from this man. Even more, he possesses the primary determinant of what always appears to surround and enclose the man: in space, his moral environment; in time, his fate, that is, the quintessence [*Inbegriff*] of possibilities belonging to him and him alone. Nothing in nature which is independent of man can confront him and have an effect on him even as a stimulus, of whatever kind or degree, without the cooperation of his *ordo amoris*.

Man is encased, as though in a shell, in the particular ranking of the simplest values and value-qualities which represent the objective side of his *ordo amoris*, values which have not yet been shaped into things and goods. He carries this shell along with him wherever he goes and cannot escape from it no matter how quickly he runs. He perceives the world and himself through the windows of this shell, and perceives no more of the world, of himself, or of anything else besides what these windows show him, in accordance with their position, size, and color. The structure and total content of each man's environment, which is ultimately organized according to its value structure, does not wander or change, even though he himself wanders further and further in space. It is simply filled out anew with certain individual things. However, even this fulfillment must obey the law of formation prescribed by the value structure of the milieu.[5] The goods along the route of a man's life, the practical things, the resistances to willing and acting against which he sets his will, are from the very first always inspected and "sighted," as it were, by the particular selective mechanism of *his ordo amoris*. Wherever he arrives, it is not the same men and the same things, but the same types of men and things (and these are in every case *types* of values), that attract or repulse him in accordance with certain constant rules of preference and rejection. What he actually notices, what he observes or leaves unnoticed and unobserved, is determined by this attraction and this repulsion; these already determine the material of *possible* noticing and observing. Moreover, the attraction and repulsion are felt to come from things, not from the self, in contrast to the case of so-called active attention, and are themselves governed and circumscribed by potentially effective attitudes of interest and love, experienced as readiness for being affected.

Even prior to the unity of perception, a value-signal experienced as coming from things, not from us, announces, as though with a trumpet flourish, that "Something is up!" This is how the actual things as a rule announce themselves at the threshold of our environment and take their place in it from the far ends of the world. This phenomenon of "annunciation" emerges clearly just at that point where we do not follow the attraction of things, where we do not arrive at any perception of the point of origin of this attraction, since we purposely resist it when its efficacy is at this level. Or the annunciation emerges when a stronger attraction nips a weaker one in the bud.

However, man's *ordo amoris* and its particular contours are behind each such case of attraction and repulsion. As little as the *structure* of environment changes with whatever happens to be the actual environment at any one time, so little is the structure of a man's fate changed by any novelty in his future life, by any new thing he wills, any new activity or creation in the future, or by any novel thing he encounters. Fate and environment rest on the same factors of man's *ordo amoris* and are distinguished only by their assignment to the

5. [See *Formalismus*, III, on "the structure of the environment" = the structure of the value-environment.—ED.]

dimensions of time (in the case of fate) and space (in the case of the environment). The law of their formation always and everywhere follows the *ordo amoris*. The study of this formation belongs to the most important problems of an intensive study of the moral being "man."

The significance of the theory of the disorders in the *ordo amoris* to the understanding of human fate will be shown later.[6] Here I shall simply state what is the only thing we are entitled to call our "fate." We are certainly not entitled to call everything that happens around us and in us which we know to be freely willed or produced by us "fate"; nor can we call everything which comes upon us purely from the outside "fate." This description covers much that we experience as too accidental to be reckoned to our fate. We do require of fate that it come upon us unwilled and, for the most part, unforeseen; however, we also demand that it present something other than a series of encounters and actions subject to causal necessity. Namely, we demand that it present the unity of a persisting and unvarying sense which presents itself to us as an essential correlation between the individual human character and the events around and within him. The specific nature of fate thus comes to this: when we survey a man's whole life or a long sequence of years and events, we may indeed feel that each single event is completely accidental, yet their connection, however unforeseeable every part of the whole was before it transpired, reflects exactly that which we must consider the core of the person concerned. What is revealed to us in this uniform sense [*Einsinnigkeit*] of the course of a life is a harmony of world and man that is completely independent of will, intention, and desire, on one hand, and of accidental, objectively real events, independent of their conjunction and reciprocal action, on the other. For as surely as fate embraces that content which "befalls" man and is therefore beyond will and intention, so surely does it also embrace only that content which, when it "befalls," could "befall" this one moral subject alone. We should thus call man's fate only that which lies within the range of certain possibilities of experiencing the world circumscribed by his character and the concrete events which appear to fill this range. These ranges

6. [Scheler makes several references in the text to later parts which were not found among his manuscripts.—ED.]

vary from man to man and from people to people, even when outward events stay the same. In this more precise sense of the word "fate," it is the way a man's actual *ordo amoris* is formed—in accordance with definite rules for gradual functionalization [7] of primary love-objects in his early childhood— that governs the unfolding of the content of his fate.

Having explained in a preliminary fashion the intuitive, normative, and descriptive senses of *ordo amoris,* I must now discuss the concept of a disordering of the correct *ordo amoris,* the various types of disorder ("désordre du coeur," in Pascal's expressive phrase), and the process which leads from an ordered state [*Gesamtzustand*] to a disordered one; that is, the concept of a *confusion* of *ordo amoris.* Finally, we must inquire into the nature of the dynamics of this kind of confusion and ask how a solution can be found for the basic forms and types of confusion we are going to describe. In other words, we must ask how the correct *ordo amoris* can be restored, if that is possible. This last question belongs to the province of pedagogy, the special character of which is still far from being clearly recognized and precisely circumscribed, and to the therapeutic technique for human salvation. Its answer will naturally depend, first, on the idea of salvation held by the particular subject concerned (which arises simultaneously from the intuitive and universally valid *ordo amoris* and from the individual's conception of salvation), and, second, on the psychodynamics of confusions mentioned above.

However, we do not want to separate the queston of conceptual clarification from the concrete investigation, and therefore, before we begin the latter, we wish only to say what "individual destiny" means in relation to milieu and fate.

The idea of a correct and true *ordo amoris* is, for us, the idea of a strictly objective realm independent of man, the objective order of what is worthy of love in all things, something we can only recognize, but cannot "posit," produce, or make. Similarly, the individual destiny of an individual or collective spiritual subject is no less objective, although its particular value-content has this subject and only this subject in view. It is not something we have to posit, but something we have to recognize. This "destiny" signifies [*ausdrückt*] the place which

7. [On functionalization, see "Vorbilder und Führer," chap. II, *Schriften aus dem Nachlass,* and "Idealism and Realism," below, note 23.—ED.]

belongs to this one subject is the plan of the world's salvation. Thus it also signifies his special task, his "calling," in the old, etymological sense of the word. The subject can deceive himself about this, he can (freely) fail to achieve it, or he can recognize and actualize it. If we are searching for any complete moral judgment and measure of a subject, we must have continually before our minds, besides the standards that hold for everyone, the idea of his individual destiny which belongs to him and not to us or to any other subject. I have tried to show elsewhere [8] how and by what means we can grasp this idea by looking at the outward expressions of his life and by extracting the central tenor of his moral intentions from its empirical realization (which always remains merely fragmentary). In this way we can obtain a total picture of him.

It is part of the essence of the ethical cosmos to exhibit itself, even, or indeed, precisely, when it has reached its greatest conceivable perfection, in an immeasurable abundance of unique, individual formations of value, of persons, and of good, although still within the framework of objective goods which are available to everyone. It is equally part of its essence to exhibit itself in a series of historically unique moments of existence, action, and work, where each moment is what "the day" or "the hour" demands. Consequently, what ethically ought-not-to-be is not this absence of uniformity; on the contrary, it is the uniformity of all standards for men, peoples, nations, and societies of every sort. All individual destinies must find their place only within the *general framework* of the universal and common destiny of man as such and, even more, of rational spiritual creatures in general. Moreover, an individual destiny is not "subjective" in the sense that it can be recognized and realized only by the person whose destiny it is. Rather, it can very well be that another knows my individual destiny more adequately than I do myself. Also, another can energetically aid me in achieving my destiny's realization. Sharing a life in common, working and producing together, sharing beliefs and hopes, living for one another and respecting one another are themselves a part of the universal destiny of every finite spiritual being. Therefore it is also a part of the essential nature of individual destiny (and everyone recognizes in his

8. [See *Formalismus,* primarily VI, B. On the following discussion of solidarity, see VI, B, 4, *ad* 4.—ED.]

own special case that each man has such a destiny) that the individual shares the responsibility for the comprehension and realization of each man's individual destiny. Thus the idea of individual destiny does not exclude, but includes, the reciprocal solidarity of responsibility for the guilt and merit of moral subjects.

It goes without saying that the whole of man's actual life, just as it can deviate from universally valid norms, can also deviate to the greatest possible degree from his individual destiny. Here it is of some importance for us that his individual destiny can be partly in harmony with, partly in opposition to, the structure of his environment and his fate (and can be so in every possible degree), even though his environmental structure and fate are still entirely different from what simply impinges upon and affects him from the outside. Above all, therefore, the individual destiny of man is not his fate. Only the assumption that fate and destiny are the same deserves to be called fatalism. Fatalism is not the acknowledgment of the fact of fate itself. Fatalism could gain currency only as long as men *reified* fate, as the Greeks did with their *Heimarmenē,* or tried to reduce fate, together with destiny, to a preworldly selection made by God, as in the concept of predestination held by Augustine and Calvin. However, environmental structure and fate (in the sense defined above) have a natural and basically comprehensible origin; they are not merely the accidentally actual and effective [*Wirkliche und Wirksame*]. Fate, to be sure, cannot be freely chosen, as some extreme indeterminists have supposed, in ignorance of its essence and of the strata of freedom and non-freedom in us. The spheres of choice, or the objects of the act of choice, are determined by fate. Fate, however, is not determined by choice.[9] Nevertheless, fate *grows up* out of the life of a man or a people, as it continually nourishes itself with content and in turn functionalizes the contents of some preceding time. Fate shapes itself for the most part in the life of the individual or, in any case, in the life of the species. And the same applies for the structures of the milieu.

If fate, like the structure of the milieu, is not freely chosen, a man can still relate himself to it as a *free person* in totally

9. [On the sphere of choice and fate, see the essay "Zur Phänomenologie und Metaphysik der Freiheit," *Schriften aus dem Nachlass.*—ED.]

different ways. He can be so much under its spell that he does not even recognize it as fate (like fish in an aquarium); but he can also, by recognizing it, stand *above* it. Furthermore, he can surrender to it or resist and oppose it. Indeed, in principle he can, as we shall show, completely cast aside or transform the structure of his environment (not only its accidental contents at any one time) as well as his fate. Of course, he can do so only through acts and modes of behavior which are essentially different from those through which he accomplishes so-called free choice.[10] Even more important, he can never do this by himself; he requires the help of beings who stand outside his fate and milieu. Thus humanity as a whole, individual man and the collective person,[11] so far as it is their fate to have to resist the universal destiny of man *in general,* can do so only with the help of God.

Fate, like the milieu-structure, grows out of effective, goal-directed processes of the psycho-vital subject in man. It does not arise from active, free, and conscious acts of judging, choosing, preferring. It arises out of those automatic processes which can be diverted if we have others to help us. In contrast, *individual destiny* is a *timeless and essential value-essence* [*Wertwesenheit*] in the form of *personality.* And, since it is not formed or posited by the spirit in man but is only recognized, since its fullness is only successively unveiled, as it were, in the course of our experiences of life and action, it exists only for the spiritual personality in us.

Individual destiny is, therefore, a matter of *insight,* while fate is only something to be confirmed, a fact which in itself is *value-blind.*

There is a certain type of *love* which must precede the knowledge of individual destiny. This is genuine *self-love* [*Selbstliebe*], or love for one's own salvation, which is fundamentally different from all so-called love of self [*Eigenliebe*]. In love of self we purposely see everything, even ourselves, through our "own" eyes only. We refer every datum, even ourselves, to our sensuous states of feeling, without having a

10. These acts of free choice lie within the limits of his milieu and fate and cannot escape the range of these. [This sentence originally stood in the text.—TRANS.]

11. [On the "collective person," see *Formalismus,* VI, B, 4, *ad* 4 (pp. 509–48).—TRANS.]

distinct and clear awareness that this is what we are doing. Thus, we can, in clinging to these states of feeling, make even our highest spiritual capacities, endowments, and powers, even the supreme subject of our destiny, the slaves of our body and its conditions. We "do not grow rich with our money"—we squander it. Covered with a web of many-colored illusions and phantoms, woven out of stupor, vanity, ambition, and pride, we see everything, including ourselves, in the light of love of self. It is quite different in genuine self-love. Here our spiritual eye and the ray of its intention is focused on a transworldly spiritual center. We see ourselves *as if* through the eyes of God himself; and this means, first, that we see ourselves quite objectively, and second, that we see ourselves as a part of the whole universe. Indeed, we love ourselves, but always only as what we would be before an all-seeing eye and only so far as we could stand before this eye. Everything else in us we hate—all the more strongly, the more our spirit penetrates into this divine image of us, the more commandingly this image springs up before us, and the more strongly our spirit turns away from any image we find in ourselves other than God's enduring image of us. The self-shaping, creative hammers of self-correction, of self-education, of remorse and mortification strike away all the parts of us which project beyond that form which is conveyed to us by this image of ourselves before and in God.

Certainly, the mode of givenness of the particular material, the unique content of individual destiny (which is released from its shell and shown to us only by acts of self-knowledge, in the Socratic sense), is peculiar to each man alone. There is no positive, circumscribed image of it, still less a formulatable law. The image of our destiny is thrown in relief only in the recurrent traces left when we turn away from it, when we follow "false tendencies," in Goethe's sense.[12] The image emerges, as it were, along the lines enclosing the points where these traces are left, binding them together into a whole, into a figure of the person. But this fact (which indeed is a shortcoming as far as the formulation and expression of the image are concerned) constitutes the eminently positive motive force this image exercises on us. It goes without saying that what is

12. [On "false tendencies," see J. P. Eckermann, *Gespräche mit Goethe,* the conversation of April 12, 1829, ed. H. H. Houben (Leipzig, 1948), p. 289.—TRANS.]

always present to us and is secretly at work in us, what always directs and leads us without forcing us, cannot be perceived as a separate and distinct content of consciousness—which is always only a "process" which stops, then starts up again. Obviously the eternal wisdom which speaks in us and guides us is not loud and commanding, but a still and merely monitory wisdom. However, it speaks all the louder, the more we act *against* it. The self-knowledge of our individual destiny works in a manner similar to the so-called method of negative theology.[13] In negative theology, rightly understood, the negations do not define the nature of the object sought or exhaust its meaning, but intend only to make it visible in its fullness through successive abstractions. Therefore, the greatest practical accomplishment of destiny is not so much a positive shaping as a pushing aside, a mortification, a "curing" of "false tendencies" (or of everything against which an objection is raised, so to speak, by the felt-points of coincidence or conflict between the image of destiny and our empirically observable self). We shall have more to say later about this technique.

How different fate and milieu are from individual destiny is also shown by the fact that a tragic relation of conflict between them is possible, a relation of which the subject can be distinctly conscious. For it is not when the contingent actuality of a man, a people, etc., is in opposition to its destiny, but when destiny and fate themselves are at odds and in conflict with one another, where the independent scope of further possibilities of life is, as it were, denied to the destiny we have recognized, that this conflict becomes *tragic,* in the preeminent sense of the word.[14] A tragic relation exists where we see men, even whole peoples, whose fate itself forces them to act against their destiny, where we see men who do not "fit in," not only with the contingent and momentary content of their milieu, but with the very *structure* of that milieu. This is what forces them always to select a new milieu with an analogous structure. We shall be concerned later with the extent to which these disharmonies can be resolved when our interest turns to the

13. [On "negative theology," see Scheler, *On the Eternal in Man,* trans. Bernard Noble (London: Student Christian Movement Press, 1960), the essay on "The Problems of Religion."—ED.]

14. [See "Zum Phänomen des Tragischen," *Vom Umsturz der Werte,* 4th ed. rev., *Gesammelte Werke* III (Bern: Francke, 1965).—ED.]

general question of the analysis [*Auflösung*] of the powers which specifically determine fate in us.

We turn now to a more precise investigation of the *form* of correct *ordo amoris* and of the way in which the human spirit takes possession of it or finds itself related to it, for only when we have formed specific and clear ideas on this subject can we arrange the basic types of the confusion of *ordo amoris* and explain their origin. This is the chief theme of the present study.[15]

[II] THE FORM OF ORDO AMORIS

ELSEWHERE WE HAVE TREATED IN DETAIL the essence of *love* in the most formal sense of the word.[16] We abstracted from the psychological and organizational peculiarities and from all the accompanying phenomena which either distinguish or degrade that love of which man is the bearer. Then the essential definition that remained was that love is the tendency or, as it may be, the act that seeks to lead everything in the direction of the perfection of value proper to it—and succeeds, when no obstacles are present. Thus we defined the essence of love as an edifying and uplifting [*erbauende und aufbauende*] action in and over the world. "Who in stillness looks about him, learns how love uplifts," as Goéthe says. Man's love is only a particular type, a partial function, of the universal power active in and on everything. Love, in this account, was always a dynamic becoming, a growing, a welling up of things in the direction of their archetype, which resides in God. Thus, every phase in this inner growth of the value of things, a growth which love produces, is always an intermediate station on the way of the world toward God, however distant it may still be from its goal. Every love is love for God, still incomplete, often slumbering or self-infatuated, often stopping, as it were, on its way. If a man loves a thing or a value, such as the value of knowledge, if he loves this or that formation of nature, if he loves a man as a friend or as anything else, in every case this

15. [No manuscripts dealing with this "chief theme" have been found. —ED.]

16. [See Scheler, *The Nature of Sympathy*, trans. Peter Heath (London: Routledge & Kegan Paul, 1958), pt. B.—ED.]

means that he emerges from his merely bodily unity [*Leibein-heit*] and stands forth in his central unity as a person. It means that in and through the action of this unity he joins the other object in affirming its tendency toward its proper perfection, that he is active in assisting it, promoting it, blessing it.

In our account love was thus always the primal act by which a being, without ceasing to be this one delimited being, abandons itself, in order to share and participate in another being as an *ens intentionale*. This participation is such that the two in no way become real parts of one another.[17] What we call "knowing," which is an ontological relation, always presupposes this primal act of abandoning the self and its conditions, its own "contents of consciousness," of *transcending* them, in order to come into experiential contact with the world as far as possible. And what we call "real" or actual presupposes that some subject wills the realization of something, while this act of willing presupposes an anticipatory loving that gives it direction and content. Thus, *love* is always what awakens both knowledge and volition; indeed, it is the mother of spirit and reason itself.[18] The One, however, who participates in everything, without whose act of willing nothing real can be real, and through whom all things somehow participate (spiritually) in one another and enjoy solidarity with one another; the One, who creates them and toward whom they aspire, striving with one another within their proper and assigned limits; this One all-loving, and thus all-knowing and all-willing God, is the personal center of the world as a cosmos and as a whole. He eternally loves and contemplates the goals and essential ideas of all things before they are created.

Thus, the *ordo amoris* is the core of the world-order taken as a divine order. Man, too, stands within this world-order, as the freest and most worthy servant of God, and only in this capacity should man be called the lord of creation. Here we shall mention only that *part* of the *ordo amoris* which properly belongs to man.

Man, before he is an *ens cogitans* or an *ens volens*, is an

17. [See "The Essence of Philosophy," in *On the Eternal in Man.*—ED.]
18. [See *Formalismus,* index under "Liebe," "Vernunft," "Erkenntnis"; and "Liebe und Erkenntnis," *Schriften zur Soziologie und Weltan-schauungslehre,* 2d ed. rev., *Gesammelte Werke* VI (Bern: Francke, 1963).—ED.]

ens amans. The fullness, the gradations, the differentiations, and the power of his love circumscribe the fullness, the functional specificity, and the power of his possible spirit and of the possible *range* of contact with the universe. Of all that is actually worthy of love—the essences of which circumscribe a priori the concrete goods which are accessible to his power of comprehension—he has access to only a part. This part is determined by the *value-qualities* and *value-modalities* which man can grasp in general and thus in things whatever they may be.

The things and properties of which he can have knowledge do not define and delimit his value-world; his world of essential values circumscribes and defines the being he can know, raising it up out of the sea of being like an island. Where his "heart" is attached, there, for him, is the "core" of the so-called essence of things. Whatever is at a distance from this object strikes him as "illusive" and "derivative." His actual *ethos,* that is, the rules of his value-preference and value-depreciation, defines the structure and content of his world-view and of his knowledge and thought of the world, and, in addition, his will to submit to, or be master over, things. This is true of individuals and of races, of nations, of cultural circles, of peoples and families, of parties, of classes, of castes, and of professions. Within the world-order which is valid for all men, every particular form of the human is assigned some definite range of value-qualities. Only the harmony of these, their fitting together in the structure of a common world-culture, can display the whole greatness and expanse of the human spirit.[19]

All that is worthy of love [*die Liebenswürdigkeiten*], from the viewpoint of God's comprehensive love, might have been stamped and created by this act of love; man's love does not so stamp or create its objects. Man's love is restricted to recognizing the objective demand these objects make and to submitting to the gradation of rank in what is worthy of love. This gradation exists in itself, but in itself it exists "for" man, ordered to his *particular* essence. Loving can be characterized as correct or false only because a man's actual inclinations and acts of love can be in harmony with or oppose the rank-ordering of what is worthy of love. In other words, man can feel and know himself to be at one with, or separated and opposed to,

19. [On ethos, value-perspectivism, and solidarity in the realization of the realm of values, see *Formalismus,* V, 6.—ED.]

the love with which God loved the idea of the world or its content before he created it, the love with which he preserves it at every instant. If a man in his actual loving, or in the order of his acts of love, in his preferences and depreciations, subverts this self-existent order, he simultaneously subverts the intention of the divine world-order—as it is in his power to do. And whenever he does so, his world as the possible object of knowledge, and his world as the field of willing, action, and operation, must necessarily fall as well.

This is not the place to speak about the content of the gradations of rank in the realm of all that is worthy of love. It is sufficient here to say something about the *form* and *content* of the realm itself.

From the primal atom and the grain of sand to God, this realm is *one* realm. This "unity" does not mean that the realm is closed. We are conscious that no one of the finite parts of it which are given to us can exhaust its fullness and its extension. If we have only *once* experienced how one feature which is worthy of love appears next to another—whether a feature of the same object or of another—or how another feature of still higher value appears over and above one which we had taken till now as the "highest" in a particular region of values, then we have learned the essence of progress in or penetration into the realm. Then we see that this realm cannot have precise boundaries. Only in this way can we understand that when any sort of love is fulfilled by an object adequate to it the satisfaction this gives us can never be definitive. Just as the essence of certain operations of thought which create their objects through self-given laws (e.g., the inference from n to $n + 1$) prevents any limits from being placed on their application, so it is in the essence of the act of love as it fulfills itself in what is worthy of love that it can progress from value to value, from one height to an even greater height. "Our heart is too spacious," said Pascal. Even if we should know that our actual ability to love is limited, at the same time we know and feel that this limit lies neither in the finite objects which are worthy of love nor in the essence of the act of love as such, but only in our organization and the conditions it sets for the occurrence and *arousal* of the act of love. For this arousal is bound up with the life of our body and our drives and with the way an object stimulates and calls this life into play. But *what* we grasp as *worthy of love* is not bound up with these, any more than the *form and structure* of the realm of which this value shows itself to be a part.

Love loves and in loving always looks beyond what it has in hand and possesses. The driving impulse [*Triebimpuls*] which arouses it may tire out; love itself does not tire. This *sursum corda* which is the essence of love may take on fundamentally different forms at different elevations in the various regions of value. The sensualist is struck by the way the pleasure he gets from the objects of his enjoyment gives him less and less satisfaction while his driving impulse stays the same or itself increases as he flies more and more rapidly from one object to the next. For this water makes one thirstier, the more one drinks. Conversely, the satisfaction of one who loves spiritual objects, whether things or persons, is always holding out new promise of satisfaction, so to speak. This satisfaction by nature increases more rapidly and is more deeply fulfilling, while the driving impulse which originally directed him to these objects or persons holds constant or decreases. The satisfaction always lets the ray of the movement of love peer out a little further beyond what is presently given. In the highest case, that of love for a person, this movement develops the beloved person in the direction of ideality and perfection appropriate to him and does so, in principle, beyond all limits.

However, in both the satisfaction of pleasure and the highest personal love, the same *essentially infinite process* appears and prevents both from achieving a definitive character, although for opposite reasons: in the first case, because satisfaction diminishes; in the latter, because it increases. No reproach can give such pain and act so much as a spur on the person to progress in the direction of an aimed-at perfection as the beloved's consciousness of not satisfying, or only partially satisfying, the ideal image of love which the lover brings before her—an image he took from her in the first place. Immediately a powerful jolt is felt in the core of the soul; the soul desires to grow to fit this image. "So let me seem, until I become so." Although in sensual pleasure it is the *increased variety* of the objects that expresses this essential infinity of the process, here it is the *increased depth of absorption* in the growing fullness of one object. In the sensual case, the infinity makes itself felt as a self-propagating unrest, restlessness, haste, and torment:

in other words, a mode of striving in which every time something repels us this something becomes the source of a new attraction we are powerless to resist. In personal love, the felicitous advance from value to value in the object is accompanied by a growing sense of repose and fulfillment, and issues in that positive form of striving in which each new attraction of a suspected value results in the continual abandonment of one already given. New hope and presentiment are always accompanying it. Thus, there is a positively valued and a negatively valued *unlimitedness of love,* experienced by us as a potentiality; consequently, the striving which is built upon the act of love is unlimited as well. As for striving, there is a vast difference between Schopenhauer's precipitate "willing" born of torment and the happy, God-directed "eternal striving" in Leibniz, Goethe's Faust, and J. G. Fichte.

A love which is by its essence infinite, however much it is interrupted, however much it is bound to and particularized by the specific organization of its bearer, demands for its satisfaction an *infinite good.* Thus, the object of the idea of *God* (considered here from the formal side of the two predicates of "good" and "infinite form of being") already underlies the thought of an *ordo amoris,* by reason of this essential character of all love. "Inquietum cor nostrum donec requiescat in te." [Our heart is unquiet until it rests in thee.] God and only God can be the apex of the graduated pyramid of the realm of that which is worthy of love, at once the source and the goal of the whole.

Wherever man, individually or communally, believes he has attained in a *finite good* an absolutely final fulfillment and satisfaction of his love-drive, we have a case of delusion, a stagnation of his spiritual-ethical development. He is enchained by an impulsive drive; or, better, that function of the drive by which love is aroused and its object held within limits is perverted into one which enchains and *represses.* We would like to use the old expression "infatuation" to designate the most general form of the destruction and confusion of *ordo amoris,* to which the more special forms of confusion can, in a certain sense, be traced. *Infatuation* is a word that quite plastically signifies both that a man is carried away and enraptured by some finite good without regard to his guiding center of personhood and that the character of this behavior is delusive. We shall speak of *absolute* infatuation when a man finds the value of a *finite* good or type of good occupying the *absolute position* in his actual consciousness of value, a position which is always necessarily present in everyone (but is not necessarily for that reason a matter of judgment or reflectively known in any other way). We shall call a good absolutized through delusion a (formal) idol. (The process of idolization will concern us later, as will the redemptive process of smashing idols and the dissolution of infatuation.) On the other hand, we shall speak of *relative* infatuation when a man, in accordance with the actual structure of loving peculiar to him and with the fashion in which he prefers one value over another, transgresses against the objective rank-ordering of what is worthy of love.[20]

However, the merely factual restriction of the parts and provinces of the realm of value that are accessible to a subject by virtue of his essential capacities for love should not be called "infatuation," nor should its consequence be called a confusion of *ordo amoris*. These terms are even less appropriate to the (arbitrarily great) restriction of the concrete goods [*Güterdinge*] which exemplify the value-region to which that subject has access, for some sort of simple restriction in the worlds of value and love is natural to a finite being. The degree of restriction decreases as we move in the hierarchy of value-perceiving beings from the worm to God; it is only in the case of God that no such restriction exists. Indeed, it belongs to the essence of that objective realm of values that the realm of that which is worthy of love can be mentally represented only in a limitless profusion of different types of spiritual individuals and, within the domain of human spirits, only through different singular and collective individuals, families, peoples, nations, and cultural circles *of unequal value*. Only because we represent that realm in this way can we know the things and events which are bearers of what is worthy of love and put them into effect. Similarly, it is of the essence of this realm that it is exhibited over the course of time in the form of a unique ethical history [*einmaligen Geschichte des Ethos*]. This entails that the unique *collective destiny* of the individual "mankind" can be fulfilled only when this exhibition reaches completion in a simultaneous (social) and successive (historical) conjunction,

20. [See the essay "Absolutsphäre und Realsetzung der Gottesidee," *Schriften aus dem Nachlass.*—ED.]

bringing together love [*Miteinander des Liebens*] within the various regions of value ordered in accordance with the *ordo amoris*. It is only when loving is restricted to one *part* of what the subject is essentially capable of attaining that we have a case of confusion. The ultimate cause of confusion here is one of types of infatuation. To this extent there is a *guilty* emptiness of love in the human heart. This can be an individually assumed as well as ancestrally and communally assumed guilt; it can be as much tragically and fatefully assumed as, in the common sense of the word, "freely" assumed guilt. The constitutive restriction of the realm of love is not detrimental to the essential unlimitedness of loving itself, for we experience this unlimitedness even in the more or less conscious discovery of a limitless, but "empty," field of things worthy of love—as it were, in back of those given to the subject at any one time or given as still attainable. *Infatuation,* on the contrary, is present only where this empty field, this "*outlook*" [*Aussicht*] toward hope, presentiment, and faith, in other words, where the *metaphysical perspective of love,* is missing in experience; conversely, it is the beginning of the dissolution of an infatuation that announces itself in the growing consciousness of this emptiness.

The unity of this realm of love lies, therefore, on another plane. It consists objectively in the unity of the lawful character [*Gesetzlichkeit*] of its graduated construction in the two directions of what is more and more and what is less and less worthy of love. It consists in the strict and law-governed gradation of essential values that remains constant throughout every phase of the infinite process. On the side of human personality, this unity consists in the lawfulness of insightful preference and depreciation of values and things of worth. This lawfulness is inherent in the acts and capacities of love and it is through this that the act of love directs itself to things [*Dinge*] in which these values and things of worth come to light for our heart and spirit [*Gemüt*].

For what we call "the basic moral tenor" [*Gemüt*], or figuratively the "heart" of man, is no chaos of blind feeling-states which are attached to, and detached from, other so-called psychic givens by causal rules of some sort. The heart is itself a *structured counter-image* of the cosmos of all possible things worthy of love; to this extent it is a *microcosmos of the world of values.* "Le coeur a ses raisons."

Whole schools have arisen which pose for philosophy the problem of "connecting the claims of the understanding with those of the heart and spirit in a unified world-view." There are those who, like illusionists, base religion entirely on "wishes of the heart," "postulates," "feelings of dependence," or similar conditions. All courageous thinkers, all genuine and thorough-going rationalists, have rejected with appropriate emphasis those modes of thought which are still illusionistic even in their most subtle form. "The devil with heart and feeling"—these illusionists say—"when it comes to a question of reality and truth!" But is this the meaning of Pascal's thesis? Its meaning is exactly the opposite.

The heart possesses a strict analogue of logic in its own domain that it does not borrow from the logic of the understanding; laws are inscribed on it—as the Ancients' doctrine of the *nomos agraphos* had taught—which correspond to the plane on which the world is constructed as a world of value. The heart can *love* and hate blindly *or* insightfully, no differently than we can judge blindly or insightfully.[21]

The "heart" no longer has its reasons after the understanding has pronounced on the same subject. "Reasons" in this case are not reasons, that is, objective determinations and genuine necessities, but are only self-styled reasons, namely, motives or wishes! But the emphasis in Pascal's saying lies on the "ses" and "raisons." The heart has *its* reasons, "its," of which the understanding knows nothing and can never know anything; and it has *reasons*, that is, objective and evident insights into matters to which every understanding is blind—as "blind" as a blind man is to color or a deaf man is to tone.

Pascal's saying expresses an insight of the most profound importance, an insight which today is slowly struggling its way up from the rubble of misunderstandings: there is an *ordre du coeur*, a *logique du coeur*, a *mathématique du coeur* as rigorous, as objective, as absolute, and as inviolable as the propositions and inferences of deductive logic. The figurative expression "heart" does not designate, as both philistines and romantics think, the seat of confused states, of unclear and indefinite agitations or some other strong forces tossing man hither and thither in accord with causal laws (or not). Nor is it some

21. [See *Formalismus*, II, A, on the establishment of emotional apriorism.—ED.]

static matter of fact silently tacked on to the human ego. It is the totality of well-regulated acts, of functions having an intrinsic lawfulness which is autonomous and rigorous and does not depend on the psychological organization of man; a lawfulness that operates with precision and exactness. Its functions bring before our eyes a strictly *objective sphere* of facts which is the most objective, the most fundamental of all possible spheres of fact; one which remains in the universe even if *Homo sapiens* is destroyed, just as does the truth of the proposition $2 \times 2 = 4$. Indeed, it is more independent of men than the validity of that proposition.

If not only this or that individual man but whole generations have forgotten how to see this, if entire generations see the whole of emotional life as a dumb, *subjectively* human matter of fact, without a meaning on which objective necessity can be based, without sense and direction, this is not something engineered by nature but is the responsibility of men and ages. It comes from the *general slovenliness in matters of feeling,* in matters of love and hate, from the lack of seriousness for all the depths of things and of life itself, and, by way of contrast, from the ridiculous ultraseriousness and comical busyness over those things which our wits can technically master. Had you said, with eyes on the heavens, "Alas, these flashes of light up there are only states of sensation, just like stomach-ache and fatigue," do you think that that sublime order among these facts which astronomy has devised would have then existed for you? Who would have searched for this order? Who tells you that there where you see only a chaos of confused states, there is not also an order of facts hidden at first, but accessible to discovery: "l'ordre du coeur"? A world as spacious, as vast, as rich, as harmonious, as blindingly clear as that of mathematical astronomy, a world accessible only to a very few gifted men and of even less utility-interest than the world of astronomical bodies!

The most basic reason why men have not looked for any evidence, any conformity to law [22] within the life of feeling and the sphere of love and hate, and have denied feelings any connection with the apprehension of objects, is the unscrupu-

22. Conformity to law is distinct from the causal connection of certain states of feeling to objective impressions. [This line originally stood in the text.—TRANS.]

lousness and inaccuracy with which they are pleased to treat all questions which cannot be decided by the understanding. Men regard all distinctions here as "vague" and as "subjectively" valid only. Everything that concerns "taste" in aesthetic matters, everything that has to do in any way with value judgments, everything that touches upon "instinct," "conscience," every evidence not established by the understanding that this or that is right, good, beautiful, that this or that other thing is false, evil, ugly—all this is held to be "subjective" and deprived from the start of any more rigorous and binding force. A retreat to these mental powers counts as "unscientific" and thus, for the fetishists of modern science, as a lack of "objectivity" as well. Within the artistic and aesthetic region the commonly prevailing opinion—despite one or two aestheticians who think otherwise—is still simply this: It is a matter of each man's taste what is genuinely beautiful and ugly, what is artistically worth-while or worthless. Jurists and national economists try to avoid "value judgments," since such judgments are by their nature unscientific. In morals the principle of "freedom of conscience" holds sway. Not only does every positive generation, self-confident of its values, know nothing of this "freedom of conscience"; but the principle is one which, as Auguste Comte has rightly said, in the end represents nothing else than a pure surrender of moral judgment to pure arbitrariness. It is a purely negative, critical, and dissolvent principle, in which all objective ethical values are denied once and for all.[23] What would one say if anyone in any of the sciences stood on his freedom of opinion? Is there an analogue of freedom of conscience in mathematics, in physics, astronomy, even biology and history? Does it not simply represent—as it is commonly understood—a renunciation of any sort of strictly valid ethical judgment?

Modern man thinks that in general there is nothing fixed, nothing definite or binding, there, where he simply does not take the trouble to look seriously for something of the sort. The Middle Ages still knew a *cultivation of the heart* as an autonomous concern, completely independent of the cultivation of understanding. In more recent times, even the most primitive presuppositions for this are missing. People no longer understand the whole of emotional life as a meaningful symbolic

23. [See *Formalismus*, V, 7, on the principle of "freedom of conscience."—ED.]

language. They no longer see that objective connections are unveiled in this language that, in their changing relationship to us, *govern the sense and meaning of our life.* Rather, they take our emotional life to consist in a series of totally blind happenings which run their course in us like any natural processes; happenings which eventually one must have a technique for managing in order to get some use from them and avoid harm. However, they do not think that we have to learn to listen to these happenings when we are considering what they "mean," what they wish to say to us, what they advise against, what their goals are, or to what they point! There is a *hearkening* to what a feeling of the beauty of a landscape, of a work of art, says to us, or to what is conveyed by a feeling of the characteristics of a person standing in front of us. That is, there is a heedful going-along-with this feeling and a serene acceptance of what stands at the point where it ends, so to say. We can have a good ear for what stands before us and a sharp testing of whether what we experience in this way is clear, unambiguous, determinate. We can cultivate a critical sense of what is "genuine" and "not genuine" here, of what lies in the line of *pure feeling* and what is only a wish which, when directed toward certain goals, adds an element of will or reflection and judgment. All of this has been lost in the constitution of modern man. He has no trust in, no seriousness for, what he could hear in these areas.

One consequence of such an attitude is that the investigation of the entire realm of emotional life is surrendered to *psychology.* The objects of psychology, however, lie in the direction of inner perception, which always involves a reference to the *self.* The only aspects of emotional being we can find in this way are the fixed, motionless *states* of the self. Nothing which is an *act and function* of *feeling* is *ever there* when observation takes this direction.[24] I shall give examples to show what I have in mind. If a person standing before a beautiful landscape or a picture looks in upon his self, to see how he is touched or moved by that object, or upon the feeling which he has in the presence of this picture; if a lover, instead of grasping his object in love and becoming absorbed in the loved object, looks in upon all the states of sensation and feeling, the

24. [*Formalismus,* VI, A, 3, b, on "act," "person," and the object of psychology.—ED.]

longing, etc., which are caused in him by the beloved object; if someone at prayer turns from that directedness to God, the unitary intention which holds sway over all his single thoughts, his feelings, the motions of his hands, his act of kneeling, and makes a unity out of this murmuring of words, these feelings and thoughts, and applies himself to these feelings *themselves*—then he is always behaving in the way we label with the words "inner perception." That is, such a person is always answering the question: "What is happening in consciousness when I perceive a beautiful object, when I love, pray, etc.?" To the extent something found in this way still has some relation to external objects, this relation is always produced through two distinct acts of comprehension, one comprehending those states and processes in the self, the other grasping the pertinent external objects. In other words, it is produced through a judgmental or inferential act of thought which is based upon two acts of perception, one of inner perception in which, for example, the pleasure I get from the beautiful picture is given to me, and one of external perception. And, indeed, this relation is always a causal relation of some sort, perhaps the effect of the beautiful picture or of the loved object, whether real or imaginary, on the state of my soul.

It has now become clear to philosophers that the *spirit* [*Geist*] seeks another way of looking at things than that presented above. However, in keeping with traditional rationalism —to which we are much more deeply attached than we know —this way is followed only in the case of thinking. Logic investigates the laws which can obtain when objects in general and their relations are substituted for one another. The acts of thinking in which these objects and their relations are grasped must serve as the basis of an investigation which does not conceive of them as objects of inner perception, but seizes them in the course of their actual execution [*lebendigen Vollzug*], so that we can look to see what they *mean* or intend. However, when we do this, we must abstract them from their concrete connection with the individual who is thinking and focus only on the difference between their essences, so far as this difference goes hand in hand with a difference in the facts and connections of fact grasped in these acts. Logic's task is to investigate the structures of ideal objective connections, of propositions, of provable relations between propositions and deductive theories, or, alternatively, of the acts through which we can grasp these logical connections.

It is, however, an act of unequaled arbitrariness to carry out this investigation only in the case of thinking and to hand over to psychology the remaining part of the spirit. In doing so, one presupposes that any immediate relation to objects belongs to the act of *thought* alone and that any other relation to objects through *intuition* and its modes or through *striving, feeling, loving, and hating,* comes about only indirectly, by means of an act of thinking which relates a content given in inner perception (e.g., a feeling-state in the emotional sphere) to objects. In fact, we live with the *entire fullness of our spirit* chiefly among *things;* we live in the *world.* In all our acts, even the non-logical ones, we have experiences which have nothing at all to do with experiencing what is being carried out in us during the performance of the act. The experience which discloses itself only in ethical wrestling with the resistances offered by the world and by our nature—the experience which shows itself in the performance of religious acts, acts of believing, praying, honoring, loving, and which becomes ours in the consciousness of artistic composition and aesthetic enjoyment—immediately gives us contents and connections of content which are *simply not present* for an attitude of pure thought, notwithstanding the fact that we can convert some such content into an object of thought once it has grown dim to us. Nor can such contents and connections be found in us, that is, in the direction of inner perception.

A philosophy which fails to recognize and a priori denies the claim to transcendence which all non-logical acts make, or allows this claim only in the case of acts of thought and those acts of intuitive cognition which furnish the material for thought in the domain of theory and science, condemns itself to blindness to whole realms of facts and their connections, for access to these realms is not essentially tied to acts of mind proper to the understanding. A philosophy of this sort is like a man who has healthy eyes and closes them and wants to perceive colors only with his ear or his nose!

To be sure, the order of the heart does not contain an arrangement of all the actual goods and ends which we can love and hate. Rather, even within the world of values and goods and the acts of love related to them, there exists a fundamental distinction between *contingent* and thus *variable,* and *essential* or *constant* legitimacies of rank-ordering and preference. Essential and constant laws of rank and preference exist only in relation to those value-qualities and their modalities which have been separated from their contingent, actual bearers. On the other hand, the way these qualities are combined in actual goods, their existence or nonexistence in a man's or a society's concrete system of goods, their tangibility [*Fühlbarkeit*] for the circle of men in question, the way they are parceled out among things presently in existence, their becoming or failing to become norms and goals of the will—all these can vary *ad libitum* from subject to subject, from age to age, from society to society. This kind of variation is no longer open to understanding; it can only be described and causally explained on the basis of induction and always in a merely probable and hypothetical way. This is the miracle of our world: through a *knowledge of essence* and knowledge of essential structure obtained from the forms of this actual, real world, we can know the constitution of every *possible* world, including even that reality which is shut off from our limited organization in life and hence transcendent to us. Here, therefore, in the region of the heart and its goods, we can, as it were, see through the accidental movements of the heart and through our familiar, contingently real realms of goods, to an eternal architecture and scaffolding which encompasses all possible spirits and all possible worlds of goods; an architecture which is reflected only here and there in our world. It is in no way *read off* this world by way of inductive abstraction and induction or by deduction from universal propositions which are valid in themselves or are reached by induction. Thus, *in* the experiences of the psychophysical living unity "Man" we find the idea of a spirit which itself contains nothing of the limitations of our human organization; and in concrete goods [*Güterdingen*] we find ranking relations between values that are valid independently of the particular form of these goods, independently of the material out of which they are made and of the causal laws in accordance with which they come to be and pass away.

The important distinction between the essential and the contingent, the constant and the variable, between what is valid beneath and above our possible real experience and what is limited to this circle of experience—this distinction has *nothing to do* with the utterly different distinction between *the individual and the universal.* For instance, the former has nothing to do with the distinction between singular and universal judgments of fact and relation, e.g., the so-called laws of nature. All the laws of nature also belong to the sphere of "contingent truths" and have only a probable certainty. On the other hand, an evident cognition of essence can very well aim at a unique, individual existence or value [*Wertsein*], depending on the region of being or value certain objects inhabit. Consequently, we can imagine that the scale of what is worthy of love, both as it exists for everyone generally and, within this, as it exists for each single and social individual, is of such a kind that every object, when its contingency is stripped away and its essence is considered, occupies a completely determinate and *unique position* on this scale, a position to which a completely precise and nuanced movement of the spirit corresponds. If we "fit" this position, then our love is *correct* and in order; if the positions change places, if under the influence of passions and drives the hierarchy of levels is overturned, then our love is *incorrect* and disordered.

This "correctness" is subject to different kinds of measurement. I shall mention only a few of them here. Our spirit finds itself in "metaphysical confusion" when an object which belongs among those in any way and in any degree *value-relative* is loved in the manner appropriate only to objects of *absolute* value; that is, when a man identifies the value of his spiritual, personal core with the value of such an object to the extent that he stands to it basically in the relation of faith and worship, and thus falsely deifies it, or rather idolizes it. At a particular level of value-relativity, (which is, as such, correctly felt and judged), an object of lesser value can be preferred over another object of greater value. An object can be loved with the correct kind of love, but in such a way that the full measure of its worthiness of love, ranging from nothing to the greatest fullness, is not, or is not *completely,* apparent to the spirit. In this case the love is *not adequate* to the object. These degrees of adequacy can increase from that of blind love all the way to completely adequate or evident, clear-sighted love.[25]

25. [See "Absolutsphäre und Realsetzung der Gottesidee," *Schriften aus dem Nachlass,* on the subject of "idolization." On the analogues within

However, it always holds true that the act of *hate,* the antithesis of love, or the emotional negation of value and existence, is the result of some *incorrect* or *confused* love. However rich and various may be the motive of hatred or the state of valuelessness which exacts hatred, *one* form of lawfulness runs through all cases of hatred—every act of hate is founded on an act of love, without which it would lack sense. We can also say that, since love and hate have in common that they do not fall within the zone of indifference [26] but take a strong interest in the object as the bearer of some value, this is *primarily* a case of taking a *positive* interest in, of loving, so long as there are no reasons for the opposite to occur—especially none which lie in some false toning down of interest.

To be sure, this principle of the *primacy of love over hate* with the denial that the two basic emotional acts are equiprimordial has often been *falsely interpreted* and, still more often, falsely substantiated. For instance, it should not be taken to imply that we must previously have loved anything which we hate, that hate is always love in reverse. While we can often observe this, particularly in the case of love for persons, the opposite happens just as frequently, namely, that a thing awakens hatred the first time it is given, a man is hated as soon as he appears. However, when the man in question is the bearer of a state of affairs without value [*Unwertverhalt*], that is, of a countervalue [*Gegenwelt*] corresponding to some state of affairs with positive value, it is a law that the latter must have formed the content of an act of love, if the act of hate in question is to be possible. Consequently, the principle which Bossuet expressed in his famous chapter on love is valid: "The hatred which one feels for anything comes only from the love which one has for some other; I hate sickness only because I love health." [27] To this extent, hate rests on a *disillusionment* [*Enttäuschung*] concerning the existence or nonexistence of a value-state which one had intentionally in mind (thus, not yet in the form of an act of expectation). (The existence of a

---

the theoretical domain to adequation, fullness, level of relativity, etc., see "Phenomenology and the Theory of Cognition," below, sec. IV.—ED.]

26. The zone of indifference is only an ideal "cut" which is never completely reached by our varying emotional attitudes.

27. See *Traité de la connaissance de dieu et de soi-même* (1722), chap. I.

state of valuelessness, as well as the absence or lack of a positive value-state, can be the motive of this hatred. Consequently, this principle does not assert that the states of valuelessness are any less positive states than the (positively) valued states but are, perhaps, only the absence of the latter. That is a completely arbitrary assertion of *metaphysical optimism;* analogously, the assertion that all value-states rest only on the disappearance of states of valuelessness is an equally arbitrary assertion of *metaphysical pessimism.*) A contradiction would arise only if every time we became cognizant of a (positive) evil, hatred also had to be awakened, which is in no way the case. For such evil can also be merely acknowledged. Indeed, in certain circumstances it can even be loved to the extent that, as an evil of a lower rank, it represents the condition which makes possible the existence of a good of higher rank or an ethical good and represents this not only accidentally, but essentially.

Hate and love are, thus, two antithetical modes of emotional behavior, and this precludes the possibility of both loving and hating *the same thing* with respect to the same value and in *one* act. However, they are not equi-primordial modes of behavior. *Our heart is primarily destined to love,* not to hate. Hate is only a reaction against a love which is in some way false. The frequent, almost proverbial saying, "Who cannot hate, cannot love either," is not correct. Rather, it is true that the man who cannot love cannot hate either. This also affects the law to which the origin of *ressentiment*-love is subject, namely, that everything which is "loved" in that way is loved only because it is the opposite of something else which one has already come to hate; only a *pseudo*-love comes into being, not a real love. Even the *man of ressentiment* originally loved the things which in his present condition he hates, and only his hatred at not possessing them or at his powerlessness to acquire them comes subsequently to irradiate these things.[28]

Moreover, we should not conclude that hate is necessarily a matter of personal guilt in the sense of being the guilt of the one who hates. The confusion of the order of love in virtue of which A hates need not be caused by A himself. It can also be brought about by B, C, D, etc., or by the societies to which A belongs. Since it is essentially necessary for love, *ceteris*

28. [See Scheler, *Ressentiment*, trans. William W. Holdheim (New York: Free Press of Glencoe, 1961).—TRANS.]

paribus, to determine counter-love and shared love, and for hate to determine counter-hate and shared hate, hate can, in principle, take its start anywhere in the whole human community where a confusion of *ordo amoris* occurs. Its starting point can be separated, so to speak, from *A* by arbitrarily long causal chains which intervene between them. Thus, it is not the case that every instance of hate which follows upon a "confusion" is determined *by* the one who hates. Our principle says only that if hate is in the world, so too must there be a confusion of the order of love in the world.

Hate is always and everywhere a *rebellion of our heart* and spirit *against a violation of ordo amoris.* It makes no difference whether it is a matter of some barely perceptible stirring of hate in an individual heart, or whether, as in the course of vast revolutions, hate covers the earth as a phenomenon of the masses and is directed upon the ruling classes. Man cannot hate unless he sees the bearer of what is commonly considered a non-value take or pretend to take over the place which belonged to a bearer of a value in that objective order in which things are assigned their position in the scale of worthiness of love; or unless a good of lower rank takes over the place of a good of higher rank (and conversely).

We have discussed elsewhere the relation between the acts of love and hate and cognitive acts and acts belonging to the sphere of striving and willing.[29] We have established the primacy of the former vis-à-vis the latter types of acts. "Taking an interest in," which is identical in the acts both of love and of hate, proved to be the fundamental condition for the occurrence of any sort of cognitive act, whether in the sphere of images or in that of thought. This "taking an interest in" is, in the last analysis, what directs and commands even the value-blind acts of attention. Only to the extent that this "taking an interest" itself is originally more an act of love than of hate could we properly speak of a primacy of love over cognition. While acts of desire and loathing, as well as genuine acts of will, proved to be founded on acts of cognition (involving representation and judgment), the value-orientation of the latter was, in turn, dependent on acts of "taking an interest" and thus on acts of love or hate. Acts of cognition get this

29. [See *Formalismus* (subject index), and the essay "Liebe und Erkenntnis," *Schriften zur Soziologie und Weltanschauungslehre.*—ED.]

orientation independently of any *cognition* differentiating between love and hate. In neither of these cases did we have to call into question the specific nature of acts of cognition and desiring, together with the legitimacy peculiar to them, or conceive of them as combined out of, or otherwise derived from, acts of love and hate. We intended to characterize only an *order of foundation* in the origin of acts from out of the whole of the personality and its capacities.

However, besides these basic classes of mental-psychic acts, we have the feeling-states [*zuständliche Gefühle*] which have no value-intention and the very complex affects and passions. Let us make a few remarks on their relation to love and hate.

The coming-to-be and passing-away of these (value-blind) feeling-states,[30] the simplest of these processes, depend as much on acts of love and hate as they usually do on acts of striving and willing; however, these feelings are not immediately and directly dependent on acts of representation and their correlative objects. These feelings always indicate the relation that obtains between the qualities of value and non-value aimed at in acts of love and hate, and the realization of these values (whether merely within the soul or in real fact) by means of the different modes of striving. For instance, we do not simply get pleasure from the satisfaction of a desire or loathing whenever it occurs; we take pleasure in this only insofar as our desire is a desire for something loved, and our loathing, a loathing of something hated. The satisfaction of a striving for something hated can be bound up with the strongest displeasure and sorrow; equally, if the striving remains unsatisfied, this can give us pleasure, *if* the object of striving is something hated. In this way, passive feelings are the indexes of the disharmony or harmony between the world of our loving and hating and the course and outcome of our desires and acts of will.

Love and hate, therefore, can never be reduced, as people have so often tried to do, to the release of passive feelings in the presence of objects of representation and thought. Instead, the release of these feelings depends on acts of loving and hating with a certain direction, goal, and value, and on the world of objects given in these acts. We feel pleasure when a loved thing exists or is present, or when it comes into our

30. [On "passive feelings" in contrast to intentional feeling [*Fühlen*] as a type of emotional act, see *Formalismus*, V, 2.—ED.]

possession, if its nature permits, through our will and action. On the other hand, we feel pleasure when a hated thing ceases to exist or is put at a distance from us or is destroyed by our will and action. Moreover, this holds true of ordered love as well as of disordered and confused love. Passive feelings are, in the first place, merely the echo of the experience of the world we get in loving and hating things; second, they are the manifestations [*Erscheinungen*] of our success and failures in the volitional and active life we lead in the world and they vary as a function of these. Our life is in turn based on the ways our love and hate are directed onto the world (and here our body and the inner psychic world which can be the object of inner perception are surely to be counted as belonging to the world). The most direct source of feeling-states is thus, more than anything else, the harmony or opposition of actual desires along some one direction of love or hate. The feelings have no "being" [*"sind" zwar nicht*], but rest on the changing relations between acts of striving (and not, therefore, on those between representations, as Herbart quite wrongly says). These acts always have a teleological reference to something loved or hated. Thus, there is absolutely no question of acts of love and hate "conforming" to passive feelings or to acts of desiring and willing. Love and hate are more original than both, even though acts of love and hate command the life of desire more directly than they do these feelings, which are already dependent variables of our experiences of striving.

The life of our feeling-states thus does not depend on objective contents of representation, perception, or thought. According as *A* strives for or loathes the very same contents of "representation" (in the widest sense of the word), and according as his striving or loathing is in or out of harmony with the orientation of his love and hate, these contents and their relations awaken fundamentally different states of feeling. This explains why a (humanly) uniform pleasure, in the Golden Section, perhaps, traces back to a uniform love for this object. No one can doubt the existence of states of feeling which are objectless or in some measure without a definite or distinct object. One frequently asks oneself, to which and what kind of occurrence should a given state of feeling be referred? Finally, there is the fact which Nahlowsky has emphasized and which has recently been confirmed again in the case of "sensations of feeling" (especially pain), namely, that there are phenomena of feeling totally without any basis in sensation and perception.[31] These are often given before the sensation which is commonly given along with them emerges and often persist after the sensation has disappeared. All these facts prove the thoroughgoing independence of the facts of feeling from the existence and network of representations.

The existence of states of feeling which we experience as directly excited by objects, even though there is no antecedent striving or resistance whose satisfaction or non-satisfaction they could represent, constitutes a decisive objection only to the familiar volitional theory of feelings. It does not count as an objection for us, since love and hate and the interest always given in them, in other words, value-apprehending attention, are still present even in the states of feeling we are describing. Interest always helps to determine the representations of the object, while the feeling of pleasure or displeasure this object excites depends on the quality of the interest, on whether it is love or hate. In these cases, too, the state of feeling does not depend on striving for or against something; it very much depends on the stirrings of love and hate, in keeping with the principle that what is loved gives us pleasure and what is hated, displeasure, and that the quality of the passive feeling changes once our love and hate have changed. Love of pain, for example, cancels out everything in the feeling-sensation of pain over and above that which is proper to sensation itself, everything which goes beyond the piercing, cutting, burning, stabbing character of pain, including even its genuine "painfulness," and transforms it into something agreeable.

The extraordinary diversity of these states of feeling among different individuals, peoples, and races in the same environmental circumstances can be fully explained only by their dependence on love and hate. It is by virtue of this that the states are either signs of the relation between the objects of perception, representation, and thought, and the changing orientation of a man's love and hate, or signs of the varying success or failure he has in attempting to see the values given in loving and hating realized, inwardly as well as outwardly, in

31. [See W. Nahlowsky, *Das Gefühlsleben in seinen wesentlichen Erscheinung und Beziehungen* (Leipzig, 1907).—TRANS.]

objects of representation and perception respectively. The actual structure of the gradations of interest and the directions of love and hate within an experiencing [*erlebenden*] subject mark off from the start the range and scope of his possible states of feeling. When these gradations and directions change, so does his range.

Not only the feeling-states, but affects and passions as well, are ruled by love and hate, which should not be themselves reckoned under these classes. I understand by "affects" the acute discharges of strong feelings of essentially sensuous and vital provenience. These affects are combined in typically different ways on each occasion and are exhibited in typical expressions, accompanied by strong driving impulses and organic sensations which pass into the expression. Accordingly, they possess a characteristic value-blindness in regard to the objects which evoke them and have no characteristic intentional relation to these objects. The passions, on the other hand, are something entirely different. In the first place, the passions permanently bind a man's involuntary striving and counterstriving (situated in a sphere beneath that of the selective will) to certain domains of function, activity, and action distinguished by a particular category of value-quality through which the man predominantly looks at the world. The affect is acute and essentially *passive;* the passion is a lasting capacity and by its nature is *active* and aggressive. The affect is essentially a blind and passing condition; passion, although one-sided and isolating, has an eye for value and is a strong and perpetual movement of our drives in the direction specified by this value. Nothing great without great passion; everything great, surely, without affect. The affect is predominantly an occurrence in the sphere of the embodied ego [*Leib-Ich*], while passion has its starting point in the deeper vital center of the "soul."

In terms of this study, affects recede into the background, while the passions are of the greatest importance. For this reason, I shall make a few remarks about the latter alone.

"If you take love away, no passion remains; if you bring forth love, then you let them all arise" (Bossuet).[32]

32. [The manuscript breaks off here.—ED.]

[III] The Kinds of Love and Their Demand
for Fulfillment

IN ORDER TO CHARACTERIZE the various confusions of
ordo amoris in the actual being and behavior of men, and to
understand their causes and the means for removing them, we
must examine more closely the ways man's spirit is specifically
related to the objective *ordo amoris*.

Above all, we must avoid the chief errors which have long
confused this question. The first of these consists in what we
can call (in the widest sense of the term) the Platonic conception of love, the theory that we have innate ideas of the objects of love. The second is the empiricist conception that the
particular formation of the directions of a man's love and hate,
in addition to the parallel formation of the "normal" man,
first arises from his actual experience of his environment,
especially its pleasant and unpleasant effects on him. The third
error is the theory which has recently become quite prominent,
that all kinds of love and hate are nothing but transforma-
tions of a single love-force which originally rules over men on
its own. When we first consider this monistic theory, it
makes no difference *what* this force is, since the monism itself
is precisely what is false here. In a kind of monistic metaphysics of love, one can consider this single love-force to be
love of God and see in the forms of love for finite objects only
different restrictions of this love brought about by human
drives,[33] or, conversely, one can make this force the libido
which "sublimates" and transfigures itself through all sorts of
repression and inhibition into higher and more spiritual forms
of love. In both cases, one denies the primitively and irreduc-
ibly different forms of the essence of love. Even if these forms
are distinguished from one another only in the course of man's
development one after the other and become actual only at
particular times (on the basis of certain release mechanisms),
still, they never emerge from one another.

The first of these views, the doctrine of the innate ideas of
the objects of love, scarcely needs refuting today. Instead,

33. Spinoza's acosmism comes very close to this conception; see,
especially, his remarks in the introduction to his essay "De intellectus
emendatione."

we need to rescue and protect the elements of truth it contains. We possess no innate ideas of the things we love and hate, whether consciously or unconsciously. We have no innate idea of God, for example, or one of a human type whose bearer inspires us with special love, or, finally, an innate idea of a thing which inspires us with inclination and disinclination, fear and hope, trust and mistrust. Even what we call the "instinctive" forms of inclination and disinclination in animals and men—e.g., man's aversion to the darkness, to certain odors, to what is disgusting, the inclinations and aversions of different races, the chicken's fear of the hawk, etc.—all these, while undoubtedly innate, are certainly not based on innate *ideas* of these things. All objective representations of what we love or hate arise from or in the experience of those objects which come to us by way of the senses, or by communication and tradition, or in some other demonstrable fashion. If we do possess general ideas of what we love and hate, these are only formed later, through comparison and reflection. This is true, for example, of our ideas concerning the natural things and events which we especially love, or the sexual types which especially attract or repel us.

Consequently, it makes no difference which one of the countless versions of this doctrine one gives: whether one thinks that they were acquired once upon a time during some previous existence of the soul or given to the soul as a divine dowry, or whether one assumes, in a purely naturalistic vein, that the material conditions in which these ideas are formed under the influence of stimuli which trigger them have passed over into the organism through heredity.

The first version is too mysterious to require refutation. In addition, at a decisive point it falls into the error of empiricism, that is, the second of the theories listed at the start concerning man's relation to the *ordo amoris*. For empiricism, too, wants to reduce the primitive and spontaneous directions of love and hate to the reproduction of earlier impressions made by our experience [*Erfahrungseindrücke*].

The second version would be religiously offensive, since there can be no propriety in tracing back to God the ideas of those things so often of lower value, even silly and foolish, to which the heart of man attaches itself; for God is the refuge of all wisdom and goodness.

It is the third, naturalistic, version of this theory of innate ideas of loved objects that can more readily lay claim to proof. What speaks *against* it is not its emphasis on the hereditary character of certain directions of love and hate, for this has been put beyond doubt by all the factual material concerning the hereditary character of instincts in animal and man, the unquestionably inherited inclinations and aversions of different species toward and against one another. Preferences for particular types in sexual selection run through long chains of generations of families and clans. If it is difficult to decide in individual cases what is to be laid to the account of tradition and what to that of heredity, in every case there are facts which are unintelligible unless heredity is assumed. An old Japanese idea, closely connected with the cult of the ancestors, says that the sexual selection of young lovers is exclusively determined by the inclinations and aversions, the desires and loathings, the wishes and signs, of the lovers' ancestors. When individual features, external and inner attributes, a way of walking, a laugh, a look, a character trait which the ancestors desired, loved, and longed for come together in an individual of the opposite sex, then the lover is inflamed with love and his love grows in the same measure as the number of those features increases and this longing is strong and unambiguous.

However characteristic of the Japanese way of thinking this omission of genuine individuality and, correspondingly, of individual love may be, however closely this omission and the mosaiclike composition of a man out of the mere sum of individual features is connected with the absence of the higher, Christian, and romantic love of the soul, still the only thing false in this doctrine is the notion that these conditions are *exclusive*.

It is correct, however, that certain ranges of erotic choice are innate and hereditary. The so-called copying of the father by young girls and of the mother by young boys in their later sexual selection, emphasized so strongly by psychoanalysts, does not need to be traced back to erotic experiences in the early childhood of the individuals in question. It seems to me rather to favor the view that this copying is the result of the hereditary transmission of the principle of preference from the mother or father to the child of the same sex. This explanation seems particularly required where a principle of preference runs through several generations and always recurs, despite different childhood experiences. Boys choose or find pleasure in women who are like their mother, since the same direction of erotic love which led the father leads them too, *ceteris paribus*. If we had more and better experiences of this fact of heredity than we do at present, we could indeed prove what we can now only suspect in some particularly conspicuous cases: Quite definite *schemata of erotic fate* and arrangements in which female and male individuals are matched with one another [*gegenseitiger Kollokationen*] recur through the sequence of generations, taking the form of hereditarily transmitted rhythms of the discharge of erotic impulse and seeking in the individual only, so to speak, the indifferent matter for their realization. Here the drama, or at least its structure and inner composition, is so often prior to those who not only have to perform it, but must write it with their life's blood.[34]

34. [The manuscript breaks off here.—ED.]

Phenomenology and the Theory of Cognition

[I] INTRODUCTION

THE EDITORS OF *Geisteswissenschaften* have invited me to make some brief remarks about the work and goals of the recent philosophical movement whose representatives have found a certain alliance in the *Jahrbuch für Philosophie und phänomenologische Forschung*.[1] I can respond to the invitation only with two reservations.

The first is that the cognitive value phenomenological discoveries have in all areas of philosophy is entirely independent of any explanation of the general essence of "phenomenology" and any statement of what phenomenology is and desires. Only a form of rationalism opposed to phenomenological philosophy cannot imagine any fruitful and valid knowledge of a realm of fact unless a definition of the relevant science has already been furnished and certain basic principles of its method have been established before any work has been done on the subject. However, definitions of this kind have in fact always been *secondary* in any development of knowledge. There is not, up till now, an accepted definition even of mathe-

Translated from "Phänomenologie und Erkenntnistheorie," *Schriften aus dem Nachlass: I, Zur Ethik und Erkenntnislehre*, 2d ed. rev., ed. Maria Scheler (Bern: Francke Verlag, 1957), pp. 379–430.

1. [The periodical *Die Geisteswissenschaften*, in which Scheler's essay was to have appeared, was only published from October, 1913, until July, 1914. A separate edition was planned in 1914, but this came to nought because of the war.—ED.]

matics, physics, or chemistry, not to mention biology and the human sciences. Methods (i.e., the consciousness of the unity of the investigatory procedure) always come after long years of fruitful work on the subject, if the controversy about them is not ephemeral. The concrete unity of investigation required by the subject alone in no way depends on a clear *consciousness* of this unity, to say nothing of the formulation of this consciousness in judgments. Phenomenological philosophy is still young; consequently, we have the less right to demand of it a fixed and inviolable formulation of the unitary procedure of research practiced in its positive work. After all we ask in vain for a formulation of this kind from the oldest, most uncontested sciences.

My second reservation is that the following remarks on the nature and spirit of phenomenology claim only to report my own viewpoint. There is no phenomenological "school" which would have to offer commonly accepted theses. There is only a circle of researchers, inspired by a common bearing and attitude [*Einstellung*] toward philosophical problems, who take and bear separate responsibility for everything they claim to have discovered within this attitude, including any theory of the nature of this "attitude."

1. *The phenomenological attitude*

In the first place, phenomenology is neither the name of a new science nor a substitute for the word "philosophy"; it is the name of an attitude of spiritual seeing in which can see [*er-schauen*] or experience [*er-leben*] something which otherwise remains hidden, namely, a realm of facts of a particular kind. I say "attitude," not "method." A method is a goal-directed procedure of *thinking about* facts, for example, induction or deduction. In phenomenology, however, it is a matter, first, of new facts themselves, before they have been fixed by logic, and, second, of a procedure of *seeing*. The goals in behalf of which this attitude is practiced are furnished by the problematic of the world as it has been formulated by philosophers over the last few centuries. This is not to say that the practice of this attitude cannot alter the more precise formulation of these problems in many ways. We can *also* understand by "method" a particular procedure of observation and investigation, with or without experiment and with or without instrumental support for our senses, in the form of microscopes, telescopes, etc. In such cases it is also a question of obtaining new facts; nonetheless, the attitude is always the same, namely, "observation," whether physical or mental facts are at issue. Phenomenology, however, has a fundamentally different attitude. That which is seen and experienced is *given* only in *the seeing and experiencing act itself,* in its being acted out [*Vollzug*]; it appears in this act and only in it. It does not simply stand there and let itself be observed so that now this feature, now that, stands out in relief without any alteration in the object. It does not matter how one comes to *see* something. This can, e.g., occur also via an experiment, but if it does the experiment does not have any inductive sense but is like the so-called illustrative experiments of the mathematicians which confirm the "possibility" of a previously defined concept. And there is also an act of seeing in fantasy-representations.

A philosophy based on phenomenology must be characterized first of all by the most intensely vital and most immediate contact with the world itself, that is, with those things in the world with which it is concerned, and with these things as they are immediately given in experience, that is, in the act of experience and are "in themselves there" only in this act. The phenomenological philosopher, thirsting for the lived-experience of being, will above all seek to drink at the very *sources* in which the contents of the world reveal themselves. His reflective gaze rests only on that place where lived-experience and its object, the world, touch one another. He is quite unconcerned whether what is involved here is the physical or the mental, numbers or God, or anything else. The "ray" of reflection should try to touch only what is *"there"* in this closest and most living contact and only so far as it *is* there. In this sense, but only in this, phenomenological philosophy is the most radical *empiricism* and positivism. It looks for a content of lived-experience which "coincides" with all propositions and formulas, even those of pure logic, for example, the principle of identity. Any question of the truth and validity of these propositions is suspended as long as this requirement is not fulfilled.

This requirement radically distinguishes phenomenological philosophy from the most prevalent form of rationalism, which takes some concepts or formulas, or even science itself, as the

basis of its procedure, and then seeks to reach the "presuppositions" of science by reduction or to bring "its results into a
consistent system." Phenomenological philosophy has a great
interest in the explanation of science and its objects, no less
than it has in the explanation of art, religion, and ethics. However, to presuppose the validity of science or of any of its
propositions is not to explain its essence but to obscure it. Moreover, to make such a presupposition is to make philosophy into
the *ancilla scientiae,* and this is the same error for which
scholasticism is rightly reproached, although now mathematical physics or historical science (scientism) is substituted for
theology. The existence of this kind of tribunal for the special
sciences is not justified, since these rightly claim to be able to
fix their own presuppositions. However, this "fixing" must
change every day as these sciences develop and undergo constant alteration.

As wide a gulf separates the radical empiricism of phenomenology from any and every kind of rationalism, insofar as
phenomenology, by virtue of its principle of cognition, rejects
the notion of giving priority to the problems of *criteria* when
it deals with any question. A philosophy which does give criteria
priority is rightly called "criticism." In contrast, the phenomenologist is convinced that a deep and living familiarity with
the content and meaning of the facts in question must precede
all questions of criteria concerning a particular domain, no
matter whether these concern the distinction between genuine and false science, true and false religion, genuine and
worthless art, or even involve questions like "what is the
criterion for the reality of an intended object [*eines
Gemeinten*] or for the truth of a judgment?" He who is always inclined to ask for a criterion first of all—a criterion of
whether this picture is an authentic work of art, say, or
whether any extant religion is *true* and which one it is—is a
man who stands outside, who has no *direct* contact with any
work of art, any religion, any scientific domain. He who has
not expended labor on some domain of facts is the one who
starts off by asking for the criteria of this domain (Stumpf).[2]

The criterion question is posed by the eternally "other," the
man who does not want to find the true and the false, or the

2. [See C. Stumpf, "Die Wiedergeburt der Philosophie," *Berliner
Rektoratsrede* (Berlin, 1907).—ED.]

values of good and evil, etc., by experiencing, by investigating the facts, but sets himself as a judge over all these. It has not become clear to such a man that all criteria are first derived from contact with the things-themselves, that even *the* criteria are to be so derived. Thus the meaning of the antitheses "real-unreal," "true-false," as well as antitheses of value, must be *phenomenologically clarified*. The only thing that remains is something with a sense similar to that of the word "true," something elevated above the antithesis of true and false which belongs only to the sphere of propositions. This is the "self-givenness" of an intended object [*eines Gemeinten*] in the immediate self-evidence of intuition. This is the truth of which Spinoza speaks, in these great and profound words: "The Truth is the criterion of itself *and* of the false," a truth which he reserved for his intuitive knowledge. The truth is never to be obtained through the critique of other doctrines. Moreover, "self-given" is not the same as "indubitable" or "irrefutable." This "truth itself" is the original basis of that truth which is the opposite of falsity and which is valid in the sphere of propositions and judgments. Thus, self-givenness and evidence (insight) are ideals of cognition which *are prior to* truth and falsity. Naturally, the man of criteria once again asks: "What criterion is there then for self-givenness?" And then, in psychologistic fashion, he searches for a *feeling of evidence* or a special *experience* which will always automatically recur like a minor miracle or sign when something is evident in this way. Naturally, such a thing does not exist. Or he asks for norms to which judgments correspond. But the idea of a "criterion of self-givenness" is already inconsistent, since all questions about criteria make sense only when a *symbol* is given in place of the thing-itself which it symbolizes.

Nevertheless, this genuine positivistic and empiricistic principle of phenomenology is in no less stark contrast to everything that up till now has been called *empiricism* and *positivism*. The philosophical doctrines which have these names do not, in fact, examine purely and simply what is *given* in living experience [*Erleben*]; instead, after having taken as their basis an altogether narrow concept of experience [*Erfahrung*], namely, the concept "experience through the senses," they explain that everything which would count as given must be traced back to "experience." Phenomenology rejects the notion that a "concept" of experience ought to be made its basis and demands that even the concepts "sensation" and "sensible" prove themselves phenomenologically. Certainly everything given rests on experience [*Erfahrung*]; but every sort of "experience of something" also leads to a *given*. The trivial and narrow empiricism of the sensationalists fails to recognize this last principle. That empiricism simply suppresses every given which cannot be made to coincide with an impression or with something derived from an impression, or it explains the given *away*. Thus Hume explains away causality, thing, ego, etc. For Kant the given must be composed of sensations and thought. Now there is nothing we have more difficulty in bringing to self-givenness, even indirectly, than just that "sensation" with which this pseudo-empiricism so blithely starts off, as if it were the primary given.[3]

Phenomenological philosophy is fundamentally different from this kind of empiricism in still another sense. It is precisely phenomenology's radical principle of experience [*Erfahrung*] that comes to justify and, indeed, vastly extend the a priori to all the areas of philosophy. Positivism and empiricism, on the other hand, are anti-aprioristic and inductive. Everything which rests on an immediate self-intuition, that is, everything which "is there" "itself" in lived-experience and intuition, is also given a priori as a pure whatness or essence for every possible observation and induction from observation. Propositions which are fulfilled by something given in this way are also a priori true; propositions which run counter to it are a priori false. Experience should no more be equated with sense-experience [4] than with induction.

The apriorism of phenomenology can completely absorb what is correct in the apriorism of Plato and Kant. Yet a gulf still separates it from their theories. The a priori does not become a constituent part of experience through an "activity of formation" or synthesis and the like, much less through the

3. [See the critique of sensationalism in *Der Formalismus in der Ethik und die materiale Wertethik: Neuer Versuch der Grundlegung eines ethischen Personalismus*, 5th ed. rev., *Gesammelte Werke* II (Bern: Francke, 1966), chap. II, sec. A; and in "The Theory of the Three Facts," below.—ED.]

4. Sense-experience is a mode of intuition responsible for selecting. [Namely, contents and objects of perception. See *Formalismus*, pp. 410, 413, 445.—TRANS.]

acts of a "self" or a "transcendental consciousness." Rather, the foundational order in which phenomena are given as the contents of immediate lived-experience, an order which is not based on an "understanding" but on the *essence* of these phenomena, is responsible for the fact that, for instance, all propositions which are based on "spatiality" also hold true of bodies, that all propositions which hold true of values also hold true of the goods and actions which bear these values in themselves. That is, everything that holds true of the (self-given) *essence* of objects (and of *essential relationships*) also holds true a priori of the objects which have that essence. What holds true of the essence of an inanimate motion holds also in a case of observable motion; what holds true of the essence of an object as such also holds for this particular object. The case is analogous with essential relationships, as, for example, that the noble is to be preferred to the useful, or that $3 + 3 = 6$. In addition to the so-called *formal a priori* of the basic intuitive facts of pure logic, every discipline, number theory, set theory, group theory, geometry (including the geometry of colors and tones), mechanics, physics, chemistry, biology, psychology—each reveals, upon closer inspection, a whole body of *material a priori* propositions which rest on essential insight. These extend the scope of the a priori tremendously.[5] And in these cases a priori in the *logical* sense is always a *consequence* of the a priori *intuitive facts* which constitute the objects of judgments and propositions (e.g., the principle of contradiction).

Thus, the phenomenological apriorism stays clear of all the various matches made by the theory of the a priori in the dominant trends of philosophy, with all the forms of idealism, subjectivism, spontaneism, transcendentalism, Kant's so-called "Copernican standpoint," rationalism, and formalism.

At the same time, phenomenological philosophy is distinguished from the prevalent forms of empiricism *and* rationalism by the fact that it is interested in the total mental experience which takes place in intentional acts, or in any of the forms of "consciousness of something," not only in the "representation" of objects. (The word "representation" is used here not in contrast to perception, but as signifying the unity of

5. See *Formalismus*, II, A.

"theoretical" behavior.) In principle, the world is given in lived-experience as the "bearer of values" and as "resistance" as immediately as it is given as an "object." Consequently, we should also be concerned with the essential contents which immediately leap to the eye in acts (and only in the acts) of having a "feeling for something," for example, for the beauty or loveliness of a landscape, in acts of loving and hating, or wishing and not-wishing, of religious longing and believing. We should be concerned with these contents in contrast to everything which I merely come upon in myself as a mental state, a feeling, e.g., everything I come upon, if I have the "opportunity," not in acts of the former sort, but in re-presentational [*vor-stelligen*] acts via inner perception. And here, too, the a priori and essential content should be distinguished from the contingent content of the object of possible observation and induction.

Just at this point it seems to many people extremely difficult to distinguish the content of lived-*experience* and the fullness of what shows itself in it and only in it [6] from the life which has simply been lived [*von dem bloss gelebten Leben*]. The life which has simply been lived, as a lifeless accompaniment or a residue of experience, can be simultaneously or subsequently observed in the form of a so-called "mental experience." And yet these two are not only relatively distinct, in the sense that the one belongs to the so-called actually present, and the other, to the immediate past; they are *absolutely* distinct facts [*Tatsachen*].

[II] PHENOMENOLOGY AND PSYCHOLOGY

SOMETHING CAN BE *self-given* only if it is no longer given merely through any sort of symbol; in other words, only if it is not "meant" as the mere "fulfillment" of a sign which is previously defined in some way or other. In this sense *phenomenological* philosophy is a continual *desymbolization of the world*.

Neither the natural world-view nor (especially) science

6. This content is not one whit less objective because its appearance and givenness depend solely on acts of the former type. [This parenthetical comment originally was made in the text.—TRANS.]

ever leads to self-givenness. Science, to be sure, rejects the special content of the natural world-view as the "basis" of its own statements; yet science can explain this content and its origin with its own presuppositions and with the help of its own objects and forces. However, science in doing so still retains the basic form of the natural world-view.

In the natural view of nature, colors and tones, for example, never come into play themselves. Instead, visible qualities are intuited only insofar as they have a representative function that is used in distinguishing and assessing the unities of things or processes and their "properties." These are unities with a certain usefulness, practical unities of meaning, such as "clock —time to get up." However, every content, for example, the phenomenon of the essence "real," or that of "thinghood," etc., is intuited in the same fashion. Thinghood does not appear as an essence in the things of natural perception but is wholly consumed in marking out this or that as a thing. Analogously, psychic stirrings [Regung] are only given, only raise themselves in their unities out of the stream of life, to the extent that some sort of possible behavior is thereby modified or distinguished from another unity of behavior. Thus, the natural world-view is full of symbol and of the accompanying *transcendence* of that which is symbolized.

Science frees itself from the various considerations of material utility that rule the entire organization of the contents of natural perception as they do natural language and its unities of meaning. Science frees itself from the pragmatic perspective of the concepts and concrete unities of natural perception. On the other hand, the symbolization of what is still given in science is significantly increased. For science, colors and tones, for example, are totally transformed into mere *signs*. In physics, colors become signs of the motions of a particular substratum on which science also bases the light ray and its refractions by certain substances. In physiology, colors are signs of the chemical processes in the optical nerve; in psychology, they are signs of so-called sensations. The color *itself* is *not* contained in these. In the natural world-view, a *red* in the green tree is given only insofar as it is needed for revealing the cherry which a man intends to get. Similarly, colors come into consideration in the three relevant sciences only insofar as they are unambiguous *signs* for the differences between such motions, nervous processes, and sensations. However, in the presence of science the colors *themselves,* their pure content, turn into a mere X. In each case this means: This color red, for example, is the X which corresponds to this motion, this nervous process, this sensation. X, however, is not given itself. Thus draft after draft is drawn on *red,* so to speak. So long as we remain within science these drafts are negotiated in infinitely varied ways against other drafts which are drawn on *red,* but they are never definitively redeemed.

Now, phenomenology is, in principle, that mode of cognition which retraces, step by step, the process of this complicated negotiation and ultimately redeems all the drafts. Its deepest intention is to redeem not only all those drafts which science draws, but all those, too, which the complicated existence and life of every civilization and its symbolism draw on human existence. Phenomenology has reached its goal when every symbol and half-symbol is completely fulfilled through the "self-given," including everything which functions in the natural world-view and in science as a *form* of understanding (everything "categorial"); when everything transcendent and only "meant" has become *immanent* to a lived-experience and intuition. It has reached its goal at the point where there is no longer any transcendence or symbol. Everything which elsewhere is still formal becomes, for phenomenology, a material for intuition. And the attitude phenomenological philosophy has toward a religious object or an ethical value is exactly the same as the one it has toward the color *red.*[7]

Thus, what constitutes the unity of phenomenology is not a particular region of facts, such as, for example, mental or ideal objects, nature, etc., but only *self-givenness* in *all* possible regions.

This clearly shows that phenomenology has just as much and just as little to do with *psychology* as it has with mathematics, with logic, with physics, with biology, or with theology —and not a bit more. Unless, of course, independent phenomenological investigation should lead to the result that the essence of the *mental* is given immediately, while the physical object or other kinds of object are given indirectly. Phenom-

7. [See Scheler, *Formalismus,* and "The Problems of Religion," *On the Eternal in Man,* trans. Bernard Noble (London: Student Christian Movement Press, 1960).—ED.]

enology, however, can prove just the opposite.[8] The only thing which deserves to be called "mental" is not any sort of object of a "consciousness of something," of an intentional act; the real astronomical sun is such an object, as are the numbers 3 and 4, which are not mental. Only such objects are mental as are given as lived-experiences of an experiencing ego [*Erlebnis-Ich*] and to whose givenness a special direction and form of "consciousness of something" or of intentional act essentially belong. This is the direction and form of "inner perception." Inner perception is distinguished from "external" perception as much by its direction [9] as by the form of the manifold of what is given in the two cases. In external perception, this form is spatiotemporal separation and apartness [*Auseinander*]; in internal perception, togetherness in the ego. Moreover, it is no less distinct from the perception of the lived-body. The givenness of the lived-body does not consist in the coordination of the facts of the external perception (of the corporeal body) with those of the inner perception (of the ego); the lived-body presents a particular essential givenness (the phenomenon of the lived-body) not based on the corporeal body or on the ego.[10] Finally, the mentally real, as explanatory causal psychology understands it, is just that which is hypothetically *projected into* the datum of inner perception for the sake of certain explanatory goals.[11]

Certainly psychology, like every science, requires a phenomenological foundation. In psychology, too, what is self-given must be kept *separate* from everything that is only symbolically and indirectly given. Essences are present in mental experiences and there are essential interconnections between these essences. In psychology, also, there is a wide domain of the non-formal a priori which no inner observation can either verify or remove; on the other hand, every possible understanding of the sense of another's mental expressions of life, an

8. See my essay on "The Idols of Self-Knowledge" [translated above].

9. Inner perception is not distinguished from external perception only by the contents of the perceiving act, or only in relation to what is outside and inside for a body [*Leib*]. Their distinction is independent of the institution "lived-body." [This originally stood in the text between dashes.—TRANS.]

10. [See *Formalismus*, VI, A, 3, e, f, g, on the mental, the givenness of the lived-body, the ego, etc.—ED.]

11. There are thus three concepts of consciousness: (1) "consciousness of"; (2) phenomena of inner perception; and (3) the real life of the soul. [See "The Idols of Self-Knowledge."—TRANS.]

understanding, for example, of the statements of the "experimental subject" in psychological experiments, must presuppose this a priori domain.

All the basic concepts of empirical psychology and their presuppositions, namely, the experience of a stream of experience in objective time, the assumption of so-called basic mental classes, the concepts of reproduction, association, etc., must be brought to absolute clarity by the phenomenology of the mental.[12] However, one thing is completely clear from the preceding comments: the lived-experiences investigated by psychology are already real processes and things which can be "meant" in a multiplicity of acts and in acts of different individuals; in the course of these there can be characteristics and features which are not experienced and thus go all the more unnoticed and unobserved. Such acts can never be "self-given," any more than a corporeal thing can be "self-given" in the natural perception of the external world. Furthermore, just as there is a distinction in the physical sphere between illusion and reality (sometimes with physical conditions, as in the case of rainbows, Fata Morgana, mirror images, the brokenness of a stick in water, and sometimes with physiological conditions, as in the case of the objects of optical illusions—for instance, the longer appearance of the vertical line in a visual object), there is the same distinction in the mental sphere between real and illusory pain, real and illusory feelings, real and illusory perception (e.g., genuine hallucination).[13]

Thus it would be a great mistake to think that the mental sphere coincides with the *immediately* given, which does not permit any genuine illusions (as distinct from mere errors, for example, those committed in judgments which subsume lived-experiences under concepts). It would be a mistake to think that inner perception has some sort of evidential advantage over "external" perception, as if, perhaps, the existence of the ego were a shade more evident than the existence of matter or a corporeal world. Instead, every possible sort of sham-ego [*Scheinichs*] exists, for example, the "Hamlet-self" of an actor on the stage, the self of social roles, or one of the selves of divided consciousness (schizophrenia). Each and every empirical perception is *eo ipso* not-evident and always gives its ob-

12. See pt. II, *Formalismus.*
13. See my study, "The Idols of Self-Knowledge."

ject only more or less *symbolically* and always as an object which *transcends* the content of perception.

Phenomenology breaks directly with every idealism of the ego such as one finds in the theories of Descartes, Berkeley, Fichte, and Schopenhauer, all of whom confuse phenomenological immediacy with mental givenness or, as it may be, with relatedness to an ego [*Ichbezogenheit*]. Phenomenology rejects both. On the other hand, there do exist *physical* phenomena, in the strictest sense of the word, which exclude the possibility of illusion (or a distinction between semblance and actuality) just as much as certain mental phenomena do. For example, illusion is impossible in the face of the absolute distinction between the pure essences [*puren Washeiten*] in which something is given as dead or alive, as physiological [14] or as belonging to the external world, as material or immaterial (e.g., as a shadow). The physical as such, together with the essential distinctions within it, never shows itself to be in any way created or "formed" or even "inferred" by an act of thought from the mental, which is allegedly the only thing *immediately* given. Nor is the sphere of mental being merely left over as a residue or remainder, that is, as that which remains over and above those alleged "objectifications" in which the organization of the mental would presuppose a reference to the natural object and to the distinctions given in it (Natorp, Münsterberg, *et al.*). Rather, the mental has its *own* way of being given in inner perception, a way which can neither be denied (as a mode of perceiving distinct from external perception) nor be reduced to external perception, as those would do who believe they can create the mental from the relation of an environmental content to an organism (Mach, Avenarius, and others).[15]

Thus the phenomenology of the mental is completely and absolutely distinct not only from any *explanatory* psychology but also from any *descriptive* psychology. There is no description without an observation of single processes. In the phenomenological attitude, however, *something meant* is brought

14. [Scheler uses *physisch* here in the narrower sense of "physiological," i.e., the physical which is dependent on the lived-body. See *Formalismus*, p. 157, n. 1.—ED.]

15. [See *Formalismus*, VI, A, 3, e.—ED.]

to sight [*er-schaut*] and nothing is observed. Every description is directed to a single empirical fact, that is, to something phenomenologically "transcendent"; a description always selects its object in advance in accordance with those features which are important for a possible explanation.

This fundamental relation between phenomenology and psychology and between the phenomenology of the mental and psychology, excluding, as it does, every so-called psychologistic conception of phenomenology, does not imply that phenomenology need not display the most abundant concrete connections with all that is pursued today under the name "psychology." In the most diverse investigations—for example, those of Bergson, Dilthey in his *Ideen über eine beschreibende und zergliedernde Psychologie,* W. James, Natorp in his *Einleitung in die Psychologie,* and what Münsterberg calls "subjectivizing psychology"—one finds rich and interesting chapters belonging entirely to the phenomenology of the mental, even though the investigators are not conscious of this fact and usually mix up their phenomenological results with empirical psychological results.

Indeed, of a few investigators, Bergson, for example, we may even say that, confronted with the task of the phenomenology of the mental, they lose sight of the proper and specific tasks of empirical psychology, while, on the other hand, they fail completely to recognize extramental phenomenological facts, and so finally fall into psychologism.

Far richer and even more fruitful are the concrete relations between the phenomenology of the mental and the physical and the works which are usually published nowadays under the rubric "experimental psychology." These works, and even more the true results they contain, do not all have an inductive meaning, in the sense that the experience which is evoked by the experimental technique can be identically repeated or observed and that inductive conclusions can be obtained from these observations. In many ways the psychological experiments they perform are only "illustrative experiments" through which one essential stage in the formation of the experiential content in question is brought to immediate intuition. Or they are like Bühler's thought experiments which supply examples of phenomenological insight into the essence of *meaning*

[*Bedeutung*], as opposed to that which is only signitively "meant" and to all imaginative representations.[16] Thus, in the works of D. Katz on the modalities of color phenomena, of E. R. Jaensch on the space of visual perception, of P. Linke and M. Wertheimer on illusions of movement, of N. Ach on the activity of the will, of K. Mittenzwey on abstraction, of C. Stumpf on acoustics, of F. Krüger and especially W. Köhler on the vocal qualities of tones, to name only a few,[17] one finds a great many sections, belonging partly to the phenomenology of the mental, partly to the phenomenology of qualities, and partly to the phenomenology of the simplest physical phenomena, which vastly enrich our phenomenological knowledge. To be sure, these researchers (with the exception of Stumpf, who sharply distinguishes phenomenology from psychology, but in limiting himself to the phenomena which he calls "sensory" unduly restricts the former) for the most part lack a clear consciousness of the unity of phenomenological investigation, so that the phenomenological element is never clearly contrasted with what is empirically ascertained and subsequently explained. Furthermore, the phenomenological results often appear to be the outcome of experiments with an inductive import and, as it were, slip casually into the investigation. However, this appearance in no way prevents the two from enriching and fertilizing one another. Moreover, it does not keep many things which belong to the phenomenology of the sensible form in which physical phenomena are given (and, consequently, many things which

16. See also A. Messer, *Empfindung und Denken* (Leipzig, 1908). [Scheler probably has in mind Karl Bühler's "Tatsachen und Probleme zu einer Psychologie der Denkvorgänge," *Archiv für die gesamte Psychologie,* 1907–8.—TRANS.]

17. [Scheler probably had the following works in mind: David Katz, *Der Aufbau der Farbewelt* (*Zeitschrift für Psychologie,* Supplement VII), 2d ed. (Leipzig, 1930), English translation by R. B. MacLeod, *The World of Colour* (London, 1935); E. R. Jaensch, "Über die Wahrnehmung des Raumes," *ibid.* (Supplement VI, 1911); Paul Linke, "Die stroboskopischen Taüschungen und das Problem des Sehens von Bewegungen," *Psychologische Studien,* Vol. III (1907); Max Wertheimer, "Experimentelle Studien über das Sehen der Bewegung," *ibid.,* Vol. LXI (1912); N. K. Ach, *Über die Willenstätigkeit und das Denken* (Leipzig, 1905); Karl Mittenzwey, "Über abstrahierende Apperzeption," *Psychologische Studien,* Vol. II (1907); Carl Stumpf, *Tonpsychologie,* Vols. I–II (Leipzig, 1883–90); Felix Krüger, "Die Theorie der Konsonanz, (Teilen I–III)," *Psychologische Studien,* Vols. I–V (1906–10); Wolfgang Köhler, "Akustische Untersuchungen," *Zeitschrift für Psychologie,* Vol. LXXII (1915); and Köhler, *Gestalt Psychology,* new ed. (New York: Liveright, 1970).—TRANS.]

belong to the phenomenological foundation of the physiology of the senses), from appearing in these works as "psychology," even though the investigated phenomenon is not given in an experienced relation to the ego.

The reason for this confusion is that these psychological researchers think they can delimit the domain of the mental without introducing the fact of the ego and the concept of the ego, failing to recognize not only the special task of psychology, but also the whole extent and unity of the problems of a phenomenology of the environment of an embodied creature, of which the phenomenology of sensible phenomena forms only a small part.[18]

The influence of phenomenology on a few younger psychiatrists is especially exciting and reacts powerfully on phenomenological philosophy itself. The introduction of the objective characteristics of the images produced in illusion and delusion (which deviate more or less widely from the objects of normal, inner, and external perception and representation as well as from emotional functions and acts) often affords the most surprising insights into the essential constituents of the corresponding normal act-complexes and the essentially necessary structure of their correlative objects. These insights give extraordinarily useful support to the essential distinction between *understanding* and *explaining* the life of another's soul and another's behavior, as well as promoting a solution to the problem of the phenomenology of the *modes of givenness of the other person* and the other's consciousness. For those who want to go into these matters in more precise detail, I can cite my work *On the Phenomenology and Theory of the Feeling of Sympathy and of Love and Hate;* K. Jaspers' "Zur Analyse der Trugwahrnehmungen," "Die phänomenologische Forschungsrichtung in der Psychopathologie," "Kausale und verständliche Zusammenhänge zwischen Schicksal und Psychose bei *dementia praecox*"; W. Specht's "Zur Morphologie der Halluzinationen und Illusionen"; and, finally, my two short works, "The Idols of Self-Knowledge" and "Zur Psychologie der sogennanten Rentenhysterie." [19]

18. [See the following essay, "The Theory of the Three Facts," sec. I.—ED.]

19. [The second essay appears in *Vom Umsturz der Werte*, 4th ed. rev., *Gesammelte Werke* III (Bern: Francke, 1955), pp. 195–309. Jaspers' work

[III] PHENOMENOLOGICAL CONTROVERSY

A FEW YEARS AGO Wilhelm Wundt subjected Edmund Husserl's *Logical Investigations* to an interesting critique.[20] I shall go into only one point of his critique here, because the relevant statement represents a typical misunderstanding to which phenomenological investigations, especially published ones, are subject. Wundt remarks that in *Logical Investigations* he often observed that Husserl never really says what the investigated things *are*, what, for example, a judgment or a meaning or a wish is. Instead he is always saying, at length, what they are not. Thus, there are sentences of this kind: "Judgment is not a representation plus a recognition, it is not the synthesis or analysis of a 'representation,' " etc., and if such a statement is made then the conclusion which follows is an empty tautology, e.g., "Judgment is—just judgment."

Wundt's remark is itself an interesting phenomenological example of the fact that a statement can be true and yet completely empty of understanding. In fact, many phenomenological discussions, and not only in Husserl, take the formal course which Wundt formulates here. What follows from this? That one must read a phenomenological book with a completely *different attitude* than Wundt adopted and as it is in fact necessary to adopt for books which communicate observations and describe what is observed, or that want to prove something inductively or deductively. If a book with such an intention contains so many negations and then caps things off with a tautology, then one should judge it even less favorably than Wundt judged the *Logical Investigations*. One ought to toss it into the fire! However, what Wundt did not consider is nothing less than the possible sense of a phenomenological discussion. This sense is only: to *bring* the reader (or listener) to see that which, by its essence, can only be "seen"; it is in view of this that all the propositions which occur in the book, all the con-

appears in altered form in *General Psychopathology*, trans. J. Hoenig and Marion Hamilton (Chicago: University of Chicago Press, 1963). The actual title of Specht's work is "Zur Phänomenologie und Morphologie der pathologischen Wahrnehmungstäuschungen," *Zeitschrift für Pathopsychologie*, Vol. II, no. 2 (1912–13).—TRANS.]

20. [This critique can be found in Wilhelm Wundt's *Kleine Schriften*, Vol. I, (Leipzig, 1910), chap. VI, "Psychologismus und Logizismus,"—ED.]

clusions, all the provisional definitions which are introduced as they are needed, all the provisional descriptions, all the chains of argument and proof, have simply the function of a "pointer," pointing to what is to be brought to sight (Husserl). However, what is to be brought to sight can never be present in any of the judgments, concepts, or definitions in the book itself. There it is necessarily the X which circulates through everything which stands in this book, until the tautology instructs the reader: "Now look there, then you will see it!" What Wundt takes to be a mere "tautology" has this sense.

We can readily understand that until this concluding exhibition takes place various negations are present. Their function is successively to illuminate the various complexes in which the phenomenon occurs and to delimit the phenomenon on all sides from all the other ingredient factors in these complexes until nothing more remains than—it-itself. Its resistance to every possible attempt to define it first shows it to be a genuine phenomenon. In a book of positive science what the author has in mind is never given in itself but is always there for the investigation only as an object bound to other objects by certain *relations*. In a book of phenomenology what the author has in mind is never there, because the object must first be brought to sight by means of all the propositions, concepts, etc., in the book. Thus the author can proceed only by delimiting and paring away, only by purifying and rejecting all hasty and premature definitions (by showing that they are circular). Even images which are immediately and clearly given *as* images, not those *clandestine* images which stealthily substitute themselves for the matter at hand, can be used to bring about the seeing of the phenomenon if they reciprocally limit one another.

To be sure, the special cognitive goal of a phenomenological investigation is the source of a special problem of the possibility and method of *communicating* what is known in this way. This problem should not be concealed. It does not exist for any philosophy which openly or—as is mostly the case— covertly starts by assuming that the only fit subject of knowledge is that about which one can *talk* in unambiguous symbols, that which can be socially communicated to anyone one pleases, that which can be the subject of debate, etc. The problem does not exist for a philosophy which proceeds from the supposition that this phonetic complex "object" means the same as "what several individuals can *identify* through symbols" or that "object" equals the X about which *universally valid* statements are possible. However, this social conventionalism must face another problem in place of the phenomenologist's problem. It must answer the question whether, in any or all the speakers, the *sense* of the utterance fulfills itself in *something given* and whether the object which is obtained in this way is perhaps merely a universally accepted *fable convenue*, completely empty of insight and cognition. The problem, to put it figuratively, is whether there are sufficient funds to cover all these great transactions of exchange and speech! Phenomenology rejects on principle that falsification of the idea of an object according to which the object must first cross the hurdle of symbolic identifiability in order to prove that it is indeed an object.

Identifiability follows from the essence of the object, not vice versa. Still less is an object that about which a universally valid statement is possible, nor is it simply a so-called compound representation "universally" valid and necessary in all cases. These descriptions fail to distinguish an empty convention from a cognition. Philosophical theses, too, have their special ethical pathos, and it is true that phenomenological philosophy is the antithesis of all rapidly produced talk-philosophy. One speaks here somewhat less, is silent more, and sees more, perhaps that aspect of the world which can no longer be discussed. To say that the world exists in order to be designated with univocal symbols and to be arranged and talked about with their help—indeed, that it is *nothing* before it enters into this talk—is to capture far too little of its being and its sense!

The essence of an object and of being (which can be the being of an act as well as the being of a value or a resistance) does not exclude the possibility that only *one man* in *one* act brings something to self-givenness for himself. Indeed, it does not even exclude the possibility that a particular object can be given in this way to *one person* alone. The essence does not exclude the possibility that something is true and good for an individual and thus that an absolute truth and insight is essentially valid for one individual and yet strictly objective. Only the subjectivistic volatilization of the object into identifiability, of truth into "universally valid statements," of a genuine insight into the necessity of judgment (whose essence is negative), excludes these possibilities.[21]

Nonetheless, this does not mean that the discussion of phenomenological issues cannot enter into the question of universally valid truth or into the problem of how we can still *understand* an individually valid truth in spite of its individual validity—contrary to what the opponents of phenomenologists like to claim, not in order to refute phenomenologists but to silence them. For this much is clear: If what is *seen* by A is a *genuine essence*, then everyone must be able to see it, since its inclusion in the content of all possible experience is essentially necessary. The question can only be: "What happens when B, after A has made an attempt to show him this, asserts that he does not see it?" This can have the most diverse causes. For example, A claims that he has seen something which, in fact, he has only observed in himself; he deceives himself in the phenomenological sense of the word, that is, he claims to have insight where he has none. Furthermore, the way he goes about exhibiting the phenomenon can be poor and inadequate. B can fail to have understood A. B can "deceive" himself phenomenologically. There is no so-called universal criterion here. Each case must be decided on its own. Certainly a phenomenological controversy, since it has to do with asymbolic knowledge which must, in turn, be transmitted and agreed upon via symbols, is considerably more difficult to settle than a controversy over things which are themselves defined as mere possibilities of fulfilling symbols and conventions. It is a deeper and more radical controversy. The symbol is used in phenomenology in an entirely different sense than in positive science, which can begin with more or less arbitrary definitions. However, phenomenological controversy is not beyond settlement, except in the case of individual truths, where it makes no sense to raise a dispute—where, instead, the only sensible conduct is to appreciate that this is a truth or a good for him who asserts it to be such.

21. [See the critique of the concepts of object and truth mentioned in the text in *Formalismus,* esp. pp. 373–76, 394; and *Ressentiment,* trans. William W. Holdheim (New York: Free Press of Glencoe, 1961).—ED.]

[IV] PHENOMENOLOGICAL PHILOSOPHY
AND THE THEORY OF COGNITION

1. *Limits and task of the theory of cognition*

IN ONE QUITE ESSENTIAL POINT phenomenological philosophy has a deep affinity with the various forms of the so-called transcendental theory of cognition. Phenomenology's procedure is such that its results remain completely *independent* of the particular organization of human nature, the concrete organization of the bearer of the acts, the "consciousness-of" which it studies. In a genuine phenomenological investigation we abstract from two things when we execute the so-called phenomenological reduction (Husserl): First, the *actual performance of the act* [*realen Aktvollzug*] and all the accompanying phenomena which do not come within the sense and direction of the act itself, along with all the characteristics of its bearer [*Träger*] (animal, man, god). Second, we disregard any *positing* (belief or unbelief) *of the particular coefficient of reality* with which the content of the act is "given" in natural perception and in science (e.g., actuality, appearance, imagination, illusion). This coefficient of reality itself and its essence remain the object of investigation. We do not bracket *them*, but rather the explicit or implicit judgments in which they are posited. Thus we do not bracket the possibility of positing them, but only the positing of them in some one mode. Only what we encounter directly, that is, in an experience with such and such an essence of a content having such and such an essence, is a topic for phenomenological investigation.

The distinctions between the essences and "foundations" of acts, e.g., the distinction between perception and memory, are independent of the particular organization of their bearers and would remain in force whatever changes this organization might undergo. Similarly, the essential connection between the essence of an act and the essence of its content, for instance, between seeing and color, enjoys this independence. We discover in this way the structure and intrinsic relations of spirit [*Geistes*] which belong to every possible world. Although we study this spirit in men, just as the principle of the conservation of energy can be studied in men and indeed was discovered in men by Robert Mayer, this spirit is still completely independent of human organization. This independence is what entitles us to form for ourselves an idea of "God." On the side of the content, we find a structure of interconnected essences belonging to a world which all the empirical facts of our human world or of our empirical milieu merely exemplify. The structure of this world and the structure of the spirit form one essentially connected structure in all their parts. It is not possible for us to look upon the world-structure as merely a "product" of the spirit or as merely the result of the laws of our experience of the world or the laws of spiritual experience in general. Even the "ego" is in every sense only an *object* in the world, the constituent element of the "inner world"; in no sense is it the condition or correlate of the world.[22]

That which can be exhibited and brought to sight, after the most scrupulous phenomenological reduction, as an essence and essential connection cannot be confirmed or disconfirmed by any possible empirical research, observation, description, induction, deduction, or causal research (in the domain of the real). However, when anything is being empirically established we must pay attention to this essence.

The method for bringing genuine essences and essential interconnections to sight is as follows. If the question is whether something already given [*vorgegeben*] is a *genuine essence*, it is evident that if it is such, any attempt to observe the pregiven is impossible. For in order to direct observation upon the object and its nature, we must already *presuppose* that we have seen the pregiven exemplified in some object. We cannot observe "that something is color," "that something is spatial," "that something is alive"; we can observe that *this* colored surface is triangular, that this body is oval-shaped, that this living organism has four legs. If I try to observe "that something is a color," I find that in order to circumscribe a circle of possible objects for observation I must look to everything which is of this *essence*, which consequently is already seen. If, on the other hand, it is a question of distinguishing essences from mere concepts, then an essence is everything

22. [On person, world, and self, see *Formalismus*, VI, A, 2.—ED.]

which inevitably and intrinsically becomes entangled in a *circular* definition whenever we attempt to define it. Thus, an essence as such, as a pure what-ness, is in itself neither universal nor individual; both universality and individuality are concepts which first make sense in relation to objects depending on whether the essence comes to light in several objects or only in one. Thus, in this sense, there is an essence also of individuals. An essential connection, however, proves to be distinct from any merely factual conjunction by virtue of the fact that when I try to confirm the factual relation I must make use of the pregiven connection which I have seen. An essential connection is distinct from an inferrable connection, since every search for proof inevitably *presupposes* the pregiven as a law in accordance with which the proof is carried out. Every proof becomes circular, or, in the case of allegedly causal connections, becomes a circular explanation.

Essential connections and essences in this sense have an ontological [*ontisch*] meaning from the start. And in this sense the *ontology of spirit and world* precedes any theory of cognition.

A problem of cognition or valuation [*Werthalten*][23] first comes up when the phenomenological reduction is once again annulled, step by step and in a fixed order, giving rise both to the question of how what is or can be phenomenologically given is selected on the basis of the concrete organization of the subjects of acts [*Aktträger*] and their particular cognitive goals, and to the question of the existential relativity or absoluteness of the relevant types of objects vis-à-vis the various basic characteristics of the bearers of acts. Only insofar as these basic characteristics of the bearers of acts (e.g., man) rest in turn on essences (e.g., finite spirit, living creature in general), and not on empirical determinations (the excitation thresholds of sensation, the range of humanly audible tones), does this investigation belong to the theory of cognition and not to the technique of cognition and methodology. Thus the theory of cognition must ask, for example, whether similarity belongs to absolutely existing objects as much as identity and difference do, or whether it belongs only to objects existentially relative to a living creature; it must ask whether spatiality is given as

23. [On the appreciation and apprehension of values, see *Formalismus*, esp. pp. 100 ff.—ED.]

absolutely as a purely extensive quality of redness or whether its existence is relative to a living creature's external perception.

The theory of cognition, therefore, is a discipline which does not precede or ground phenomenology, but follows it. We should not think that the theory of cognition, in its most comprehensive form, is limited to "theoretical" cognition. It is the theory of the apprehension and elaboration in thought of the objective contents of whatever is. Consequently, it is also the theory of the apprehension of values and the judgment of values, in other words, the theory of valuation and evaluation. However, any such theory presupposes the phenomenological investigation of the essence of that which is given. Cognition and valuation are themselves particular forms of a "consciousness-of-something" built up from the immediate consciousness of self-given facts. Accordingly, cognition, if the word is used meaningfully, always has to do with the act of thinking which selects from the given what it copies or reproduces; it has nothing to do with any production, formation, or construction of the given. There is no cognition without prior recognition [*Kenntnis*]; there is no recognition without the prior existence and self-givenness of the things recognized.

Any theory claiming that the object must first be determined or even produced by the methods of cognition runs counter to the self-evident sense of cognition. So, too, does any theory which wants to decide how cognition is possible before spirit [*Geist*] and concrete data [*Sachgegebenheiten*] have been phenomenologically examined. (Of course, it should reach this decision before affirming a particular real world existing independently of cognition.) There is no way we can refute the old objection, which Nelson acutely formulated recently, that any such theory of cognition is circular, since it must presuppose the possibility of cognition as such and the possibility of a particular type of cognition if it is to achieve cognition of the faculty of cognition.

If we understand by the phrase "theory of cognition" simply a theory concerning the relation between conscious thought, that is, conscious judgment, and a world *already unified and held together* by *prelogically* given essences and their connections, and do not presuppose that this world has a certain empirical constitution, then such an undertaking is meaningful. The specific task of the theory of cognition here is to bring into relief within every region of objects and within every mode of cognition that which functions in the given as the starting point for logical treatment and elaboration. However, the given itself is not given simply *as* the starting point for possible thinking (or as the sum of all pertinent problems). It is no less of a contradiction to acknowledge what was just said (namely, that thought does not simply come upon a completely unorganized *mē on*, the mere sum total of all "problems," as, e.g., Hermann Cohen consistently asserts from his standpoint), to acknowledge that a "description" of the data must precede the posing of the relevant problems, *and* to assert at the same time that the data to be "described" must themselves be regarded as standing under the dominion of "transcendental" laws of thoughts, which have only to be found. As pleasing as it is in itself that eminent scholars like Nicolai Hartmann, Emil Lask, and (although in a quite different sense) Richard Hönigswald wish to grant phenomenology its own domain, within the theory of cognition itself, it has not yet become clear to them that by making these concessions, which are originally alien to their own point of departure, they deprive themselves of the right to let a critical theory of cognition precede phenomenology.[24] With these concessions the embarrassing *mē on* is simply removed to the sphere of that which is given to judgmental consciousness as something formed and ordered in it by the categories of objects. They fail to recognize this as the absurd consequence of a false starting point, and thus maintain the theory that cognition is the copying of the object by judgmental consciousness. Only the fundamental insight that any question of a criterion presupposes at least that we have in view that of which it *is* the criterion can help us beyond this halfway standpoint.

The theory of cognition still faces an abundance of independent problems. Before applying itself to providing a foun-

24. This comes out quite strikingly in the critique Ernst Cassirer addressed to the last works of Emil Lask. [See Emil Lask, *Die Logik der Philosophie und die Kategorienlehre* (Tübingen, 1911), and *Die Lehre vom Urteil* (Tübingen, 1910); and E. Cassirer, "Erkenntnistheorie nebst den Grenzfragen der Logik," *Jahrbücher der Philosophie,* Vol. I (1913).—TRANS.]

dation for the different branches of science and to bringing the data and basic concepts of these into relation, first, with the corresponding regions of fact in the natural world-view (whose "forms" science preserves) and, second, with the phenomeno-logically reduced content of the pertinent region of fact, the theory of cognition must first of all clarify the general *stand-ards or measures of cognition* which are applied in every theory of knowledge.

2.   *The measures of cognition*

The absolute measure of every "cognition" is and remains the *self-givenness* of a fact. This means that a fact is given in the self-evident unity of coincidence between what is "meant" and what is given in experience (in the act of "seeing") ex-actly as it is "meant." Something given in this way is at the same time absolute being; and an object whose being is of this sort exclusively, an object with this kind of pure essence, is given with ideal *adequation.* That is, everything in the natural world-view and in science which plays the role of "form," "function," "selective factor," or everything which functions as the real act [*Aktualität*] or the orientation of the act and for this reason is *never given here, is given* as part of the content of a phenomenological intuition in an act of pure, formless in-tuition. An object which is given only in a pure act of this sort, where nothing in the way of form, function, selective factor (not to mention the organization of the bearer of the act), stands between the pure idea of the act and its object, is and is called "absolute existence."

In contrast, all objects which essentially can only be given in acts with a certain form, quality, or orientation, etc., are called relative, namely, *existentially relative.* They are existen-tially relative to the bearers of those cognitive acts, while these bearers in turn are essentially associated with these forms, etc. The concept of cognition, in contrast to the concept of an object, presupposes the existence of a bearer having some essential organization, whatever that may be. To be sure, the content of cognition continually passes over into the con-tent of self-givenness when it is completely adequate and com-pletely reduced. Nonetheless, the two remain essentially distinct, since cognition can never become the very being [*Selbstsein*] of the object itself, while this being is given when the object is given "in person."

Despite the absolute distinction between absolute and relative existence, the existential relativity of different types of objects forms a graduated series of levels. The theory of cognition must establish the place each type of object, especially the object of science and the sciences, occupies in this series. It encounters here a task of almost inexhaustible scope which up till now has scarcely been grasped with any precision. The levels in this series are distinguished through the fact that the less relative objects are connected with a bearer of increasingly less definite organization, a bearer whose nature is less and less onesidedly grounded in other essences. The idea of God might serve as the limit concept of the bearer of the adequate cognition of all absolute objects. In this way we are able to establish which objects are relative, for example, to a finite bearer in general. We can ask this question of the object "equality," of the object "law" (in the one case, law = functional dependence, in another, causal law in the sense of temporal succession), of the form of a thing (which as thing is never self-given in perception), of spatiality and temporality, of the distinction of true-false, etc. For example, does "God" also use "laws," or do they fall away for an omni-intuitive being? Are laws objects of cognition only for finite beings? Or does a law or a particular type of law, the mechanistic causal law, only become a particular object for bearers of knowledge who are living creatures and possess bodies? or only for bearers with human organization? This is what pure nominalism thinks, which sees in laws only a way of economizing on human sense-perception and thinks that they can be replaced by an (uneconomical) accumulation of sense-perceptions. As we can see in these examples, these questions are finely and richly differentiated, and, unfortunately, a single example cannot show us exactly how they are to be posed and solved. We shall even pose the question of the level of relativity of all the basic objects of mathematics, sets, groups, number, the object of geometry, in order to decide one day whether Plato was right when he said "God does geometry."

The question of what is *existentially relative* to a *living creature generally* or to anything whatever which is a bearer of the essence "vital movement" and "vital form" (corporeality) proves to be quite fruitful. Regardless of this relativity, a realm of such objects (and we have good reasons for taking the whole object-world of mechanistic physics and association-istic psychology to be one) can be completely independent of the existence of man and man's concrete organization.[25] Indeed, since "life" is not an empirical concept but an essence we can see, and since it is the seeing of this essence in certain objects that first *makes* us add them to the realm of organisms, a realm of objects *of this sort* can, in general, be independent of the existence of every earthly living thing organized in a certain way. The ideal content of this object-world and thus a perfect science of it could be completely independent of our sensory organization. In principle it could be translated into every possible language of a being with a sensory organization, yet this whole object-world would still not be an absolute being, not even one existentially relative to a pure transcendental understanding in Kant's sense. It would remain relative to the active, basic tendency of a possible life in general. This whole world would first "vanish" not before the eyes of God, but before those of a finite, cognitive being, whose body we imagine to be completely reduced.

There is, in principle, no definite limit to the degree of additional relativity we can find in the course of determining the levels of existential relativity. Thus, we can set out types of objects which are existentially relative to a normal human organization, for example, all the contents of man's natural world-view, a visual object [*Sehding*] like the moon or the sun there in the sky, or all normal objects of illusion, like the vertical line which appears to be longer in a square. Indeed, we are forced to go further and further in this direction. There are objects which are existentially relative to certain races, based on the particular forms in which they comprehend the content of the inner and external world. These come to our notice especially in the phenomenology of the structure of languages. Similarly there are structures of lived-experience relative to a particular cultural epoch. These structures hold sway in all the formations of this epoch and can be discovered in them. A phenomenological doctrine of world-views, such as

25. [See *Formalismus*, VI, A, 3, g.—ED.]

the pioneering genius of Wilhelm Dilthey and his school tried to set up as the foundation of all the cultural sciences, first obtains its exact foundations from a phenomenological investigation into this context. We can also exhibit objects and the corresponding structures of experience which are relative to man and woman, or, again, objects relative to inner and external perception, as well as to the givenness of the lived-body. Finally, we find, in a hallucinated object, for example, an object which is relative to a *single* individual during a definite interval of time. I have shown elsewhere that this way of treating things is also necessary in the case of values.[26]

It is clear that this relativity of objects has absolutely nothing to do with what is commonly called "subjective," just as this whole body of theory concerning existential relativity has nothing in the least to do with psychology. Indeed, the objects of the inner world and of self-reflection, the objects of experience of the self and of others, have different grades of existential relativity, just as the objects of the external world or religious objects do (e.g., actual feeling and illusory or hallucinated feeling, imagined pain and actual pain). The psychologist is just as much subject to the structure of experience of the inner world proper to his cultural epoch as the natural scientist is to the structure of this epoch's experience of the external world. The associationist psychology of the seventeenth and eighteenth centuries, together with the dominance of a mechanistic metaphysics of nature, is the result of a structure within which this epoch generally experienced the world, a structure the phenomenologist can grasp with precision. The mechanistic-individualistic conception of society and history during this period and the organization of the world of religion manifest in the experience of the deists demonstrably correspond to this structure.

Thus, as we carry out the theory of the existential relativity of objects, it is important to note that relativity to *human organizations* in no way plays a special role but only forms a transitional point. In particular, any theory (e.g., agnosticism, as well as the Kantian theory of the "thing-in-itself," or of the distinctions between illusion-phenomenon-thing-in-itself which rest on this) which would like to limit the cognizable in general

26. See *Formalismus*, V.

to the objects which are relative to a human organization or to a so-called transcendental understanding become patently meaningless. A vast series of different levels of existential relativity leads from the absolute object which is essentially completely cognizable [27] to the object of hallucination, passing at varying intervals through the objects of all regions of fact. In this sense there are no so-called limits of cognition in general, but only limits relative to the particular mode and quantity of cognition achieved by certain active agents. In saying this we are presupposing that we can phenomenologically exhibit this mode of cognition as such and thus achieve a cognition which is not "relative" in the same sense and on the same level, an absolute cognition of the essences constituting these agents.

Thus, strictly speaking, the only thing which is "relative" is never cognition but only the *existence* of the objects and the *limits* of cognition. The "limits" are more or less relative, not cognition itself. Thus, there certainly are "limits" to the content of *man's natural world-view*. For example, we do not find among its objects, which we designate collectively the "environment" (milieu) of men, the kinds of radiation with which we are acquainted from physics. The particular content of this natural object-world should never be taken as a given to which science would have to pay heed. The *"facts" of science,* and not only its "things," its atoms, ions, electrons, and constants, forces, and laws, are never contained in the facts of the natural world-view, nor can they be *abstracted* from them, as the older empiricism assumed. They are entirely new "states of affairs" [*Sachverhalte*] selected in accordance with principles of selection germane to the science in question, from all the pure or phenomenological facts that have been reduced to the level of states of affairs.[28]

Naturally, these principles never determine the content of those states of affairs, but as inner laws of the "observer" they do determine *which* of those states of affairs come to be facts of this or that science. They determine which ones having

27. We leave open here the question of the degree of adequation with which even absolute objects can be cognized. [This sentence originally stood in the text between dashes.—TRANS.]

28. [On this and what follows, see the following essay on the "Three Facts."—ED.]

to do with colors come to be facts of the physics of colors, or facts of the physiology of color, or of the psychology of color, or of the history of color-vision. Never and nowhere does science start from so-called sensation, as if it had to seek causes of this; it always starts from *states of affairs*. Sensation itself is only one single fact which falls to the lot of scientific explanation. Just as little does science take its start from the environment, as the older form of empiricism thought. On the contrary, the environment comes to be quite a "problem" for biology, something biology must clarify.

Just because we can give a complete explanation of why, for example, we see just this visual object in the sky with all its particular properties as the sun, no "property" of the natural thing can be considered a given fact which science would need to explain. On the other hand, this fact is still one which science does explain, no differently than it explains the rainbow, for example.

If the spokesmen of the Marburg school meant nothing other than this when they rejected the notion that the content of the natural perspective along with the unities of natural language (the idiosyncrasies of which are explained by historical philology) is the reservoir from which the "facts" of science are drawn, then they could be assured of my agreement. But they ignore the existence of a sphere of pure facts beyond those of the natural outlook and those relative to certain sciences, facts which form among themselves an organized realm, not a "chaos" and certainly not a chaos of sensations. Natural as well as scientific facts must be considered selections from the stock of these pure facts. Because they are ignorant of this, members of the Marburg school suppose that the progress of research first "creates" the scientific fact as a problem, an X to be determined. The scientific fact is, for them, the "end-point" of research, and its whole content depends on a function which an unstructured chaos exercises, so to speak, in providing a "filling" for "problems" and "questions." Naturally, this makes the origin of the problems themselves completely incomprehensible; the scientific logos, however, seems cloaked with the dignity of a Creator-God. Moreover, the principles and categories which guide the determination of the "indeterminate," the existentialization [*Existentialisierung*] and "positing" of the *mē on* [i.e., nonbeing] which lacks both existence and determinateness, give no other proof of their identity than the fact that they can be shown by reduction to be the "presuppositions," the "foundations" of the science in question.

This whole way of looking at things overlooks the fact that all the forms and structures which adhere to the objective region of the *natural* world-view (independently of thinking in the sense of judgment and independently of the objects and principles of pure logic and wholly contingent in relation to them) also enter into the scientific object-world, without giving up even a trace of their essence. Science preserves without change the notions of thing, force, energy, causality, the real and the unreal, space and time, the reference of words in natural language in which the content of natural intuition, that is, the environment, is articulated. (This reference can be the same despite the change of meaning in the definitions, e.g., of the sun in the sky and the astronomer's sun.) Science is never able to explain these forms and structures. It explains only the special content of the *human* milieu as distinct, for example, from the special content of the milieu of different animal species. It never explains the milieu-structure in general which, in fact, is *relative* not to pure thinking and pure intuition, *but to the living creature.* The atom is just as much a "corporeal thing" as that chair over there and consists of the same strata: visual thing, tactile thing, materiality, mutual externality, spatiality, and temporality, quite independently of whether it crosses the thresholds of our senses. The atom is a corporeal thing and not a concept. The sensation which physiology and psychology say possesses intensity and quality is a genuine thing having properties, even if the sensation is only hypothetically assumed. The object answering to the subtlest concept of force in science contains the same phenomenon of effective action [*Wirkens*] [29] which confronts me, within the natural world-view, in a waterfall when it beats against a heap of stones. No sort of "determination," no conceptual definition, no distinction between "hypothetically given" and "observed," makes the least change in the identity of the structure and constitution of the two kinds of object. And this identity can never be dissolved into

29. [See Appendix A in the following essay.—ED.]

logic and mathematics. The sciences of the real remain essentially separated from the sciences of ideas.

However, the natural intuition of *ideal objects* (magnitudes, continua, numbers, spatial figures) and the science of these, positive mathematics (which is wholly distinct from the philosophy of mathematics, i.e., the theory of the essence of number, set, group, magnitude, etc.), not only have the *same* objects of cognition; natural and scientific intuition also follow the *same* essential connections and the *same* laws governing the foundations of data, even if mathematics infinitely surpasses natural intuition in definiteness and extent. All the objects of both are contingent from the standpoint of pure logic. Analogously, there are strict limits based on the essence "sign" and the symbolic function in general, and these limits are respected by natural languages no less than by the learned terminology which rests on conventions, limits which no psychology can "explain."

Thus, the distinction between the object-world of the natural world-view and that of the scientific does not rest on these forms and structures, but only on the *content* and the *level of existential relativity* of the objects on either side. The existence of the objects of the natural world-view, in keeping with their purely phenomenological contents, is relative to *human* organization. This constitutes the narrowness and constriction of this "world-view," which in turn simply provides the framework within which the experiential structures of man and woman, of race, of cultural unities of different epochs, brand their objects with still higher levels of relativity. But the natural view is infinitely richer than the world-view of science in the fullness of the content of every object relative in this way and in the corresponding "adequation" of cognition. At the same time, the natural world-view is essentially the intuition of a human "community" [*Gemeinschaft*] which we define as a group of men whose mutual understanding is built up independently of the observation of their physical bodies [*Körper*], their movements, and their properties, and does not come about by means of inferences from what is observed in this way. Instead, the natural world-view is built up from the perception of the expressive unities in the manifestation of their lived-bodies [*Ausdruckseinheiten ihrer leiblichen Ausdrucksäusserung*]. This enables us to join in intending the state of affairs intended in these manifestations, and this is the second condition of mutual understanding.[30] Any technical terminology and any conventional arrangement essentially presuppose this "mutual understanding" and a communality of group existence in general. Natural language is the most important form of this natural expression and its words and syntax are the units in which the expression is articulated.

In contrast, the scientific way of looking at the world is trained upon the objects which are not relative to the organization of the species *"Homo";* these objects are relative to all the organizations living things can possibly have. They ought to be considered "absolute" objects. Accordingly, their existence and constitution do not depend on the particular sensory and kinetic organization of man, nor does their effect on human bodies [*Körper*], which obeys exactly the same laws as their effect on all other bodies, act as a stimulus on the sensation and the possible kinetic intention of man taken as a whole. Precisely for this reason the same laws govern the effect these objects have, not only on one another, but also on the bodies of all living creatures, even those with quite different systems, those whose sensation and acts of movement require quite different stimuli.

These objects can, in principle, be obtained, on the basis of the formal and structural principles of the natural outlook and on the basis of pure logic and mathematics, from the particular sensory and kinetic organization of *any* organism; they are, so to speak, translatable into all the languages of the senses. We could, in principle, obtain knowledge of the sun and the planets even if the sky were continually covered with clouds. Today we recognize a multitude of sub- and supra-sensible realities whose activity has no stimulus-value for our power of sensation; we are on the way to basing mechanics on the theory of something which has no stimulus-value for us, namely, the theory of electricity. It is similarly certain that in principle we could have come to know even those objects of physics whose activity *does* have a stimulus-value for us, if by chance they had not had any at all. All this does not in the least exclude the possibility that this

30. [See *Formalismus*, VI, B, 4, *ad.* 4, on "lived-community" and "society."—ED.]

whole domain of objects is completely relative to the lived-body [*Leib*] and to life and to feeling [*Empfinden*], to sensibility and vital movement *in general*. However, since these concepts are concepts of genuine essences, as phenomenology shows,[31] and not empirical abstractions from any sort of earthly organism, the existence of the whole world of physics and chemistry is not necessarily bound to the existence of this earthly world of organisms itself. However, it still remains bound to the existence of objects with the essence "life."

All this constitutes the breadth and unboundedness of the scientific orientation. Science frees us from the limits of the human environment. On the other hand, the scientific picture of the world remains far behind the natural in the adequacy of its cognition and the corresponding "fullness" of the content of its objects. It becomes *merely symbolic* in proportion as it escapes those limits, that relativity of objects to the specific organization of man.

Let us take careful note of the following. Adequation and inadequation constitute a standard of cognition entirely independent of the level of relativity of the objects of cognition, on the one hand, and of the *truth* and falsity of the judgments about these objects, as well as the "correctness" of judgments in the sense of pure and so-called formal logic, on the other. One limit of the adequation of every intending [*meinenden*] act and the corresponding absolute fullness of its object is its self-givenness. This principle holds equally for all acts whose content is an image or a sign; even the latter acts are not purely signitive, but can be fulfilled through an imageless [*bildlose*] and, as it is often called, nonintuitive meaning [*Bedeutung*]. The other limit is the absolute inadequation of the act which merely intends, in which the object is present as "only intended," merely as what is required to fulfill a sign or symbol. In between these are all possible grades of adequation. If every measurement of adequation can be made only by comparing several acts in which the same objects are given in varying grades of fullness, still a definite adequation and a definite fullness belong from the start to every act.

Now, in the first place, we simply cannot reduce the levels of relativity of objects to mere distinctions in adequation and

31. [On lived-body, life, etc., as essences, see *Formalismus*, VI, A, 3.— ED.]

to the corresponding differences of the fullness with which the absolute object may be given; nor, conversely, can we define the richer object as the one which lies closer to the absolute object on the levels of relativity. Rather the two standards are independent variables; only in the case of self-givenness do absolute object and complete adequation of givenness coincide. For example, a relative object which, like an obsessive idea or hallucination, is relative to *one* individual alone, can in principle pass through all grades of adequation and can be present in all grades of fullness.[32] The hallucinating individual can notice and attend now to this, now to that, feature of an hallucinated chair; he can take more or less of it into his perception or, again, he can penetrate more deeply or less deeply with vision and touch into the relevant visual and tactile thing. This is the case on all levels of relativity and with respect to all the different domains of objects. Apollo and Zeus are religious objects relative to the Greek people; but surely the grade of adequation of the perception of these gods and the grade of adequation of the feeling of their holiness (i.e., the piety of the Greeks) were diverse and dissimilar among the Greeks.

Despite the fact that the fullness of an object and the level of its existential relativity are independent variables, they are nonetheless bound to one another in another direction. Existential relativity as such yields nothing; it is, in the last analysis, only a selection of the phenomenological content of the absolute objects. Thus, we should think of all the *environments* of the different animal species, including that of man, as contained in the absolute world, insofar as we think of the absolute world as completely reduced phenomenologically. These environments all represent realms of choice out of the phenomenologically reduced world. Thus we can say that each level of the existential relativity of an object, in comparison with some level on which the same object is less relative, contains less of the fullness of the whole world or the world-thing [*Welt-dinges*]. We can also say that every cognition of a more relative object is a less adequate cognition of the world than the cognition of a less relative object, one lying closer

32. Up to self-givenness, in which this "I hallucinate this object" with all its intuitive features becomes the total object. This object is then an "absolute object."

to the absolute object. To this extent, the entire arrangement of levels of existential relativity can be reduced to differences in adequation and to the corresponding differences in the fullness of the cognition of the world and in the fullness of the world itself.[33]

In addition, the adequation and inadequation of a cognition are equally independent of the *truth* or *falsehood* of the judgment passed on an object (and even more independent of its "correctness"). One cannot, as Spinoza tried to do, make the absolute antithesis of true and false a matter of degree, and then equate true cognition with adequate cognition, false cognition with inadequate. For it is clear that any degree of adequation of cognition and any amount of fullness of its object can be conjoined with true as much as with false judgments. A judgment does not concern simply the given aspects of an object, but the object itself with all its features. Only in the case of self-givenness is the judgment not only true but also evidentially true. In other cases judgment can be false, however high the degree of adequation. Conversely, a judgment can be true even when the object stands before us as merely intended and completely devoid of fullness. The results of the operations which a calculating machine carries out are as "true" as a man's judgment based on his own calculation. However, the increasing adequation of the cognition of an object cannot be reduced to an accumulation of true judgments about it—though the partisans of Criticism [*Kritizismus*] seem to think it can. We can only say that a more adequate cognition of an object and a correspondingly greater fullness of the object afford greater opportunity for both true *and* false judgments; or we can say that there are a greater number of true and false "propositions-in-themselves" (in Bolzano's sense) concerning the object of greater fullness.

33. The fullness of an object cannot be reduced to the number of observations we make of it; instead, the content and number of these observations depend entirely on the fullness with which it is given. Still less can its fullness be reduced to the sensations we have of it. Rather, the fullness with which, e.g., a concrete physical thing as such is given also determines what elements of its fullness enter into the associated visual, tactile, and auditory object. Correspondingly, the seeing or hearing of this thing (or event) can for its part be more or less adequate when the same sensations are felt.

It scarcely needs to be said that truth and falsity have nothing to do with the level of the relativity of an object. A man who hallucinates a brown chair and issues the judgment "This chair is yellow," or subsumes it under the concept "table," judges falsely, while he judges truly when he says "This chair is brown," or "This is a chair." For although the existence of the object, that is, of its underlying subject, is posited along with every judgment, the level of the relativity of its existence is in no way posited together with this. Who would doubt that a man can make true as well as false judgments in a mythological study of Zeus and Apollo? Thus, it is self-evident that one can issue true and false judgments concerning the things within the natural world-view that are relative to human organization, just as much as one can issue true and false judgments concerning those of physical science, which are not relative in this way. A man who says, "The sun has risen," when it has not yet risen, judges falsely; while he judges truly when he says "It has not risen." In spite of this, since Copernicus there is no longer any sun in the world of science which rises and sets; there is only the earth's rotation about its axis. But how senseless it would be to say that the meaning of the words "true" and "false" can be elucidated only by looking to science and its objects and methods!

From this it is also clear that if we have contradictory propositions of the form $A = B$, $A = nonB$, then one must be false only if the A in both propositions designates the object on the *same* level of existential relativity. Otherwise both propositions could be "true" or both "false" without violating the law of noncontradiction and the essential connection on which it is based, namely, the incompatibility of the being and nonbeing of an object. This is a basic principle of the greatest importance to the theory of cognition, one which Kant has already correctly applied in his antinomies.

Finally, we shall call any supposition that an object A lies on the level R of existential relativity, whereas in fact it lies on the jointly given level $R - _1$ or $R + _1$ (where "−" means increased, and "+" means diminished existential relativity), a *metaphysical illusion*. We shall call any supposition that an object which is inadequately given is self-given an epistemological [*erkenntnistheoretisch*] illusion; and any supposition that an object *A* is given in the same fullness as a jointly given object *B*, although it is given with greater or lesser fullness, a *common illusion.*

We oppose the whole sphere of illusion to that of possible error which has its seat only in the relation of judgments to states of affairs. Illusion, on the contrary, lies always in the way in which states of affairs come to *givenness.*[34]

Now observe that judgments are absolutely "true" if and only if (1) no illusion occurs with respect to their object; (2) the state of affairs "meant" by them does obtain; (3) they are "correct," that is, they observe the laws of formal logic. And judgments are "false" if they fail to meet any one of these three conditions, no matter which. Only when the last two conditions are not met do we have the right to speak meaningfully of "error," of *material error* in the first case, of *formal error* in the second. A judgment and its corresponding proposition can be false as much because of an error as because of an illusion. However, an illusion can never rest on the falsity of a proposition or on an error, any more than it can be removed through cognition of the error and cognition of the falsity of a proposition. All illusions are in this sense *pre-logical* and occur quite independently of the spheres of judgment and propositions. In *one* sense, however, all falsity rests on illusion, and all truth, even the truth that there is "truth itself," rests on insight. Similarly, each and every error rests on self-deception, namely, when we deceive ourselves into thinking that the state of affairs intended by a judgment does obtain, whereas it does not obtain (material error), or into thinking that the incorrect judgment is correct (formal error).

It is only the "common illusions" of relative adequation that lead, as shown above, to false judgments. Metaphysical illusions, for example, the supposition that the objects of mechanical physics are absolute objects, do not influence the truth and correctness of the propositions of this science, in the sense that their logical content must be altered if we see through the illusion. Physically everything remains the same, whatever degree of absoluteness the physicist ascribes to his object; it makes no difference whether he believes, for exam-

34. [See "The Idols of Self-Knowledge," sec. II, on illusion and error.—ED.]

ple, in Poincaré's charming simile, that the world, even for God, is a game of "billiards," or, like Mach (and no less erroneously) he regards his objects as pure symbols used to simplify complexes of sensation. To this extent the representative of positive science is gratified by the independence of his results from philosophical controversy. But he fails to recognize that the truth of his propositions within the level on which his objects are relative does not remove his fundamental illusion about the world, since it is about this level that he is deceived. He fails to see that, in principle, this truth and the harmony of his entire science do not yet distinguish him from the hallucinator who makes true and correct judgments concerning his object within his hallucinated world. One can be greatly learned and still be the opposite of a wise man, namely, a philosophical fool. We shall thus have to say that all the propositions of such a physicist are metaphysically false, although scientifically they might be perfectly true. Indeed, his "science" itself, in the cognitive function he assigns to it, is a false science and becomes a true science only when illusion is removed.

On the other hand, every material error itself rests on a metaphysical illusion, namely, on the illusion that the intended state of affairs obtains on that level of the relativity of objects with which the judger is in fact concerned. It makes no difference whether or not he knows this explicitly. All states of affairs, even in the case of illusion, *are* [*sind*], in the sense in which that which is meant has being [*in Sinne des Seins des Gemeinten*], but not all "obtain" [*bestehen*]. And it is only the "obtaining" [*Bestehen*] [35] of a state of affairs that constitutes the material truth of the judgment. Therefore the basis of every material error is the illusion which arises when someone intends a state of affairs in judgment which "is" and is thought to be on a level of being which he has mentally in view, although it is not in fact on that level.

Error, in the *formal* sense, rests on a kind of *epistemological illusion*. That all concepts, judgments, and argument must satisfy logical principles and laws is a condition of the truth of the relevant propositions generally, independently of ma-

---

35. The being and nonbeing of this are incompatible only for the unity of *one and the same* level of relativity, no matter which. [This line originally occurred in the text.—TRANS.]

terial truth. Consequently, these principles and laws themselves can no longer be called "true" in the same sense in which their obtaining is the condition of true propositions and in which their satisfaction in thought is the condition of the correctness of judgment. And yet they are still "true," in the plain and simple [*schlichten*] sense of the word, a sense that is prior to the distinction between the material truth of a proposition (= the obtaining of the intended state of affairs) and its correctness (= the satisfaction of the pure principles of logic by all the unities of the relevant logical formations). They are "intuitively true," that is, their truth is given in these principles themselves.

3. *The two basic principles of the theory of science*

Let us return now to "science" and its objects. Its objects, as we saw, are on another level of relativity than those of the natural world-view. They are "absolutely there," as regards human organization; but they are relative in regard to life in general. Science passes beyond the content of the human environment; indeed, it explains this content on the basis of facts which are not contained in it. But it does so relatively to life and preserves the formal and structural laws of an environment in general. We can thus define science straightaway. Science is cognition of the environing world, as opposed to philosophy, which is cognition of the world (or "world-wisdom").

At this point I shall be readily understood if I say that in virtue of the relations between the standards of cognitions we have just explained, the adequation of scientific cognition must diminish in exact proportion to the independence of its objects from the content of the human environment; that is, it becomes, in the same proportion, *cognition by means of symbols.* Since the existential relativity of objects is in general reducible to the fullness and adequation of our cognition of the world, and since natural objects have greater fullness, the natural world-view in principle comes closer to the world and its fullness than science does. A greater *fullness,* out of the total fullness of the world, enters into the world-view's content, although, to be sure, the selection of this fullness is made according to laws belonging to human organization alone. The world-view's object is the human environment, but within this its content is that of the world. The object of science is the world as it exists independently of man and his organization; but, out of the fullness of this world, its object is only the structure of an environing world *in general*. Here there is a narrow and restricted "daylight view," there a wide and unrestricted "nighttime view." Both are certainly not what "philosophy," what "world-wisdom" is seeking. For philosophy seeks a wide and unrestricted daylight view, restricted only, to be sure, to the *essences* of the world and the essential structure of the being of the world. The world plainly and simply, in its absolute objectivity and in its fullness, remains transcendent to the cognitive power of finite and embodied [*leiblicher*] beings. It is—God's.

Still another thing belongs to "science." As little as its facts stem from the sphere of natural facts, so little does its conceptual apparatus stem from the sphere of meaning of natural language together with its units and syntax. Instead, it is essential to science that *technical signs* and conventions about their meaning be established, chosen in such a way that, first, all scientifically relevant facts can be *univocally designated* (the principle of the univocal determinability of all facts through signs), and, second, the smallest possible number of such signs and the smallest possible number of forms of their combination are chosen to designate the greatest number of facts and combinations of facts (the principle of economy). The conventions which ensue from these basic principles of the constitution of that institution we call "science" are drawn up by the learned who as such do not form any kind of lived-community but a technical society. By "technical society" I understand any group whose members, having no natural understanding of one another (in the sense defined earlier), come to understand one another's judgments only on the basis of certain definite signs. For a fact to be a scientific fact, therefore, it must not only be selected in accordance with the structural forms of the natural view and in accordance with the particular "principles" of the science in question; it must be universally determinable by these signs, in accordance with the basic rules of the scientific constitution mentioned above.

This constitutes an essential distinction between scientific cognition, in the pregnant sense of the term, and natural cognition, on the one hand, and philosophy, on the other, a distinction which has rarely been sufficiently perceived. *Philosophical* cognition, by its essence, is asymbolical. It seeks to know a being just as it is in itself, not in its role of simply providing the filling for symbols applied to it. The very function of signs thus becomes a problem for philosophy. In fact, philosophical investigations should not presuppose the existence either of natural language and its system of meanings or of any technical system of signs. The object of philosophy is not the *addressable* [*beredbare*] world, that is, the world already under the obligation to make univocal agreement concerning itself possible and to assure that there must be a univocal determination of its content in several acts of an individual and in the acts of several individuals. Philosophy's object is not the content of the world already selected and articulated with a view to attaining a "universally valid" knowability [*Erkennbarkeit*]. Its object is the *given itself*, including all possible signs for that given. Certain philosophy, in trying to reach this goal, makes use of language, both as an instrument of discovery and as a means for exhibiting results. However, philosophy never calls upon language for help in determining its own object; philosophy uses language only in order to bring *to sight* that which is essentially indeterminable by any possible symbol because it is determined in itself and by itself. In the course of its investigations, philosophy makes use of language in order to rid its objects of everything functioning merely to fulfill a linguistic symbol and therefore not itself given. For the natural perspective, the world is given straightaway, so to speak, only as the fulfillment of possible linguistic symbols. The philosopher, by keeping up a resolute fight against the tendency to let the given be given only in this form, discovers the *prelinguistically given* which is, as it were, still untouched by language, and, thus, he sees what aspect of the given functions as a mere fulfillment of language. It is by just this means that he discovers the force of language and its selective, articulating power. However, the philosopher may make even less use of the technical language of science in the way science does, or of the presupposed univocal determinability of facts by a technical system of signs.

Let us now clarify the relation between the principle of

univocal determinability of all facts and the second principle of the constitution of the scientific institution and the *standards of cognition* with which we just now became acquainted. These were (1) self-givenness, (2) adequation of cognition, (3) the level of the existential relativity of objects, (4) simple truth—being-true [*schlichte Wahrheit–Wahrsein*], (5) material truth and falsity, and (6) correctness and incorrectness. The standards which follow one another in this way form a series with the property that the sense of each of the following standards *presupposes* the sense of those which precede it. The concept of adequation and fullness first comes to acquire meaning through the approximation of a cognition to self-givenness. The existential relativity of an object can be reduced to the increasing and diminishing fullness of the world [*Weltdinges*]. Simple intuitive being-true is the self-givenness of the coincidence of the state of affairs meant in judgment and posited in the proposition with the state of affairs which in fact obtains. Material truth and falsity presuppose simple "intuitive being-true" and concern the relationship of simply true propositions to the object of judgment. "Correctness," on the other hand, pertains to the conduct of the subject, to the act of judging insofar as it leads to the truth in the simple sense.

However, it is by this time clear that a given cognition can be precisely determined in accordance with all these standards without our also being able to determine the object of cognition *univocally* and in the most economical way. Thus, whether there are signs which can univocally or equivocally determine something [36] in fact does not make the slightest change in the value of this cognition, a value which is to be ascertained according to these standards. Thus, taken strictly, those principles in general are not principles of the theory of cognition but are basic articles of the institution "science" resting on the philosophical theory of the essence of signs. That is, they do not belong in epistemology but in the theory of science, a branch of applied epistemology. Accordingly, we could, in principle, achieve a cognition of the world in ac-

36. For when we talk of construing something in one or in many ways, the sign-function is present. This is itself a phenomenological datum and has essential laws of its own. [This parenthetical statement originally stood in the text.—TRANS.]

cordance with all these standards, without having even one of the pertinent objects or even one pertinent fact univocally determined. Even concepts and judgments of law [*Gesetze-surteile*] do not have the least to do with the univocal determination and formulation of their objects. It is only a mistaken nominalism that continually confuses the most frugal and univocal designation of concepts and formulations of laws with the concepts and laws themselves, that confuses the methods of measuring magnitudes, the units of measurement used, and the manner of reckoning with them, with the precise magnitude of the things [*Sachen*] themselves, and that confuses the clothing a logical principle wears, for instance in symbolic logic, with the principle itself.[37] The exhibition of our mechanical knowledge in a few basic principles and basic magnitudes and their numerous and complex consequences, or alternatively, in several independent basic principles and their more simple consequences, is not identical with the independent cognitive content and truth-content of this knowledge.

On the other hand, we could succeed in univocally ordering the content of the world in a vast system of signs, following the conventional rules for combining the elements of complex signs; this ordering could be such that we could univocally determine every fact and all the relationships of facts to one another by means of the combination of these signs. And yet we still would not have to ascribe any sort of *cognition*, measured by any of the standards mentioned, to the "model" of the facts obtained in this way (in the sense of mathematical "modelling"). Univocal determination and economical ordering have nothing in the least to do with *cognition*. Our cognition of the world is in no way enlarged if the content of the world is univocally determined in this sense; it is not enlarged if every complex fact (and every complex relation of facts) is exhibited with the aid of the combinations of these signs and the laws for operating with them, which function analogously to the rules, for example, of the game of chess. Indeed, if it were enlarged in these ways this would make it possible to sketch out in advance a symbolic model

37. It is in particular the case that the "principle of the univocal determinability of facts by means of symbols" is not identical with the principle of identity.

of every complex fact (together with its consequences) which is to be produced in practice, and to picture in the model, as the engineer and architect do in their blueprints, everything which is going to play a part in the realization of the project, and to see beforehand how well it will work out there. A paradox results: For the *practical* vocation of *mastering things,* such an ideal, univocal symbolic ordering of the content of the world and the relationships immanent to it would be perfectly sufficient; just as in the case of the smooth functioning of signals it is sufficient for a watchman, when this or that colored signal appears, to pull this or that switch, without needing to know that this train or that is coming. A consistent "pragmatist" could be content with this solution to the problem. For it is also obvious that pure cognition (measured by the standards mentioned) as such is totally without importance for all technical activity. It becomes important only to the extent that the sameness or difference or other relations of the object known also bring about reactions in our activity [*Handlungsreaktionen*] which correspond to these various relations. Thus, if any system of *symbols* for objects and relations is substituted for the cognized objects and relations with which they are univocally coordinated, this is everything a possible practical goal could require. And yet this symbolic system does not contain any element of cognition. Certainly such a system of signs for the univocal ordering of the world exists only as an ideal. But that does not concern us here. It is important here simply to show how fundamentally different and independent from one another these two tasks in principle are: to have cognition of the world, and to order the world univocally.

It must now appear to the phenomenologist to be the greatest mistake of all to place the two articles of the constitution of "science" at the apex of the *theory of cognition* and then to equate the being of the world itself with that which is univocally determinable by science (as the most consistent representatives of the Marburg school do). To do this is nothing less than to make a basic article of the institution "science" into a condition of *being itself.* What comes last in the series of the standards of cognition and no longer plays any real role in determining the value of the cognition, but merely decides whether the cognition in question belongs to science, now takes over first place: nothing can count as being [Sein] which cannot be shown to be univocally determined. No wonder that people have spoken here of the production of being in thinking. Kant's thesis, "the understanding prescribes its laws to nature," has been "trumped." For not only does "produce" take the place of "prescribe"; even what Kant set in contrast to thinking as the given, namely, the forms of intuition and the material factor of cognition, is to count as something which must be determined through thought. If, however, we consider what has been said, we get an essentially different conception of these relations. A prescription, in the strict sense, cannot be imparted [erteilt], as Kant held, to "nature," nor, in general, to objects and facts, but only to the *signs* we employ for the latter. Everything else must be considered "given." The "understanding," to speak with Kant, creates nothing, makes nothing, forms nothing.

4. *The a priori and the order of givenness*

What Kant spoke of as "forms of intuition and of understanding" are for phenomenological experience givens which can themselves be put on display [aufweisbare Gegebenheiten]. They are never "given" in the natural world-view or in science, but are *operative* [wirksam] in them as principles and forms of selection.

What does this mean? It means that there is a fixed *order of foundation* in which phenomena are given in both kinds of experience, so that a phenomenon B cannot be given if a phenomenon A is not given "beforehand," in the order of time. Thus, spatiality, thinghood [Dinghaftigkeit], efficacy [Wirksamkeit], motion, change, etc., are not added onto, any more than they are abstracted from, a given by the so-called understanding as forms of its synthesizing and relational activity. Instead, all these are *non-formal phenomena* of a special sort; each one is the object of a careful and painstaking phenomenological investigation. No thinking and intuiting can "make" or "structure" them; all are *encountered* as data of intuition. However, our natural experience is such that these phenomena must at any time *already be given* in it, if *other* phenomena—e.g., colors, tones, qualities of smells and taste—

are to be given. Spatiality is thus given prior to, and independently of, figures in space, the place and position of any things whatever, and, more than anything else, the qualities these things have. Thus, thinghood, materiality, and corporeality of a particular corporeal thing are given prior to its nature [*Washeit*] and to the material properties it actually has. The immediate phenomenon of motion is thus given prior to a change of place and the indirect identification of what is moving; prior even to the comprehension that what is moving is a body or a thing or a visual object (e.g., shadows, a streak of light moving itself). Thus, figures are given as identical and different, as similar, etc., independently of the relations between their qualities and prior to, and independently of, these qualities themselves (Bühler).[38] Furthermore, perceivable relations, like "similar," are given prior to and independently of their *relata;* indeed they are given as the principle by which that which enters into the content of our perception of the relata, that is, that which can serve as the basis of this perceived similarity, is selected. A vast field of investigation opens up here concerning the law of the formation of natural perceptual givenness, a field far more extensive than the one Kant established, in part correctly, in part falsely, and penetrating far more deeply into the nonformal domain [*ins Materiale*]. For instance, the fact that we connect the physics of color with the theory of light is ultimately based on the fact that the experience of the different levels of brightness *precedes,* in the order of givenness, the experience of the quality of color, that the experience of the unity of a solid thing functions only as a symbol for the colors, and, finally, that the experience of the spatial extension of a surface (not that of extension itself) is given prior to the experience of the source of the color. It is only in this way that it becomes possible to treat color-phenomena in physics as dependent on different refractive properties of dense media and on different rays with different component parts. (I have not mentioned all the presuppositions of this.)

Once this order of selection is firmly established, any cognition is a priori the material [*Materie*] of which must be ante-

38. [Scheler probably had in mind Karl Bühler's *Die Gestaltwahrnehmung: Experimentelle Untersuchungen zur psychologischen und ästhetischen Analyse der Raum- und Zeitanschauung* (Stuttgart, 1913).—TRANS.]

cedently *given in the order of givenness,* if the object in respect to which this cognition is a priori, is to be given. For instance, geometry and number theory are a priori for any knowledge of the phenomena of nature and, moreover, for the whole world of physical bodies, because the intuitive material which both sciences presuppose (over and above pure logic) for the constitution of their objects occupies a clearly defined level in the formation of any possible perception, representation, or even fantasy-representation of a physical body. Set theory is a priori with respect to geometry and number theory. Its objects of investigation are the intuitively given relations between bare pluralities in a field of pure apartness [*Auseinander*] [39] where this field has not yet been defined as either spatial or temporal. However, these relations are embedded in any multiplicity of elements within one of the more specialized forms of apartness and must be so, in accordance with the order of givenness. The ordering of the temporal manifold, in turn, has a hand in constituting number.

The principles of mechanics are never verifiable or controvertible by the observation of bodies in motion and are a priori for these bodies, since the pure phenomenon of inanimate *motion* [*Bewegung*] can already satisy these principles. To comprehend this we do not require a body or thing, but only the immediate identification of "something solid" which has *reversibly* changed the way it occupies space [*im umkehrbaren Wechsel der Raumerfüllung*]; this datum *precedes* the givenness of any observable motion of bodies. The *irreversible* change or fluctuation of something which is solid yields the image of alteration [*Veränderung*].[40] Thus, I will not be able to picture to myself, even in fantasy, any possible

39. [On the phenomenon of pure externality, see *Formalismus,* VI, a, 3; "The Idols of Self-Knowledge," and the following essay, "The Theory of the Three Facts."—ED.; and translator's introduction, note 42.—TRANS.]

40. [Scheler distinguishes in this passage three phenomena: *Bewegung* (motion or movement), *Veränderung* (qualitative alteration or change of state), and *Wechsel*. It is quite impossible to translate *Wechsel* in such a way as to capture all the nuances Scheler read into the word. It is meant to designate a phenomenon given prior to both movement and alteration. From the examples Scheler provides elsewhere it is reasonably clear that he has in mind any pattern of fluctuating change, of undulatory or oscillatory variation. I shall use makeshifts such as "fluctuating change or variation." See "The Theory of the Three Facts" and "Idealism and Realism," below, for further details of Scheler's notion.—TRANS.]

observation of bodily motions which would, were it executed, ever give me a reason for giving up the propositions which are called the "principles of mechanics."

It is of the essence of *inanimate motion* that the moments ingredient in all motion—(1) tendency and fulfillment, (2) immediate identification of the logical object, and (3) continuity in the variation of place—are given as founded on a variation of place (which is, therefore, already given). In inanimate motion, unlike the case of vital movement, we do not apprehend every difference in topical variation as built upon a previously given variation in tendency; on the contrary, we apprehend every change in tendency and direction as built upon a given change of place. The object tends from point A to point A_1, because it (as immediately identified) is, after the lapse of a certain time, at A_1. Any definition of direction or tendency comes about, so to speak, *post festum*, or in looking back from the momentarily given place. In the perception of vital motion, however, we *primarily* follow the *tendency* and see where it leads the object. In vital motion, change of place as the content of perception is the "consequence" of the motion of what "moves itself." Since, in the case of inanimate motion, our mind, as it were, runs ahead of the moving thing and starts by catching sight of the point reached in the next phase, this inner law governing our comprehension of inanimate motions has no limits even when what is moving has in fact come to rest. That is, there must be a positive reason for rest, a cause that checks the continuation of motion. One component of the principle of *inertia* is given in this: In order to keep a moving body in motion, no new cause of moving is required, but rather one is required for its transition to rest. Thus, the principle of sufficient or deficient reason does not lead to the principle of inertia; only the given *phenomenological insight* into this can lead to it. The rectilinearity of movement which the principle expresses is again intuitive, for if the experience of movement is built upon a given variation of place of something solid, then the tendency of movement at every instant and in every phase must be rectilinear, for two distinct places necessarily can always be linked by a straight line, i.e., by a line with this uniform figure [*dieser Gestalteinheit*]. In whatever way a body might in fact be moving itself, according to our observation, since it belongs to the *essence* of the phenomenon of inanimate motion that its course be in a straight line and to the *essence* of a corporeal unity that it be the unity of a solid thing, we must be able to analyze every possible motion of a body in such a way that this principle continues to be satisfied. The same thing holds true of the identity of direction of inanimate motion, which is always built upon the parallelism of the line segments traversed. Finally, the uniformity, that is, the equality of distances traversed in equal time, is also intuitively evident from the essential form of an inanimate motion. We can divide any straight line into equal parts; this is geometrically evident. Let *different* time-intervals correspond to the intervals between the points on the course which mark off these equal parts; then one and the same change in the occupancy of space by that which has the quality "solid" no longer underlies one and the same motion. However, every phenomenon of motion is founded on the phenomenon of a reversible variation in the manifold of mutual apartness. And in this field of mutual apartness in general that which is given is not yet distinguished into a spatial and a temporal manifold; this same datum turns into a temporal, qualitative *alteration* of a segment of space [*Raumstück*] when there is an irreversible change or variation [*Nechsel*] and into the *movement* of something in space in the case of reversible change or variation. Every identical line can become both a space-line and a time-line. However, this means that to every phase in the change, so far as movement is built upon change, at least one phase of movement corresponds in the parts of which equal space-lines must be connected with equal time-lines.

Indeed, a great deal can be gathered from the essence of an inanimate motion. I shall not go into this here. It always holds true that what is self-evidently true of the *essence* of inanimate motion itself is *a priori true of all the possible* movements of bodies we can observe. Hence the possible givenness of these is tied to the givenness of this essence of inanimate motion.

Thus, in principle, as we have seen, the a priori is no addendum, no connection created by our minds; the a priori simply follows from this, that the facts contained in the world —all thought of as phenomenologically reduced—are given to us in a fixed order.

[V] PHENOMENOLOGY AND SCIENCE

PHENOMENOLOGICAL PHILOSOPHY claims to furnish *pure, presuppositionless,* and *absolute* cognition. And just because positive science does not and cannot do this, phenomenological philosophy stands in contrast to it as an independent kind of cognition.

Nevertheless, it is indispensable for phenomenology also to show how the problems and cognitive goals of positive science come about. I must honestly confess that phenomenology up till now has altogether lacked a solution to this problem. Thus a situation has arisen in which it appears that, for every problem, there are a phenomenological *and* a positive, scientific truth—*two truths,* so to speak. It is not enough to say, "Yes, 'genetically' the case might be thus and so, but that just doesn't interest the phenomenologists." In the end, the totally naïve question arises: *Who is right?* Is the world of objects which has been completely reduced phenomenologically, the absolutely, ultimately existent, and true world; or is the true world of nature what physics, chemistry, and biology assert it to be? Is the soul in truth what empirical, genetic psychology maintains it is? If phenomena are the absolute existents, then everything else is to be reduced to them. How, then, can phenomenology exempt itself from this task? If, on the contrary, phenomena are mere "appearances" behind which positive science (and a rationalistic metaphysics in which science culminates) finds or constructs the so-called true and actual, then even phenomenology is, as it were, a foreground view of the world, and the phenomena are mere epiphenomena of an absolute real, causal nexus of things and forces.

Naturally, the phenomenologist is convinced of the first standpoint. But conviction is not enough. If he cannot, from his own position, comprehend science and its world and furnish them with meaning [*Sinn*], he ought not to wonder if someone says "You have to do 'only' with 'phenomena' "—in other words, this someone has already imported the sense of "mere appearance" into the word itself. And yet phenomenology wishes to be the exact opposite of so-called phenomenalism, the theory that our cognition is only cognition of the so-called appearances of realities lying behind these appearances. It even wants to show how this distinction comes about (Goethe's theory of colors). Then it must also show how one gets from phenomenological facts to the basic concepts of explanatory science, for example, to the concepts of the mechanical explanation of nature, to the basic concepts of positive biology, life, environment, stimulus, reaction, death, growth, heredity, to the basic concepts of descriptive and explanatory psychology, and to the basic concepts of the sciences of culture and of spirit.

Let us concentrate briefly on the problem of the mechanistic theory of nature (and on associationistic psychology), outlining its basic ideas.

As is well known, philosophical views on the meaning and cognitive validity of the mechanistic view of nature are quite diverse.[41] Without exhausting these views, one can list the following types:

1. Some philosophers, Wundt, Münsterberg, and Natorp, among the more recent ones, hold that the idea of natural science, namely, the reduction of all the appearances and variations in nature to what depends on motion, is already implicit in logic. They think the mechanistic view is the uniquely "uncontradictory view" of nature. A particular tone, or a particular color, can be strictly identified by two men who see it or hear it, only if its mechanistic definition is substituted. To think of nature and to think of nature mechanically mean the same thing for these scholars. For them, therefore, the so-called subjectivity of qualities, values, and forms, especially the form of the organism, is not demanded first by the results of physics and physiology, but is straightaway required by logic. It is another question what sort of reality they ascribe to the objects furnished by the mechanistic reduction once they have made this assumption. The answer to this depends on whether one believes that thinking in general can posit something real. If one does ascribe this competence to it, then one must hold to a mechanistic account even of the *absolutely real*. Külpe and Stumpf, in the end, aim at doing just that, in contrast to Wundt, who escapes this consequence only by

41. [See the later study "Erkenntnis und Arbeit," in *Die Wissensformen und die Gesellschaft,* 2d ed. rev., *Gesammelte Werke* VIII (Bern: Francke, 1960).—ED.]

means of his nominalism. (Planck, among the physicists, does the same.)

2. Kant does not go so far. For him the mechanistic view of nature is the result, first, of presupposing that space and time are forms of intuition which are prior to any qualities, as are the laws governing them, and, then, of the constitutive principles of transcendental logic. Looked at closely, this logic already contains in itself everything that leads to the mechanistic view of nature, particularly the principle of the conservation of something permanent in space and the principles of the regularity of temporal succession and of the reciprocity of action and reaction. It is not difficult to show that taken together these two imply the mechanistic view of nature. For it is only in the phenomenon of motion that a strictly continuous and regular temporal series of stages is given, together with the identity and spatial determinateness of the object traversing the series. What is missing in this phenomenon is change of state [*Zustandsänderung*] which implies a succession of different qualities. The latter takes place both discontinuously and, in the case of a change of state, without falling under any law. For Kant, too, qualities, values, and forms remain subjective. But, since space and time are to be forms of human intuition and of man's transcendental organization, the mechanistic account remains *existentially relative to man*. Independently of man there is the sphere of the "thing-in-itself," in which practical reason places the objects answering to its postulates.

3. The man most opposed to the first view is the one who sees the mechanistic view of nature as a *historical accident*, resting on the fact that people first studied phenomena of motion and then "explained" the relatively less known by way of the better known. But "explain" means nothing other than this. There is no question of discovering ontological grounds [*Seinsgründen*] or causes (i.e., in the real order). Accordingly, if people had studied acoustical or color phenomena first, if Huyghens and Newton had lived before Galileo, then an acoustical and optical view of nature would have been possible, in which changes of colors and tones would have been the independent variables. According to this view (Mach), qualities are as objective as quantities, and changes of state are as objective as motions. The ideal of

physics, however, would be to strip away the contingent, historical-psychological career of knowledge and to put in the place of any mechanistic reduction of phenomena mere *symbolic* formulae expressing their functional dependence and the variations of their magnitudes and qualities. This would be the more objective picture of nature, as opposed to the one we get in the mechanistic view. According to this position, the mechanistic view is to be explained psychologically and historically and possesses only an economical value. Under this assumption, according as one equates qualities with the contents of sensation or distinguishes these from one another, one is led either to a psychologistic metaphysics or to one which is at the same time realistic, like that of Aristotle. Ernst Mach understands the matter in the first sense; the French physicist, Pierre Duhem, who calls himself a formalistic Peripatetic, understands it in the second sense. Still, let us note that the phenomena of life do not constitute, for these scholars, any region with its own peculiar lawfulness or any new quality and form.

4. I mention a fourth view, which has been slowly developing and to which Lord Kelvin, Maxwell, and Oliver Lodge among the physicists were already inclined. It was given a rigorous formulation by Boltzmann and was brought to completion on the philosophical side by so-called pragmatism (James, Schiller, Bergson). These scholars assert that, in contrast to the third type, only the mechanistic reductions give an "understanding of nature." "It seems to me that the true sense of the question, 'Do we understand something or not?,' when it is a physical question, is: Can we make for ourselves a mechanical model that corresponds to the facts? If I can make one, then I understand; if I cannot, then I do not." Thus, these scholars agree with the first and second position, over against the third, that only the mechanistic view constitutes a genuine understanding. And yet the advocates of these two positions are worlds apart. For they immediately add that it is evident that one can make *infinitely many models* of any phenomenon which univocally determine it. It is not logic and mathematics that lead to the mechanistic view of nature, but something else. Hence, the mechanical model never has the sense of a true image of nature, agreeing with the real objects, any more than it has merely the sense of a univocal

symbolic determination. This symbolic determination is indeed possible according to the third view, even without such models. On the fourth view, the model gives us something different; it shows what "plan" and what "blueprint" we would have to follow if we were commissioned to produce the phenomenon in question. Therefore it is neither "theory" nor "hypothesis," but a *picture* of the technical production of a phenomenon of nature which is on the whole possible. A technical production which is on the whole possible—that is, no matter whether we take it to be desirable, no matter whether it is in fact possible for us or not. The point is not that the natural researcher has to think about certain technical applications and uses when he is doing research. The thought is rather the reverse: his understanding *itself*—its categories and inner laws, the mental apparatus of research—is of such a kind that the feasibility of producing the phenomenon under investigation, by means of human movements and human activity and in accordance with a picture or a model, is precisely the condition for his assertion that "he understands." Pragmatism started from the same thought and then carried it further. At one extreme, William James and Schiller went on to the well-known pragmatic concept of truth and knowledge generally: thoughts are identical or different, according as they lead to the same or different practical reactions; they are true, when they lead to the desired reactions. Bergson, in contrast, attempted to reduce all logical categories (even identity), as well as space and time in mechanics, to the needs of life, a life which itself can no longer be understood with the help of the categories which arose from it but is meant to be accessible only to an intuition and empathy of a very unclear sort.

I can only suggest here my attitude to this problem and my opinion of how phenomenology may overcome it. All four positions must be called extraordinarily crude in comparison.

I take the first three versions to be utterly mistaken. There is no basis for the assertion that the *contradictions* which result once we have posited the reality of perceptual contents, qualities, values, or forms, lead us to subjectivize everything, including the data of the mechanical theory of nature. This assertion is a consequence of the tacit introduction of certain assumptions into the principles of identity and of contradiction or into their application. These assumptions are that what is identical must be (1) a thing, (2) a solid thing, and (3) in space and time. Existential propositions concerning pure qualities or pure values or pure forms cannot contradict one another; they cannot do so even if we take these qualities, etc., to be properties of things. It only leads to a contradiction if we do not *perceive* [*anschaut*] these as such, but take them to be *univocal symbols* for solid things in space and time (and natural intuition had already paved the way for this move), and at the same time presuppose the essential interconnection between color and extension. This connection excludes the possibility that the same point in space can be both blue and green. That is, the contradiction does not *lead* to the mechanistic reduction, but *presupposes* that only what it furnishes is real.

Let us take a more precise example. Someone says that on the assumption that *objective temperature* consists in the spatial extension of a body or in the motion of its parts (and is not merely measured by it), one comes upon the *contradiction* which results when one allows the qualities belonging to the sensation of temperature to subsist as objectively existent. For it is a contradiction, someone says, that in the realm of quality $a = b$, $b = c$, and a is less than c; but this is nonetheless the case if I make the qualities of sensations objective. Therefore, quality can belong only to sensation. In fact, this contradiction simply induces us to distinguish quality and its continuous intensification from the sensing [*Empfinden*] of a quality, never to subjectivize the quality itself. In the second place, exactly the same contradiction is found in the case of extension and this contradiction does not lead us to subjectivize extension. Here, too, we distinguish extension and its decrease and increase from our apprehension [*Erfassen*] of them. Third, a contradiction does not exist between the sensations of temperature; one arises only when the sensation is taken as a univocal symbol of something objective which continuously increases—in other words, as a symbol of objective temperature. In themselves the qualities of sensation form a continuous series; gaps appear in this series, and the qualities become discrete only when they are taken as symbols of some objective being whose condition is being continuously altered.

This presupposes that this objective being is a fixed thing which has objective temperature as a property whose content varies.

Fourth, we already have a phenomenal distinction between "I am warm," or "I am freezing," and "It is warm or cold here," etc. That is to say, temperature sensations and objective temperature are phenomenologically distinguished. Furthermore, the connection between objectively warmer and colder and the increase and diminution of extension is not an inductively established result, resting on observation and measurement, but is *presupposed* whenever an inductive confirmation is sought. It is already given in the comparative relations between "being-warmer and more extended" and "being-colder and less extended"; that is, in the relations between these "states of affairs," independently of whether a corporeal body of definite magnitude is given or presupposed. In exactly the same way that the quality of any bright color, blue or yellow, for example, diminishes when its extension decreases, until it becomes totally obscure and disappears; and just as the brighter a surface, the greater its magnitude; just as everything larger is from the start given as heavier, while anything smaller is lighter—so, too, an increase in extension is phenomenologically linked to an increment in the state of affairs: "It is warmer." For just this reason, an objectively smaller body which has the same temperature as an objectively larger body seems to be warmer than the latter, just as an objectively larger body seems lighter than a smaller body of the same weight. The sensations of traction [*Zug*] and of temperature are not the foundations for these phenomena and comparative relations; rather, those sensations are the dependent variables of these phenomena. Consequently, it is neither the observation and measurement of bodies, nor a pure convention (as Mach thinks), that causes us to choose extension as the measure of temperature.

The same point holds good of any application of the *method of contradiction* to *color*. Only when we presuppose that color is a *univocal symbol* (representative function) of the equality, similarity, or differences between the properties of solid things do we run into contradictions; that is, only when we presuppose what we wish to *prove* with the method of contradiction. Even to assert that two individuals can never have evidence that they are hearing the same tone, or seeing the same color, or that a single individual is now remembering the same tone that he heard five minutes ago, is groundless.[42] In applying the mechanistic reduction, we presuppose precisely that this *is* possible, for this reduction gives us the utmost assurance that the function of tone or color is the same whenever it symbolizes the same solid thing. The concept or identification of color-blindness does not constitute an objection to our thesis; it, too, presupposes the strict identity of this function.

Furthermore, it is precisely Herbart's errors which have shown that this false method of contradiction can just as well be turned against the data of the mechanistic view itself and thus against the objective existence [*Existenz*] of the corporeal thing with its properties, movement, and alteration (Mach). These are errors because it is precisely the phenomenological exhibition of thinghood and materiality, and of the phenomena "variation," "movement," "alteration," that removes a contradiction which would arise if these material phenomena did not exist. That is, in the logical sense even these data are *specific material items* [*besondere materiale Etwasse*]; while on Herbart's assumption there are only sensations and logic. But all of these data are *material,* asensual phenomena. From Herbart's point of view motion, for example, involves the contradiction that the same thing is at the same time at place *a* and not at place *a*. But, first, the phenomenon of movement is not based on the difference of place of an identical something; movement is still given even between points which can be distinguished only as long as some movement is taking place between them. In the second place, the phenomenon of movement is not based on the givenness of continuity, as sudden discontinuous movement shows. Third, it is not based on something immediately identical (Wertheimer).

If neither logic nor mathematics, neither the essential connections discovered after the phenomenological reduction has been completed, nor any experience we get through observation, can adequately substantiate the principle of the mechanistic view of nature; if, however, science nonetheless claims that with this principle it can explain the content of the natural outlook as something merely relative to men, then the

42. [See *Formalismus,* VI, A, 3, g.—ED.]

question becomes all the more pressing: "What authority and what *sense* does this principle possess?"

In themselves, the two basic articles of the constitution of "science" no more lead to the principle of the mechanistic view of nature than do (1) the universally valid real principle of causality; (2) the universally valid logical principle of the sufficient (or deficient) reason for something's being other than it was [*Andersseins*]; and (3) the functional principle which expresses the essentially necessary interdependence of all variations in the sphere of mutual externality and is a priori and universally valid for "nature" in general. Those basic articles can never do more than determine the univocality and purposefulness of the signs and combinations of signs applied in the world of scientific communication. If the mechanistic view of nature is also symbolic insofar as only a very few elements are selected out of the sphere of the phenomenally given (e.g., solid thing, motion, causal contact in space and time, and the functional interdependence of variations in the magnitude of these basic facts), and if everything else is univocally symbolized by these and only these, then this just means that the "given" is exhausted by the object answering to this view. And this is the *given* by which every other given is symbolized. But then the question arises: "How is this possible?" Why can all the others be univocally symbolized by just these givens? Why not by others? It is impossible that this given, too, rests on a free choice or on a convention. For we are not free univocally to determine or not to determine the observed facts through the movement of solid things and the effect of their contact on one another. Instead, it is only this determination that lets us, in Lord Kelvin's striking expression, "grasp" what is observed.

Still, what does it mean here to determine something "univocally"? Does it mean that the *entire* content of what is observed is univocally determined by the *mechanical model*? This is what the rationalistic theory assumes. According to it, a unique and independent world should lie "behind" the observed facts, a world defined and "conceived" in the mechanistic theory of nature. The effect of these real objects on the psychophysical organism should first bring forth the observed facts and, once again, bring them forth univocally. However, it is just this presupposition that is erroneous. It is the preeminent service of the English school of physicists that, notwithstanding their adherence to the view that we can understand nature only mechanically, they nonetheless saw and proved that while we can imagine producing only a single mechanical model which allows us to grasp the facts, we could always produce an *infinite number* of other mechanical models which would allow us to grasp these facts equally well. This possibility would naturally be excluded if there were a one-to-one correlation between the model and the observed facts we grasp via the model, that is, a correlation of such a kind that a complex of facts corresponded to every model, and a particular part of the model, to every part of the complex of facts and conversely. Nonetheless, the determination of any complex of facts through any one of the infinite number of models is strictly univocal. It is so, not in the sense that every positive and perceivable content in the facts generally is determined (much less univocally determined), but in the sense that to "comprehend" any difference [*Anderssein*] in the complex of facts or in any of its elements requires a different series of different models which are once again infinite in number.

This is the peculiar sense that "univocal determination" has here. And now, in light of the foregoing, how is this peculiar relation to be understood in terms of the theory of cognition? My answer is as follows. We can make univocal determination comprehensible, first, by means of the fixed and inviolable order of selection any living creature follows when it comes to act effectively "upon" the world (where the world is imagined to be phenomenologically reduced), and, second, by means of the order in which pure facts and their interconnections reach [*zugeht*] the creature's essentially sensory and body-dependent [*leibbedingten*] intuition. This second order is founded on the first; it becomes intelligible in its own right by virtue of the value it has for the goal-directed striving of life *qua* life in general, for life as such strives to exercise a growing power and mastery over everything in the world which can be turned into a part of its environing-world.

This much should be clear: the paradox contained in the two simultaneously valid propositions, that the mechanistic theory univocally determines observed nature and that, nonetheless, there are infinitely many such theories which do this, is dissolved if there are any *objective* conditions [*Sachbedingungen*] for the observed facts (i.e., objective and real grounds by which they are explained) which are at the same time *cognitive* conditions for the possibility of perceiving and observing these same facts. It is a phenomenological truth that the structural relation between the factors in any possible content of sensory perception (leaving aside the special functional and anatomical organization of the animal's senses) is of such a nature that in every perception an abundance of self-subsistent intuitive facts comes to us in varying degrees of adequation. These facts have nothing to do with the movement of solid things or with the effects of their mutual contact in the field of spatiotemporal externality. At the same time, it is also true that the order in which these facts "come to us" is so constituted that the following states of affairs must reach us and be given to us "first of all": the solidity of something, the thinghood of something, the movement of something, and the spatiotemporal contact of something with something else (plus whatever else belongs here; this list is not exhaustive). These must occupy the first place in the order perception follows in selecting the pure content of the world, *if* (and insofar as) we are to have access to any other states of affairs whatever, e.g., being-blue, being valuable, having this or that form, etc., and indeed have access to them in the same place in the world. Consequently, nothing can be given through sensory perception that would not also be univocally determined once the movement of solid things, their contact in the field of externality, and the mathematical concepts [*Begriffswelt*] which govern this manifold a priori are positively determined. If this were not the case, that would imply a break in the order of advent [*Zugang*] and selection.

On the other hand, it is also obvious that everything in the total perceptual content that goes beyond the "aspect" of the movement of solid things in space and time is never determined in its being and nature [*Sein und Sosein*] by this aspect on any occasion when it is present. What *is* determined is only that just "this" and not "some other thing" can "have some influence" on the motion of a lived-body and thus takes on value and significance for the essential tendency of a lived-body. Thus, there must always be not one way, but infinitely many ways, of substituting a mechanical model in place of some content. This "substitution" becomes completely independent of the degree of cognitive adequation to which the content is brought in philosophical cognition, up to the limit of self-givenness. However, the objects which any cognition of this sort possesses will always be necessarily relative to life; they will form a realm of possible resistances to a living creature in general. Therefore they are at one and the same time real, and exist independently of man and his organization, and yet have no reality for a finite mind, for its reason and pure intuition. For this finite mind they are only possible models living creatures follow in fashioning a plan of possible technical activity leading to mastery over their possible environment and to the manufacture of things which might possibly be useful to them.

This shows that if we leave aside the basic articles of its constitution (i.e., the univocal and the most economical determination of facts), there can be no doubt that the science of inanimate nature has the task of seeking and furnishing *truth* and nothing other than truth. Every one of its propositions must agree with the states of affairs "meant" in these propositions; that is, every one of them must be *materially true.* All of its theses, inferences, deductions, and inductions must be *correct* and therefore subject to a normative legislation based on pure logic. Leaving aside the basic articles of its constitution, which have no validity in philosophy, science naturally shares these standards of cognition with every form of cognition, including the cognition exercised in our daily affairs from the perspective of the natural attitude. Science obviously shares them with philosophy as well. Thus, science is to this extent an institution for the cognition of truth. A researcher whose research is guided by something other than the investigation of truth, one who aims at useful or technically applicable results, lacks the primary ethos of the researcher and does not deserve that honorable name.

However, precisely because the researcher shares the goal of knowing the truth with so many others, his peculiar cognitive goal is completely indefinite. It is determined only after we have said what kinds of facts are "meant" by the propositions which must enter into his judgments. The answer to this turns out to be: (1) facts which can be univocally determined by symbols and facts for which there is no individually valid, but only universally valid, truth; (2) facts whose objects are relative to life; and (3) facts which are such that some living movement might by acting upon them produce some sort of alteration in the environment, some alteration, whatever it may be, which hovers before the mind of the creature as having value to his life.

This means that the truth which science provides is, like every truth, "absolute." However, the cognitive objects with which scientific truth is concerned, while not relative to men, are existentially relative to life. And this distinguishes science from the natural outlook, on the one hand, whose objects are all relative to man, and from philosophy, on the other, which aims at absolute objects. Second, the selection of the facts and truths which are called "scientific" is already dominated by a principle which no longer has anything to do with knowledge [*Kenntnis*] of the world. We may now call this the "principle of setting possible technical goals." This principle already has an influence on the order of selection of those elements of the phenomenologically reduced world which enter into the content of the natural outlook, always within the limits of the milieu of the species *Man.* The facts which are bound together by the reactive effects [*Reaktionswirksamkeit*] they might possibly have on human activity (in other words, the contents of the milieu of the human species) make their appearance in every act of perception, memory, and expectation, in accordance with the degree of their importance to life. Science frees itself from the limitations of this existential relativity to man; but the price it pays is the adequacy of its cognition. Henceforth scientific cognition concerns only that "aspect" of any possible environment which we need to know in order to gain mastery over everything which, without belonging to the milieu of man, is nonetheless contained in the sphere of existential relativity to life.

Philosophy, on the contrary, seeks the truth of a cognition which is as adequate as it can possibly be, a cognition that finds its ideal perfection in self-givenness. If it is obvious that the cognitive goals of philosophy and science can never interfere with one another, it is equally clear that the cognitive goal of philosophy is set over that of science.

What is furnished by the mathematically determined mechanism of nature is also factually present in nature, so far as those facts which fulfill the basic concepts of this science are concerned. This is not stamped upon or prescribed to nature by any legislation of the understanding or by forms of the understanding and intuition which "lie in readiness in the subject." The intuitive materials for these basic concepts are not freely chosen over all the rest, contrary to the opinion of Ernst Mach and the members of the pure symbolic school, Henri Poincaré, for example. They are already present as the independent variable in the structure of every natural perception and in the structure of any vital milieu; independent, because present as what is primarily "given."

However, the construction of any of the particular mechanistic schemes [*Mechanismen*] which we carry out with these materials and on the basis of principles already lying in the intuitive essence of these materials is a free mental or spiritual construction. (And insight into these principles may be obtained only by means of this essence.) These constructions should not aim at "depicting" anything "behind" things. Rather, all of them collectively should simply produce a "plan" by which nature can in principle be moved and steered toward any arbitrarily variable goals; steered not by us men with the powers we happen to have at the moment, but by persons who are free, although still encumbered with a lived-body [*durch freie, aber leibbehaftete Personen*].[43] It is obvious that a plan for the possible control of nature need not be "equivalent" to, or a "model" of, that which is there to be controlled, nor could it be. It is also obvious that there always are and must be not merely one plan, but infinitely many plans, of this kind.

On the other hand, the idea of a plan by which it becomes essentially possible for a living creature to move and control nature obviously may never be equated with a plan drawn up for reaching some one definite goal or utility-goal, such as the actual production of a thing, a house, for example, or a bridge or machine, by men. In between these there is a gaping abyss, the abyss between *science* and *technology*. From the start, the plan we have had in mind is not existentially relative to man and his organization. The plan defines and circumscribes every possible setting of technological goals and thus

43. [It is not clear whether Scheler's emphasis on the body here is as "negative" as the translation may convey. On the relations between man, lived-body, and persons, see *Formalismus*, VI, B, 2, pp. 472–74.—TRANS.]

does not take its start from any one goal or from any collection of these. The spirit which sketches out this plan is guided not by the utility-value of any piece of work to be produced, but by the vital power-value which lies in the mastery life achieves over nature and is totally independent of the application of this power to this or that technical goal.

This interpretation does not put the "conceptual" understanding (which Kant mistakenly took for a "pure" and "transcendental" understanding) at the service of a goal or utility-value. Rather, from the foregoing remarks we are brought to an understanding of the origin of this conceptual understanding itself. The conceptual understanding has its origin in the pure spirit, on the one hand, and in the essential and primal tendency of life to extend and master its environment by exercising its power, on the other. Ethics teaches us that power is better than utility. However, it also teaches that power is not and should not be allowed to be the motivation of research; only the knowledge of truth can play this part. Again, it teaches us that knowledge of truth, since it is a purely spiritual value, is a "higher value" than any form of power.[44]

Nonetheless, our question at the moment is not about the motives of the researcher or the necessity that his results, i.e., the theses of science, be true. The problem is to know the precise origin of the "understanding," not in the sense of a "faculty," but as the sum total of the basic concepts and principles with which the construction of mechanistic physics is carried out and to know how its objects arise. The motives the researcher has for his subjective application of this understanding are the business of ethics, not the theory of cognition. And the problem is exactly one of determining how the true statements within mechanics itself can achieve in addition something so totally different than being-true [*Wahrsein*] in relation to the data corresponding to them: how all the phenomena of inanimate nature come to be univocally determinable in virtue of these truths. We are concerned not with mechanics as a special science, but with the mechanistic view of nature.[45]

44. [See *Formalismus*, II, B, 5.—ED.]
45. [The manuscript breaks off here.—ED.]

The Theory of the Three Facts

[I] PHENOMENOLOGICAL OR PURE FACTS AND NONPHENOMENOLOGICAL FACTS

A PHENOMENOLOGICAL OR "PURE" FACT is one which comes to givenness through the content of an immediate intuition. We call the content of such an intuition a "phenomenon," where this term has not the least to do with the "appearance" (of something real) or with a "semblance." Intuition of this kind is phenomenological intuition, "phenomenological experience," or "essential insight." The "what" furnished by this experience (namely, essences, essential connections) is "given in person" [selbstgegeben]. The essences and essential connections brought to sight are "given" (a priori) before any inductive experience.

Phenomenological experience in this sense furnishes the facts themselves and does so directly, that is, without symbols or signs, in contrast to any nonphenomenological experience, for example, natural intuition, or scientific experience. Phenomenological experience is asymbolic experience. The phenomenological fact is, in the first place, an asymbolic fact.

At the same time phenomenological experience is an immanent experience; that is, only that which can itself be intuited in an act right now belongs to it, in contrast to every

Translated from "Lehre von den drei Tatsachen," *Schriften aus dem Nachlass*: I, *Zur Ethik und Erkenntnislehre*, 2d ed. rev., ed. Maria Scheler (Bern: Francke Verlag, 1957), pp. 433–502.

[202]

"transcending," nonphenomenological experience, in which something is "meant" or "supposed" [*vermeint*] which is not intuitively given in it. The phenomenological fact is, second, an *immanent fact,* that is, it is the content of an experience in which "what is meant" or "intended" ["*Gemeintes*"] and "what is given" coincide. It is in the coincidence of what is meant and what is given that the "phenomenon" appears and the content of the phenomenological experience is fulfilled.

Facts, therefore, and not constructs of an "understanding" (Kant), are the material bases of phenomenological philosophy. Kant's basic error was to equate the material (= "the given") with the merely "sensory content," thus equating the a priori with the formal element or "thought," or what reason "adds on" to the sensory content. This is an error he took over from English "sensationalism." "Sensory content" designates nothing which might be a determination of the content of a color or a tone, say, but only the *way a content reaches us.* The error is that instead of simply asking what is given in the meaning-intention, one mixes in objective and even causal theories, which deal with what goes beyond the intentional.

If one asks, for example, what is "given" in the perception of a physical cube, sensationalism's answer, that the "perspectival side view" of the cube or the "sensuous content of sensation" is given, is fundamentally wrong. What is given is the cube as a complete *material thing* with a definite spatial unity of form. It requires a series (a gradual building up) of acts of natural perception before one can arrive at the point from which the sensationalistic epistemologist so naïvely starts. It is precisely the concepts "sensory content" and "sensation" that are most in need of phenomenological clarification. "Contents of sensation," in the strict phenomenological sense, are only those contents whose appearance or disappearance makes for some kind of variation in our own bodily condition, for example, hunger, thirst, fatigue, etc., along with those sensations which are localized in particular bodily organs. These are genuine "sensations" in the strict sense. Afterward, one can also call elements of the perceptual world, such as color, tone, etc., "contents of sensation" in an extended (analogical) sense. However, "contents of sensation" in this extended sense are never "given" in any sense of the word. "Sensation" is only the name for a variable relation between a bodily condition and the phenomena of the external (or internal) world. It is the task of philosophy to purify the contents of intuition from the organic sensations accompanying them.

The attempt to reduce all the intuitive content of the world (both the external and the internal worlds) to the elements of bodily states, and then to reconstruct them out of the latter, represents an illusion. The theory that sensation is that which is "given" passes off what is merely a (theoretically possible) projection of the content of the world onto the bodily states of an organic being and their variations, as the "essence" and unique constituent of the content of the world. And, since everything which belongs to the sphere of sensation is indeed relative only to the body and its particular organization, the whole content of the *world* becomes relative to the body, which is itself only a minimal constituent of the content of the world. At the same time a pure symbol, a hypothetical and instrumental concept belonging to a special science, namely, the psychology and physiology of the senses, is used to define what must be as far away as one can imagine from anything merely symbolic and instrumental, namely, the "immediately given." Such a science, if used fruitfully, should represent only the unity of a discipline concerning organic sensations in general.

Once the content of the world is made thoroughly relative to the body, then only four possibilities remain for winning back the world of *objects* and, in particular, the world of *reality*.

The first possibility is the complete abandonment of this world, with the explanation that the universe is a great sensation-complex, while objects, real things, etc., are only symbols for this complex and its parts (Mach).

The second way is to let "real things" in a completely transcendent sphere correspond to the relativized content of the world. One can say about these real things only that the order, the difference, in short, all the relations of the parts of the world-content are also found among them; beyond that, one can only designate them as X, Y, Z. Naturally, since one has put a symbol, namely, sensation, in place of the content of the world and has tried to construct the world out of "symbols," the *real* must in turn become so empty that it itself melts into mere symbols. Someone thinks he can still get hold of what is behind the relativized world-content and does so—what does he have? A completely contentless and meaningless world of signs,

X, Y, Z, which can never, in principle, be satisfied in the content of any intuition he can exhibit. The journey to the transcendent world ends—with our making obeisance to the signs we have fabricated.

The third way is the way of the Kantians. Since every content of the world is relativized, and since the essence of any science consists in obtaining a realm of "objects," a realm whose sense and validity are independent of our organization, one resorts to the hypothesis of synthetic "functions of thought" which establish unities of every sort, to "acts of a pure thinking, willing," etc., through which a realm of "experience" is to be constituted. The contents of this realm indeed remain relative and subjective, but its forms, although first created by those mental functions, ought to restore the objective character of the world.

Pragmatism, finally, has taken the fourth way, substituting practical needs and the actions corresponding to them for the mental functions of a transcendental understanding. These needs and actions are to be the architects of the realm of experience.[1]

The starting point of all these theoretical systems is the erroneous theory of the given which we reject here.

Let us return to the point at issue. If we ask how the "given" or the "facts" within natural intuition (of the external world) are related to the "sensibly given," then we can no longer doubt that it is nonsense to say that these facts are given to us as "sensory contents" or as complexes of these. However, it makes *good* sense to ask to what extent those facts which analysis can show to be mere "sensory contents," in the genuine or analogical sense, are found in the content of natural "facts" in natural things and events and their causal relations.

The answer would be that the things are never given to us "in person" in natural intuition (this is only possible in phenomenological intuition), but neither are the sensory contents associated with these things given in natural intuition. Rather, it is characteristic of the facts of this sphere that their content is as far removed, so to speak, from the things-themselves as it is from the sensory contents objectively associated with the

1. [For Scheler's treatment of pragmatism, see "Erkenntnis und Arbeit," *Die Wissensformen und die Gesellschaft,* 2d ed. rev., *Gesammelte Werke* VIII (Bern: Francke, 1960).—TRANS.]

natural experience of these things. In place of the intuitive contents of a corporeal thing which an ideally successful phenomenological intuition could obtain, in the object of natural intuition only that part of these contents is given which can function as a sign of the bodily states linked with the experience of this object. These bodily states in turn become the points of departure for an action directed upon these objects. Second, these contents are built upon, "founded" on, one another in such a way that, in the order in which they reach us, those which point to the concomitant bodily states which are most important for our action take precedence over the others.

On the other hand, if we compare the content of the facts of the natural outlook with the sensory facts an analysis can discover in the experience of these natural facts, we will discover two things. First, only those sensory contents enter into the content meant by a natural perception that can count as signs for *things* constituted in such and such a way. (Some, namely, those belonging to "sensation" in the analogical sense of the term, enter into this content directly; others, those belonging to sensation in the strict sense, do so only by way of an empathetic projection [*Einfühlung*].) Second, these sensory contents are founded upon one another in such a way that the very first to enter into the concept of perception are those which can be signs for the properties of things which are most important to life. However, this does not mean that the properties themselves are necessarily given.

The "fact" belonging to the natural outlook is a *middle realm* between things-themselves and the states we are in when we experience things-themselves. It is, so to speak, an answer given by the world to the inquiries put to the universe by our bodily states and their unities or by our needs. In contrast to the "pure facts," it is doubly symbolic: A symbol for the thing itself as well as a symbol for our bodily states.

This last remark is of the greatest importance. It shows that the idea which has prevailed among almost all physicists since Descartes, namely, that it is the task of physics (in the widest sense of the word) to make those assumptions about the real which will allow us to explain "sensations," the only things which are given to us, as the effects this reality has on us (or the idea that one has to understand sensations and their relations as "signs" for the real and its relations), is completely mistaken. Furthermore, it confuses physics with physiology. Not only are the epistemological facts of the case falsified; biology and physiology also maintain an utterly false relation to physics. People have failed to see that the "facts" of the physiology of the senses are derived from the world of natural facts just as originally as those phenomena which turn into the datum of physicalistic thinking. Instead, people believe that physicalistic reality must already be constituted—that colors and tones, for example, must be physicalistically reduced before we can pose the relevant physiological problems. This is not the case at all, as Hering showed, especially for colors. Rather, what is given is the state of affairs of external natural intuition, and this can be accounted for by two equally primordial explanations, one physical *and* one physiological (or biological in the wider sense of the term), at least to the extent that science can in general "explain" anything here. In any case, this state of affairs is always simultaneously a sign for a physical *and* a physiological process which is the correlate of those "genuine" organic sensations which are interwoven with the content of any act of natural perception. An investigation of the sensation of traction [*Zugempfindung*] and its physiological correlates as well as of the objective (physically defined) weight must take its starting point in the physical phenomenon of the heaviness of a weight which I lift. By no means should we consider the "sensation of traction" as the given and then wish to get to the objective weight by way of this datum [*Datum*]. In fact, the sensation of traction itself varies with the natural phenomenon of heaviness, which, on its part, is in turn conditioned by the magnitude, look, and form which belong to the object of the natural perception of some physical body.

The foregoing is even more important for our understanding of the essence of sensibility and the sense-functions in general. The data of cognition are never furnished by these functions; they are furnished by the unitary act of intuition performed by means of these sense-functions. These functions "make" nothing and produce nothing; they simply *select out* those sides and parts of the actually existent reality which can be made to serve as signs for the vital functions which preserve the body or for the reactions which have to be executed. The body does not determine the content "red" or "blue," but it determines the fact that this content becomes a sign for this particular thing. The sense-functions have an exclusively analytical meaning.[2]

Only if we radically distinguish the physiology of the senses from all epistemological [erkenntnistheoretischen] and psychological problems and incorporate the physiology of the senses into the concrete context of physiological problems can we destroy the fundamental error of thinking that the sense-functions have a *cognitive* meaning or that they provide us with the material for any cognition. Their meaning is, in fact, quite different. Through signs, they make known to the organism the presence or absence, the proximity or distance, the advantages or disadvantages of the objects (things and events) surrounding it. By this means sense-functions institute processes such as glandular secretions or impulses to certain reactions. We must completely undo that strange mystification of the sense organs and their functions which leads to the idea that they should be something quite different than an apparatus for the reception and analysis of environmental stimuli. Only gradually and through specific achievements serving to preserve the organism are sense organs distinguished from other organs, such as the liver and the spleen. The sense organs have been formed out of the general sensitivity of the entire organic body. The idea that we are attacking here holds that sense organs are the apparatus for something as indifferent to life as "cognition" and that the sense-functions, instead of being connected to the universal functions of the organism, ought to be "functions of cognition." The knowledge of the world which ensues on the occasion of this dialogue between the environment and the organism[3] is not given through the sense-functions but through an act of *pure intuition*. The performance of the act of intuition is merely triggered when the dialogue occurs and is placed in the service of life's goals.

2. See Pavlov, "Naturwissenschaft und Gehirn," *Ergebnisse der Physiologie*, Vol. XI (1911); Bergson, *Matière et mémoire* (Paris, 1908). [English translation, *Matter and Memory* (New York: Humanities Press, 1962)]; Uexküll, *Umwelt und Innenwelt der Tiere*, 2d ed. (Berlin, 1921).

3. The dialogue of organism and environment is nothing more than a particularly complex form of the interplay of stimulus and reaction, or, as Pavlov says, "an increasing conditioning of the reflexes," and an increasing independence of the movement to be performed from immediate mechanical contact with the objects to which the movement of fleeing or seizing is directed. [This statement was originally in the text.—TRANS.]

Thus, intuition of the world is never a coefficient of the sense-functions, nor are the contents of intuition ever a summation of sensations. The sense-functions simply assign to intuitions a place in the play of organic functions and reactions; they refract, as it were, the unitary ray of intuition into a multiplicity of single rays, namely, into the functions whose corresponding contents are merely signs for that whole of things which intuition would furnish in the absence of this biologically purposive refraction. Intuition (and its particular qualities, such as perceiving, representing, remembering) furnishes the *positive* data of knowledge. The sense-functions never have a positive, creative role in this but only a *negative*, selective, suppressive, and analytical value.

This interpretation takes on considerable importance for the understanding of the developmental history of the sense-functions both as a whole and within the special domain of the comparative physiology of the senses. It is totally inconceivable that life in the course of its history would have fashioned organs and functions which should serve to procure cognition and truth, goals which are quite meaningless to life, instead of promoting, like all the other organs and functions of life, the introduction and unfolding of processes and reactions which serve its growth and preservation. If the sense-functions and organs are conceived as "instruments of speculation" (Bergson), then they are deprived of all the explanatory principles which could give us a developmental understanding of all the remaining parts of the organism. It makes no difference whether or not they have given us one up till now. Nothing seems clearer to me than these two principles:

1. Cognition of the environment can become biologically important to a creature only if the actual process which, in causal fashion, makes this cognition possible for the creature (e.g., stimulus, nervous process, excitation of the brain) also introduces a process or a reaction which leads the creature to gain some advantage or to avert some disadvantage.

2. However, if the real process can introduce such processes and reactions, then the concomitant cognition of this real process, or better, of its starting point, is an addition which makes no difference at all to the preservation of life. Consequently, a "cognitive function" or an "organ of cognition" is developmental nonsense: it would be an isolated *factum, toto*

caelo distinct from every other biological factor, projecting its way into this world as though it had come from another.

Once the essential acts which can lead to cognition are given, we can easily understand that the *choice* between the particular contents they may have for living creatures—insofar as living creatures are the bearers [*Träger*] of these acts —comes about through vital functions and the organs specifically organized for these functions, namely, the sense-functions and sense organs. Then the value of the sense-functions and organs for life as a whole is that they distribute possible cognition throughout the organic realm according to the grade of its vital importance to the various action-systems which constitute a species and a genus, etc. In this case, the "action-system" of a living creature guides the formation of the sense-*functions*, while the sense organs are first developed within the scope of these functions and the lawfulness peculiar to them by reason of the particular features of the real world and its effects on the creature.

The "action-system" determines the anatomical structure of the organism as well as its "milieu"; neither is the effect of the other, although they are exactly adapted to one another. They are "adapted" only because they go back to a third cause which determines them both. We see this cause in the "totality of the forms of life and intentions of vital movement," the structure of which constitutes the essence of an organism. By "milieu" I do not mean a "subjective image," a "perception," or a "sensation" of the organism, or the environment which objectively surrounds the organism and affects it. I mean, rather, that part or those aspects of that objective environment whose variation brings about a modification in the organism's vital processes (whether inner organic processes or reactions). Only processes of this sort should be called "stimuli," for not everything which has a real influence on the organism is a stimulus. All the mechanical, chemical, and electrical effects which impinge on the organism and have only physical and chemical effects are not stimuli. Conversely, a process can become a part of the milieu and a stimulus, even if it does not influence the body of the organism via a continuous chain of mechanical effects (e.g., a flash of light, a red cloth, the rearrangement of the pictures and chairs in a room, etc.), so long as it brings about such modifications (Pavlov's laboratory). All "milieus" are, so to speak, only side views of the world considered as one thing [*des Weltdinges*] and should not be confused with parts of the world. We can call the reality corresponding to natural world-view the "milieu of the species man." These milieus are accessible to a strictly objective study.[4] No "animal psychology" is needed for that (Uexküll).

An organism's milieu determines the scope of the world within which the organism's sense-functions can provide it with contents—I mean here the sense-functions as they are when still independent of the particular organization of the sense organs. The arrangement of these organs and the subjective organic states associated with them (*sensations* in the genuine sense) are themselves determined within the scope of the sense-functions. We can see, hear, smell, and taste only that which belongs to our *milieu*, or, to put it more sharply, the only qualities of the world that turn into sense-qualities are those which can become signs for the independently determined things and events within this milieu. We now know, especially after Pavlov's investigations and countless experiments, that any sense-content linked with another sense-content which triggers a physiological function is itself capable of instigating the same process. For example, either the sight of a lemon, or a certain tone frequently connected with this visual content, can trigger the process of salivary or gastric secretion, if either one of them is linked with taste, pressure, and temperature of a piece of food in the mouth or on the tongue. All these visual or auditory contents are simply signs *a, b,* and *c* for those properties of the lemon, *e, f,* and *g,* on account of which the process, e.g., one particular type of secretion, occurs. However, the contents which serve as signs need not be identical with the objective properties of the thing or fulfill them, even though it is these properties to which just this and no other form of secretion—for example, salivation—is suitable. Even where the given content, the optical appearance of the lemon, belongs to the thing in question (and this is not true in the

4. [On organism and milieu, see *Der Formalismus in der Ethik und die materiale Wertethik: Neuer Versuch der Grundlegung eins ethischen Personalismus,* 5th ed. rev., *Gesammelte Werke* II (Bern: Francke, 1966), chap. III.—ED.]

case of the simultaneously sounding tone), it is there only as a sign for the properties which are not given themselves. The sense-contents which arise in a natural way (without artificial instruments) do so only to the extent that they can take over the functions of such signs.

It would, therefore, be quite senseless to think that the sense-functions are formed and function completely for themselves and for the goal of cognition, quite independently of the vital processes of the whole organism. Clearly, the assumption that people seem to have had up till now, that a creature first possesses a definite range of sense-qualities and then perceives just those things whose properties are fulfilled by such qualities, is not valid. It is *because* a definite circle of things and events has importance for its reactions that the creature grasps with its senses only those qualities which can be signs of these things.

Therefore it holds true, in the comparative study of the sense-functions of animals, that the formation of the quality ranges which the various sense-functions have at their disposal is totally bound up with the expansion and contraction of the milieu. The lizard, for example, reacts to the phenomenon of a rustling noise by turning its head and fleeing. In contrast, it shows no reaction of any kind when, say, a weapon is fired over its head. Its sense of hearing is constructed only to grasp those tonal qualities which can occur in the phenomenon, so important to it, of a "rustling sound." It would be completely arbitrary to say that the lizard does indeed hear the discharge of the weapon as well, but that no reactive movement is bound up with this, since the sensory termini are not connected with its motor centers. Rather, it is the use that can be made of the sensory impression, its association with some phenomenon which is important to the lizard and its mode of life, that directs the formation of the organs capable of perceiving qualities within those ranges which the animal has at its disposal. It would be an unbiological and unphysiological way of looking at this matter to try to test the limits of sensibility and the thresholds of its power of discriminating certain qualities without paying attention to the "milieu." The animal does not start out with sense-functions and organs which provide it with certain qualities within certain limits and then go on to perceive all the possible things which have these qualities as properties; instead, because the animal perceives certain *things,* the qualities which can be used in comprehending those things are also given to it.

"Self-given" and "indirectly given" should not be equated with the distinction between what is "given at present" and what is given as past or future, any more than they should with the distinction between "sensory content" and "non-sensory content." People frequently describe matters as if only a tone sounding at present can be "given in person," while the continuation [*Nachdauern*] of this tone in so-called immediate memory or of a past tone given only in memory cannot be given "in person," as though that which is part of the present instant of consciousness has any advantage in evident self-givenness over that which is not part of the present but a part of a past consciousness. For instance, this is what Lipps has in mind when he says: "At the junction with my here-and-now lies the pivotal point of all certainty in general."

It can easily be shown that a complete phenomenological reduction has not taken place here. Once we abstract the intentional act from the individual, disregarding whether its content is posited as actual or not, and looking only at what appears along the direction this act takes, then we cannot, on the whole, speak of a "present act" at all. In order to decide whether an act is present or past we must refrain from carrying through this reduction. The concept of "present act" cannot be fulfilled in any other way than by our thinking of an individual who exists in objective time performing this present act; only because this individual is "in the present" is the act which he performs also "in the present." Any "being-present," "being-past," or "being-future" is already contained in the phenomenal content of the pure act. The distinctions we draw between perception, memory, and expectation, which are essentially connected with the intuition of the present, the past, and the future, are already distinctions between qualities of acts. No doubt these qualities are variable functions in relation to the content which we perceive, remember, or anticipate; nevertheless, they belong to the "phenomenal content" when we observe them in an act of unqualified intuition. We must thus sharply distinguish that which is given *in the acts themselves as* past, present, or future, and that which is *objectively* "present," "past," or "future." [5] Unquestionably these are completely *different* things. Real experiences of the objective past, or, better, one factor in these, for example, a feeling of sadness which they awake, can be given "as present." This is continually the case in experiences which have been suppressed and forgotten, although they color the felt-content of what is given as present and so are themselves given "as present." Through critical reflection we sometimes discover what it is that is making us sad or depressed and see that this has nothing to do with our present life. A man lives in one phase of his youth as though it were "in the present"; his interests, feelings, and ideas correspond to the situations of the eighteenth year of his life. This is a case of memory without any consciousness of the act of "remembering." So, too, an anticipated experience which objectively lies in the future can be given "as" present even though the act of anticipation does not stand out in relief. This happens, for example, when we are cheerful because in three days something joyous is going to happen, without our "picturing" this event to ourselves at the moment. This happens whenever we anticipate anything, e.g., when we feel pain at the mere sight of the enemy's drawn sword, indeed, already see the blood flowing.

Objective concepts are always to be regarded as *derived* from *phenomenological* concepts. There is *not* a "present consciousness" which has as its real components all acts and contents, including those which we remember or anticipate. Nor is it the case that since the contents cannot be present [*anwesend*], "representatives" or "symbols" for them must be on hand, the so-called memory images and anticipatory images—i.e., genuine and integral parts of the actual image-content which point to the past and the future only by means of certain "symbolic functions." Rather, from the start acts are present in *every* unity of consciousness in which some contents are given "as present," others "as past," still others "as future." What the psychologist calls "present consciousness" is only what he has added as a real process to that one part which is given "as present" and

5. [On the phenomenology of present, past, and future, see *Formalismus*, VI, A, 3, g, and the remarks on intuition and sensory perception which follow in the text.—ED.] [See also "Idealism and Realism," below.— TRANS.]

what he sees in the phenomena taken as signs of these processes.

Every "present ego," quite like every present physical phenomenon, is given from the first against a background which is lost in both directions of time as in a mist. The ego does not arise from the synthesis of many "momentary egos"; instead, the momentary ego is a part of the content of consciousness given at any one time. Indeed, the momentary ego is that part which has a certain conspicuous relationship to the body [*Leibe*] (whether the inner or external body) in virtue of which its variations depend on those of the body. If the body did not exist, the qualities of the temporal directions present, past, and future would make no sense. These temporal qualities are relative to the body.

We can now add a third distinction that obtains among facts which have been divided into phenomenological or pure and nonphenomenological (natural and scientific) facts. The phenomenological fact is a *pure* fact, that is, one from which all possible elements of sensation have been eliminated. Phenomenological seeing is "intuition" or pure intuition, in which the sensory functions no longer play a (intentional) role. We can also say that "phenomenological acts" are those whose unity and content are completely independent of the sensory functions by means of which they are given or with whose cooperation they are given.

Thus, the first thing required for identifying phenomenological facts is the radical *elimination* of any form of unity which is not based purely on the things-themselves but is only assigned to these because the unity of a *sensory function* allows us to grasp these things. As long as we simply exercise an act of seeing, hearing, smelling, these two forms of unity are not detached from one another and our perception is a sensory perception. It is quite different if this act of seeing, hearing, or smelling becomes part of the content of an act of intuition. This act of intuition is now no longer a sensory perception, but a *pure* perception.

Even though this fact already shows clearly that there does exist a pure act of perception in general, nevertheless, this act of intuition does not furnish the phenomenological fact generally. Indeed, the act does furnish one type of phenomenological fact, namely, the sensory function itself; but it does not furnish the state of affairs in phenomenological intuition which corresponds to the object of such a function in sensory perception. It does indeed make it possible for us to distinguish the unities "color," "tone," etc., and the unities between acts and individuals from the unities which they receive only because they are phenomena of seeing or hearing, accompanied by this or that sensation, this or that law of increase and diminution, of localization, etc., based on the functions of seeing and hearing. However, this view does not tell us what the pure *phenomenological content* in these phenomena themselves is. At the most, it leads only to the assertion that this is the residue which remains in the phenomenal content after one has removed the unities situated in these functions, together with the products of choice. However, this is a negative definition. It does not tell us directly and positively what the facts which are objects of the sense-functions *are* in pure intuition after the sense-functions have been removed. It achieves only the reduction of the phenomenon to its sensory content, not an *adduction* [*Adduktion*] of the phenomenon to exactly that content which is *independent* of the sense-functions and the unities they form.

Is such an adduction generally possible? Is it not reminiscent of every kind of mysterious assumption and undertaking to try to bring facts to intuition independently of our sensory constitution? We could not, so they say, get out of our own skin and see how things stand, if we did not possess this sensory constitution. Yet these objections completely overlook what is at issue here. The fact that the phenomenologist has eyes and ears and visual and auditory functions is a fact that not even he can dismiss. There is no real and experimental elimination of the sensory character [*Sinnlichkeit*] of our perception, any more than there is an elimination of the circulation of the blood, the heartbeat, and digestion, when perception occurs. The phenomenologist can no more do phenomenology without these things than he can do without eyes and ears. But it is a totally different question whether the phenomenologist as a cognitive being, in his mode of knowing and in the intentional intuitions of facts he performs, is necessarily bound to the intentional existence of eyes and ears, seeing and hearing, as much as he is to their *real* existence.

This question is not affected by our inability to get out of our own skins. Rather, two things are completely clear. First, even if there is a pure intuition of facts, a pure non-sensory intuition of them (which is as far removed from mediated thinking and inferring as it is from sensory perception), such an intuition, insofar as a living being performs it or is its bearer, can never be realized other than through and by means of a sensory organization. In other words, it could be realized only if this constitution brings it into the service of the needs, drives, reactions of this creature. Precisely because of this, however, the real dependence of intuition on a sensory constitution never provides the least proof that such a pure intuition of facts *does not* exist. Nor does the fact of this dependence prove that intuition is exhausted in the combined activity of the sensory functions or that its objects are exhausted in the complexes or partial contents of these functions, or, finally, that the sensory function is not *only* the condition of the *realization* of intuition for a living creature, but belongs to the *essence* of intuition. For this reason establishing these real or causal connections completely misses the point of the question occupying us here.

We must also mention another objection. The assertion that there is such a thing as a pure intuition, since it is surely not observable by the senses, is either itself clear in turn through pure intuition or only becomes so through mediated thinking, that is, through a procedure in which we vary the phenomena under different sensory conditions and see the positive element which remains identical in all these. The first alternative is impossible, since no act can be confirmed by another act of the very same type. If, however, the existence of a pure intuition and its factual content is confirmed only after the greatest efforts in mediated thinking, comparison, variation, paring away, etc., then the facts ascertained thereby are no longer "facts," much less "pure facts." They are mere abstractions produced by our analytical and comparative thinking, which takes its start from the facts of sensory perception—the only "true facts"! It is a strange intuition of "facts" which cannot itself be intuitively discovered but only comes to givenness through mediated thinking! What pass themselves off to it as "facts of pure intuition" are in reality only products and results of a mediated thinking which is essentially unintuitive. This is what someone *could* say.

Nevertheless, this objection is no more sound than the first and rests on the equation of the method of confirmation with the essence of what is confirmed. For again, it is clear that *if* a pure intuition exists through which a state of affairs becomes accessible, the reconstruction of this state of affairs can nonetheless be bound up with mediated thinking, with analysis and comparison and variation, with deduction and inference, owing to the fact that this intuition is necessarily thoroughly mixed with the psychological constitution of its bearer. That is, it is possible that what is immediately given through pure intuition comes into our consciousness in its purity *as* immediately given and *as* given through intuition only through a mediated process of thought. In every perception, including sensory perception, in every act of representation, memory, and expectation within the common world-view, pure intuition is present [*anwesend*] as that which spiritualizes all these acts, what furnishes everything purely positive in their contents, and institutes their intentional connection and their identical relationship to "the same." Nevertheless, the reconstruction of states of affairs which are given via this unitary intuition only after the particular modes, forms, and directions of its activation have been removed can be bound up with a procedure which is itself not pure intuition, but "mediated thinking." The methodological role this "thinking" plays would in no way be creative or synthesizing, as, for example, in Kant; it would be merely an unavoidable *means and tool* for bringing something to intuition which in its purity is at all other times indissolubly combined with factors which result from the sensory constitution of our nature, whether forced to do so through association or in some other way. Thought does not "create" or "produce" these states, it simply *purifies* them.

The foregoing shows that these objections do not place the goal, namely to bring the facts themselves to intuition, beyond reach. On the other hand, that such intuition is possible is no positive proof that a non-sensory intuition exists. All that has been shown is that the actual cooperation of intuition and sensory functions is an incontestable fact which speaks neither for nor against the existence of a pure intuition, for everything here hinges on the *kind* of connection and necessity which obtains between intuition and sensory function. Is it a necessity rooted in the essence of both, like the connection between extension and color, for example, or is it a necessity of an exclusively causal, for example associative, nature? Is our ability to grasp the facts themselves grounded in the essence of our intuition, or is it only a condition of the realization of intuitive acts by the real bearer, "man," "animal," etc., that the sense-functions play a definite and unavoidable role here, that they appear as analytical factors in between the act of pure intuition and what is intuited?

Only phenomenology itself can decide these questions. If, after the phenomenological reduction has been undertaken, facts and connections between them still remain, we have proof that there is a "pure intuition," that the facts are "pure" facts, and that their connections are "essential connections" which defy all merely causal explanation. If facts and their interconnections do not remain, then no intuition exists, and the constitution of our picture of the world is relative to the sense-functions.

We can now adduce four essential characteristics of "pure facts" from what has been said:

1. The pure fact must maintain itself as a positive something [*Etwas*] and as an intuitive identity when the sense-function through which this fact actually reaches us is varied, provided that the sense-function itself is brought into our intuition and is then varied within the sphere of the phenomenological reduction. What accounts for the differences between these facts must not be explainable in terms of the differences between the sense-functions through which they in fact become accessible to us. The connection between these facts must be absolutely inexplicable in terms of the concrete physiologically and psychologically real connection between our sensory functions.

2. The pure fact must have the character of an ultimate *foundation* of the merely sensory components of natural facts. In other words, when other pure facts are added the specific sensory content of the phenomena is altered, while the addition of an altered sensory content does not alter the pure fact. Or, more briefly: if pure facts exist, then they must be the *independent variable*, while the sense-content is the dependent variable. The possible, indeed, even the actual, sensory appearances of the intuited object must be determined only by

its purely objective nature, even though these appearances are univocally determined only when we include the actual performance of the sense-functions belonging to the percipient creature. However, it can never be the case that the nature of the intuited state of affairs changes when the manifold sensory contents which enter into it change—contrary to what sensationalism teaches.

3. The identity and difference of pure facts must be completely independent of all the *symbols* with which it is possible for us to designate them and of the symbols which are used in presenting the facts of which they are parts. Equally, their connections must be totally independent of the connections which we have created between the symbols for them through convention, stipulation, or custom. Furthermore, their connections must be independent of those which the component parts of these facts have only because it is their function to represent what is not given in person [*Nicht-Selbstgegebenes*].

4. We want to divide pure facts into two classes: first, the totality of "phenomenological facts in the broader sense," then a class of "phenomenological facts in the narrower sense." Phenomenological facts can be facts which lie in the essence of an *object in general* as well as facts which differentiate the essences of objects. The first class coincides with the basic facts of pure logic; the phenomenology of this class is the basis of pure logic or the theory of objects. The second class is that of phenomenological facts in the narrower sense. It is clear that anything which differentiates or diversifies phenomenological facts can never lie in the content which they have only in virtue of being objects pure and simple. It is also clear that the connections between them are intuitive essential connections and for this reason must be "necessary" for anything which becomes their bearer. Nonetheless, pure logic alone cannot gain insight into these connections. Thus, from the standpoint of pure logic, the connections would be incomprehensible and, so to speak, accidental or contingent. As against any inductive necessity, however, they would be intuitive and grounded in the essence of the facts themselves. These essential connections which are not purely logical may be labelled "essential connections in the narrower sense." The principles of pure logic would not take precedence over them, since these principles themselves only

represent a *limiting case* of essential connections, namely, those that hold between objects simply because they are objects and nothing more. Even the principle of noncontradiction [*sic*], the principle that one of the two propositions "*A* = *B*" and "*A* = not-*B*" is false or that a proposition of the form "*A* = not-*A*," whatever stands in the place of *A*, is false, would have its ultimate basis not in itself but in the incompatibility of the being and nonbeing of an object. And this is a phenomenological and ontological insight. On the other hand, there can be countless instances of incompatibility which are not intelligible from the principle of noncontradiction or the incompatibility on which it is based.

These four characteristics must, I say, be proper to "pure facts" in the narrower sense. They constitute their essence. Phenomenology stands or falls with the assertion that such facts *do exist* and that these facts and their connections are genuinely what lies at the basis of all other facts and connections, those of the natural and scientific world-view.

One note on the second characteristic. Perhaps nothing distinguishes our view of phenomenology so fundamentally from prevailing views, even from theories which in other respects stand quite close to phenomenology (e.g., the theory of "Gestalt-qualities," or the views expressed by Carl Stumpf in his *Erscheinungen und psychische Funktionen*), even, indeed, from Edmund Husserl's theory of "categorial intuition"[6] than the second characteristic of the essence of pure facts. We cannot spare all these views the reproach that they share the *prōton pseudos* of the sensationalistic theory of cognition. This error does not seem to us to lie simply in the radical sensationalistic thesis that the entire content of intuition can coincide with the sensory material or with any transformation of this material through psychic development, but rather in the presupposition that sensory contents *furnish the foundation* of every other content of intuition. Some of these thinkers admit non-sensory but still intuitive contents which in no way reduce to relations and which are not instituted or produced by the activity of thought, as in the cases mentioned above. Nonethe-

6. [See Husserl, *Logische Untersuchungen* (Halle: Niemeyer, 1900; rev. ed., 1913), II, 40–46, English translation by J. N. Findlay, *Logical Investigations* (New York: Humanities Press, 1970), II, 773–88.—TRANS.]

less, they think they can still say (I cite here Husserl only) that although "categorial intuition" is indeed an independent function vis-à-vis sensory intuition (and thus is never intelligible in terms of some transformation of the latter), and although it is distinct from all "thinking" which is merely a significative "intending" [bloss signifikativen Meinen] (e.g., the *intuition* of equality, similarity, unity, totality, thinghood is distinct from the identically named *meanings* which are fulfilled only in such intuitions), nonetheless, every categorial intuition is "founded," whereas only "sensuous intention" is unfounded intuition. This theory is not essentially different from the theory of "Gestalt-qualities."

I have a twofold objection to make here. First, the consistency of a purely phenomenological procedure is suddenly interrupted here, once when the concept of "sensory" intuition is introduced without examination, and then again when the objective presuppositions of the "perception" of the objects of categorial intuition are identified with what is "given in person" in this perception. This means that the phenomenological reduction is not scrupulously carried through. This might be the reason why, in the second place, a host of indubitable facts remain concealed which speak in favor of the opposite view, namely, that the contents of categorial intuition "found" the contents of sensory intuition. This is in fact the case provided that the expression "to found" is understood, not as the temporal order in which the component parts of a particular intuitive object which is already posited as real (that is, in the case of an incomplete "reduction") become accessible to us as beings with a body and a soul [als leiblich-seelischen Wesen], for in that case founding is confused with causality, but as the order in which certain intentional acts and the contents they embrace are built upon one another in accordance with their essence. It makes no difference which bearers of acts are involved here or whether the things [Sachen] at issue are real or unreal. Only those inner, objective relations of dependence which lie in the phenomenologically "given" order of phenomena should be called relations of *founding*, if we are going to use this term to designate something distinct from the genetic order of the course of perception.

In recent times Kant's theory has sometimes been interpreted along these lines.[7] I think that it is completely mis-construed in this interpretation. The sense of Kant's theory remains the thought that in the "material of appearance" only what shows itself suited to fulfilling "forms," "modes and laws of comprehension," and certain basic relations which are already inherent in the essence of human understanding can be given. The "structure" of experience precedes all sensory contents. Its parts and elements cannot themselves be derived from pure thought and must simply be exhibited. This structure limits and circumscribes a priori the range in which sensory facts can possibly be given to us. Thus far phenomenology can, in principle, acknowledge Kant's results. Phenomenology rejects only the derivation of such a structure from the modes of activity of the human mind, since it demands that even this structure must be accessible to an intuition and experience and thus cannot be the condition of every "possible experience." It becomes the *object* of phenomenological intuition; the latter overcomes the relativity of natural *and* scientific experience, since it makes this structure itself the object of intuitive inspection. Moreover, the phenomenologically elucidated theory of cognition distinguishes between natural experience and scientific experience, while in Kant they merge into one another and become indistinguishable.

One final remark about the third requirement. Phenomenological interconnections must be independent of any factual connection which occurs only because of connections between symbols designating facts and, beyond this, between symbols whose bearers are situated in the facts *themselves*. These are the symbols in which facts "present themselves" without our having added on some arbitrary symbols.[8] It is not a basic peculiarity of natural intuition alone, as we have shown, that bodies, events, etc., present "themselves" in so-called phenomena where the content is partly given, partly consumed, as it were, in its twofold function of symbolizing both things and our sensory condition; the very same thing holds true of the *connections* between natural facts.

7. See E. von Aster, *Immanuel Kant* (Leipzig; 1909).
8. [See (2) of the next section of this essay, "Transcendence and Symbol."—ED.]

[II] THE DISTINCTION BETWEEN THE FACTS
OF THE NATURAL OUTLOOK
AND THE FACTS OF SCIENCE

1. *Things, events, and states of affairs*

IT IS CLEAR AT FIRST SIGHT that *natural* experience
and *scientific* experience are very different things. Even someone
who wants to furnish sound theoretical proof that in the end
they are different only in degree, must admit this. Scientific
experience, with regard to external nature, for instance, leads
to a complicated mechanism of motion. Neither this mechanism itself nor its parts and the real things supposedly underlying them are found in the content of *natural experience.*
There are no atoms, molecules, or masses in natural experience
and no attempt is made there to replace colors and tones with
vibrations. In natural experience there is no "space" and no
"time" in the sense in which geometry and chronometry have
strictly defined these structures. What is there is an at least
halfway intuitive world of colors and sounds, a world which
surrounds us, articulated into unities of things and events.
Science begins its work by destroying this world. A stone is
here no complex of molecules, no "something" continually exchanging energy with its surroundings, no mere unity of mass
with a definite magnitude; it is just a stone, a unity complete
in itself which answers to an act of natural perception. This
world is neither a continuous whole from which we extract only
artificial parts, nor a sum of homogeneous, simple particles.
Bodies have their vague differences of size, without being
measured and expressed numerically. However, these sizes are
not constant. Bodies become larger and smaller with distance
and proximity. This world contains distinctions like that between reality and unreality; things have a causal effect on one
another, come into being, and pass away. There are capacities
and powers of every kind, distinctions between the animate and
the inanimate. The objects of this world are not "complexes of
sensation" or "representations" or "contents of consciousness"
or anything else of this sort. This world also includes states and
peoples, for instance, which one cannot see with the eyes nor
hear with the ears.

Whatever theories one has, one always returns once again to this "natural world." Primordial and indestructible by thought, this world always returns, as though automatically, whenever we try to imagine ourselves looking at things differently. It is the medium in which we live and carry on our affairs. Today the sun still rises and sets in this world, sometimes red, sometimes white. Despite Copernicus, this world is the stable immovable ground beneath us on which we stride, a surface curved and bent in numerous ways, the "earth" with a certain horizon. About us the stars shine at night, and the moon is now full, now a crescent. This world is "real," and we are absolutely convinced that things remain on the table as they are when we leave the room. We do not merely expect to see them again when we reenter the room. We do indeed expect that, but only because we believe that they are also there when we do not perceive them.

One can consider the natural world from two points of view: that of *natural perception* and that of *natural thinking*, which we can call "sound common sense." We meet with this sound common sense objectified in a certain sense in ordinary language, in its categories and the corresponding parts of speech, in the units and structures of meaning through which perceived things and events, etc., are named and through which they are distinguished from one another, if only in a vague way. There exists here a "natural" way of judging and inferring, a "natural" way of examining and experimenting with things. Just as an equally spatial and temporal perspective pervades the entire world of natural perception, just as all things appear indefinite and indistinct when they are at a distance from the lived-body and the here and now and become smaller and smaller in the visual world, until they disappear into a nothingness which is in some way surrounded by an unknown, so, too, a kind of perspective pervades the "world of meaning" which an individual (or a people, etc.) has at his disposal. The more important objects are to his most elementary needs, the more urgent the essences of these needs are, the more precise are the distinctions he will draw between them and between their similarities and their differences. We sharply distinguish among animals or plants which are useful to us, while other animals and plants are designated only by quite vague "concepts." In natural "space" there are an "above" and "below," an "ahead" and "behind," a "right" and a "left." In natural "time" there are, above all, past, present, and future. A finite segment of indeterminate magnitude of both space and time is present in this natural world, where these two are the same for things as well as events. An empty and a filled space, an empty and a filled time are also present in that world.

I would like to give only a few examples of how this natural outlook should be received. First of all, one must guard against importing theories into it. For example, it is nonsense to ask, as Berkeley did, "Does the 'common man' believe in matter or not?" in order to go on to prove that the common man is an "idealist" and does not believe in it, in short, to conclude that matter is an "invention of the learned." The common man does not have the object "matter" and he has neither a positive nor a negative conviction about it.

Passing on to *science*, we must call its world-view "artificial" as opposed to the "natural" world-view. In place of the simple natural perception of things and events, in science "observation" comes into play, and this is something quite different from natural perception. Observation furnishes contents where natural perception has no more to give. It is not essential in science for a voluntary effort of attention to precede observation, for this occurs in the natural world-view as well. It *is* essential, however, that "observation," in contrast to perception, is always accompanied by an intention trained on something which I want to observe. Furthermore, this "something" is always the idea of some *state of affairs* and I want to see whether this obtains or not, or what it looks like in this or that thing or event. A judgment or a question need not be present to guide my observation. Rather, my judgments and even my questions can change because of observation. It would thus be much too much to claim that observations serve only to verify judgments which have already been completed or that observations are only means to lead us to other judgments. It would be saying too much to assert that a definite question must precede any scientific observation, whether a question of "if" or of "what." Observation is not merely a means for solving questions; often entirely new questions arise from a so-called accidental observation. But observing is never a blind gazing into space, however attentive it may be; it is never merely a matter of "paying heed to something." As the prefix "ob-" indicates, in observation I am directed toward "something" which I intend, which I grasp by anticipation, with the mind's eye. And this "something" is never a quality, for I can never observe a quality but can only see it [*erschauen*]. It is never a "thing" or "event" "on" which I am making my observation during the time I perceive it (without, for this reason, observing either in the strict sense). Rather, that which I observe is a "state of affairs," the state of being-red or being-blue or being-hard, etc., a state of affairs which is only meant or intended. The target of observation is the obtaining or non-obtaining of this state of affairs, its being thus-and-so or being otherwise.

Thus the first characteristic of scientific facts is that they are chiefly "states of affairs" and not qualities or things or events. This does not mean that science does not assume and recognize "things" and "events." However, it is essential that science not make things and events into its direct and immediate objects of inspection, but only construct these as the requisite "bearers" of states of affairs. It constructs them, as will be shown shortly, according to the requirements of a certain nexus of states of affairs which is itself a priori for the experience of the pertinent science. This nexus is not derived from individual states of affairs but follows from the essence of the states of affairs and those of their ingredient qualities with which this one science is concerned. Scientific things and events thus need not be accessible to perception. This holds true as much for the bodies, masses, and distances, which astronomy constructs in thought as the bearers and starting points of the phenomenal states of affairs which alone are accessible to observation, as it does of atoms and molecules, etc. These are not, in the strict sense, "scientific facts," but *explanatory assumptions* needed to support facts and render them intelligible. While, therefore, things and events are "given" in natural intuition, in the scientific perspective they are not "given" but constructed and indirectly thought.

There is absolutely no recognition of this fact in two "popular" theories whose common failing is ignorance of the nature of states of affairs. The first is the theory which equates "facts" with complexes of sensation or perceptual contents and then says either that science must content itself with the search for lawful connections between these (Mach) or that it must suppose that realities underlie them that are only conceptually and unintuitively comprehensible. Accordingly, this theory must assume that the objective connection between these realities corresponds to the subjective connection between sense-contents (Külpe). Against this theory, we must say that there simply is no law which obtains among the contents of sensation and contents of perception. The physicist begins his work precisely by eliminating what is due only to his sensations. Only through such an elimination does some form of lawfulness arise in the context of his "facts." The perceptual contents follow one another without rules. As for the second theory, if nothing exists besides perceptual contents and "realities" of the sort already mentioned, it is impossible to see on what sort of *evidence* [*Anhaltspunkte*] the assumption of objectively subsisting relations between these realities is based. At this point one could only resort once again to the relations between perceptual contents. However, if these clues already lie in perceptual contents, what additional purpose is served by assuming those relations and the objective connection between them? Is it not obvious that here one abandons the very starting point of the investigation which originally led one to assume these realities, namely, that no conformity to law holds sway between perceptual contents? If this conformity does not exist in them, how, then, are strict and unambiguous "clues" for the assumption of objective relations between realities going to exist in them? One is obviously turning in a circle. It is altogether different if the elimination of contents of sensation leaves behind unities of "states of affairs" which are completely independent of these contents. Then these states of affairs can serve as starting points for the construction of realities, while their connection, which already subsists objectively, can do the same for the real causal connections which are not "given."

Theories which totally deny that there is a world of "scientific facts" independent of the sphere of judgment and its laws [*Gesetzmässigkeiten*] are opposed to these forms of empiricism and realism.[9] Here a "fact" is always only the X which satisfies an imposed relational nexus of conceptual meanings (the X which, metaphorically speaking, "satisfies" an equation). On this view, science *creates* its own "facts" and these can

9. See Paul Natorp, *Die logischen Grundlagen der exakten Wissenschaften* (Leipzig, 1910), pp. 92, 94.

deviate as much as one likes from natural facts. It is only the context of thoughts and thought-elements which guarantees the truth of each one of these facts. Any talk of scientific judgment's having to conform itself to "facts" no longer makes sense. Conform to what facts? Science should not be tied down to the "facts" of the natural world-view. On the contrary, science should explain the content and existence of this natural world-view with the help of its concepts, principles, and methods! "Scientific facts" are always only demands to form new connections; they are factors promoting the procedure of pure thought. It is not surprising that, according to this view, the "objective side" [*das "Objektive"*] of the universe consists in a purely relational structure which is not anchored to anything, while its *termini* can be arbitrarily varied. But relations of this sort which are not attached to anything are absurd. The world is something else besides a mathematical equation which here has the dignity of a *noumenon*. And there is an *essential* distinction between "scientific facts" and scientific concepts and propositions. I cannot define a "scientific fact" as an X of which an existential judgment holds true. The *concept*, the meaning of "existence," is something other than existence *itself*. To strive for a formalization of all of science, as the Marburg school does, is to do impossible violence to all the exact sciences.

Nevertheless, a correct insight, or a whole series of correct insights, does underlie Natorp's arguments, which is not recognized by the first group of researchers mentioned above. The first insight is that the scientific fact is no more contained in the natural fact than it is reducible to the contents of sensation, to sense-contents. We can understand readily enough that someone who sees both these points and, for the rest, recognizes nothing besides an activity of conjunction which is regulated by logic and has its seat in the sphere of judgment and deduction, must deny the "factual nature" of scientific facts. Such a thinker also sees, quite rightly, that scientific facts cannot consist in the concrete things and events of the natural outlook (not even as a partial content), since the scientific view presupposes that these things and events have been destroyed. In addition, he rightly sees that the scientific fact represents something new vis-à-vis the facts of simple perception, something not contained in simple perception as well as something bearing the marks of an "intellectualization" [*Durchgeistigung*] which "natural facts" lack.

However, it is completely in error to assert that the "scientific fact" is only the X which must be extracted from the given which has already been established by judgment and that it is, therefore, nothing which can be given in the absence of this sort of confirmation. Rather, phenomenal states of affairs exist independently of the sphere of judgment and of everything which can be laid to the account of thinking. Whether I "assert," "assume," "inquire into," or "leave undecided" some state of affairs which I have seen makes no difference at all to its existence. It is the obtaining or non-obtaining of this state of affairs or of its content that I observe in any thing or "event."

In this, too, Natorp is right. Things, events, and forces are, in the "scientific outlook," only the bearers of facts and their relationships, constructed according to a priori laws which do not lie in these as such (for they presuppose that these things, etc., are known), any more than they do in the content of perceptions and sensation. But it does not follow that these laws must be equivalent to laws of the acts or functions of thought, such as judging and deducing—in a word, to the laws of the operation of an understanding, as Kant asserts. Rather, although these laws precede "things" and "events," although they guide our assumptions concerning things and events as bearers of the states of affairs, assumptions which must hold true of "all" things insofar as they are the bearers of such states of affairs, nonetheless, they can still be *objective* [*gegenständliche*] and *ontological* laws, based on the essence of these states of affairs and not on a mere processing [*Bearbeitung*] of the states of affairs in thought.

I must add one more remark. I am by no means asserting that only things and events are to be found in the natural outlook and its objects, and not states of affairs, or that states of affairs have their place only in science. The distinction between the natural view and the scientific view rests much more on the *direction* in which we proceed from the one to the other, that is, from the state of affairs to a thing or conversely. In the natural perspective, we move from things to states of affairs; in the scientific, we start by leaving the question of things, events, and forces undecided and proceed from states of affairs to things.

Thus, the first characterization of scientific fact which we require is that it is a "state of affairs" which appears only in observation. Just as "observation" takes the place of perception, so "natural" experimentation or any investigation in the course of work or play is replaced by the "technical" experiment, where the conditions under which some phenomenon can be observed and identically reproduced are methodically isolated and varied. Let us leave this out of account for the moment, since it is not characteristic of the essence of science.

2. *Transcendence and symbol*

The two kinds of facts in question here, the facts of the natural outlook and those of science, have something in common as well as something which distinguishes them.

It is common to them, first, that both kinds of facts, in principle, can never be brought within an act of cognition. Instead, it is characteristic of both kinds that the intentional act which apprehends them (whether it is of a conceptual or an intuitive nature) intends [*meint*] something *more* than the content present in the act as it is being performed. This meaning-something-more and meaning-something-beyond what is phenomenologically immanent is what we call the *transcendence* of the act. Accordingly, the two kinds of facts are to be called "transcendent facts." I may look at a corporeal object, for example, from every side in succession; I may open it, divide it, investigate as much as I like; in every act of apprehending it I *mean* more than what I know about it at any one time. This holds not only of intuitive and real objects, but also of pure objects of thought and ideal objects, for example, the number 4. Even when I am thinking this number under the meaning "3 + 1" or "2 + 2" or "5 − 1," I have in view the number with all its properties, even though I do not need to be thinking of all of them. Thus what we are here calling transcendence is not limited to the real. Consequently, we say that the two kinds of facts are *phenomenologically transcendent*.

They have another feature in common in addition to their transcendence. They are never themselves given in the present or "in person"; what is given in them (in quite different ways in the two cases, as we shall see) is either *simply* a *sign* or a *symbol* for them, or contents which stand as signs or symbols for them, although this does not mean that the facts disappear completely. Consequently, these facts are always necessarily given *indirectly* [*mittelbar*], never directly. This holds true of physical, mental, and ideal facts.

What we are here calling "indirect" or "mediated" should not be taken to mean "inferred." The inferred is only one species of the indirectly given. Everything ought to be called indirectly given which does not lie in the phenomenological content of the corresponding act. Certainly in an act of common sensory perception the physical object as a whole, together with its back side, its inside, etc., is intended. However, this whole is not given directly but only by means of the *appearance* of this physical object. In natural perception the content of this appearance is at the same time a symbol for this *intended* whole. For this reason, however, the intended whole is by no means inferred from the appearance. We *infer*, for example, that there is fire when we see smoke rising. But fire is not inferred from the red, flickering light which I see there in the distance; rather I perceive the fire *in* this appearance and, as it were, through it. Second, "indirectly given" should not be equated with "given only by means of a sign," in other words, by means of some real fact, such as a phonetic complex which constitutes the unity of a word, or a figure in a table which is not related to the thing it designates but merely stands for it on the basis of convention, definition, or custom. Naturally, what is given in this way is only indirectly given. Indeed, this indirectness is, as it were, the ideal limit of the indirectness with which something can be given at all. In this case the phenomenological content which is given in the intentional act is nullified and the content or object which serves as a sign pulls completely free of what it designates. The lines, colors, and forms furnished by the physical objects themselves serve as signs for what natural perception, which is performed wordlessly, intends. It is in the physical objects and not in quite new things like sounds, letters, etc., added by us, that the intended wholes of things express themselves, as it were.

We shall call the second feature of the two kinds of facts discussed here the *symbolism* of natural and scientific experience. This common feature of the two types of facts is the *indirectness of their givenness*.

We must now emphasize as strongly as we can a point

which people have continually failed to appreciate. This failure has done the greatest harm to the theory of cognition. The distinction between self-givenness and symbolic givenness defined here has nothing to do with the opposition between "sensory content" and "non-sensory content." Thus, what I have said on no account entails the assertion that "sensory contents" are "self-given," while non-sensory contents are indirectly given, or that what is immediately given in the total content of the natural perception of a physical object, for example, coincides with its sensory content. Such an assertion is made by every sort of sensationalism and would have to be proved. However, the whole orientation of the concepts "sensory" and "non-sensory" has nothing in the least to do with our orientation. What we designate as indirect and direct or immediate must always lie *in* the intended object. It is intended in this object and it is given in this object, whether symbolically or directly. Thus, the color red, which is a property of a cherry, is given to me directly, when I look at a cherry with a particular shape. The inside of the cherry, which is also intended, is not given to me directly, but only symbolically. But something like "sensory content" or "content of sensation" is never given to me in the cherry. Coloredness [*Farbigkeit*] is perhaps given to me in the red color, but "sensory content" is still not given. That red as a matter of fact is a sensory content is not given to me in the intention of the act of perception either immediately or symbolically. It is just as extraneous to the act of perception as the fact that it is a man who performs this act, or that this man has lungs, a heart, and two legs. The expression "sensory" can in general never signify a feature which can be found in tones and colors. This nuance of color has the color-tone yellow, this brightness, and that saturation, it is warm or cold; but to say that it is "sensory" is a meaningless assertion. Sensory content and "sensation" are precisely those concepts which most require a phenomenological analysis, in other words, a reduction to that which is immediately given by what these concepts intend. Consequently, they should never be presupposed and applied in a phenomenological analysis. Furthermore, these concepts tell us only *how* any definite content, whether given directly or symbolically, reaches us as men, through seeing, hearing, tasting, etc. However, the manner in which they do so can never be found in the content itself.

When we are trying to establish what is contained in a fact which appears in the natural or scientific mode, any theorizing about what *can* and what *cannot* be given, on the basis of this explicitly or implicitly presupposed theory, must withdraw before the straightforward establishment of what *is* given in this fact. However, this rule is violated if, along with the sensationalists of every sort, we start from the unclear thought that only sensory facts can be given to us and therefore *are* given to us. For, or so one thinks, that for which there are no sense-functions and no special and appropriate sense organs, or, finally, that for which there are no special *stimuli,* cannot be given to us. Once a person has entered upon this false way of seeing and arguing, he must naturally conclude that any part of the content found in the objects of natural and scientific experience that projects beyond those of its elements we can identify as contents of sensation, and thus cannot coincide with such contents, is something that we added on in some way or another, the result of our activity, a product of our shaping or fashioning, etc. Relations, forms, space, time, objectivity, being and nonbeing, values, thinghood, unity, plurality, multiplicity, motion, and change, causal operation, the distinction between the mental and the physical, etc., must then one and all be reduced to an addition of this kind, to a product of our shaping or fashioning.

Much more important, however, is the question of how scientific and natural facts are distinguished with respect to their transcendent and symbolic character. Both are transcendent and symbolic in the sense we defined. They are never "given themselves" in contrast to the phenomenological fact. And yet there is a vast difference in the *mode* of their transcendence and symbolism.

We begin with the mode of "transcendence." Science unfolds for us a picture of the world whose objects are transcendent not only to *phenomenological* intuition but also to *natural* intuition, which itself already far transcends the immediately given. Thus the heaven of astronomy is completely transcendent to the natural world-view. Masses of the size astronomy hypothesizes, the distances which it posits, temperatures like that of the sun, are completely inaccessible to natural perception and representation. In what does the difference of transcendence consist? Let us take some simpler examples.

How does the distance between two bodies differ depending on whether that distance exists for science or for the natural outlook? How does a particular metallic sphere differ in the one case and the other? Let us start by considering both only from the side of intuition, leaving out the sphere of judgment.

I said earlier that the physical object belonging to the natural outlook has a doubly symbolic function. This holds true insofar as the appearance falling within perception is in any way present to begin with and has a definite content but at the same time functions as a sign first for the whole "intended" physical object "intended" or "meant" in the act of perception and then for our bodily condition. Thus, it is not the case here that the "phenomenal content" completely disappears in the face of the symbolic representational function which it also possesses. I do see the red gleaming in the greenery as a sign for the cherry, but I also see the "red"; I "see" it, even though not in the same way I would see it if I grasped it as the quality it is *for itself* (and not as the property of a thing). Thus, too, I always see "the same" distance between the chair and the table, despite the fact that the appearance is strictly speaking lengthened or shortened with every movement of the head. I notice this fact about this appearance only with great difficulty, since I pay attention only to the representational function of the appearance and this refers to the "same" distance between the two bodies in each of the changing appearances. The presentational functions of the appearances have the same orientation and all intersect "in the distance between the bodies." And yet, these appearances are still given to me in conformity with the content each of them has. Together they belong to the notion of "distance" germane to the natural outlook.

However, I can assume a different attitude. I can completely rob the "appearance" of its own content which it always has in natural perception and grasp it artificially as a *symbol* only: a symbol, first, of a "sphere" [*Kugel*] the whole of which, including the side turned toward me, now lies completely outside the content of perception, and then as a symbol of a "state" in me. I take this state to be the basis of the different modes of givenness of the side of the sphere turned toward me and the side not turned toward me. The "appearance" has now completely disappeared. What remains is, first, the objectively existing sphere and, second, a state in me. What is this objectively existing sphere? Certainly nothing which can any longer be intuited. From now on it is only the identical object of all possible statements which can be made about it. The series of these statements is essentially infinite and can never be concluded.

I call the reduction of the natural sphere-thing [*Kugelding*] undertaken here a "scientific reduction." It is diametrically opposed to the phenomenological reduction. The phenomenological reduction seeks to strip the content of appearance of all signs and representational functions and get it *directly* into sight. Only in this way does the "appearance" become an absolute "phenomenon." The scientific reduction, on the contrary, eliminates the appearance insofar as it has a content of its own and leaves only its "empty" representational function. Now, for the first *time*, a "man in a certain state" stands over here and a "sphere" stands over there. These can no longer be "given" to one another but are from now on only parts of reality which can *affect* one another, without the man's knowing any more of this than the sphere does.

Thus, the "scientific object" corresponding to the sphere is reached when the appearance of the sphere has lost the privilege it possessed in natural perception over the sides and parts which are simply intended. That which entered into the appearance in natural perception now belongs to the sphere in the same way as that which does not appear at all. It, too, is only intended and intended exactly in the way its inner parts are. The scientific object, to express it paradoxically but intelligibly, is present where the front side is given exactly as the back side is. Since the sphere now no longer "presents itself" through an appearance, if we are still going to direct an intentional act upon it, there remains nothing for us to do but to represent it through something which lies completely *outside* of it, in other words, through a thing produced by us which serves as a *sign* for it; namely, a word or some other kind of sign. We can say, therefore: (1) the phenomenological object is "self-given"; (2) the object of natural intuition is symbolically given, but it "represents itself"; and (3) the object of science is only symbolically intended and is represented by an artificially established sign.

"Object" and "fact" are thus sharply distinguished. While the "facts" of science are "states of affairs," the bearers of these facts are only *symbolically meant objects*. These objects contain a definite content only in virtue of *scientific definition*. "Definition," therefore, is in fact an indispensable constituent of the "scientific object." Definition does not find the object before it but "constructs" it, although it constructs it on the basis of facts or states of affairs which are combined into a unity in the object. Thus, one should in fact say that the straight line or the circle of geometry, the sulphur of chemistry, etc., are, as objects of science, only "given" through their definitions.

The "definition" under consideration here must be strictly distinguished from something else which is frequently given the same name. In the first place, the "definition" must be distinguished from the specification of *what a word means in ordinary language* [Volkssprache]. Just as science is not bound to natural perception for its intuition, neither is it bound to the meanings of the words of ordinary language for the meaning of its own concepts. The assertion that in the end science always must have recourse to the words of ordinary language (an assertion which is defended by those who see science merely as a completion of the natural world-view) is completely inadmissible.[10] Mathematical and chemical symbols are not necessarily linked to ordinary language. If we call the specification of what a word in ordinary language means a "definition," then this is something completely different from scientific definition in the above sense. For giving a "definition" of a word in ordinary language is always a question of analyzing a preexistent "meaning," and the results of this analysis can be "true" or "false." What we achieve with this sort of "natural definition," as we want to call it, is never the new constitution of an "object," but always only a clearer insight into the limits of the range within which the presupposed meaning legitimates the application of the sign bearing this meaning to the facts.

Scientific or technical definition, on the contrary, freely raises up totally new unities out of the sphere of meaning, guided only by the idea that the conjunction of states of affairs

10. [See Appendix B, below.—ED.]

in one of these new objects should be as expedient as possible. For this reason, such a definition is never "true" or "false." It constructs a unity of meaning on the basis of the essential interconnections between object, being, thinghood, corporeal unity, etc., to which an object which itself can never be "given" must correspond. Likewise, such a definition must be distinguished from the determinations of scientific terms which take place on the basis of constructive definitions of this sort. These "definitions" no doubt also display the element of choice which lies in constructive definitions; however, once constructive definitions are presupposed, then these "definitions" can be true or false. Thus, one can give very different scientific "definitions," in this sense, of a "straight line," so long as a constructive definition, for example, that a straight line is a line uniquely determined by two points, is presupposed.

This example shows that the scientific world-view, even in its logical character, is not bound to the rules of "sound common sense" and thus not to any sort of logic which might be built upon the observation and description of natural thinking. Its artificial abstraction of classes and laws does not presuppose the "natural abstraction " of these, which is carried out involuntarily. Its inferences (deductive and inductive) and its "method" do not presuppose the natural forms of the movement of thought. Instead, science has a "logic of its own." To be sure, this logic must do justice to the *phenomenologically essential* relations between objects in general, which already underlie ordinary logic, but it need not conform to any principles of a "logic" which presupposes linguistic meanings which have already been defined. Thus, there is no one "principle of noncontradiction" which is to be found in both scientific and natural logic or to which scientific logic would have to pay heed; there is only a phenomenologically essential relation which must find a certain logical wording in both forms of logic.[11] Accordingly, the purest form of scientific logic is *symbolic logic,* which erects its structures with total freedom while respecting those phenomenological relations, and is not tied down to a philosophical logic.

11. [See "Phenomenology and the Theory of Cognition," p. 136.— TRANS.]

3. Natural and scientific selection

I want to point out still another difference between the natural outlook and the scientific outlook. This is the difference between their *bearers* [*Träger*]. The bearer of the natural view is the natural *lived-community* [*Lebensgemeinschaft*] of a people at any one time.[12] The bearer of the scientific view is an *institution* with the name "science"; its members are called "savants." Just as the unity of the objects of science rests on artificial and constructive definitions, so the basic content of this "institution," its constitution, is built up from generally acknowledged "convention." Taken together, these conventions form the "dogma of science"; among these conventions are, for example, all the technical rules concerning a common terminology, common measures and units of measure, as well as methods of measurement. While it belongs to the essence of natural language to be *national* and to represent a plurality (a fact which can no more be annulled or replaced by the single artificial language of which the partisans of scientism dream than the natural world-view itself can), it belongs to the essence of the technical, scientific language to be international. This is possible because scientific language is in no sense bound to natural language.

The institution science finds its ultimate expression in two rules: (1) all "facts" should be *univocally determined* through selected symbols and symbolic systems; and (2) this should take place in the most *economical* way possible, that is, in such a way that a minimal number of symbols is applied.

The goal of science is cognition of the truth within quite definite limits. Specifying these limits is a special task of the theory of scientific cognition which, in turn, presupposes the general theory of cognition.[13]

From this we can provide a final characterization of "scientific fact." If its phenomenological nature [*Sachnatur*] is that of a "state of affairs," still, not all states of affairs are "scientific facts." Only those states of affairs which can be grasped on the

---

12. [On Scheler's concept of lived-community, see *Formalismus*, VI, B, 4, *ad.* 4 ("Einzelperson und Gesamtperson").—TRANS.]

13. [See sections IV and V in "Phenomenology and the Theory of Cognition," above.—ED.]

basis of the constitution of the scientific institution (whose content changes in the course of history) are scientific facts. What belongs to the essence of a "scientific fact" is not that it in fact be recognized, but that it be recognizable by science. At the same time, this recognizability is always bound up with a social condition which as such has nothing at all to do with truth, fact, being, objecthood, or objectivity [*Gegenständlichkeit, Objektivität*]. For facts of observation, this social condition is that we must be able to *produce* such facts in a specific way, that is, through a technique; for concepts and propositions, the condition is that we must be able to communicate them either directly, by applying symbols conventionally valid for all savants, or indirectly, by undertaking operations with these symbols which conform to the basic conventions of deductive symbolic logic.

The scientific fact must in this sense be a "universally valid" fact, for its "verifiability" [*Nachprüfbarkeit*] helps to constitute its essence. Of course, that it is a fact at all is not based on "universal validity," "verifiability," or "communicability"; these underlie only the selection of "scientific facts" from among facts in general. Facts which do not meet this condition—which are not communicable, for which no technique or production can be provided, which no one or only one man or only a few men, experts or non-experts, see—naturally exist just as much as *scientific* facts do. On the other hand, scientific facts must also be facts; they do not first turn into "facts" by virtue of the universal validity of the judgments establishing them. However, they do become *scientific* facts only when the institution of experts acknowledges them. A magnitude, for example, is only a scientific fact once a means for measuring it has been produced and acknowledged. But it was a fact before this; "this same" fact, this same magnitude can be measured in quite different ways, by different methods, in different units, and by different ways of coordinating numbers with these units.

"Universal validity," "verifiability," and "communicability" are relevant only to the members of the institution of science, not to all men or to all rational beings. It is clear that even today a poll of all men concerning truth or falsehood with respect to scientific questions would count for less than the actual results of science. To be sure, the content of the natural outlook is no less "socially" conditioned than the content of the scientific. But here the ground for "common acknowledgment" is created not by conventions and selected symbols, but by tradition and involuntary imitation, and by natural language, with its units and forms of meaning and its syntax, instead of artificial symbols. Since these forces are "involuntary," sharing this feature with what is grounded in our assumptions [*Annahmen*] in a purely unbiased way, the facts of the natural outlook have a stability and obtrusiveness which scientific facts lack. However, stability and obtrusiveness do not give natural facts any "objective" grounding or make them more firmly grounded [*gegründeter*]. Nor do these two features imply that the particular concrete contents of the natural outlook are any less "relative" to a people and a language and to the stages of their history. On the other hand, the scientific fact, which lacks this stability and obtrusiveness, is independent of a people and language and is "universally valid."

However, only with the "pure fact" is a "fact" given which is also totally independent of all social conditions, whether these have a natural or an institutional form. The pure fact enjoys this independence because it is essentially asymbolic and independent of both artificial and natural symbols. Naturally, this in no way excludes the possibility of communicating such facts, of discussing them, of providing instructions for how one can bring them into view. They are even less "individually" conditioned than they are "socially" conditioned. Nor is a pure fact's nature as "pure fact" ever conditioned by any kind of "universal validity." For this reason, the import of language (which the phenomenologist naturally uses too) is reversed when the phenomenologist speaks with others about pure facts or when he writes books and stands in contrast to the use of language among savants or by a man of the people. The meaning of the words which the phenomenologist applies and the significative unities of his spoken or written sentences do not "say" what he means in such a way that the addressee or reader thereby comes to recognize a thought with which he was not previously acquainted. Words and sentences here are only expediently chosen stimuli, as it were, inviting the one addressed *to see for himself* what the phenomenologist means when he is speaking. The phenomenologist presupposes that the other could have seen it without words and communication. While elsewhere, in science and in life, all "showing and demonstrating" serves only as a prop for the understanding of the thought-content immanent in the utterance, in phenomenology all talking is only a means for showing something, for *exhibiting* something. Deductive inferences are not used here to prove or construct something, but only to exhibit something. If *B* asserts that he does not see what *A* shows to him, then a dispute arises which cannot be settled.[14] For just this reason, the "pure fact" is deprived of the stability and obtrusiveness of the natural fact as well as of the univocal definability of the scientific fact; the former because of the involuntarily effective powers of tradition and imitation, the latter because of the voluntarily established symbolism and conventions. In return, however, the pure fact alone is a strictly objective fact, the pure fact which is the *ultimate basis* of *all* other kinds of fact, the fact in which *all* symbols are for the first time fulfilled and redeemed.

If we adhere to this view, then it is a factual question whether the following assertion holds true: when non-sensible features of the intuitive content are varied, the sensible content of the whole intuitive fact is altered, but never the converse. If the sensible content, by its essence, has a characteristic advantage over the non-sensible content (for instance, the content of an intuition of a relation in impressing itself on the sphere of intuition), still, this has nothing at all to do with "founding." Whatever the sensible content in something intuited may be (an appearance of brightness and darkness, one of color and tone, etc.) and regardless of this advantage (which it enjoys only as a *sensory* content, not as the nature or the substance [*Inhalt*] of this sensibly given appearance), it can still be altered depending on the exhibitory function which this content exercises for the intuition of the *whole* intuitive content. However, the whole content, on its part, is *primarily* determined precisely by the non-sensible content of intuition (that is, the content which in general cannot be given by the senses). For instance, the appearances of the whiteness of snow and the whiteness of blossoms differ *qua* "appearances," even though they contain the strictly identical *quale* "white." They are different because they are integrated into different forms of space and because they exhibit quite different things.

An unprejudiced phenomenology of sensory appearances is

14. [See *ibid.*, sec. III.—ED.]

the best means for expelling this sensationalistic assumption. Such a phenomenology shows us not only how relations, relationships between temporal and spatial forms, and phenomena of motion can be given in the most thoroughgoing independence of the relata, the content of the spatial and temporal forms, and the subjects [*Träger*] and directions of motion. It also shows us that the content of these relata and subjects changes when the relations or motions do. Phenomenology shows us, for example, that the quality and intensity of sensory contents are not independent of their phenomenological extension and duration but are altered along with these; that alteration can be given even if we do not apprehend the qualitative states that succeed one another in it and that these qualities, when they are of different phenomena of alteration, constitute different phenomena. Such a phenomenology shows us that the sensation of traction changes with the changes in the phenomenon of the "heaviness" of a body we lift and look at, and not the converse; that the phenomenon of the warmth or coldness of a room allows the sensation of temperature to change. It shows us that in cases where we can immediately identify forms with different sensory content, say, a melody at different pitches, or a spatial figure with differently colored borders, these forms are *independent* phenomena which are by no means founded on sensory data. On the contrary, I believe that a complete survey of the facts that are pertinent here will lead one to a basic point of view totally opposed to sensationalism. This will be the view that only those phenomena can become *sensory* phenomena for a particular kind of animal, or for man, or for an individual, which can fulfill, so to speak, or "clothe" [*bekleiden*] (if I may speak figuratively), the relations, the forms, the categorial contents, like thingness, corporeality, etc., which the creature in question can intuit *first of all* and in such a way that these provide the foundation for the sensory phenomena themselves. The sum total of these at any one time would be for a creature what I have elsewhere [15] called the "milieu-structure of a species." Precisely in these matters phenomenology should uphold the incontestable right of what Kant has already correctly seen and defended against Berkeley, Hume, and others, namely, that in all experience cer-

15. [See *Formalismus*, III, and *"Ordo Amoris."*—ED. and TRANS.]

tain forms, relations, and categorial unities "precede" sensory data, marking out in advance the structure within which an experience of these data is possible. This does not mean that we must concede any significance whatever to the enumeration of those unities in Kant's philosophy, or, what is naturally much more important, in any way consent to his explanation of these facts in terms of functions of the understanding which are inherent in human nature. In other words, we do not have to consent to the subjectivistic inflection Kant gave the a priori. On the contrary, it seems to us an enormous step backward behind Kant when anyone takes seriously the assertion that every categorial intuition is an intuition founded on "sensory intuition." Whoever says this will always fall back into the error of thinking that thinghood, for example, can be understood as a mere "connection" of appearances which have sensory content, as a "lawful mode of combining" these, or, indeed, as the expectation of a connection between a sensory content which is given and one which is not given.

The nature of the connections between natural facts is such that through these connections certain relations between facts are displayed which have a certain *value* for the creature perceiving them and, at the same time, objectively existing relations are manifested in them. We can also say that the phenomenal contents of natural facts display not only these facts themselves but also other facts; they function not only to exhibit the thing or the event itself but also to exhibit something else along with this thing or event. Indeed, both these exhibitory functions and the exhibitory power as such provide the *limiting* condition under which the content of a phenomenological or pure fact can enter into the phenomenal content of the natural fact. For instance, if we reduce the perception P and the perception P_1 of a natural fact, say of a stone lying here, to their *phenomenal* contents ph and ph_1, then we have obtained two new objects which are not identical, nor even equivalent, but only *similar* to one another ($ph\ a\ b\ c\ d\ e\ f\ g\ h$ and $ph_1\ a_1\ b_1\ c_1\ d_1\ e_1\ f\ g\ h$). No sort of "similarity" is given in the natural perception itself; only "one and the same thing," namely, the stone. Only the factor consisting of the elements $f\ g\ h$, the common possession of which makes up the similarity of ph and ph_1, enters in both cases into the *phenomenal* or *exhibitory* content of the natural perception of the stone. We perceive here only *that part* of the pure fact which is "similar" to remembered and expected *pure* facts. I add "expected" and thereby set our assertion apart from those who say that in natural perception we perceive anything new as "similar" to something already "known" or to a "modification" of some such thing. Expectation, or even the attitude which remains after the act of expectation has been performed, determines what we perceive *at present* no less than memory does.

Our assertion must be distinguished from an erroneous interpretation which has been given to it. This interpretation arises when someone fancies that in natural perception itself the difference and bare similarity of ph and ph_1 are given, on the assumption that ph and ph_1 first come fully into consciousness in the two acts of perceiving the stone, and that ph then evokes ph_1 through "association" or that the dispositional stimuli belonging to ph merge with the new stimuli of ph_1 and lead to an "assimilation" of the object of sensation to what is merely imagined or to the "elements" of this. Such an interpretation is wrong, since what is effective here is precisely *not* the similarity between two facts of *consciousness* but the objectively subsisting similarity between two facts not give to consciousness, facts which we obtain only through phenomenological reduction. What corresponds to this in our consciousness or in the content of perception is "one and the same" perceptual content which itself is completely simple and not at all complex. "Natural perception" does not make an addition to what is first of all given, as one says, in "sensation," an addition of a reproduced fact or remembered fact. Natural perception subtracts from, or makes a selection from, the content which is given to a "pure" intuition. Natural perception is, therefore, a *suppression* of objectively existing *differences* in favor of *likenesses,* a suppression of the factual content itself in favor of its mere "similarity." The relation of similarity does not hold between the contents of natural perception or its components (sensations) either successively or simultaneously; on the contrary, what at the level of pure facts is mere "similarity" at the level of natural perception is *one and the same* appearance. And it is not several appearances of the same thing that stand in this relation of similarity, so that the one evokes the other by association, but every *single* "appearance" is already a relation of similarity between "pure" facts that is not given *as* a relation of similarity but *as* an identical object. The "law of similarity" we have in mind here is a law of the *mode of formation* of natural perception, not the law that obtains between its contents or the "elements" of its content. This law from the first determines what enters into the content of natural perception; it does not come to pass in the development of what has already entered into that content.

It is also clear that these two interpretations have completely different results in regard to the cognitive value of this process. The interpretation we reject lets natural perception appear more as "illusion" as more components are added to the facts of "sensation." The further our mental life develops, the more "full of illusion" our picture of the world would become. On the other hand, according to our conception, the suppression, the selection of "pure" facts, is diminished to the degree that the similarities ingredient in the content of perception cease to be vague and superficial similarities and become more determinate, more differentiated, and more essential; and, second, as the store of the pure facts grows, these help the perceived fact to come to light by virtue of their similarity to its phenomenal content. In this way natural perception progressively gives more and more of that reduced content of perception which is "similar" to the reduced contents of the same object as it is in memory and as it is when it becomes manifest. In doing so, it causes the fullness of the phenomenal content to increase.

Our argument does not establish a onesided dependence of perception on memory or on expectation, contrary to what pragmatism thinks. It is true that we perceive only what is objectively similar to that which is remembered about the same object; it is also true that only what is "similar" to something perceived and present enters into our natural memory. This is demonstrated only in the *phenomenological reduction* of the acts of expectation and memory. Through this reduction we become aware of contents which are never on hand in natural expectation and memory, since expectation and memory have already completed the process of elimination which removes the pure facts and leaves in their place only the foundational role they play for the relation of similarity.

However, in our opinion one thing is clear. What the pure content in the phenomenal content of natural perception *is* and likewise what the pure content in the phenomenal content of natural memory and expectation *is* discloses itself only in the "coincidence" of those acts leading to the unity of the *cognition of an object*. Only in this "coincidence" does the objectively "true" object itself appear; and the greater the number of acts of perception, expectation, and memory which are trained on it, the *greater* is the fullness of what appears "in person." That "identity" of the relation of expectation, memory, and perception to "the same" is, however, an essential law of these acts, that is, a law of the essence of these acts.[16] Such an identity could never "develop" if it were not originally present. What can be extensively "developed" is the coordination of contents of memory, expectation, and perception, experienced as directed upon identical objects, with the same events and things in the real sphere. Only here are deceptions and errors possible. To ask through which "genetic" process the case expressed by the sentence "I hear the tone *C* which I expected" or "I remember the tone *C* which I perceived yesterday" comes about is to put a senseless question. The contents of memory still deviate widely from perceptual contents (when, for example, what is perceived suffers wide-ranging objective alterations) without losing their identity with these, an identity of which we are immediately aware. They can be similar to one another up to the point of complete equality, without this identity having to be *given*. Thus, I am not perceiving at the moment any object other than the one I am simultaneously remembering.

Phenomenology, therefore, must decline to answer any question which is posed in the manner I shall now describe. Someone asks: How do I know that the memory-image of the tone *C*, which I now have, involves the "same" tone *C* which I heard yesterday? How can I know this, since only this "image" or this "present experience of memory" is "immediately" given to me, but not the tone *C* heard yesterday? Yesterday's tone is given only indirectly, through a symbolic function! No! we say: Nothing like a so-called memory-image is immediately given to me. In the phenomenological fact we do not have the tone *C* which is heard and a "memory-image" of it; we have one identical tone *C* which I have reason to analyze into two

16. [See *Formalismus*, VI, A, 3, g.—ED.]

tones or into two separate objects only when I reflectively attend to my hearing and memory as separate modes of the consciousness of this tone. It is only this which induces me to assign the tone remembered in the phenomenal past, against the background of "yesterday" and its vaguely perceived content, the status of a tone which I heard [als einen gehörten] and to assign the very same tone the status of a tone which is now "being remembered." That "image" is on the whole nothing "real," but only the reified phenomenon of the tone C in memory, a psychological symbol. It is here a matter of indifference whether "the tone C" means a determinate tone which has continued to sound from yesterday until today, or the "general object" which can be built upon hearing and memory. There is also a phenomenon of the tone C which is such that I can be in doubt whether I am hearing the tone or only remembering it. This happens quite frequently when a tone is fading away. Here I have the tone C with complete clarity, but doubt occurs as to whether I am "hearing" or "remembering" it.

This case shows that there exists an *overarching [übergreifendes] consciousness* of objects, so to speak, which is only secondarily divided into the various modes of consciousness, that is, into perceiving, remembering, and expecting. This overarching consciousness gives to all our acts and functions a primitive *unity* of intention [des Meinens] which is never the result of development, etc. (Brunswig).[17]

One further remark. The content of perceptions, expectations, and memories can naturally be *mental* as well as *physical;* there can be contents of inner *and* external intuition. For this reason, the connections to be considered here are as much a priori vis-à-vis any variation in mental experience as they are vis-à-vis variations in physical experience. They constitute "mental reality" just as much as they do "physical reality." To mental reality belongs the total course of mental events in objective time, whatever man perceives or fails to perceive of them.

Let us return to the context of the natural outlook. Perception and memory are originally directed to the *same* objects; however, the content given in both, compared with the full content of reduced acts of perception and memory, is only a fragment, *selected* according to an a priori relation of simi-

17. [See Alfred Brunswig, *Das Vergleichen und die Relationserkenntnis* (Berlin and Leipzig, 1910).—TRANS.]

larity. "A priori" means here only "determining natural experience" and not being determined by it. Natural perception, and not only scientific observation, furnishes us more with certain relations between the true and absolute facts than with these facts themselves. But natural perception does not give them "as" relations but as *marks* of things [*Sachen*]. Natural perception conceals the facts, so to speak, beneath the bare reciprocal symbolic function they have as signs for one another's appearance and disappearance.

From this two problems which have previously mocked everyone's ingenuity become clear for the first time. First, the problem of the presence of the *universal* and of universal meaning [*Bedeutung*] in the natural outlook. Second, the problem of the three most important modes of connection among natural "facts," namely, the spatial, the temporal, and the causal.

Ad 1. *The universal and meaning in the content of natural perception.* Along with the full content of every natural perception, regardless of the level of a creature's mental development on which it occurs, a "meaning" is given which as such is of a completely non-sensory nature. I perceive "a table," "a house," "a stove," and so forth. Or I recognize a perceived X, of which I know a priori "that it has a meaning," "as" a table, "as" a house, or "as" a stove. What does this mean? Let us start by rejecting two answers, both of which make this matter a little too easy.

The first is the assertion that there is nothing like a "meaning" in the content of natural perception. The only thing I can perceive is a certain optical or other sensory content, for instance, the side view of a house, these forms, lines, colors, and planes. Several of these can succeed one another and can do so in such a way that certain expected and remembered connections between these views can grow up and endure on the basis of experience and practice. Apart from this, we still have the word "house"; it has a fixed connection with those side views and their successive order and, in fact, stands *for* their order. It does not designate something "independent" (here, real) but a mere "order," a set of relationships which can be realized at any time in memories and expectations. Nevertheless, who has ever thought that when he perceives a house in natural perception he is perceiving an "order" and not a determinate *thing* with this meaning? When he is in doubt, he might perhaps know whether it is a house or not by the "order" in the sequence of his intuitions, but he will never admit that what he *means* by "house" in this sentence is an "order." And for what is the *word* "house" needed? One does not need to know the word "house" or some equivalent sign in order to "perceive a house." If a man applies the term, then he does so, as he clearly thinks, only because it *is* a house which he perceives. And he does not perceive a house in these planes and forms because he feels an impulse to utter the word "house." Rather, it is clear that "the house" presents itself to him in every single side view, in the first as much as in the last and, indeed, in the immediate identity: "the same house."

Others say "no!" More is *already* found in perception. A *judgment* is present there. One recognizes what one sees "as" a house or "as" something which falls under the "general" meaning "house," or recognizes it as something which bears the marks *a, b, c,* of the general object "house." Simultaneously, one acknowledges the *existence* of something constituted in this way, something which is an example of the general idea of "house." Let us leave aside, for the moment, the positing and non-positing of its existence and restrict ourselves to the nature [*das Was*] of the object. Again we must ask: How is this "judgment," which gets read into the simple perception, distinguished from the case where someone likewise "perceives the house" and, *in addition*, asserts "this is a house"? We can find no answer to this. What a marvelous construction! We are continually perceiving a thousand things, without finding a trace of this sort of judgment and assertion, much less a trace of the thought of a "general object." What are called "judgments" in these two cases are fundamentally different things. The house stands there as an individual real thing, it has mortar, floors, a roof, and windows; it has real parts, every one of which is sensibly present in a side view no differently than any other, no differently, in fact, than the whole house itself. A "general object" is neither an individual, nor a real thing, nor are these predicates ascribable to it. And is it not clear that the man who remarks that this house which he is seeing can be subsumed under the meaning "house," or that the marks of the concept "house" are found in it, must have already perceived this real thing, the house?

The first theory "sensifies" [*sensifizert*] or "nominalizes" the meaning, or, better, the meaning-content which lies in natural perception. The second theory "logicizes" [*logifiziert*] natural perception and attributes to it something which it does not have.

A solution to this question must separate as sharply as possible the questions: (1) Is the given *given as* "universal" or *as* "singular," as "general" or as "individual"? And is the given perhaps universal in another sense? (2) In which sphere of the three facts *is* the given either universal or singular, general or individual? (3) How are universal and singular, general and individual, related to *essence*?

Nothing is more certain than that *natural* perception gives everything which it does give us as a singular and individual object. Any attempt to "logicize" or rationalize perception miscarries because of this plain and simple fact. Even if a few or many of the generic features of a tree should be present in the content of my perception of it, nonetheless, the tree is always meant in them as single and individual. And, conversely, a man who knows maples may have a thousand cases of this species of tree representatively in mind when he is thinking of the general object "maple," he may even be perceiving the trees as examples of this species (things which someone who simply perceives such a tree does not see); nonetheless, what he means is a universal and general object. It is not the abundance or poverty of the generic features present in the intentional object that decides what is singular and individual or universal and general. This is rather a distinction of character introduced by the various modes of *meaning* [*Meinens*]. A child who calls any object to which the phenomenon of flying adheres "bird," for example, a butterfly or a moving shadow, perhaps, or who calls the vanishing of any object behind a solid wall "cuckoo," when he uses the word nonetheless means a *single* and *individual* object. A "universal" is not given to him (according to our definition of "given"), something single and individual is. That for the adult *exactly the same* phenomenon of "flying" becomes the content of a universal *meaning* under which the flight of the bird and the flight of the butterfly are subsumed is an entirely different matter and should not be read into what is given in the act of meaning [*Meinung*].

If natural perception gives us everything "as" single and individual, then one can still ask how that which it gives us is related objectively and logically to the pure factual content which the same object has after it has been phenomenologically reduced.[18]

18. [The manuscript breaks off here.—ED.] [The appendixes have been added by the editor from additional manuscript material, each one dealing with questions or themes announced in the main text.—TRANS.]

APPENDIX I

Pure fact and causal relationship (phenomenology and causal explanation)

PHENOMENOLOGY HAS A THREEFOLD RELATION to any *causal explanation*.

In the first place, everything which is to be phenomenologically exhibited sets an absolute limit to causal explanation. Causality has the same extension as existent reality. Each and every real thing, however, is *eo ipso* phenomenologically transcendent (leaving aside the *essence* of the real).

The intentional relationship, the "consciousness-of-something" which is the fundamental fact of all phenomenological study, is *opposed* to every sort of causal relation and is presupposed by any instance of causality.

Act and object do not stand in any causal relation; they are *connected in virtue of their essence*. Between acts there are relations of "founding"—an original relation which again has nothing to do with a causal relationship but only decides which act, with its particular essence, serves as the foundation for which other act, with *its* particular essence. Thus, the intuition of a self "founds" the intuition of mental facts. The essences of acts do not have any kind of temporal determination. The performance of acts of a particular essence occurs within a temporal *order*, but it does not have any duration in time. Time and temporal duration, however, are fundamental to causality. The performances of acts do not stand in any causal relation. Between pure facts there are connections of essence and foundation which correspond exactly to the foundational relations between the [correlative] acts.

Whenever we are in doubt whether a fact is a *pure fact* or one of the two other kinds of fact, the criterion for deciding this consists in establishing whether we must have *already seen* the fact in order to be able to unify the objects which bear this fact, *or* whether it is possible to define this unity independently. It can be shown that I can only discover what triangles or living things are if I have already seen the *phenomenon* of triangular-

[253]

ity and the phenomenon of life and say: all objects or things are triangles or living beings which become the bearers of these phenomena. On the contrary, there is no phenomenon of tree-ness or cowhood. I can, indeed, form the essential concepts of these, but only by way of a definition or the vague meaning of the word in language. I can also say that a pure fact is one such that when I try to define it I fall inevitably into a *circulus in definiendo*.

The case of *essential connection* and *causal connection* is analogous. Essential connections are connections which *I must have seen* in order to verify causal relations in a particu-lar region. For instance, the principles of the geometry of colors and tones are presupposed by physical optics and acoustics; the self-evident essential connections between eth-ical values are presuppositions of the historical and psycho-logical explanation of a stage or level of morality. In the sphere of real objects, the criterion of the presence of an essential con-nection is whether when I am looking for a causal explanation I fall inevitably into a *circle* where I have to take *A* to be as much the cause of *B*, as *B* is the cause of *A;* or, if *A* and *B* are merely functionally dependent on one another, I have to take *A* as well as *B* to be the independent variable. Essential connec-tions are revealed in these abortive attempts.

The second relation between essential connections and cau-sal ones follows straightforwardly from this. Intuitive connec-tions between essences can *never be annulled* or destroyed by the discovery of continually new causal relations between things and processes. Thus, a real combination of two things with two other things can never destroy the proposition $2 \times 2 = 4$, even if three or five or six things come about when we produce this combination. This would only mean that one must look for previously unnoticed causes which have pro-duced the new things. But $2 \times 2 = 4$ remains true even in a world in which, as a rule, five things result from the real com-bination of two things with two others. Essential connections must thus hold good of all the bearers of this essence, whatever they might be and whatever causal connection might hold be-tween them. Thus connections between pure qualities are valid regardless of the states of affairs into which these qualities enter; connections between states of affairs are valid, regard-less of the things in which they come to light. And for just this reason, these connections obtain among states of affairs and things, insofar as they are the bearers of these essential contents. The essential connections between founding objects and acts also hold true of the objects and acts they found.

The preceding holds true of *every* causal explanation, mental as well as physical, natural as well as scientific. Phenomenology initially had to fight for its right to exist as the phenomenology of the mental. Accordingly, it had to start by keeping genetic psychology and inductive-experimental physiological psychology within their proper bounds. However, what holds true of them also holds of *each and every* causal and explanatory science, of all the individual natural and cultural sciences as well as the historical sciences. Each science—for instance, mechanics, optics, acoustics, etc.—possesses its special phenomenological foundations which are independent of any causal explanation. The establishment of these foundations has nothing to do with psychology or even with the phenomenology of the mental. I cannot understand what the phenomenological foundations of the principles of mechanics or of biology can possibly have to do with the phenomenology of the mental. The unity of phenomenology consists solely in this, that in all objects and values phenomenology searches for the ultimate, *intuitive basic facts* and connections of fact. Phenomenology provides the ultimate intuitive facts, etc., for explanatory and descriptive psychology, no differently than it does for all the other sciences, including all the descriptive sciences. All "description" can be traced back to observation and is at the service of any causal explanation which is to be carried out. Phenomenology, however, does not rest on "observation" but on *bringing to sight* an intentional object; it does not "prepare the way" for causal explanation but is already the *basis* of this as of every other preparatory undertaking. This is at least the case with "critical" phenomenology. "Positive" phenomenology, however, is so far from being a preparation for causal explanation that it rather goes behind all causal connections and furnishes the absolute facts themselves. Consequently it strictly coincides with metaphysics. In both cases it is the exact opposite of a "description."

The third relation between phenomenology and causal explanation consists finally in the fact that the former has to *clarify the concept and the essence of the causal relationship* and its subspecies. The causal relationship belongs among both the facts of the natural *and* the scientific outlook at once; both kinds of causality are in need of a foundation in *pure* facts and in relations [*Beziehungstatsachen*] of a simpler sort which must be brought directly into intuition. We scarcely need say that the fact that something like a causal conjunction exists cannot itself be causally explained. This fact can nonetheless be traced back to its *constitution;* all the factors ingredient in it can be brought to sight, and the role they play in the composition of this kind of conjunction can be understood.

It is precisely this question about the *essence of causality* which is genuinely phenomenological. We shall turn to it in what follows.

Above all, it is important to establish once and for all the facts of the *natural intuition of causality* in their purity, still unmodified by scientific concepts of causality. One does do so when, for instance, one begins with the "regular course" of natural processes. That this beginning is mistaken is shown first by the fact that the starting point of the natural idea of causality does not lie in any kind of "regularity." Just as the first glance at a physical thing does not yield an independent "appearance" which leads to the assumption of the thing only after other "appearances" have been coordinated with it; just as, on the contrary, the physical thing exhibits itself in every appearance, so, too, the repeated succession of the events A and B does not lead to the idea of a causal connection. Rather, this connection is already given in *every single* case in which one thing *has effect* on another. Through its action [*Tun*] and the suffering [*Leiden*] of the other the special unity of a process stands out from the vague plenitude of the environment. A falling stone breaks a glass, a flood destroys a town; in every case of this kind the causal connection between the parts of the process, the operative activity of the one thing and the change of state in the other thing as a result of suffering this activity, is fully given. For this purpose we do not need a recurrence of the same process or of its parts; moreover, any expectation of this kind of regularity in the natural outlook is *based upon* the intuitive fact of such acting and suffering. If A is the active and B the suffering element, then in keeping with the foundational relation which prevails here, when the same A recurs B must follow; an equivalent B must follow an equivalent A; a similar B, a similar A. Consequently, the facts here are exactly analogous to what they are in the case of things. The unity of the thing does not consist in the coordination of remembered contents of previously given appearances with an appearance which is presently given. It has its unity from the fact that we intend [*intendieren*] the *whole* of the thing in every appearance, that, in the case of a physical thing, for example, we also perceive that it has another side, that it has an inside, that it has this and that form, that it is actual. Similarly, when we perform certain activities (such as opening a door, walking around, etc.) we expect to experience the complete sensory fulfillment of these intentions. The case is quite analogous here. We do not expect B when A is given *because B* regularly follows A—and this tension of expectation would be the fact which we call "having effect." Rather, *because* we perceive the effect of A on B, when A recurs we have the expectation that B will follow.

So the matter clearly stands, at least in the natural worldview. It may be the case that, to the extent the regularity of the conjunction is experienced, it defines more precisely, modifies, completes, or reduces the particular unities of the perceptual contents which things already yield and which later enter into the intuitive relationship of acting and suffering. However, this is not the origin of the *idea* of acting or of the essential connection: "What acts must, if it recurs, act in the same way." Rather, this experience merely accounts for the variation in the content of the particular, intuitive unities (and these, only so far as their sensory fulfillment comes into question) which serve as the foundations of the intuited relationships. This is an enormous distinction. On the other hand, those sensory contents which do enter into the episode of acting and suffering are not "given" first of all; they are given only after they have been *chosen* to serve as *signs* for the particular character of the given case of acting and suffering. This character exists independently of the things which are acting and suffering and can be given *before* these are.

Acting-and-suffering is not always the same being [*Sein*] which is divided into a plurality only by the particular things which are suffering and acting. Each case of acting and being-active [*Wirken und Tätigsein*] is *distinct* from every other, quite independently of their bearers. Each is a *particular case* and has as little to do with the concept of acting as intuitively similar things have to do with the *concept* "similar." Every "pressing on something," "thrusting of something," "pulling of something" can be brought to intuition as a particular mode of acting, independent of the determination of this "something" as this specific thing. However, something identical remains in all acting-and-suffering and must be brought to intuition at a level on which it is no longer qualified by these various tendencies. This is *pure acting-and-suffering.*

A "process," in the natural outlook, is always to start with the *uniform whole* of an acting-and-suffering, which takes place in two or more things. The *primary* natural causal connection exists not between processes but between acting-and-suffering *things.* "Processes in things" are really changes of state and are erroneously called "processes." Only when we intuit the alteration, the qualitative change in some one state of affairs and *disregard* the things among which this change takes place, can this alteration turn into an independent "process." Even lightning, the rolling of thunder, rain, which encounter us as independent events, are still split up into active and suffering *things.*

It is important, because characteristic of the *natural* way of thinking about causality, that every causal relationship here is based on things and is bound up with relations between things. Things and only things act and suffer. This also makes it comprehensible that a rigorous dualism of *cause and effect* arises here. When the thing *A* acts, the thing *B* suffers and the "effect" [*Wirkung*] is the result of this, the state into which *B* comes. If in the scientific world-view the principle of the *plurality of causes* acquires meaning, it does so only because here the substratum of things and the qualitative contrast of acting and suffering *disappear,* as we shall show.

A proof that causality is founded on *things* also lies in the fact that things "come to be" and "pass away." This fact belongs incontestably among the facts of the natural outlook. The natural man stands in the presence of the commencement and cessation of the being of a thing (which is what the above phrases mean), without feeling the slightest need for a causal explanation. It is "self-evident" that new things are always "arising," that they come into being out of nothing, and that new things are sinking back into nothing. The natural man first becomes aware of causality in the acting-and-suffering of things present which have a certain duration. And only a thing's change of state can wring from him the question, "What thing was acting upon this and 'effected' this change?" On the contrary, the *arising* and *passing away* of things have no cause. It is a simple matter of fact which *founds* the causal relation but is itself quite causeless and without effect.

Science can deny "coming to be" and "passing away" only because science grasps the "process" as an *independent state of affairs* no longer founded upon things. The new formation still has a beginning and an end of being; it begins to be and ceases to be. But "arising" and "perishing" no longer belong to it. One cannot say of a process that it "arises" and "perishes." On the other hand, since all alterations now become parts of a *continuous* process and are accommodated in this alone, the "things" of science become absolutely enduring and unchangeable "substances" which can no longer arise and perish. Only because of this has the distinction between arising and perishing, which in the natural world-view is an absolute fact, become merely *relative* to the beholder. For the cessation of part *A* of the event now falls in the same point of time at which part *B* begins. Any case of "perishing," from another point of view, is the "arising" of something else.

We discover here a distinction between the *natural* and the *scientific causal fact* which is quite analogous to that between things and states of affairs. Scientific facts are, as we said, states of affairs provided by observation.[19] Science, unlike natural perception, no longer has as "given" the things in which it first discovers states of affairs; it proceeds from states of affairs to "things" while the content of these "things" now becomes purely symbolic. Science comes upon "states of affairs" and construes all things so that they can become "bearers" of states of affairs. Analogously, science no longer proceeds from active-and-suffering things to the unity of the event, as natural intuition does; science starts from processes as states of affairs [*Vorgangssachverhalten*] and seeks in them relationships of regular succession, in order to construct substances and forces in the manner these relations require.

The facts established here also exclude an interpretation which competely misses the essence of causality, the interpreta-

---

19. [See section II above.—ED.]

tion that would place the root of the causal concept in the fact of the *alteration of a thing* (Herbart, Lipps, von Aster).

People say that if a thing A, a tree in summer, for example, is given together with the properties a, b, c, and afterward the same thing A, the tree in winter, for example, is given with the properties f, g, h, then an objection is thus raised against the natural assumption of identity, namely, that a thing is and remains what it is. Thus, there is a *contradiction* between the assumptions that A is the same thing and that it is not the same. And now the conversation of the inviolable *axiom of identity* demands either that we look for some new thing B whose action allowed the thing A to suffer that alteration, or that A be so divided that the reciprocal effect of its parts explains the change from A (a, b, c) to A (f, g, h). The first would hold in the case of a cause acting from outside the thing itself, the second, in that of *immanent* causality. However, what we have said makes it clear that the scientific concept of substance, instead of being explained, is falsely *presupposed* and is already substituted for the natural concept of a thing. Within the natural world-view the alteration of a thing is no more a "problem" or a "contradiction," that is, a violation of identity, than its coming to be and perishing is. The natural world-view knows no absolutely enduring and constant substances. For this reason, the alteration of a thing is never a fact which leads objectively to causality. At most, the alteration can become a subjective motive for asking after a cause, *once* causality has been given through the acting-and-suffering of two things and the twofold change of state connected with this. The principle of identity holds true only of *objects generally* and not of things as things, to say nothing of the principle's requiring the duration of things and the uniformity of their content. Rather, things can be created and annihilated, arise and perish, and change "of themselves" as much as one likes, without violating this principle.

When science abstracts from things which are active and "suffer," the qualitative distinction between these disappears, as I said. This is the distinction which divides the whole of the active operation into two parts. What remains after it disappears is the *idea of an active operation* which now no longer has its seat in one of the two things, but takes place *between them*. As long as things precede the intuition of causality and are the foundations for the comprehension of causal conjunction, the active thing, even when it is not acting, is still able to act or has a *capacity* for acting. Now, in contrast, this acting is no longer seen as the real possibility of a thing's being active; it becomes an intuitive *datum* for the concept of "force," which is already a scientific concept. While "capacity" still belongs wholly to the thing which has the "capacity," the "force" is completely detached from things and expresses itself in both things simultaneously, in conformity with the *spatial* and *temporal* relationships between them. These relationships become the varying *conditions* for that expression.

In this way, acting-and-suffering things give way to *substances, operations, forces,* and *conditions* as a result of one and the same scientific reduction of everything which is given to states of affairs. One notices in this that the concept of force has just as much objective grounding as the concept of substance and that the concept of substance does not have the slightest advantage over it. In the natural world-view *neither* one exists. In the natural world-view things exist, things which act-and-suffer and have certain capacities for doing so, capacities which are no more constant and enduring than the things themselves. The notion of constant and enduring essences which remain the same over the duration of time maintains its position only in the concepts of force and substance.

People have often contested the assertion that *active operation* is a real fact which we *immediately* encounter in the facts of external perception, where it is a matter of the operation of physical things. Now it is indeed true that we cannot bring the concept of *force* immediately into coincidence [namely, with an intuition], for force is the constant and real condition for the occurrence of an operation which follows a definite law and for just that reason it is never given otherwise than symbolically. However, the assertion that force is nothing other than the constant condition for lawful alterations, or, as Helmholtz says, the "hypostasized law," is quite wrong. No inference and no logical operation can lead from lawful alteration to the assumption of a force, if the *active operation* is not present as an *immediately* given matter of fact. Only the lawbound effectiveness of the operation [*Wirksamkeit*] leads to force. Also, assertions like "force is an hypothetical addition to lawful appearances, an element of thought which is never given," are quite illusory, since mere thinking can never create a wholly new material item like force out of nothing. It may be hypothetical that we assume this or that force, for which the operation immediately given to us is missing; but force itself is nothing hypothetical, any more than actuality or the external world.

Furthermore, it is empty talk to say that there is no immediate datum of external intuition corresponding to force, except for a sensation of muscular tension experienced on the occasion of our own movements. It is wrong to say that we either immediately impute this sensation to the external phenomenon or that we start by falsely making it into the antecedent condition of our movements (from which, in fact, these sensations result), and then impute this self-deception to the external phenomena themselves.

Finally it is empty talk to say that force is an activity immediately experienced in our ego and that once this activity has collected together and combined the phenomena, it is then falsely "projected" onto these phenomena or onto the things which are their bearers.

The first of these assertions is nonsensical. How should a sensation of whatever sort be the fact in which concepts like force and activity can be fulfilled? The phrase "sensation of muscular tension" completely deceives one as to the fact that this sensation itself is seen as the sign or the result of a "tensing," that is, of some kind of activity. In other words, the first assertion acquires the semblance of sense only when that dynamic element is presupposed in order to fix the boundaries of the type of sensation. We experience the activity of the movement of our muscles as a fact which is quite *independent* of the muscular sensation that follows upon it. Localization and dependence on some organic condition do not belong to this activity as they do to the muscular sensation itself. This activity has a direction; the sensation certainly has none.

The second view as well, which goes back to Descartes and Berkeley, where activity and operation are ascribed exclusively to selves and souls, is completely unjustified. We find forces in a storm at sea, in a swift torrent, in a thunderstorm which wastes our fields. These run counter to any of the merely potential efforts which we could possibly "impute" to things and in magnitude and power, they far surpass all the activities we can bring about by ourselves! And we are aware of the pull of something, when we lift a weight known to us, or the push of a body pushing against us, prior to and quite independently of the tactile sensations connected with them. Yet these sensations must be given before anything else is, if we are to be able to "project" our sensation.

In every experienced *resistance, we are aware of the operation* and the forcefulness of something which does not and cannot stem from ourselves. And we very quickly divide resistances into those which our own body [*Leib*] offers to us and those offered by something independent of the body. "Resistance" is here a unique *phenomenon* which should not be equated with a so-called sensation of resistance or with a subjective experience which we glimpse through some perception. The phenomenon of resistance comes to light only as directed against an activity we perform and, indeed, only in the exercise of this activity itself. It is not a necessary condition of this phenomenon that this activity be performed *by us*, that it flow out of the self, to say nothing of actual contact between the body and what is resisting it. That actual contact is not involved is shown by the fundamental difference between cases in which, as in certain phenomena of *aboulia* [namely, willessness] a man cannot *will* a movement of the arm and those in which he simply cannot *execute* this movement, for example, because his arm is injured. In the latter case he still experiences the resistance of his arm; in the former case, he does not experience this resistance.[20] The *body* [*Leib*] *cannot* be the *presupposition* of the phenomenon of resistance, since the body itself can be the *bearer* of this. But the same consideration holds for the *self*. In ethical conflict we experience a resistance offered by our own self, our "character," and not only detached cases of pressing or pushing. When we say that things resist one another, for instance that the mass resists movement in proportion to its magnitude, or when we define the mass in terms of resistance to movement (as the physicists do), the phenomenon of resistance is given in a single case of this sort. The assertion that we find only accelerations of different mag-

20. [On the "phenomenon of resistance," see *Formalismus*, III; further, see the remarks on the problem of reality in section VI in the later work, "Erkenntnis und Arbeit" (1926).—ED.] [See also "Idealism and Realism," below.—TRANS.]

nitude in the same motion and that resistance is only an anthropomorphic, or at least subjective, addition to this fact, is quite arbitrary. Even if we were to eliminate the body and the self, the phenomenon of resistance would still be given to intuition. Only if we interpreted this phenomenon as the outcome of a "striving" in the resisting bodies [*Körper*] would this be anthropomorphic or at least subjective, in the sense of the projection of feeling (which itself would not necessarily be an anthropomorphic projection).

Effective action is therefore an ultimate intuitive fact and, indeed, that fact which forms the uniquely absolute and constant feature of causal conjunction. Both propositions must now be proved more rigorously.

I see how a stone shatters a glass which it hits as it plunges downward. I assert that what is present in the intuitive fact is not only the stone which continually changes its position as its velocity increases, not only the glass and the alteration of it which occurs when it makes spatial and temporal contact with the stone, but also the *effective action* of the stone *on* the glass. This is clear without further ado, if I envision a case where the glass, at the moment the stone touches it, cracks apart "of itself" or through some other cause, for example, an increase in temperature from a source of heat not manifest to me. In such a case all the intuitive facts mentioned before are given, but the total situation which was given to me before is different. What is missing now is the effective action of the stone on the glass. Even if I were to assume that the fall of the stone is *regularly* followed by the cracking apart of the glass, since it constantly triggers that heat-source which causes the glass to crack apart, one could say that we cannot decide, or can decide only with great difficulty, whether the stone is having a causal effect or not. However, the same radical distinction remains present in both states of affairs insofar as they are intuitively meant. The action or the inner mode of the production of the effect is, in fact, intuited along with the rest, since everything is intuited whose removal causes the intuitive situation to *vary*. We do not have to decide at this point whether this fact of "effectiveness" was noticed here or simply perceived. Certainly it is not merely thought, and certainly it cannot be made to coincide with all the merely potential sensory contents of intuition or with the spatial and temporal components making up their form. However, that would be an objection to our assertion only from the point of view of the "sensationalistic presupposition" we are here trying to avoid.

There is still more to be said. I am aware of the effectiveness as uniform and as one and the same, despite the abundance of the temporally different phases of the process and the different ways they are filled with content, and despite the spatially different "images" [*Bilder*] into which I can analyze the whole of the "process." I am conscious that every one of the separate images is only one of the external sides, a partial view of this uniform, inner effectiveness which represents the primarily given foundation for the comprehension of these images. Once I have left aside the things which act-and-suffer, so that only the unity of a *process* remains which I can analyze into images and phases by dividing the time and the space the process occupies, then the "effective action in general" is still left in the process. When I leave those things aside, I perform an act [*ein Akt*] in which this process as a whole comes to light, an act which itself is not temporally extended. We always require additional acts if we are to undertake those divisions of this one act which embraces the whole process. And what is primarily "divided" in all this is only *the space and the time* in which the unity of the process lies. The process is only *indirectly* divided, namely, as the X which fills this space and this time. However, the nature and the particular unity of this X are not themselves based on the unity of this space or this time and *eo ipso* not on the results of that division which leads to those images and phases. They are *grounded in the unity of the effective action*. Put differently, single process comprises everything which is united through one and the same *unity of an effective action*, and all this belongs to one process in images and phases of this sort, exactly as all those sensory contents become the contents of the properties of a thing, which can exhibit its already grasped individuality *as* a thing. At different levels of organization a cognitive creature may choose very differently between the actual unities of effective action on which the unity of processes is based, in keeping with the importance their particular features may have for his possible reaction to and action upon them. For us, what is important here is only that it is not primarily the *sensory* materials and the temporal unities demarcated by them which lead to the unity of the process and the effective action; conversely, it is effective actions already perceived which lead to these materials, through the mediation of a temporal unity.

The relation of *causal action and temporal sequence* claims our special attention.

The only temporal sequence which can be in question here is the immediately given temporal sequence, the phenomenon of B's following A. We exclude, therefore, any temporal sequences which must first be inferred. This means that we exclude, first, a temporal sequence which we infer from the different spatial images of the phases of some one content, such as the sequence of the hands of a clock; and second, all temporal sequences of spatially separated facts, since these obtain only if we presuppose that one knows what was happening simultaneously at these separate points. Then the question is whether the immediately given sequence, which in any case is a fact of immediate intuition (as much in the perception as in the memory of a process), is the *foundation* of effectiveness *or not*?

Certainly we have a well-grounded starting point for this in two respects. First, we can grasp the unity of a process in an act which itself has *no duration*. And, second, the effective operation of A on B is not only given retrospectively on the basis of B but can be given even before B is. The "unity of a process" is the unity of an *effective action*. The effective action is the core of the process, the point of crystallization, so to speak, around which all its sensory contents and spatial and temporal determinations first crystallize. Now, every "process" is temporally determined in some way or other. It has a beginning, an end, and a duration. This temporal determination, however, lies wholly *in it*; it belongs to its matter. Thus one cannot say that the process itself is *in* time or that it commences and ceases to be. Beginning and end are rather only its limits, something still *immanent* to it. No succession of any kind belongs to the process as a *whole*, exactly as it is grasped in a uniform act. Only if I divide up duration of the process does an immediate, intuitive successiveness [*Folgesein*] belong to the phases which fall within these parts of its temporal duration. On the other hand, different processes do succeed one another; nevertheless, this succession is never immediately intuitive but is based upon the duration of the processes and the relation between their beginning and end. The beginning of an event B succeeds the beginning of a process A, for example, if B has a shorter duration than A and if their endings can be joined by a line in space. The processes display the most varied relations to one another, but they can have a precise temporal relation only by way of their relations in space. In the same indivisible act of perception, I see the process V begin, for example, a man goes from place P to place P_1 and the process V_1 approach its end, for example, a falling stone reaches the ground. If I can join the two beginnings B and B_1 and the two ends E and E_1 of the processes V and V_1 with a straight line, or if there is such a straight line between B and B_1, E and E_1, then I say that the processes V and V_1 take place "at the same time." If, on the contrary, the straight line which I draw from the beginning B of the process V to V_1 hits a partial content of V_1, which "follows" the beginning of V_1 in the immediately perceived succession of its parts, then B_1 in objective time is "before" the event or the beginning of the process V_1 and thus is before B. If a straight line exists between E (the end of the process V) and B_1 (the beginning of the process V_1), then they immediately follow one another. Compare the diagrams on the next page:

This fact is completely distorted if someone says that in order to comprehend the duration of the process V which begins at B and ends at E, since only a momentary phase, e.g., E, of the process is ever given, one must at point E look back to B through recollection and thus must have B in consciousness as a memory-image. Only in this way can he then go on to assess or judge the temporal distance $B-E$, which is generally not given, in some feature of this image (possibly the grade of its brightness or paleness). First, it is an error to presuppose that only a momentary phase of the process is immediately given. What is *given* to us is always a *complete process* with its temporal extension. The act embraces the whole of this process and itself *qua* act fills no time. No judgment or inference, no kind of interpretation, no sort of conjunction of atemporal contents could give us the fact of duration, if it were not *immediately given along with* that which we experience in an event. It is therefore quite senseless for us to presuppose objective time, even for the acts themselves, and then think that the immediate intuition of time comes about

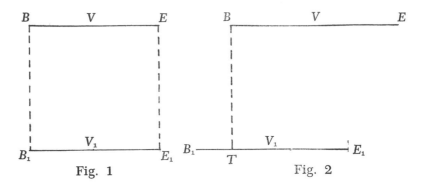

Fig. 1   Fig. 2

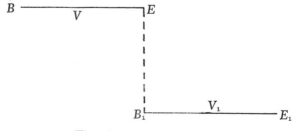

Fig. 3

in just the same way and through processes similar to those in which an indirect temporal ordering of processes takes place. This indirect ordering presupposes that immediate intuition of duration and successiveness which is immanent to the process given in one act.[21]

Let us look more closely at duration and successiveness in the process. It is obvious that they are in any case quite different from what we call, by assumption, *objective time*. Duration is, first of all, not independent of temporal content, and temporal content cannot vary independently of duration. Consequently, it is not possible to divide up the duration of the process like a piece of homogeneous time, for every division alters the phenomenal duration of the *whole*. Also, we cannot think of this same temporal duration as filled by different

21. Thus it does not require "memory" to grasp a process. We do not grasp the parts of a process in as many successive acts as there are temporal parts of the event itself. We can think about eight days' time and their content without thinking for eight days.

processes and starting and end-points; such a presupposition belongs to the essence of objective time. In addition, we cannot think of the phases of the process as shifted about in it and its total duration, *without* affecting its content. Here, it is not valid to presuppose that a simple difference in the temporal position of a process [*Ereignis*] can never change its content and that another content always points to new causal constellations which alter the process [*Ereignis*]. Rather, every phase here is bound up with the effective action given *as a whole;* its "place" in this whole is fixed by what it (as an arbitrarily extracted unity) means as a symbol for this effective action. Thus, a tone-phenomenon varies when the same objective tone *C* enters into different rhythmic unities. The succession and the sequence of the phases of the process are also bound up with the whole of the effective action. The successiveness of each phase, e.g., ph_2 after ph_1, ph_3 after ph_2, is an immediately and qualitatively changing fact; that ph_2 succeeds ph_1 also depends on the fact that ph_e (the final phase) succeeds ph_i (the initial phase).

Notice that *no succession* of any sort lies in the idea of *temporality* itself, and that, on the other hand, nothing can be present in the qualitative contents of the phases which could determine that this one qualitative content follows this other, even when the general succession of these phases and contents is presupposed. As Kant rightly saw, it is never the parts of time themselves that succeed one another; there is also time which is filled by a constantly enduring content, where no succession at all is present. It is always one temporal *content* which succeeds or "follows" another content. And, in any case, it is by an essential interconnection that temporal contents which are not identical, but different, insofar as they *are* temporal contents, occur one after the other. If we know that X, Y, and Z are temporal contents and as such different, then we also know that they follow one another. But this still does not tell us how they follow one another, whether, for example, X follows Y or Y follows X. There is nothing in the quality which differentiates X, Y, and Z that determines the order of their succession. What does determine this order, for instance, that X precede Y, is the direction which the effective action takes from one phase to the next. X, which acts, precedes; Y, which is acted upon, follows.

There is one particular phenomenon in which the order of this sequence is still undetermined, although temporality, succession, and quality are all present. This is the phenomenon of *pure fluctuating change* [*Wechsels*], as presented, for example, by a swarming throng or by any succession of a quality which I do not identify, and so cannot grasp and interpret either as a *change of state* [*Zustandsänderung*] or as a *movement* [*Bewegung*]. For instance, I can apprehend the changing reflections of light and shadow on a surface now as the same places being filled in succession, now (as in every play of shadows) as the movements of thinglike unities. Fluctuating change, however, is the phenomenon which I can still see independently of these conceptions. Or, to put it differently, fluctuating change is given when I interpret a white surface becoming blue now as a new color-quality coming to occupy the same place, now as a movement, a flowing of the blue over the surface, and the resultant covering over of the white. In truth, it is even given independently of these interpretations. If we imagine the total content of external perception reduced to the level of givenness—which runs through all change of state and movement—then we can say that both the specific successiveness of appearances and effective action are based on this fact. It can also easily be shown that the same changing qualities are now simultaneous, now successive, depending on the interpretation we add. They even succeed one another in a different order, so that now Qu_1 follows Qu, now Qu follows Qu_1, depending on which interpretation we add.

Only the differences in effective action which I see in this fluctuating change determine the temporal relation between these appearances. These alone lead to univocal sequences: the same white and black qualities succeed one another, when I trace back the fluctuating change in these reflections to the effect of a change of state; they are simultaneous, when I trace it back to the effect of a movement. What we are saying is not farfetched. It is well known that Faraday traced back the falling of a stone to the successive changes of state of the space through which it falls, changes of state which are univocally determined by the changing conjunction of spatial lines of force. There is no longer anything materially identical here which "is falling." Any sort of movement is here only a sum of the changes of state of fixed positions in space, where this sum is designated by a line of force. Between all the parts of the universe there is a continuously variable, reciprocal penetration [*Durchdringung*]; "absolutely stable mass," "movement," "action at a distance," "impenetrability of bodies" are only divisions and consolidations of facts undertaken by our senses and needs. I am far from accepting this picture of the world. It serves me here only as an example of how the assumption of other effective actions evokes a totally different conception of the specific succession of appearances and of simultaneity, where both of these are equally based on the fact of fluctuating change.

Thus we see that in the end Kant is basically right in his dispute with Hume, despite the fact that his proofs were partly false, partly deficient. Kant was right to assert that a perceived regular sequence between A and B does not lead to the assumption of a causal connection, but that, conversely, the causal connection first objectively determines what precedes and what follows.

This can be illuminated from still another side. At the level of the scientific concept of causality, we distinguish between the active *cause* and the *conditions* of its activity. Now there is no distinction of any kind between causes and conditions so far as we have in view only the effect as a fact with which we begin when we want to retrace its cause. Its occurrence is no less "necessarily" bound to the conditions than it is to the action of the cause. The locomotive can no more run without rails than it can without steam power; without a barrel and dry powder (which belong to the conditions of firing) and without the trigger's being pulled (temporally, this is the final necessary condition to be added), the bullet no more starts on its course than it does without the vital force which is called forth when the powder is ignited. And yet there is a distinction, manifested in the fact that we everywhere look for a cause, however many conditions the effect or its occurrence may have.

Nor does it do any good to strike out the cause altogether (or, what is the same thing, to equate it with the concept of conditions) or to label it merely the "most important condition." There is indeed an objective measure for the "importance" of a condition, although every condition, whether important or not, is indispensable to the effect. If we analyze the fact of the effect itself into constitutive and contingent features, and then arrange these under and over one another, we can call a condition more important, the more its variation alters the less contingent or constitutive features of the effect. Such a measure of the importance of conditions may be the only method for finding the cause among factors all of which must be present if the effect is to come about. Nevertheless, the cause is something other than the most important condition, for it is not distinguished from conditions by degree, but *essentially*. The distinction between cause and condition can be maintained only if the *action* [*Wirken*] of the cause can be *brought to sight* independently of the *effect* [*Wirkung*]. The method of varying the circumstances and weighing the importance of the conditions may lead us to see the cause in this way, but always only in the negative sense that everything which is *not* the cause is detached from the antecedents of the fact. In order to grasp the cause positively, we must see the activity. And it must be admitted that the cause can, in principle, be seen even in a single case.

From this we can also understand that the effect is univocally determined along with the cause, but not vice versa. By "cause" we never mean the activity itself which in the case of a given effect can never be more than *one;* we mean the *things* which exercise this effective action. These can be different even when the effective activity is the same. If, however, the cause is given, then the effect, *if* it comes to pass, must always be the same; for the effective action of a thing is determined when the thing-itself is. On the other hand, we cannot say that, when the cause and action are given, the occurrence of the effect is also *necessary,* for the occurrence of the effect is also dependent on the appropriate conditions. However, if an effect is given, the cause must have had effect. But the same cause need not always bring about this effect. Instead, different causes can have the same effect. Also, in cases where one action which brought about a determinate effect is opposed by another which suppresses the occurrence of this effect, the occurrence of the effect does not prove to be necessary.

Up till now we have spoken of the immediately given fact of "effective action" and the equally given fact of "temporal sequence." Any construction of an *objective causal principle* whose validity is now no longer restricted to the given, but extends to real things and events [*Ereignisse*] (which we distinguish from the unities of process [*Vorgangseinheiten*] [22] which continue to be given) rests on two essential connections: (1) that every process is the unity of an effective action; and (2) that the specific temporal sequence from *A* to *B* is determined only by the effective activity we perceive or intuit. On the strength of this principle we suppose that there is a temporal sequence and a causal relation between processes even if we never perceive them. This temporal sequence is a pure symbol.

Now, for the first time, we have an *objective time* which is distinguished from the duration and succession which are immanent to processes. Compared to that immediately experienced time, it is never intuited in any way, but is only something meant, a *symbol* through which we make the intuitively given durations and sequences comparable with another and thus measurable. This happens, as I say, by means of a passage through space. We choose a "basic process" and ask how many times its duration or that of its parts is contained in the duration of other processes. While the intuitive duration of unified processes is indivisible and cannot vary independently of the content of these, in this case we can ask how many times the basic process must take place if we are to be able to connect the end-points of this process to be measured with the end-points of the basic process by means of a straight line? This number gives the objective duration of the process we have to determine. Objective time is thus purely and simply a *numerical relation between durations of immediate time*. That objective time is continuous, homogeneous, that is, such that events are not materially altered by their temporal position, and furthermore that it is infinite and is a time which contains all others as parts, these are not essential determinations *of time itself* or of what is given in it; they are determinations of the *number series,* which are then transferred to time.

The causal relation which obtains between events now

22. [Scheler distinguishes *Ereignis* (event) and *Vorgang* (process) for the first time in this passage. Earlier his terminology fluctuated between these two terms when he was discussing the phenomenal givenness of effective action. I have translated *Ereignis* as "process" in earlier passages; hereafter it will be translated as "event."—TRANS.]

becomes no less *symbolic*. We never perceive this relation itself; nonetheless, we can fulfill the symbol we have for it with the aid of the immediate datum of effective activity. As a result we now take as our basis the essential connection which always connects the same effect with the same cause and proceed in such a way that we only infer that *A is* the cause of *B* from the lawlike recurrence "of the same" event *B* "after" the same event *A*.[23]

Consequently we ought to avoid confusing two things: A lawlike recurrence *of the same events A* and *B* and a lawlike recurrence of the *sequence* of events which themselves only need to be similar to one another, so that $A \to B$, $A_1 \to B_1$, $A_2 \to B_2$ is given. We infer the causal relation not from the regularity in the coming and going of events (e. g., day and night) but only from the regularity of the *sequence* of events.

Accordingly it would be quite wrong to say that experience [*Erfahrung*] first of all bears witness to a recurrence of the same processes and, after that, to a regular sequence between the recurrent processes, or, in other words, to the fact of a *"uniformity in the course of nature"* [*Gleichförmigkeit des Naturgeschehens*]. Rather, in the development of the natural perspective, this relation of regular succession serves as the basis for the unification of those processes which we succeed in perceiving. What is given to us here as "the same" event (or, better, the qualities, forms, etc., which are here combined into the identical unity of an event) is codetermined by the condition that it must become the terminus of a regular sequence.

Once again there is an analogue here to what we found when we were considering the "universal" in the natural worldview.[24] Events which regularly succeed one another are not given to us as "similar"; they are similar to one another only in the *phenomenological reduction* which, among other things, suspends the real causal connection, as well as any other real connection, in the sense that it leaves them undecided. On the contrary, the events which in the reduction are only similar to one another are given in the natural world-view, that is, in

23. While natural intuition infers from the fact that *A* is the cause of *B* that *B* must be present when *A* recurs, that is, infers the law from the cause, science infers the cause from the law.

24. [See above.—ED.]

unreduced perception, as "one and the same" event. Thus, that something similar follows something in sequence is a relationship which *selects* out of the *pure* factual content that which enters into the content of perception. Regular recurrence is not a result of natural experience [*Erfahrung*] but a *law of its formation.* We perceive only what simultaneously reminds us of something similar in our past and points to something anticipated, lets it be "seen in advance."

Theories concerning the basic relation of natural and scientific facts

THE FACTS WITH WHICH SCIENCE IS CONCERNED are states of affairs; its objects are only symbolically meant. Natural facts are things and processes which exhibit themselves in appearances; states of affairs are always given only indirectly through such things and processes.

At this point we encounter a problem: how are natural and scientific facts related and how are the modes of experience in which they are grasped related?

Here there seem to be two possible answers which are sharply opposed to one another.

According to the first, natural facts are the irremovable foundations of the world of scientific facts; that is, there is *no distinction* rooted in the constitution and essence of these two kinds of facts. Instead, the scientific fact is the "natural fact" insofar as the latter is completely described. Scientific experience is only the *completion*, the progressively finer and more exact development, of natural experience. Science should never detach itself from its native soil if it does not want to fall into the void. If one discovers scientific concepts which find no fulfillment even in completely perceived natural facts, then one speaks of "supplementing" the world of natural facts, of "extrapolation" and "interpolation." (Naturally these procedures must take place in accordance with other facts of the natural world-view.) When even these procedures do not seem to do the job, one talks of an "idealization" of natural facts, especially in regard to the conceptual stock of pure mathematics and mechanics (John Stuart Mill).

According to this view, the basic relation of the natural fact to the scientific fact is that of a part to the whole. Science is not concerned with objects of a different kind, with an objective world different from that of natural intuition, and it does not discover facts which would be situated totally outside the sphere of the natural world of facts. Science furnishes exactly the same objects and facts completely which natural intuition furnishes incompletely; science orders them better and distinguishes them with greater precision while in natural intuition they lack any order and are not distinguished with any precision. Even the rules which "supplementation," "interpolation," and "idealization" must follow, as well as the mode of ordering in which science orders its facts, must themselves be taken over from the concrete domain of the natural perspective and its order.

Something analogous also holds for the sphere of understanding: the logical laws of thought are only the laws of the natural movement of natural thinking, of "sound common sense," reduced to their basic rules. They were found, ultimately, through observation of and empirical abstraction from the natural processes of thought. This also holds true of the highest unifying concepts of science and of the single sciences. They are only more exact versions of natural categories. The scientific concepts of substance, for example, are more exact versions of the natural concept of a thing; the scientific concepts of force and of life are more exact versions of the corresponding natural concepts. Scientific geometry is a continuation of natural geometry pursued in the parcelling of land and the measuring of fields. The idea that science is only a higher stage in the development of the natural outlook, an advance to the rules according to which the natural outlook is formed, also belongs to this line of thought. Seemingly we can find a starting point of this kind for every science. For psychology, for instance, it will be the distinctions between inner states already recorded in popular speech, along with the practical observation of men, etc.; for historical science, it will be the historical tradition.

As simple and suggestive as this view appears, it faces an objection which is of the most basic nature. Applied to special problems relevant here, the objection forces us either to give up this view or to modify it by means of totally new distinctions. The objection states that the facts of the natural world-view cannot fill scientific concepts and meaning-intentions [*Bedeutungsintentionen*] with content because, on the contrary, the facts of the natural perspective are themselves accessible to explanation with the help and under the presupposition of scientific concepts.

I want to go into this point with somewhat more precision. My reason is that the very advocates of a theory of cognition based on phenomenology, because they began by taking into account the apprehension of the essence of phenomenological facts and the demarcation of the mode of apprehending these from both scientific *and* natural experience, were inclined to overlook the equally important distinction between scientific facts and natural facts. Consequently, they brought these two kinds of facts into an indiscriminate unity.

Looking at the contrast between these two modes of experience, we find there is a twofold relation between science and the natural world-view. Science exercises a continuing critique of the natural world-view and its claims, and at the same time science uses its own principles and basic concepts to explain, once the facts and things, forces and laws it establishes are presupposed, how exactly this natural world-view had to come about.

An example of science's critique is the Copernican view of the material universe which contradicts any natural view of the world. It is no wonder that time after time rationalist philosophers have gone into battle against empiricism armed with the history of celestial mechanics. Science reveals the natural and normal illusions, the lower and upper limits, the thresholds of discrimination, belonging to natural sense-perception. Once it has determined the true sizes and distances of the stellar masses, science shows us how we come to see the moon and the sun in the apparent sizes and distances in which we do see them, and how it happens that the moon on the horizon appears larger to us than it does when it is directly overhead. In the form of physics, science shows us that the natural events which appear in quite different contents and objects of natural perception and which determine sensations of quite different kinds must be considered essentially alike, since they take place in conformity with differential equations of the same structure. On the other hand, science proves to us that totally different real events can excite the same image-contents in natural perception. Physics quite obviously frees itself from that old division into optics, acoustics, mechanics, etc., that was made only according to the sense-functions through which we receive the real. The electromagnetic theory of light shows us a unified and continuous connection between real processes; a natural perceptual content corresponds only to certain parts of this context, while other parts are not sensibly perceived. Physics is always exhibiting facts and realities, e.g., a whole set of different types of rays, for which we have no corresponding sensory sensations.

When present-day physics erects its whole edifice on the objects and laws of the theory of electricity—that is, on the theory of something we cannot perceive—and considers even mass a dependent function of a certain velocity of electrons, it seems to be mocking any theory of cognition wanting to see scientific truth in the conformity of thoughts with the facts of natural intuition, any theory which considers science a "completion" of natural intuition. Physics seems to mock such theories when it exhibits in the chemical atom a system of electrons revolving about a mid-point, or when, in the theory of relativity, it eliminates the ether as the bearer of the movement of light and even rejects the concepts of time and space as ultimate, basic concepts, if they are meant to represent mutually independent possibilities of the variation of magnitudes. Nonetheless, physics is a science built up entirely on the observations of "facts." What kind of facts are these? With what data and through what operations does a science come to sketch a picture of nature so completely contradictory to the facts of the natural outlook? This is the question the theory of cognition must face. What is it then which fulfills the concepts of science and to which scientific propositions must conform, to the extent that they are more than bare differential equations, to the extent that they furnish the sense and physical meaning of these equations? It will not do, as I have shown, to answer either that pure sensation would still remain even if the entire natural world of things were destroyed (Mach's answer), or that physical reality consists of pure equations.[25] Physics begins its work precisely by eliminating sensations from the body of facts which its theory must satisfy and it makes progress just to the degree that this elimination is successful. Moreover, it has been shown that the same physical processes can be made perceptible [*merklich*] to different senses and that we could have reached exactly the same physical reality which we have, even with a completely

---

25. [See "Phenomenology and the Theory of Cognition," p. 136.—ED.]

altered sensory organization or in the absence of this or that sense. That formalism, however, which lets physical reality consist in equations or allows totally unknown and unknowable transcendent things X, Y, Z to correspond to these as their foundation, out of a certain metaphysical need for stability, completely dissolves physics itself into mathematics and closes itself off from any possibility of interpreting those equations. (See Hertzian equations and the way Maxwell hit upon them.)

Before we get into this question as it applies to the simplest and most elementary physical concepts, we should point out that things are no different in the other sciences, whether they are more abstract or more concrete than physics.

Not a single basic concept of pure *mathematics* is obtained by operating in any way on the facts of the natural perspective, whether this is called abstraction, idealization, interpolation, or extrapolation. The simple reason for this is that there is *not* something concrete corresponding to these concepts in the natural outlook. There is no conceivable abstraction through which anyone can grasp what we mean by the *number* 3 in three things lying at hand if he does not already have the number or find it on this occasion.[26] The number 3 is not a property of any one of these things or of the whole collection of them; it is not a relationship between them, no "coordination" of the elements of this heap of things [*Dinghaufen*]. I can coordinate them with one another however I choose, but if I do not in every case coordinate *one* ($= 1$) thing with one ($= 1$) other thing and thereby presuppose the number 1, I shall not find that for which I was looking. I do not want to repeat the refutation of this old empiricist error which was always forced to leave the infinite number totally unexplained and to limit itself at most to small, positive integers, thus making us regard all other numbers as formations with a completely deviant and purely fictitious structure. In the natural world-view we do indeed count and calculate, but this application of numbers *pre*supposes the existence and the knowledge of number, and this knowledge does not have its origin in that application. Mathematics no more counts things and calculates with things than it measures real spaces; it is

26. See G. Frege, *Grundlagen der Arithmetik* (Breslau: Koebner, 1884) [English translation by J. L. Austin, *The Foundations of Arithmetic* (Evanston, Ill.: Northwestern University Press, 1968).—TRANS.]

concerned with numbers and their laws as independent, *ideal* objects. And these objects do *not* lie among the facts of the natural outlook. Equally absent are the basic geometrical concepts and relationships as they are defined by the axioms of geometry. Only insofar as they are defined by these axioms do they bring about the unity of the concept of geometrical space with its formations and properties, where the latter deviate completely from the space of the natural outlook. The straight line, the plane, the point, simply do not lie among the facts of the natural outlook and are not to be obtained from them by any procedure of variation or abstraction, or by an idealization. It is *with the help* of scientific concepts that we come to decide how correctly the same words are applied in the natural world-view—to decide, for example, whether this stick is straight and how far it is from being strictly straight, whether the metal sphere is a sphere, etc.

Precisely the same thing holds true of the basic concepts of *mechanics:* mass-point, uniform motion, force, velocity, acceleration. Mechanics begins by destroying any classification of the different types of motion to the extent that they are taken from the natural outlook and from language, for example, falling and rising motion, quick and slow motion, celestial and mundane motion—in other words, all the distinctions among forms of motion which people in antiquity and the Middle Ages fancied were bound up with definite, qualitatively different substances, like "ether" and "matter." Mechanics destroys the natural concept of force, drawn from the intuition of organic life, according to which motions take place in forms which are present in the essence of this force; moreover, the force, in the course of its operation, ceases of itself. The "stone grows tired," as Plato says. In place of these classifications we get concepts like point-mass, ideal, frictionless motion, motion in a completely empty, uniform space in conformity with the effect of force operating only over a differential of time; and these are clearly concepts which are not found among the facts of the natural world-view, any more than the corresponding objects, namely, absolutely solid, fluid, and gaseous bodies.

Precisely the same principle holds true, moreover, of the concrete sciences. It would be a mistake to think that these remain closer to the facts of the natural outlook. The *chemist* smashes the natural unities which confront us as individual, corporeal things, as well as their generic and specific unities. He displays the same chemical substances in things as basically different as diamond and coal. He displays the same and the similar in that which is, for natural intuition, fundamentally different. He denies that "the qualitative transformation of materials" occurs when they are combined and allows only the spatial combination and separation of ultimate, qualitatively specific elementary particles. He shows that the corporeal things which confront us as compact individuals are only accidental unities bound together into aggregates by the laws of molecular processes, unities which are continuously caught up in the process of formation and decomposition, continually exchanging matter and energy with the materials [Stoffen] and forces in their environment in a manner totally unknown to natural perception. He proves that their unity, their stability, their individuality are merely subjective appearances resting on our senses, our needs, and our interests.

Once again, however, if we bring in physiology and psychology, we can explain how we got to the particular unities of corporeal things in the natural outlook. We can explain how the limits of the sense-thresholds of our different senses, the shifting application of our emotional and voluntary attention in keeping with our needs, have created the species and genera of these particular unities. The concept of "acid" [Säure], which has long since ceased to have any connection with "sour," is an example of this kind of gradual transformation of chemical concepts, an example already adduced by Mill. Today the chemical elements are so far from being definable in terms of sensory contents that, on the contrary, the sense-functions, to the extent they are to be known physiologically, are almost all reduced to chemical stimuli and processes.

Again, the same principle holds true of biology and its subordinate sciences.

If, therefore, the facts of the natural perspective do not provide any limitation on, or standard for, the truth and validity of scientific concepts and judgments, and if science can indeed explain these facts as an "illusion" necessarily resulting from our organization, the most pressing question becomes in what "facts" scientific concepts and principles *do* find their fulfillment; especially since sensation cannot furnish any such fulfillment, but rather itself can and must be explained by scientific concepts and principles or by the realities answering to these.

Once we have seen the mistake of the empiricist theory that the sphere of scientific facts and objects is in some way derived or extracted from the sphere of natural facts and objects, we can go on to think of several other basic relations between these two species of fact which correspond to extant attempts to solve this problem. One such attempt is made in *Kant's theory,* which is for the most part fairly imprecise.

Kant's conception of the relation between the scientific and the natural amounts to this, that in his concept of "experience" he does indeed start from the finished experience of science and breaks science down into its components; that is, he takes scientific judgment as his starting point and then seeks to learn to what extent "sensory contents" (a concept which he does not probe any further) correspond to the meaning-content of such a judgment and to what extent we meet with other factors in this "experience." These other factors are what Kant calls formal factors. Within them Kant again distinguishes those which, in his opinion, can be made to coincide with intuition (these are the forms of pure intuition) and those which do not admit of this (these are the functional laws and forms of judgment, the logical categories). Both kinds of formal factors, however, still exhibit precise contents in contrast to pure logic and cannot be derived from the basic concepts of logic. Together the formal factors form, according to Kant, a feature of the organization of man distinct from the concepts and laws of pure logic which hold true of objects in general, and thus of objects "in themselves" as well.

Now, although Kant, in fact, and in part consciously, makes scientific experience his starting point, he still assumes from the start that the formal structure of *scientific* experience coincides [*zusammenfalle*] with the formal structure of *natural* experience. He does not distinguish these two modes of experience sharply and in principle. He believes that both natural experience and scientific experience are built up through the same acts of synthesis and in conformity with the same laws lying in the organization of man. For example, space as it is understood in the natural outlook does not diverge widely from the space of geometry; the natural concept of a thing does not diverge widely from the scientific concept of substance. As a result, the reality of mechanical physics acquires a very obscure position within the levels of the being of objects which Kant distinguishes. Kant, as is well known, distinguishes three levels of being: (1) that of absolute objects or things-in-themselves; (2) the level of the world of appearance [*Erscheinungswelt*]; and (3) the level of subjective semblance or illusion [*Schein*]. It is characteristic of his position that the facts and objects of the natural outlook as well as the reality of mechanical physics fall on the level of the world of appearance. The stone lying before me (if I abstract from all individual and general sense-deceptions) as well as the molecular complex, or finally the complex of atoms and electrons to which science reduces the stone, are on this same level. Thus Kant assigns the rainbow to the sphere of subjective illusion, the drops of water of which it physically consists to "appearance," and the absolutely unknown X, which corresponds to it in the sphere independent of the organization of the human mind, to the "thing-in-itself." This vacillation is especially clear in the case of the much-contested scientific concept of "matter." Kant emphatically asserts its existence, against Berkeley, but does not decide whether matter lies in the sphere of appearance or in that of the thing-in-itself. His vacillation is also clear in the case of the concept of sensation, where three sorts of things are continually confused with one another: (1) sensation as content is an absolute datum, the material of appearance; (2) it is (also as content) an effect of what, in the end, are purely mechanical stimulations on the physiological organism;[27] and (3) it is an effect of the "thing-in-itself" on the "thing-in-itself" of our Self.

However, we cannot doubt that Kant committed an error when he set the forms and the structure of the natural outlook and its contents, together with the scientific perspective, on *one* level and thought that the product of the natural outlook is in essence the same as the product of the scientific world-view. There may be something identically common in

27. This is demonstrated when Kant asserts the "subjectivity" of sensation, that is, the subjectivity of its contents, but distinguishes it as subjective "a posteriori" from the subjectivity of space and time which alone can be called subjective "a priori." [This sentence was originally in the text.—TRANS.]

them, but this can be proved only after a precise phenomenological characterization of these two modes of experience
that are at first fundamentally different. Kant's error is com-
pounded if we come to identify these two modes of experience by first examining the factors and foundational relations
in scientific experience, that is, the experience already fixed
in scientific judgments, and *then* by assuming that these
same factors must be discoverable in natural experience. By
this means natural experience is *rationalized* in a completely
oblique fashion and does not come to light with the features
characteristic of it.

A second mistake is connected with this. Since Kant does
not distinguish phenomenological experience from scientific
experience but always speaks of "experience" without distinction, he cannot specify through what experience he brings
forth what he calls the *forms* and constitutions of any possible
experience. It follows that the concepts of those forms do not
in turn "agree" with facts, nor are they true forms; they appear
as the contingent means situated in the human organization
for constructing any truth and objectivity.

On the other hand, Kant's own solution has an advantage
over the more glaringly scientistic extension the Marburg
school and the pragmatists have given it. Since, according to
Kant, the same laws of synthesis are at work in the construction of the natural outlook as in the construction of the world
of scientific objects, an agreement of scientific judgments with
the facts of the natural outlook can at least be meaningfully
demanded. The facts here are still not "created" and "produced"
in scientific judgment; scientific judgment has to agree with
the facts belonging to the natural outlook, even though these
"facts" themselves are formed and determined by exactly the
same rules of synthesis which prove to be at work in scientific
judgment as well.

In contrast to the "halfway" character of Kant's theory,
the solution now offered is eminently pure and stands in the
most extreme opposition to the theory first discussed, according
to which science is only a completion and continuation of the
natural outlook, while natural facts remain the standard for
scientific facts. I shall call this theory the "scientistic" doctrine, ignoring the various forms it can take. According to this
doctrine, science represents a *total break* with the natural

perspective, as much with its individual contents as with all its forms and structure. Scientific research is not concerned with perfecting, supplementing, or idealizing what is given in the natural perspective, but with a fundamentally new construction which is produced purely by the power of the mind. The facts of the natural outlook, its forces, things, and relations, its sound common sense should in no way count as "given" for science; neither the natural outlook itself nor agreement with its facts should ever be made into a standard for the truth of scientific concepts and principles. Rather, science has, among other things, the task of completely explaining the facts and objects of the natural perspective, for example, the occurrence of a natural intuition of things, the natural consciousness of the fact of the distinction between the real and the unreal, the natural concepts of force and activity, etc., and of doing so in such a way that nothing is left unexplained. Thus science does not explain the world by taking as its foundation, if not the content, then at least the forms, of the natural outlook; these forms themselves are also an object which it explains. The content of natural perception is so little binding upon science that, on the contrary, this perception and its components should be completely explained and made intelligible with the help of the psychology of sensory memory, the physiology of the senses and the brain, plus chemistry and physics.

The upshot of this definition of the relation between science and the natural outlook is that nothing should be counted as "given" to science which constitutes a limit for science, nothing with which its concepts and principles would have to agree. A scientific fact is only the X which must be determined, the correlate of the scientific judgment. "What is given" is therefore something totally "undetermined," a "chaos of contents" which itself is to be addressed only as the limit of scientific determination and must be seen as nonexistent in the strictest sense of the term, as the *mē on*. "Given" is a term which simply expresses the infinite task of science or which says that science is still unfinished. This can also be expressed as follows: *nothing* is "given" to thought; or, everything which is given to an act of thought must be determined in turn by a new act of thought; only that is given to thinking *which it gives to itself*.

Science, therefore, in no sense comes upon a body of fact. It produces, it creates, and it constructs its context of nature in a completely free manner, without confining itself in doing so to a mere "modeling" [*Abbildung*] or "imitation" [*Nachbildung*] of a given. Science does not undertake abstractions, idealizations, or selections of antecedently given facts, but it constructs—without being held in check by a given—a system of concepts and principles through which the chaos first takes on the character of a "system of nature." Thus the object answering to a curve does not consist in an intuitive content, however precise this might be; it is given only in the analytical formula which analytical geometry develops for it. Thus the so-called fact of free fall consists in the *law* of free fall in which for the first time what "free fall" *is* gets completely expressed. Only in one of these contexts does the content represent a "fact." Apart from this fulfillment in a logical context, it melts away without remainder into the chaotic mass of the given.

The *truth of science* consists in this coherent context of concepts and propositions. The only standard of this is its inner consistency and its power of determining and articulating the chaos of this undifferentiated mass.

It does not seem to us a great distinction, as many assume, whether scientism takes on a more rationalistic or a more pragmatic form; it makes little difference whether a "pure thought," which carries in itself the legitimacy of its function and performs its acts in independence of all practical enterprises, should carry out this program, or whether the "understanding" itself should be understood as a precipitate of originally practical vital reactions whose rules have become fixed. This is the case at least in regard to the question which is here being examined.

One notices immediately how essentially the rationalistic form of scientism deviates from the historical Kant. While for him the absence of a distinction between natural and scientific experience is essential, here a sharp distinction is drawn between the two and there no longer exists any structural unity between the two modes of experience.[28]

28. [The manuscript breaks off at this point.—ED.]

Idealism and Realism

[I]

THE CONFLICT BETWEEN what are customarily called "Idealism" and "Realism" remains even today one of the basic points of controversy in philosophical ontology and epistemology (*prima philosophia*). In contemporary German philosophy as well as in that of the most recent past this fundamental conflict has taken on two more specialized subforms: it has become a conflict between "Idealism of Consciousness" [*Bewusstseinsidealismus*] and "Critical Realism." The trend in recent decades, incidentally, has clearly been toward a sharp decrease in the number of adherents to the various forms of the Idealism of Consciousness, while Critical Realism has been steadily gaining ground.

The aim of this study is twofold. First, I mean to show that it is a mistake to opt for either one of the parties to this conflict. Second, I shall demonstrate that the variants of both Idealism of Consciousness and Critical Realism rest upon three different errors: (1) on a false statement of the question; (2) on a completely unsatisfactory division of the pertinent parts of the problem; and (3) on a persistent *prōton pseudos* [primary error], i.e., on a presupposition common to both standpoints that we can show to be false. Indeed, a sharper grasp of this presupposition gives a fundamentally

Translated from "Idealismus-Realismus," *Philosophischer Anzeiger,* II (Bonn: Verlag Friedrich Cohen, 1927), 255–93.

new meaning to the whole state of the problem and leads to a definitive overthrow of the Idealism-Realism antithesis. Since in my view everything depends on this *prōton pseudos,* I place it here at the head of my remarks, even though a full understanding of it and its various forms will only come later.

This false presupposition is the assumption that we cannot separate what we call the existence [*Dasein*] or reality of any object (whether of the internal world, the external world, another self, a living being, an inanimate thing, etc.) and what we call its nature [*Sosein*] (its contingent nature as well as its essence, *essentia*) when we are dealing with the question of what is, or what can or cannot be, immanent to knowledge (*scientia*) and, further, to reflexive knowledge [*Be-wusstsein*] (*con-scientia*).[1] One of my principal theses is that in every case the nature of a being (contingent as well as essential nature) can, in principle, be immanent to and truly inherent in knowledge and reflexive consciousness [*Bewusstsein*].[2] Furthermore, it can be present there exactly as it is outside of consciousness, and therefore not only as it is represented by some image, perception, idea [*Vorstellung*], or thought. This immanence of the nature of a being to consciousness occurs, of course, with totally different degrees of adequation and on completely different levels of the relativity of its existence to the existence and constitution [*Organisation*] of the "knowing" subject. Existence, however, can never be immanent to consciousness. Rather, existence necessarily transcends knowledge and consciousness and is alien to them. Existence is essentially transcendent and remains independent of them, even in the limiting case of a "divine, omniscient Mind." In other words, the nature and the existence of any possible object are separable with respect to the possibility of their being *in mente* [*in the mind*]. The nature of a being can be *in mente* and actually is so in any evidential

1. [*Dasein,* literally "being-there," will usually be translated by "existence." *Sosein,* literally "being-thus" or "being-so," means the essential nature of an entity as well as its contingent or accidental characteristics. I shall translate *Sosein* variously by "nature" or "character."—TRANS.]

2. [Scheler stresses here and elsewhere the etymological and conceptual link between knowledge (*Wissen*) and consciousness (*Be-Wusstsein*); see 'Wissen und Bewusstsein" ("Knowledge and Consciousness," II, 2, below). Moreover, he uses *Bewusstsein* in both an active ("being conscious") and a passive ("being consciously known") sense; see below.—TRANS.]

cognition of what a thing is, which excludes cases of illusion and error. Existence can never be *in mente*. I shall speak later of how existence can be "given" despite this. Existence transcends thought, intuition, and perception, as well as any cooperation of thought and intuition in that higher form of knowledge we call cognition. Cognition is the "knowledge of something as something," the coincidence [*Deckung*] of intuition and thought.

In sum: Critical Realism and Idealism of Consciousness are the result of treating the nature and the existence of an entity as inseparable with respect to their possible immanence to knowledge and consciousness. All the representatives of the Idealism of Consciousness, e.g., Rickert and the Marburg logicians, Schuppe,[3] H. Cornelius, and the positivistic Idealists are correct in asserting that the nature of an object can "itself" be *in mente*, thus not only an "image" which refers [*hinweisendes*] to it or a "symbol" which represents it. But they draw, from the *prōton pseudos* common to Idealism of Consciousness and every form of Critical Realism, the formally correct but materially false conclusion that every possible type of existence must also be *in mente*. Thus there is no existence transcendent to or independent of consciousness. *Esse est percipi.* Consciousness (supra-individual consciousness or consciousness in general) is therefore the necessary correlate of all existence. On the other hand, all the Critical Realists, no matter how they try to prove their thesis, start from the same primary error, plus a true proposition; it is their recognition of the true proposition that gives them the advantage over the Idealists of Consciousness. This proposition states that the existence of an object is always and necessarily transcendent to every possible consciousness (including the divine) and can never become the content of knowing or consciousness. However, from these two premises they draw the conclusion, again formally true but materially false, that the nature of an object as well must always and necessarily be independent of, detached, and separated from every possible knowing and consciousness. Therefore, nothing can ever be given "in consciousness" except an "image" or a "symbol" (perception, idea,

3. [Ernst J. W. Schuppe (1836–1913). His main works were *Erkenntnistheoretische Logik* (Bonn, 1878) and *Grundriss der Erkenntnistheorie und Logik* (Berlin, 1894; 2d ed., 1910).—TRANS.]

thought) which refers to the character of the object. (We disregard the fact that they picture what they call consciousness as a "big box" and do not think of it as an "act" or "intention.") Thus both standpoints, from a common basic error and a premise which is in each case true, draw false conclusions, each contradicting the other.

Still, this is only one of the errors basic to these epistemological standpoints. I mention it first because it is the only error which is common to all forms of Idealism of Consciousness on the one hand and Critical Realism on the other. For the rest, there are considerable differences among the remaining errors in the various forms of both which we shall have to bring up later.[4]

[II] DIVISION, ARRANGEMENT, AND SOLUTION OF THE PROBLEMS PRECEDING THE QUESTION OF REALITY

THE GREATEST SHORTCOMING in previous attempts to solve the problem of idealism versus realism is the defective division and logically incorrect arrangement of the subsidiary questions which are a part of the problem as a whole. Thus our first task is to make a precise division of the subsidiary questions and to inspect their actual interdependence. The first such question concerns what I call the ordering of evidence [*Evidenzordnung*].

1. *The ordering of evidence*

In Leibniz we can already find the striking observation that *cogitatur ergo est* is no less evident than *cogito ergo sum*. Naturally, *est* here does not mean existence or reality but being of whatever kind and form, including even ideal being,

4. Of the complete work, which is to appear shortly in a separate edition from Verlag Cohen, Bonn, I present here only the second and third sections, entitled "Division, Arrangement, and Solution of the Problems Preceding the Question of Reality" (Part II), and "The True Problem of Reality" (Part III). The first part of the work provides a morphology and a critique of the forms that idealism and realism have adopted in Western philosophy. The fourth part will furnish my "Theory of Essence and the Cognition of Essence"; the fifth, a critical confrontation with Martin Heidegger's *Sein und Zeit*. [The edition Scheler alludes to never appeared.—TRANS.]

fictive being, conscious-being [*Bewusst-Sein*], etc. However, we must go even beyond this thesis of Leibniz. The correlate of the act of *cogitatio* is not, as Leibniz said, being simply, but only that type of being we call "objectifiable being." Objectifiable being must be sharply distinguished from the non-objectifiable being of an act, that is, from a kind of entity which possesses its mode of being only in performance [*Vollzug*], namely, in the performance of the act. "Being," in the widest sense of the word, belongs indeed to the being-of-an-act [*Akt-Sein*], to *cogitare*, which does not in turn require another *cogitare*. Similarly, we are only vaguely "aware" of our drives [*Triebleben*] [5] without having them as objects as we do those elements of consciousness which lend themselves to imagery. For this reason the first order of evidence is expressed in the principle, "There is something," or, better, "There is not nothing." Here we understand by the word "nothing" the negative state of affairs of not-being in general rather than "not being something" or "not being actual." [6] A second principle of evidence is that everything which "is" in any sense of the possible kinds of being can be analyzed in terms of its character or essence (not yet separating its contingent characteristics from its genuine essence) and its existence in some mode.

With these two principles we are in a position to define precisely the concept of knowledge, a concept which is prior even to that of consciousness. Knowledge is an ultimate, unique, and underivable ontological relationship between two beings. I mean by this that any being *A* "knows" any being *B* whenever *A* participates in the essence or nature of *B*, without *B*'s suffering any alteration in its nature or essence because of *A*'s participation in it. Such participation is possible both in the case of objectifiable being and in that of active [*akthaften*] being, for instance, when we repeat the performance of the act; or in feelings, when we relive the

5. [*Trieb* is a key word (along with *Drang*) in all of Scheler's late texts (e.g., "Erkenntnis und Arbeit," in *Die Wissensformen und die Gesellschaft*, 2d ed. rev., *Gesammelte Werke* VIII [Bern: Francke, 1960], pp. 336–38). No one English word—"drive," "impulse," "inclination," "instinct"—fits every context.—TRANS.]

6. The principle that if nothing is not, there must be a type of being which simply is per se, is an insight which follows immediately upon the above. This is disregarded here. See my essay "On the Essence of Philosophy," *On the Eternal in Man*, trans. Bernard Noble (London: Student Christian Movement Press, 1960).

feeling, etc. The concept of participation is, therefore, wider than that of objective knowledge, that is, knowledge of objectifiable being. The participation which is in question here can never be dissolved into a causal relation, or one of sameness and similarity, or one of sign and signification; it is an ultimate and essential relation of a peculiar type. We say further of B that, when A participates in B and B belongs to the order of objectifiable being, B becomes an "objective being" ["*Gegenstand*"-*sein*]. Confusing the being of an object [*Sein des Gegenstandes*] with the fact that an entity is an object [*Gegenstandssein eines Seienden*] is one of the fundamental errors of idealism. On the contrary, the being of B, in the sense of a mode of reality, never enters into the knowledge-relation. The being of B can never stand to the real bearer of knowledge in any but a causal relation. The *ens reale* remains, therefore, outside of every possible knowledge-relation, not only the human but also the divine, if such exists. Both the concept of the "intentional act" and that of the "subject" of this act, an "I" which performs acts, are logically posterior. The intentional act is to be defined as the process of becoming [*Werdesein*] in A through which A participates in the nature or essence of B, or that through which this participation is produced. To this extent the Scholastics were right to begin with the distinction between an *ens intentionale* and an *ens reale*, and then, on the basis of this distinction, to distinguish between an intentional act and a real relation between the knower and the being of the thing known.

2. *Knowledge and consciousness*

Only after the concept of knowledge has been based on an ontological relation [*Seinsverhältnis*] can we work out the particular kind of being from which the principle of immanence-to-consciousness (the common starting point of Idealism and Critical Realism) mistakenly proceeds as though from a primary insight. This is the being of "being-conscious" [*Bewusst-Seins*]. All being-conscious must first of all be brought under the higher concept of ideal being, or, at all events, that of irreal being. The mental item which presents itself in the experiences of consciousness may be real; being-conscious itself never is. However, the concept of consciousness is derivative in not only this sense. Consciousness also presupposes the concept of knowledge. Nothing is more misleading than to proceed in the opposite direction and define knowledge itself as simply a particular "content of consciousness," as we see if we oppose, to the particular kind of knowing and having-known which we call consciousness, another kind of knowledge which precedes it and includes no form of being-conscious. We will call this knowledge *ecstatic* [*ekstatische*] [7] knowledge. It is found quite clearly in animals, primitive people, children, and, further, in certain pathological and other abnormal and supra-normal states (e.g., in recovering from the effects of a drug). I have said elsewhere that the animal never relates to its environment as to an object but only *lives in it* [*es lebe nur "in sie hinein"*].[8] Its conduct with respect to the external world depends upon whether the latter satisfies its instinctive drives or denies them satisfaction. The animal experiences the surrounding world as resistances of various types. Hence, it is absolutely necessary to contest the principle (in Descartes, Franz Brentano, *et al.*) that every mental function and act is accompanied by an immediate knowledge of it. An even more highly contestable principle is that a relation to the self is an essential condition of all processes of knowledge. It is difficult to reproduce purely ecstatic knowledge in mature, civilized men, whether in memory, reverie, perception, thought, or empathetic identification with things, animals, or men; nonetheless, there is no doubt that in every perception and presentation of things and events we think that we grasp *the things-themselves,* not mere "images" of them or representatives of some sort.

Knowledge first becomes conscious knowledge [*Bewusstsein*], that is, comes out of its original ecstatic form of simply "having" things, in which there is no knowledge of the having or of that through which and in which it is had, when the act of being thrown back on the self (probably only possible for men) comes into play. This act grows out of conspicuous resistances, clashes, and oppositions—in sum, out of pro-

7. [The English word "ecstatic" fails to convey the nuances of Scheler's term *ekstatisch*. Etymologically, it means "standing outside of oneself." From the context, ecstatic knowledge means a relationship to the world which is prior to the emergence of self-consciousness or reflection.—TRANS.]

8. [See "Erkenntnis und Arbeit," chap. IV—TRANS.]

nounced suffering. It is the *actus re-flexivus* in which knowledge of the knowledge of things is added to the knowledge of things. Furthermore, in this act we come to know the kind of knowledge we have, for example, memory, ideation, and perception, and, finally, beyond even these, we come to have a knowledge of the relation of the act performed to the self, to the knower. With respect to any specific relation to the self, this last knowledge, so-called conscious self-knowledge, comes only after knowledge about the act. Kant's principle that an "I think" must be *able* to accompany all a man's thoughts may be correct. That it in fact always accompanies them is nevertheless undoubtedly false. However, the kind of being (indeed, of ideal being) which contents possess when they are reflexively *had* in their givenness in conscious acts— when, therefore, they become reflexive—is the being of being-consciously-known.

We must reject entirely the frequently encountered assertion that consciousness is a "primal fact," that one ought not speak of an "origin" of consciousness. The very same laws and motives in accordance with which we think of consciousness' raising itself from one level of reflection to the next will apply when we think of consciousness itself originating out of a preconscious, partly subconscious, partly supra-conscious condition of the being of the contents of knowledge. (And the motive is always suffering of some sort, suffering, as we shall see, at the hands of the real being [*Realsein*] which is ecstatically given prior to all consciousness.) Only a very definite historical stage of overreflective bourgeois civilization could make the fact of consciousness the starting point of all theoretical philosophy, without characterizing more exactly the mode of being of this consciousness.

3. The problem of the transcendence of the object and the consciousness of transcendence

The third preliminary problem for every theory of reality is that of the experience of transcendence. We saw in the case of Berkeley that his erroneous principle *percipi est esse,* and his assertion that any being which we think, just for the reason that it is thought, cannot at the same time be regarded as subsisting independently of thinking, incorporate a failure to recognize the consciousness of transcendence peculiar to all intentional acts. This is an instance of the failure to recognize that not only all thinking in the narrower sense, in the sense of grasping an object on the basis of "meanings" and grasping a state of affairs through judgments, but *every* intention in general, whether perception, representation, remembering, the feeling of value, or the posing of ends and goals, points beyond the act and the contents of the act and intends something other than the act [*ein Aktfremdes*], even when what is thought is in turn itself a thought.

Indeed, *intentio* signifies a goal-directed movement toward something which one does not have oneself or has only partially and incompletely.

Berkeley (following Locke, who was the first to make the basic philosophical error which introduced "psychologism" into epistemology) arrived at the principle *esse est percipi* by making the idea [*Vorstellung*] (and even the sensation) into a thing, an immaterial substance, and by failing to distinguish between the act, the content of an act, and the object. Furthermore, Berkeley confused the being of objects with the fact of being-an-object, even though the latter has only a loose and variable connection with the former. On the other hand, the transcendence of the intentional object with respect to both the *intentio* and its present content is common to every instance of being-an-object. It is, for instance, proper to objects of pure mathematics which are certainly not real but ideal (for example, the number 3). These are produced from the a priori material of intuition in accordance with an operational law governing the steps of our thought or intuition. Transcendence is further proper to all fictitious objects and even to contradictory objects, for instance, a square circle. All these sorts of objects, e.g., the golden mountain or Little Red Riding Hood, satisfy the basic principle of the transcendence of objects over and above that aspect of them which is, at any moment, given in consciousness, just as much as do real objects existing independently of all consciousness and knowledge.

It is precisely because the principle of the transcendence of the object is completely independent of the existential status of the objects themselves and, thus, independent of the question whether they are produced by us or subsist on their own—whether they are fictions or real beings—that the fact of the consciousness of transcendence is not even remotely qualified to solve the problem of reality. This has been misunderstood equally by W. Freytag, Edith Landmann, P. Linke, and even by Husserl himself.[9] Indeed, people have wanted to speak of an intentional realism (E. Landmann) in contrast to Critical Realism and to all other forms of realism. N. Hartmann was quite correct in emphasizing, in opposition to this, that the projection [*Hinausragen*] of the intentional object beyond the content of consciousness and its act cannot make the least contribution to solving the problem of realism.[10] If something is an intentional object, we cannot recognize from this fact alone, whether it is real or not. If the perceived cherry, the conceived triangle, a friend's visit anticipated in a dream, Little Red Riding Hood, a freely planned project, or a felt value, have entirely different characteristics and predicates than do the mental processes and the actual contents in which these objects appear, then the distinction between intentional and mental holds equally of both the real and the irreal. *Thus, the problem of what is real is not touched by the fact of the transcendence of the object,* and *percipi est esse,* in Berkeley's psychologistic sense, is laid to rest. This also frustrates attempts, such as Hume's in his *Treatise,* to derive being-an-object in general—an object as distinguished from an idea—from a psychogenetic process in which the very ideas through which this psychogenetic process is supposed to be accomplished are themselves reified [*verdinglicht*].

What is gained by the transcendence of the object is the identifiability of the object in a plurality of acts and the identifiability of what is thought by several individuals. This identifiability is not restricted to ideal objects, which are generated according to a definite operational law and are therefore producible by everyone out of the same material of intuition which is given prior to any particular sense-experience. The identifiability obtains in precisely the same way for objects of myth and folklore, of belief and artistic fantasy. Goethe's Faust, Apollo, and Little Red Riding Hood can be identified by several

9. [Willy Freytag (b. 1873), author of *Der Realismus und das Transzendenzproblem* (Halle, 1902); Edith Landmann (b. 1877), *Die Transzendenz des Erkennens* (Berlin, 1923).—TRANS.]

10. See N. Hartmann, *Grundzüge einer Metaphysik der Erkenntnis* (Berlin, 1921).

individuals and are the objects of common, universally valid statements. Indeed, exact identity of the nature of the object in question and evidential knowledge of this identity can occur *only* in the case of ideal objects. Our certainty that we all think the same number 3 in the strictest identity of its nature is much more evident than that we all think the same real object, a tree, for instance. In the case of real objects we can actually prove that it is impossible for the momentary content in which the object is represented and thought to be exactly the same in a plurality of acts and for many individuals. The only other contribution made by the fact of the consciousness of transcendence, so long overlooked in recent philosophy, to the problem of reality is this: the acts in which this consciousness is present can bring the givenness of reality, of which we shall speak later, into "objective" form, and can therefore elevate that which is given in this way as real to the status of a real "object." But with this, the contribution of the consciousness of transcendence to the problem of reality is at an end. Although N. Hartmann made the same point with respect to Paul Linke's otherwise shrewd and pertinent comments on his doctrine of reality,[11] still we should emphasize that the transcendence of the object does not *exclude* the reality of the object, not even of the *same* object in the strict sense of "same."

It is very important to note that the transcendence of the object is by no means a primitive component necessarily ingredient in all knowledge. It is missing in all ecstatic knowledge. In ecstatic knowledge the known world is still not objectively given. Only when the (logically and genetically simultaneous) act furnishing ecstatic knowledge and the subject which performs this act become themselves the content of knowledge in the act of reflection does the character originally given in ecstatic knowledge become a mere reference pointing to the "object." It is only here that the object or that which turns into an object remains from now on "transcendent" to consciousness. Therefore, whenever there is consciousness, objects transcendent to consciousness must also be given to consciousness. Their structural relationship is indissoluble. Whenever self-consciousness and consciousness of an object arise, they do so simultaneously and through the same process. The

11. *Philosophischer Anzeiger*, Vol. I, no. 2. (1926). [Scheler is referring to Linke's article "Bild und Erkenntnis."—TRANS.]

categorical form of an object is not first impressed in a judgment upon a nonobjective given, not even in a one-term, simple judgment, as some people have thought (e.g., Heinrich Maier in his book *Wahrheit und Wirklichkeit*).[12] This is a pure construction. Consciousness of an object precedes all judgment and is not originally constituted by judgment. The same holds true of consciousness of states of affairs. The consciousness of an object and the intentional object are not the result of an active [*tätige*] "forming" or "imprinting" which we perform on the given through judgments or any other operations of thought. On the contrary, they are the result of a pulling back, the result, that is, of the re-flexive act, in which an originally ecstatic [*ekstatisch gebender*] act turns back knowingly onto itself and comes upon a central self as its starting point. This central self can be given at every level and degree of "concentration" and "collectedness" in "self-consciousness." What we had hold of [*das Gehabte*] remains "as" object, while the act of reflection turns the knowing back onto the knower, as the result of a turning away [*Abwendung*] and a pulling back, and not of an active turning to [*Zuwendung*].

From what has been said, one may very well imagine that the real world could be abolished without consciousness and the self being altered or abolished thereby. But this could in no way be the case with the world of objects that transcend consciousness. Descartes as well as Lotze misunderstood this. Where a *cogito* exists, there must also be a *cogitatur* in which a transcendent object is thought. Only a being capable of reflection (*reflexio*) and self-consciousness *can* have objects. Charlotte Bühler has recently made it seem probable that the infant does not yet possess objective consciousness.[13] In waking from the effects of a drug we can follow the process by which the givenness of the surrounding world becomes objective again. There is one last point of contact between the problem of reality and the consciousness of transcendence. The consciousness of transcendence, as already indicated, shows how the

12. [Heinrich Maier (1867–1933), *Philosophie der Wirklichkeit*, 3 vols. (Tübingen, 1926–35). Scheler's reference is to the first volume.—TRANS.]

13. [Charlotte Bühler was a German psychologist and author of important works on infantile fantasies and the first manifestations of consciousness. An English translation of her work *Das Kind und seine Familie* appeared as *The Child and His Family* (New York, 1939).—TRANS.]

mere ecstatic possession of reality on the level of the immediately experienced resistance of an X to the central drives
of life passes over into a reflexive and thus objective possession
of reality. And we find similar transitions between ecstatic remembering which is merged in the being of what is past and
reflexive remembering, between ecstatic drive activities and recurrent deliberation [*Besinnung*], between ecstatic surrender
to a value and objectification of a value, between identifying
with an alter ego and "understanding" [*Verstehen*] another,
however slightly.

4. *The problem of the spheres of being*

Among the confusions which have become involved with the
problem of reality, there is the confusion of the vast and complicated problem of the spheres of being (above all, the spheres
of the so-called external and internal worlds, the physical and
the mental) with the problem of reality. Descartes became entangled in this confusion, albeit indecisively and unconsciously, as a result of his false assumption that the inner world
is given prior to the external world. Berkeley likewise became
entangled, but this time clearly and decisively. The same is
true of J. G. Fichte, W. Dilthey, and even W. Wundt, insofar as
Kant specifies that the mental be given immediately, the physical only indirectly or mediately. Still others share this confusion
(e.g., O. Külpe, P. Natorp) as a result of their equally false
theory that the external world and its objects are given prior
to the inner world. I am not going to present here a complete
treatment of the problem of the spheres, a problem both
germane and vast in scope. I will settle for indicating how
many irreducible spheres of being there are, in my opinion.
These are: (1) the sphere of *ens a se,* absolute being in contrast to relative being; (2) the spheres of the external and internal world; (3) the sphere of the creature and its environment; and (4) the spheres of the I, the Thou, and society. A
basic law common to all the spheres of being is that the being
of the sphere itself is always given prior to the individual
empirical objects which are given through the various types of
perception and intuition. Only a special investigation, however,
can decide whether in general something real can also be given
within each of these spheres. The positive sciences should

establish which objects, within the spheres in which something real can be given, are also in fact real.

For this reason, we ought to reject the phrase "reality of the external world." It suggests that there is a special problem of the reality of the external world, or that the mere acknowledgement of such an independent sphere as the external world—whether given prior to or simultaneously with the internal world—contributes something to the totally different question: can what is given in the external world also be *real?* The sphere of the external world—granting its independence and underivability—contains both the real and the irreal in a mixture peculiar to itself. Space, the form of every external world, is certainly not "real," since it cannot exercise any causality [*nicht wirkungsfähig*]. It would not be real even if it subsisted independently of our consciousness. A shadow, a virtual image, the blue of the heavens, a rainbow, the colors on a surface are, without a doubt, "appearances of the external world." Nevertheless, one cannot ascribe reality to them.

On the other hand, something is not irreal because it belongs to the mental sphere. The distinction between appearance and reality in the mental sphere is, as Kant rightly saw, exactly the same as in the sphere of the external world. A mental reality, as Moritz Geiger has recently shown, following some suggestions in my work "The Idols of Self-Knowledge," is just as distinct from the phenomena of consciousness [*Bewusstseinserscheinungen*] in which we grasp the character of that reality inadequately and only piecemeal as physical realities are from the contents of our consciousness "of them."

It is, therefore, methodologically incorrect to require, as Nicolai Hartmann has recently done, a proof of the reality of the external world before (in the sense of logical order) one acknowledges the independent sphere of external worldhood [*Aussenweltlichkeit*]. On this point Paul Linke, in his polemic against Hartmann, is completely in the right. Kant, too, distinguished the problem of reality from the problem of the existence of the external world. He requires no proof for the sphere of the external world and he considers it a "scandal of philosophy" only that none is produced for its reality. Despite this, he denied the absolute reality of any external world accessible to all our "possible experience." Today we maintain both the independence of the external world vis-à-vis the internal world and the necessity of first ordering and differentiating the internal world, insofar as it becomes an object, according to its connections with the external world as well as with other objective spheres, e.g., the products of culture.[14] What we "infer" is neither the being of the external world as a sphere (which is given prior to all particular contents in it) or the reality of the sphere "external world" itself, but only that which in each case is *real* in the "external world." Thus we can only infer particular coordinations between an already specified nature and real being [*Realsein*] and, conversely, between pregiven real being and a particular nature. To think that the external world as a sphere could be inferred from the givenness of the internal world, as Descartes, H. von Helmholtz, and Schopenhauer thought, is certainly a patent mistake. Ewald Hering proceeds correctly in his investigations into the physiology of the senses against the mode of thought, prevailing since Descartes, which holds "visual objects" [*Sehdinge*] to be experiences of the internal world which one must first make intelligible by means of physical stimuli and physiological processes.[15] Hering begins with the independence of the color and light phenomena of the external world and examines their physiological dependencies, without initially reducing these phenomena to basic physical concepts; thus to have proved the independence of the sphere of the external world is scarcely to have proved its reality. Similarly, we no more acquire our first notion of the sphere "external world" by means of reflection on the givenness of the internal world than we infer the being of the sphere "internal world" from the pregiven objects and orderings in the external world. Nor is the internal world ever present as the mere residue of things still not ordered in the external world.[16] This latter theory, which Avenarius has developed most rigorously in his theory of introjection, is certainly erroneous, for an *ordering* of the contents of what is given in the sphere "internal world" can be undertaken without

14. See also Spranger in his study "Die Einheit der Psychologie," in *Abhandlungen der preussischen Akademie der Wissenschaften*. [The correct title is "Die Frage nach der Einheit der Psychologie," Vols. XXI–XXIV (Berlin, 1926).—TRANS.]

15. [See Hering's "Über den Farbesinn," Part I of his *Grundzüge der Lehre vom Lichtsinn* (Leipzig, 1905).—TRANS.]

16. Natorp in his *Einleitung in die Psychologie nach kritischer Methode* (Freiburg, 1888). See my "Erkenntnis und Arbeit."

reference to the objective ordering of the external world—although certainly not in the descriptive, much less the genetic, sense.

A new problem associated with the division of the spheres of being arises when we ask which of the independent and irreducible spheres is immediately filled with content and actually established [*gesetzt*], while some other sphere is not yet so. It is clear that the being of ideal objects and their conformity to law are independent of and logically prior to the being of real objects. Similarly, the external world is given prior to the internal world. The socially shared world [*Mitwelt*] is given prior to the individual's own objective world. And as I have shown in detail,[17] the reality of persons is clearly given prior to the reality of living creatures, and the latter prior to the reality of inanimate creatures. Hence the reality of the inanimate world, as we see in the case of Berkeley, has always been most problematic. The idealism of consciousness, however, could take root only after modernity had displaced the organological and panvitalistic world-view of the Middle Ages and antiquity.[18]

5. *The problem of the relativity of being*

A problem whose specific character is still far from being grasped is that of the relativity of the being of an entity (as object) to the special properties of, and the place in the world occupied by, another entity which participates in it. Let me give an example: what I call the sun can have different levels of existential relativity to the man who takes part in its manner of being. For instance, if I observe the setting sun from my window, I can focus on the momentary image-content which, as an aspect of the thing-in-my-milieu (red ball of the sun) there in the sky, enters into my perception at that time. Second, I can consider the thing-in-my-milieu, "the red ball of the sun" itself, visible from this region and capable of disappearing behind the mountains without being destroyed or having to give up its identity as "the red ball of the sun," as a new level of existential relativity. The third level would be the sun as it

17. [See "Erkenntnis und Arbeit," pp. 373–78.—TRANS.]
18. On this point, see the last chapter of my book *The Nature of Sympathy*, trans. Peter Heath (London: Routledge & Kegan Paul, 1958), and my studies in *Die Wissensformen und die Gesellschaft*.

corresponds to the totality of our present-day astronomical knowledge about this fixed star, apart from any standpoint of an observer on the earth and his psychophysical properties such as sensory thresholds and so on. This would be the sun in its reciprocal causal relations with all the extended bodies in the universe. I can, if I reflect on the well-known chemical constitution of this body, proceed to imagine the molecules, atoms, electron systems, and finally, if I subscribe to a dynamic theory of matter, the centers and fields of force which underlie the electron systems, and which, though no longer spatially ordered, still determine the measurable dimensions of the electron systems. And I can imagine these centers themselves as somehow rooted in the ground of all things.

I can, in all this, always ask to what aspect of the participatory entity, man for instance, the pertinent level is actually "existentially relative" and to what aspect is it no longer relative. For example, is it relative to man as a corporeal thing or as a living creature or as a finite knowing mind? Or is it relative to a standpoint in the universe of extended bodies or to no particular standpoint at all? It is precisely in this sense that the god Apollo is existentially relative to the Greek people.

The levels of existential relativity appear in every sphere of being, for example, in the sphere of the mentally actual as well as in that of the physically actual. In the mental world the phenomena of consciousness are only signs and references to the mental *life* underlying them.[19] This distinction also appers in the sphere of the ideal and the fictive. When Kronecker said: "The Good Lord created the positive whole numbers and all the other numbers come from man," the great mathematician wittily epitomized his principle of the arithmetizability of mathematics, and thereby acknowledged the existence of different levels of being even within the domain of mathematical objects.

I consider simply mistaken any attempt to get around this problem—a peculiarly Kantian problem, but linked by Kant much too hastily to the theory of knowledge—by transforming it into the problem of the degree of adequacy, whether quantita-

19. I have already shown this in "The Idols of Self-Knowledge" (of inner perception). Moritz Geiger confirmed it in his "Fragment über das Unbewusste," *Jahrbuch für Philosophie und phänomenologische Forschung*, Vol. IV (1921).

tive or qualitative, of our knowledge vis-à-vis an existentially homogeneous world-of-things [*Dingwelt*]. Bergson once expressed himself along the lines of such a reduction. For Hartmann, too, all being lies on exactly the same level, the level of absolute being. Kant's highly significant doctrine, which I would characterize as that of the three-"layeredness" of the world ("thing-in-itself," "objective actuality of appearances" [*Erscheinungswirklichkeit*], and mere "phenomenon of consciousness"), has already been repudiated here in principle. However, it seems to me to represent progress that in ontology one now distinguishes a few more levels of the existential relativity of objects than Kant did. A return to the principle that everything which is is *either* a mere phenomenon of consciousness *or* a thing in itself, independent of consciousness, does not spell progress.

It is important to express these problems, which are so crucial to metaphysics, in a purely ontological form and not confuse them with problems of cognition. If something is relative on some level of existential relativity, still, no matter how highly relative it may be, it never becomes, because of this relativity, a content of cognition, much less a content of consciousness or something belonging to the "psychic" sphere. The red ball of the sun in the sky, the shadow whose length varies as it darts from place to place, or the broken stick in the water, none of these is what one would call a content of consciousness or something mental. We should not even label what is existentially relative to one individual in quite particular circumstance a "content of consciousness," for instance, a genuine hallucinatory object which continues to exist independently of my bodily movement and my wandering attention and moreover seems to have another side as well as an inside and can fall under the laws of optical perspective. It is precisely in the sphere of consciousness that I can turn away from it, suppress it, put it out of my sight. This thing is existentially relative to the individual in his total condition, conceived of as psychophysically undifferentiated. Similarly, the self, as the center of consciousness, does not encounter a hallucinated bear any differently than it does a real table. It can recognize it or not recognize it "as" a bear. It can make any number of false and true, that is materially consonant, judgments about it and draw whatever conclusions it pleases from its "existence." The logical consistency characteristic of the paranoiac's thinking, once he has invented the existence of a plot against him, has often been noted. At that level of existential relativity, which is called the "natural world-view," the world confronts us as something useful. Heidegger recently has appropriately characterized the world at this level as an "implement ready to hand" [*zuhandenes Zeug*], a scheme of reciprocal reference in which each thing has its "place." [20] Psychopathology shows us that one's environment can become fixed at this level of "being," as in the case of basic aphasic disorders when any further significance of these implements becomes vague and inaccessible. We can of course "handle" them as the very things they are, but we no longer grasp them as meaningful "objects." It is fairly certain that the environment of an animal is almost totally fixed on this level of "being." To define this level of being is, as Heidegger rightly sees, a purely ontological problem. It would be incorrect to characterize it as the mere *givenness* of being, for on this level there is no other being which could be *given* in this or in another way. We could perhaps speak here of the forms of the being of givenness [*Seinsformen der Gegebenheit*] but not of the forms of the givenness of being [*Gegebenheitsformen von Sein*].

When an object appears on another level of existential relativity than that on which it belongs, I call it a metaphysical phantom, and the correlative act a "metaphysical illusion," as distinct from an illusion about adequation or sense or meaning. It is clear that this phantom character and the corresponding metaphysical illusion have nothing to do with any distinction between true and false, i.e., with error in the sphere of judgment (in the formal as well as the material sense). Nor do they depend on the degree of the adequacy of the image with which something is there for me on any level of existential relativity. For example, a theoretical physicist could have fashioned for himself, within the limits of mathematico-physical knowledge, a thoroughly clear, unambiguous, and coherent image of nature, and nonetheless find

---

20. M. Heidegger, "Sein und Zeit," *Jahrbuch für Philosophie und phänomenologische Forschung*, Vol. VIII (1927), and the parallel references in my essay "Erkenntnis und Arbeit." [See *Being and Time*, trans. John Macquarrie and Edward Robinson (New York: Harper & Row, 1962), pp. 96–102.—TRANS.]

himself in a state of *complete* metaphysical illusion about the existential relativity of the objectivity of the image. The problems associated with the existential relativity of the objects of mathematical-physical knowledge have absolutely no bearing on what is true or false within this discipline. On every level of existential relativity an indefinite number of true and false judgments are possible, as well as indefinitely many grades of adequacy of the intuition of the object judged. If anyone says to me, for instance, "The sun has set," it would be absurd, within the context of objects of everyday life, to reply to him that the sun, namely the astronomical sun, cannot rise and set, and that consequently his judgment is false. We are speaking on an entirely different level of existential relativity than that of astronomy.

It is very important in developing this problem to note that the displacement of an entity among the various levels of existential relativity in no way encroaches upon its selfsameness [*Selbigkeit*]. It seems false to think, with Erich Becher,[21] for example, that we argue from the red ball of the sun to the existence of the astronomical sun by means of a causal argument; or that both objects are related to one another as an effect to its cause; or that this ball of the sun is something like a content of consciousness and its cause is the astronomical sun. Here one level of existential relativity has been incorrectly placed in a causal relation with another level, while the truth is that every level of existential relativity has a form of causal connection proper to it. Moreover, if one speaks here of "contents of consciousness," then the intentional relationship of "knowing" (that of a knower to what is known) is falsely transformed into a real causal relation.

The distinctions between semblance [*Schein*], appearance [*Erscheinung*], and the appearing [*das Erscheinendes*], which as yet have received little investigation, properly fall within the ambit of this problem. So do the problems of *ontic perspectives* and, thus, of the problems of phenomenalism. With this in mind I have developed a special theory of the existential relativity of the being of corporeal things in my study "Erkenntnis und Arbeit." I shall not go into this theory

21. [Erich Becher (1882–1929), a critical realist who wrote *Gehirn und Seele* (Heidelberg, 1911), and *Geisteswissenschaften und Naturwissenschaften* (Munich, 1921).—TRANS.]

here, where I am concerned simply with indicating the difference between the problems.

6. Cognition and its standards

It is only at this stage in the ontological problematic that the question with which people usually and mistakenly begin in philosophy makes its appearance, namely, the problem of the cognition of the world. As a starting point it requires a comprehensive theory of the standards of cognition. The notion of cognition can be traced back to that of knowledge. Cognition is knowledge of something "as" something and thus always presupposes two kinds of knowledge: knowledge through intuition and knowledge through thinking. Cognition is the unity [Deckungseinheit] in which some correlate of intuition (whether perception, memory, expectation, sensory, or nonsensory intuition), that is, an image and something thought, coincide. To cognize means to insert an image into the sphere of meaning (concept, judgment, argument). Cognition is the reciprocal coincidence of image and thought, as Hartmann has recently shown with great clarity in his Metaphysik der Erkenntnis, in the chapter devoted to the notion of criteria.

The foregoing principle holds true both against theories whose criterion of cognition is a onesided coincidence of the thought with the image, and against such doctrines as that of Plato or, more recently, of H. Cohen, which demand a onesided coincidence of the image with the thought. The scholars who tailor thoughts to images are sensationalists if, in addition, they derive all intuition from sensible perceptions. Thus, Hume demands that one provide an impression for every meaning, even categorial meanings (e.g., substance, causality), the meaning being a copy of the impression. One who accepts (correctly) nonsensible intuition but also requires that all meanings prove themselves onesidedly in such intuitions succumbs to another form of this error. For example, Husserl makes this requirement in what he calls the "principle of principles." On the other hand, those scholars who regard intuitive material in itself as completely unorganized and undefined think that it is only by means of unities freely devised by thought that any kind of definiteness, limits (horoi), and organization are imported from the sphere of meaning into that of intuitive being, which in itself is consistently designated "chaos." For instance, H. Cohen in his *Logik der reinen Erkenntnis* characteristically reaches for the Platonic expression *mē on* [nonbeing] for the "given."

We categorically reject both points of view. Cognition rather takes place in the strictly reciprocal accommodation [*Anpassung*] and identification of image and meaning, and is directed to the one intrinsically and ontologically [*ontisch*] undivided and indivisible nature of the being of the thing [*Sache*] itself. It is the character of the thing-itself which in the strictest sense is given *in* this coincidence of image and meaning. The processes by which we progressively identify all the images of the thing in question with one another and correspondingly identify the thoughts with one another (following normative rules of "correct thinking") simply prepare the way for the genuine act of cognition which takes place only in the coincidence of image and meaning. On the important point of the reciprocity of image and concept, we concur with Hartmann. However, we reject completely Hartmann's interpretation of the function of this agreement as simply a criterion for the agreement of cognition with the nature of the thing in question. Here Hartmann goes down the road of a Critical Realism. In a special chapter of the second edition of his book (chap. 10, "Critical Addenda"), he tries to provide his theory of images with a firmer foundation and to defend it once again against the attacks of P. Linke. We consider wholly inadequate any theory of cognition which is based on images immanent to consciousness alone, that is, any theory which reduces cognition to an essentially unconfirmable "agreement" with states of being [*Seinsbeständen*] which are independent of any and every possible act of knowing. It makes no difference whether one requires agreement only between the relationships of ideas and the relationships of things, or whether one also requires some measure of agreement between the relata of these relationships. All the objections of Spinoza, Kant, Husserl, and a host of other so-called idealists to these basic notions of Critical Realism are still valid today. In such a theory of cognition, as in all theories of images, what is involved is a metaphorical use of "image" in virtue of which the relation between a painting and its object is substituted for the relation between cognition and being. In this theory, no notice is taken that a relation like that of the painting to the thing painted already presupposes cognition of both objects. The painting "knows" nothing of the thing of which it is a painting. Any sort of likeness which is forever *essentially* unknowable, whatever the scope of our knowledge may be, has no meaning whatsoever for any kind of cognition. The very *meaning* of cognition, which like every form of knowing is subject to becoming, is reduced to absurdity if it signifies nothing more than a duplication of the world in another medium. If such a view were correct, then we could in no way refute the argument of idealism, the argument that in doing away with "thing-in-themselves" we make no alteration in the state of possible knowledge (not even in God's knowledge) and that, therefore, the positing of such "things-in-themselves" is groundless. But Critical Realism and even Nicolai Hartmann proceed from that very point, which we characterized as false at the outset of this essay. The nature of the existent can indeed be *in mente* and at the same time *extra mentem,* it can indeed leap into and out of mind, without its real existence, or the nature itself in the strictest sense, following these leaps.

In my opinion there are two reasons why such an excellent scholar reverted to one of the most primitive forms of epistemology (namely, the image-theory). The first has its origin in the problem of illusion.

In an illusion concerning what something is, the nature of the object itself is certainly not *in mente* but rather something which only refers to it, namely the intentional object. And the possibility of illusion must always be admitted. Hartmann therefore concludes that even in the case of successful cognition something must be present that, relative to the existent which is independent of consciousness, is only an "image." This thesis is refuted by Linke's argument that the possibility of illusion does not exclude cognitive insight into the nature itself; indeed, the meaning of the concept "possible illusion" presupposes insight, that is, insight into the thing itself. Hartmann's thesis is also refutable on purely phenomenological grounds, for we can still make it a matter of direct intuition how, in every case of disillusionment, that which was allegedly given in the preceding segment of time as the nature of the thing now turns into an image, that is, disappears as a nature and takes on the character of a mere image. And the nature of the thing-itself, after the disillusionment, now takes the place of what was just demoted to the status of an image in the process of disillusionment. It is precisely the phenomenon of disillusionment that definitively refutes the claim that such an "image" can also subsist even when cognition takes place, and that whether or not the "image" constitutes knowledge depends on an untestable relation to the things in themselves.

However, it seems to me that Hartmann's attempt to ground his Critical Realism contains still other basic errors in addition to those pointed out by Linke. Hartmann, like many others, employs an unfortunate definition of what he calls a "real object." He means by this the nature of the real object. This is the thoroughly negative definition of real being indicated by expressions like "to be independent of all intentional acts," "to be independent of consciousness," etc. Now nothing should be less open to dispute than that it belongs to a real object to be and to subsist independently of all acts of knowing. However, it is indeed disputable that the words "real being" *mean* nothing other than this independence, and it is further disputable that real being follows from the independence of being and not vice versa. The question is of great importance for our problem, not only because reality "in-itself" is independent of knowing, but also because one consequence of the mode of givenness of real being is the independence of the real from our experience [*Erlebnis*]. We shall return to this later.

In addition, the word "independent" is extraordinarily ambiguous. It can, in this context, mean the same as "it is a matter of objective indifference to real being (so far as it also has some nature), whether knowledge participates in its nature or not." We assert that the independence of being in this sense is a consequence of its reality. But it is otherwise for Hartmann. Since, for him, the independence of its being first constitutes the reality of an object, "independence" does not mean the same as "indifference." Rather, it means "the exclusion of the participation of knowledge in the nature of the thing." If we use a strict logical formulation, we can say that we consider the negation of "dependent" in "in-dependent" a case of contradiction; Hartmann regards it as a case of contrariety. Nondependence on knowledge is not, however, "independence." For Hartmann the nature of the real object is not indifferent to its involvement in the knowledge-relation.

Rather the real object, spear in hand, so to speak, *wards off* any cognition of itself. However, does the fact that the real object *can* become an intentional object, and thus have its being *in mente,* mean that the reality of the object, its existence, enters into the mind as well? Never! Reality is "transintelligible" for every possible knowing mind. Only the *what* of the being, not the *being* of the what, is intelligible. For what reasons, we shall have to see.

7. *The problem of apriorism*

Finally, the problem of reality must be sharply separated from the problem of apriorism. The problem of apriorism comes up as much in discussions of intuitive and rational cognition as it does in the doctrines of value (axiology, ethics, aesthetics), where it has a role of its own to play. This is not the place to go into the problem itself.[22] In no case does apriorism lead to idealism. Only in Kant are the two doctrines linked together, in consequence of his principle that the a priori is to be reduced to forms of thought and intuition, that is, to functional laws of the human mind which in the process of experience become formal laws [*Formgesetze*] of the being of the objects of experience as well. This presupposes Kant's erroneous theory that only sensations are given. However, if one allows, as we do, that the forms of thought and intuition belonging to the human mind first arise through the "functionalization" of insights into the essence of a thing, originally achieved in a single exemplary experience, then any such connection between idealism and apriorism falls away.[23] Even the assumption that

22. See my remarks on this topic in "Erkenntnis und Arbeit," and in my *Formalismus.* [See *Der Formalismus in der Ethik und die materiale Wertethik: Neuer Versuch der Grundlegung eines ethischen Personalismus,* 5th ed. rev., *Gesammelte Werke* II (Berne: Francke, 1966), esp. II, A, B, pp. 65–126.—TRANS.]

23. [Scheler's theory of functionalization plays a large role in his later writings. Against Kant, he maintains that the forms and patterns under which we intuit and think things are not imposed on these a priori by the human understanding but are gradually derived from the things themselves inasmuch as we have essential insights into them. These insights get transformed into "norms" or "rules" which govern our subsequent encounters with things. See *Vom Ewigen im Menschen, Religiöse Erneuerung,* 4th ed. rev., *Gesammelte Werke* V (Bern: Francke, 1955), pp. 446–67, and *Die Wissensformen und die Gesellschaft,* pp. 13, 239–40, 286, 378.—TRANS.]

the organization of the human mind is constant through human cultural history becomes superfluous. New essential insights into being itself can be functionalized.

8. *The problem of reality*

Now that we have sorted out the various problems above we are in a position to distinguish the questions contained in the genuine problem of reality. I divide them up into eight subquestions which I shall mention briefly here.

(I) What is the givenness of reality? What is experienced [*erlebt*], when anything whatever is experienced as real? This is the question of the phenomenology of the lived-experience of reality. (2) In what sorts of acts or modes of human behavior is the factor of reality [*Realitätsmoment*] originally given?

The next two questions are closely connected. (3) What kind of being is reality itself in an objective sense? (4) How does the reality of an object come to be, if it does come to be? Or can one speak meaningfully of the mode of being that is reality coming to be out of a sphere of nonobjective and not yet real being? (5) In what position in the order of givenness is the real being of a world given? For example, does it precede or follow sensible phenomena, structures, and relations, spatiality and temporality, and so on? Analogously, what position does the act furnishing the factor of reality occupy in the order in which human acts and modes of behavior are founded?

The following three questions are closely related. (6) What factual grounds and conditions must hold in order for the real being of a previously given and sharply delimited nature to subsist? (7) What cognitive grounds are there for ascribing objective reality to a state of affairs that is already determined with respect to the sphere to which it belongs, the categorial form of its being, and its character? (8) What do existence and reality signify in the so-called existential propositions and how must one conceive the relation between existential judgment and other kinds of judgment?

The existential proposition contains a peculiar paradox that until now has never been completely explained. In my opinion, only the theory of the being of reality expounded here is in a position to explain it. The paradox consists in this, that the existential proposition is undoubtedly a synthetic judgment.

Existence never follows from essence and the predicate of existence is never contained in the subject of the judgment. On the other hand, the existential judgment is in no sense an ampliative judgment, as are all other synthetic judgments, a priori as well as a posteriori. No new attribute is added to the subject. Rather, reality is predicated of the sum total of all the attributes that may belong to the subject. However, it would be a great mistake to attack the problem of reality from the perspective of the last three questions, although it is usually done. We cannot explain the existential judgment if we do not know beforehand what the factor of reality consists in, since it is this which provides the predicate "existence" in the proposition with its meaning. Without knowing this, we will never be able to elucidate the problem of the existential proposition. To conceive of reality itself as a category, whether of givenness or of the form of the judgment, as Rickert does, is a completely hopeless undertaking. To reduce the question of reality to that of the "validity" of the existential proposition or the affirmative judgment leaves the predicate "existence" completely unexplained. (See *Formalismus*.) [24]

Moreover, we should try to avoid confusing all the questions concerning either the coordination of a particular nature which has already been defined with the sphere of real being, or the coordination of an X already given as real with a particular nature, with the problem of the factor of reality and the acts which furnish it. We must not confuse such questions with the problem of what sort of being reality itself is and how it "comes to be." Such confusion has, however, been perpetrated by all the neo-Kantian schools (with the exception of Riehl's) and by all those who think they can define being real as "an object's standing under certain lawful conditions of fact" (for example, H. Lotze). These lawful conditions, besides having quite different structural forms in each of the major spheres of being making up the reality of the world (inanimate nature, the vital sphere, historical objectivity), plainly play their decisive role wherever there is a question of coordinating reality with being of such and such a nature. In the question of reality itself they play no role at all. In any event, the only thing that can be conceived, inferred, or derived from lawful condi-

24. [Scheler may have had in mind *Formalismus*, pp. 195–97.— TRANS.]

tions is the coordination of a particular nature with the sphere of the real. However, that there is reality and that a real world exists at all can never be inferred from any such conjunction of ideas. One can, indeed, infer the factual movements of a body from measurable changes of distance, once the primitive phenomenon of movement has been given. But the primitive phenomenon of motion itself can never be inferred. Similarly, one can infer that there must be *something* real or that an X given as real must be *something* in particular, if something else is given as real. We can never infer either the being of a real world or the factor of reality itself.

Epistemology until now has dealt almost exclusively with questions six through eight. It has asked: under what conditions does the reality of an object subsist [*besteht*] and under what conditions can one ascribe reality to an object? Only this explains why the neo-Kantians could seriously think that the term "being real" means no more than "standing in a lawful relationship to actual and possible perceptual contents" or that it means simply the occurrence of something within the domain of so-called lawful "possibilities of perception."

It is not those questions but the questions concerning the factor of reality itself and the acts that furnish it that are decisive for the "technique of essential insight" [*die Technik der Wesenserkenntnis*], especially insofar as it is bent on grasping the primitive phneomena ingredient in every cognition of essence. Husserl has called this technique "phenomenological reduction." For, if the factor of reality must be nullified [*aufgehoben*] in order that genuine essence may come to light, if a "deactualization" of the world must be carried out as the condition of its decomposition into essences [*Verwesentlichung*], then it must above all be clear what the moment of reality itself is and in what acts it is given. It is this factor we must strip off in the reduction and it is just those acts and modes of behavior which first furnish this factor and make real being accessible which we must suspend.

Husserl has never discussed this question with any thoroughness but has contented himself with the vague as well as false declaration that real being is synonymous with "having a place in time." Thus, although he has posed this basic problem of theoretical philosophy in a profound and original way, he has hardly clarified it, much less answered it. The "elimination" or "suppression" of the positing of reality always implicit in the natural world-view is by no means satisfactory. It is a matter here not of suppressing existential judgment, but of stripping away the factor of reality itself which fulfills the meaning of the predicate in the existential judgment. Or, it is a question of eliminating the acts furnishing this factor. Merely to suppress existential judgment is child's play. It is quite another thing to set aside the factor of reality itself by putting out of operation those (involuntary) functions which furnish it. To accomplish this requires very different techniques. However, any such lightening of the task of reduction would scarcely please Husserl. One no longer sees what ought to be altered in the "blossoming apple tree" (to use Husserl's example) through the mere suppression of the existential judgment. One does not see at all how, by this means alone, a new world of objects is to reveal itself, a world not contained in the natural world-view. The only result of bracketing the positing of existence [*Daseinssetzung*] is that the contingent characteristics of the object which has all along preserved its place in space and time emerge more clearly. We are still a long way from the essence and are forced to ask, in astonishment, "What was the good of all this?"

The situation is quite different if we assume that we have a theory of the factor of reality and the acts furnishing it. Then we understand reduction as a procedure for actually inhibiting this factor and truly putting these acts out of operation (not merely looking away from them, in the sense of logical abstraction). We are no longer dealing with a mere method, a thought procedure; but with a techné, a process of inner action through which certain functions, which are continually being carried on in the natural attitude, are in fact put out of operation. We are dealing, furthermore, with an action through which the factor of reality itself, and not only the judgment about it, disappears. However, one can still ask whether the disappearance of the factor of reality is any more suited to lead us to the essence of things than the suppression of the existential judgment. The answer is that, along with the factor of reality (or the acts furnishing it), a well-ordered series of the properties of the objects of the natural world-view necessarily disappears as well. Both the contingent characteristics and the spatiotemporal location of an object belong to this series. We shall speak later about the order in which these disappear. At the same time it will become clear that, as a result of disengaging the acts in which the factor of reality is given, not only does something disappear but something new emerges which was not contained in the natural world-view and which reveals itself to us as a basic constituent of genuine essence. The all-too-simple "logical" method of Husserl is not sufficient here.

In addition, Husserl links the theory of the reduction with his "idealism of absolute consciousness," something that is not logically required. The reduction is totally independent of the epistemological antithesis idealism-realism. Hartmann has also made this point with striking clarity. What remains after the deactualization of the world is indeed the "ideal" world of essence, but not something that can be automatically considered merely immanent to consciousness. Husserl's assertion, that "immanent essence" precedes "transcendent essence" and that therefore the essential laws of the "consciousness" of something must also be laws of the objects of consciousness (the form which Kant's Copernican revolution acquires in Husserl), in no way follows from the procedure of the reduction. It is an epistemological standpoint which comes from elsewhere and follows from the well-known principle, first expressed by Descartes, that every given is originally immanent to consciousness. We have already rejected this principle. Moreover, we shall show that the origin of reflection or the being of consciousness [*Bewusstseins*] is bound up by an essential law with the prior ecstatic having and enduring [*ekstatische Haben und Erleiden*], the experience of resistance. This experience furnishes the factor of reality. We shall also show that the particular form of being which consciousness or reflexive being has, though on the one hand contemporaneous with the experience of reality, actually is its consequence, and not its foundation.

[III] The True Problem of Reality

From these critical remarks on Husserl's theory of reality, let us turn to the first two fundamental questions in the theory of reality. Since I treated these questions thoroughly in my study "Erkenntnis und Arbeit" and do not wish to repeat myself, I shall begin by stating briefly what was discovered

there. Then I shall elaborate on the significance of these results, first, for the relation of the experience of reality to that
of space and time; and second, for its relation to causality. The
consequences which bear on the theory of essence and its
cognition will follow in Part IV.[25]

At least the germs of the idea that reality is not given to
us in perceptual acts, but in our instinctive [*triebhaft*] and
conative conduct vis-à-vis the world, or, more broadly, in our
dynamic-practical behavior, are quite old. The first traces of
the idea are to be found as early as Duns Scotus. Berkeley advances it both in support of his idealism against the notion of
lifeless being and in his denial of the existence of matter, asserting that reality can belong only to a self-active being.
Berkeley's idealism is (among other things) simply a consequence of his maintaining that souls are the only self-active
beings. In addition there are traces of the idea, as W. Dilthey
has pointed out in his well-known study, in the Scottish philosophers, Thomas Reid especially, as well as in Jacobi. The most
penetrating and rigorous development of the notion, and the
one which, at the same time, seems to come closer to the truth
than anything else written on the subject—closer even than
Dilthey's "Contributions to the Solution of the Question of the
Origin of our Belief in the Reality of the External World" [26]—
is that of the Frenchman Maine de Biran. Bouterweck,[27] a teacher
of Schopenhauer, expressed the idea with clarity and precision
and joined to it his theory of the "higher consciousness." Schelling, to be sure, did not appreciably clarify the problems of
reality which we sketched in questions one and two. However,
in his piece on freedom and evil [28] his response to the ontological
problem of what reality itself is and how it "comes to be" is
very close to our own. We can even show that Schelling's
doctrine that the real being of the world arises from a "longing"

25. [Not published.—TRANS.]
26. See Dilthey, *Gesammelte Werke*, Vol. V (Leipzig, 1924).
27. [Friedrich Bouterweck, or Bouterwek (1765–1828), erstwhile
Kantian and belles-lettrist. He published *Ideen zu einer allgemeinen Apo-
diktik* (1799) and *Lehrbuch der philosophischen Wissenschaften* (1813).
—TRANS.]
28. [Scheler would seem to have in mind Schelling's *Philosophische
Untersuchungen über das Wesen der menschlichen Freiheit* (Landshut,
1809), English translation by James Gutmann, *Of Human Freedom*
(Chicago: Open Court, 1936). However, the passages quoted do not appear in this essay.—TRANS.]

[*Sucht*] for a reality which is itself not yet real is in exact accord with the theory that reality is given via resistance. Schelling says: "There is no actually effective [*Wirkliches*] being without an actually effective willing, whatever its more detailed motivations might be, that there *be* something. Thus, I know the real being of anything whatever only from the fact that it asserts itself, that it excludes another being from itself, and that it resists any attempt to penetrate it or to suppress it. True resistance consists in willing. The will alone, of all that is in the world, is what truly resists, is what is unqualifiedly capable of giving resistance. The will, therefore, is truly the invincible. Even God, one might say, cannot conquer will except by will itself." "As little as the divine will by itself can explain the necessity of universal things, so impossible is it to explain the contingency and actuality of things by pure reason alone." Even in the case of God's real being, Schelling does not accept the principle of Aquinas or Leibniz that it is a "truth in itself" that His existence follows from His essence, much less Leibniz's formula: *Deus est ens, ex cuius essentia sequitur existentia.* "But from the essence, the nature, the concept of God nothing more than this ever follows, that God, if He exists, must exist a priori, otherwise He cannot exist; but, that He exists does not follow from that." It is likely that Schopenhauer drew his principal positions from this treatise of Schelling's. In Schopenhauer the ontological thesis that the entire existence of the world is the result of an "insistent longing" is united with the idea already prevalent in Bouterweck, that real being is given only in resistance. Several times he says expressly that for a purely intellectual spirit there is no distinction between real and irreal. This thesis does not depend upon his other epistemological positions which, in our opinion, contain the gravest errors with respect to all the problems mentioned above. Even in Fichte we find, on several occasions, the idea that reality as givenness becomes known in the lived-experience of resistance.

The notion had a rich history behind it when Dilthey took it up more recently and made it a topic for discussion in contemporary philosophy. Additional attempts were then joined to Dilthey's study in an effort to establish his conclusions at an even deeper level. For example, there are detailed arguments by Frischeisen-Köhler, in his book *Erkenntnis und Wirklich-*

keit [29] and in a lecture which appeared in the writings of the Kant Society, against the thesis that the word "reality" means "to stand in relationships regulated by law." Then, Ernst Jaensch, in the appendix to his book on the Aubert-Foerster Law, tried to confirm Dilthey's notion by way of individual phenomenological analyses. [30] D. Katz provides important material for the solution of the problem of givenness in his recent book *Aufbau der Tastwelt,* without, I fear, seeing the salient point of the matter. [31] I am starting with Dilthey's study, as I did in my "Erkenntnis und Arbeit," and shall first give the conclusions of that earlier work.

In the first place, Dilthey is still not clear that the experience of resistance [*erlebte Widerstand*] is not, in general, a peripheral sensible experience [*Erfahrung*] but, instead, the genuinely *central* experience of our life of straining and striving [*Drängens und Strebens selbst*]. This experience must, therefore, be most sharply distinguished from all the sensations accompanying it, such as those of touch and muscle tension. Dilthey, taking note of the fact that, when we prop a stick against a wall, resistance is experienced in what is being propped up, while the sensation of touch is in the hand, observes: "It is unsatisfactory to assume that this objectification is brought about through the sensations of touch and muscle tension, and in particular through the sensation of pressure (which was emphasized above as an element in the experience of resistance), all of which are localized in the finger tips. The result of this would be only a lifeless, local sensation, having nothing to do with the experience of living force in resistance." This observation is very much to the point. When, despite this, Dilthey frequently speaks of the "sensation of resistance," it is surely an inconsistency. In fact, the central experience of resistance is generally not bound to sensible sensations, as the mental experience of resistance will soon show us. When drive-based attention [*der triebhaften Aufmerksamkeit*] is ob-

29. [Max Frischeisen-Köhler (1878–1923) was a psychologist who studied with Dilthey. Scheler is probably thinking of his book *Wissenschaft und Wirklichkeit* (Leipzig, 1912).—TRANS.]

30. [The Aubert-Foerster Law states that two objectively smaller objects can be distinguished as two at greater distances from the retina than two objectively larger objects subtending the same visual angle.—TRANS.]

31. [Published as Supplementary Volume XI to *Zeitschrift für Psychologie* (1925).—TRANS.]

structed, especially in its dynamic features, the experience of obstruction and resistance can occur in conjunction with optical as well as acoustical and other sense-perceptions. It can, as we shall show, also accompany the objects of memory and thought (e.g., "The state devoted only to thoughts resists my will"). Resistance is thus centrally experienced at that level of my "self" which may be provisionally defined as the "center of vital drives" [*triebhaftes Lebenszentrum*].

However, Dilthey's insights are combined with a whole series of errors. These expose his theory and the kernel of truth it contains to extensive criticism (from Rickert, Rehmke,[32] O. Külpe, and Heidegger,[33] among others). I have discussed them in detail in "Erkenntnis und Arbeit" and only mention them briefly here to give the results of that investigation.

According to Dilthey, every experience of resistance, which as a unified experience [*Erlebniseinheit*] is in principle independent of sensations generally, will nonetheless be "mediated" through sensations when it is first given. "The primary and therefore constitutive process is as follows: an impulse to move in a specific direction lasts a long time, indeed, it grows stronger and instead of the intended external motion, sensations of pressure occur. This connecting link between the consciousness of the impulse and the consciousness of the obstruction of the intention, a link lying in the aggregate of sensations of pressure, is present every time. Therefore, we become conscious of the external world only through mediations." "One cannot facilitate the grounding of our belief in the external world with any extravagant assumption such as that the will has an immediate experience of resistance, or, in general, with the psychological fiction of an immediate givenness of some type."[34] Indeed, Dilthey straightforwardly calls the aggregate of pressure sensations the "precondition" of the experience of resistance.

However, there is a fundamental error embedded in Dilthey's statements on the relation between (1) drive and perception, and (2) the experience of resistance and the emerg-

32. [Johannes Rehmke (1848–1930), an epistemologist and ontologist. He wrote *Unsere Gewissheit von der Aussenwelt* (Heilbronn, 1892) and *Lehrbuch der allgemeine Psychologie* (Frankfurt, 1894).—TRANS.]

33. [See "Sein und Zeit," pp. 246–54 (*Being and Time*, pp. 290–98).—TRANS.]

34. [Dilthey, *Gesammelte Werke*, V, 113.—TRANS.]

ence of the imaginative [*bildhaften*] content of the intuited attribute of the "real" thing offering the resistance. And the very "immediate" experience of resistance that Dilthey denies does exist. The experience of weight and traction when one is lifting a material body is not a temporal consequence of the sensations of tension which were called forth by the deployment of muscles and sinews excited to activity by resistances to motion. The actual experiences of heaviness do not change in simple proportion to the stimuli and our sensations of them. But, as Julius Pikler has shown, the experiences are dependent not only on the stimuli but also on the exertion and deployment of force by the person having the sensations.[35] "Exertion," or the experience of exertion, is something completely different from the sensations of tension in the muscles and sinews. Exertion is the centrally experienced resistance offered by the heavy object to the deployment of the driving impulse; the occurrence of the sensations of tension depends upon this drive. The strength of sensation is, as Pikler puts it, always the expression of the magnitude of a drive-fulfillment as well. "A weakling lifting the same resistant weight feels it to be heavier than a strong man does, a child feels it to be heavier than an adult does. Conversely, in order to feel the same weight the former needs a greater stimulus than the latter."

Dilthey's appeal to Helmholtz's theory of "unconscious inferences" has by this time lost its meaning, since that theory has been rigorously refuted by Hering, Jaensch, and others. Helmholtz's theory presupposed a strict proportionality between stimulus and sensation; it has been definitively disproved in every domain to which Helmholtz applied it. The "mediate acts of thought" Dilthey thought he had to assume actually begin only when we have to determine more precisely, through the contents of sensation, the character of an X already apprehended as real. Sensation and perceiving presuppose an instinctive yearning to "open oneself" to the external world, or, at the very least, presuppose the drive to be awake [*Wachtrieb*].

Quite apart from these special questions belonging to the physiology of the senses, the problem of reality is not on the whole connected only with sensibly perceptible facts. It arises

35. [In his *Sinnespsychologische Untersuchungen* (Leipzig, 1917).—TRANS.]

as well in the sphere of what-is-past [*Gewesensein*], which can never be given to us through perception. The problem of reality also arises in the distinction between what is mentally real and what is only an appearance in the consciousness "of" the mental. The reality of something past is not given to me primarily through so-called memory images, but through a resistance and a pressure exerted on my present lived-experience by "something" that my will power can no longer alter. Thus even the actuality of the past makes itself felt primarily not as "object" [*Gegenstand*] but as the resistance [*Widerstand*] given to my life when it is trained on the future. Only when this life is obstructed does that looking back emerge which is the presupposition of any memory. We continually attempt to turn something in the "past" to practical account, whether to contend with it in, for example, the form of remorse, or to continue a past course and lead it into the present. It is in these attempts that we confer upon what is past its primary effective presence [*primäre Wirklichkeitscharakter*]. The question "What shall I do with my past?" is posed or poses itself in our exploratory activity before the question "How was the past constituted in itself?" The real being of the whole sphere of the past is, of course, given prior to any single thing in it that may give me a memory of the past. This sphere manifests itself primarily in a dynamic experience of pressure, which, as can be shown, increases as we grow older and accounts for the striking diminution in the spontaneous feeling of freedom and in the range of one's abilities in old age. Even the lines memory follows are primarily determined [36] by the fine variations in the experiences of pressure, as well as by the accompanying value-character of the contents accessible to memory within its own sphere. Individual experiences of pressure arise, with varying intensity, against the background of the total impress of the past. They are the primary determinants of what enters into the image—contained in memory—primary, in relation to all the other determinants of our memory life. They already belong to *mnēmē*, that is, memory,[37] and not only to specifically human *anamnēsis* (i.e., recollection).

In the mental sphere as well, the resistance which we ex-

36. [Reading "umbegrenzt" for "unbegrenzt."—TRANS.]
37. [Reading "der Mnēmē, das heisst Gedächtnisses" for "der Mnēmē das Gedächtnisses."—TRANS.]

perience to our conscious, voluntary doing and attending is the basic feature of reality. We have good reasons for distinguishing here "actual" friendship from "imaginary" friendship, "genuine" feelings from "spurious" ones, "really wanting to" from mere, deceptive "wishing"—from "wishing," that is, that passes itself off as will. Furthermore, we distinguish the actual motives of our deeds from the imagined motives we delude ourselves into thinking we have on account of their morally superior value. An experience proves itself actual and genuine by standing firm against attempts to eliminate or change it by means of conscious willing or arbitrary attentiveness.

Further, if the effective reality [*Wirksamkeit*] of one experience does not agree in character [*Sosein*] with another way of acting or another experience as the connection of their meanings [*verstehbare Sinnzusammenhang*] would require— for example, if a man does not act friendly toward one whom he claims to love—then in ordinary life we shall contest the actuality and genuineness of his feeling. It is necessary to maintain that, in addition to real feelings which are combined with fantasy-*images*, there are also fantasies of feeling; that in addition to real volitions, there are also the semblances of volition [*Scheinwollungen*] which one really does not will; in addition to real motives, there are also the semblances of motives. Here, too, the phenomenal experience of mental reality is that of resistance. The objective reality of the mental, however, is its efficacy [*Wirksamkeit*] in the mental context. It has rightly been pointed out that what is most efficacious is generally just what is furthest from consciousness. Principally, what is involved is not self-knowledge or self-observation, but what language terms the "finished product" [*mit sich fertigwerden*]. All attempts at making something conscious, all self-perception and observation, are only means to this more important end.

The second basic error in Dilthey's study is the conflation of his theory of reality with the false thesis that everything given is immanent to consciousness. Dilthey does not notice that the experience of reality is above all an ecstatic one, and not an ecstatic "knowledge of" but an ecstatic "having of" reality. Consequently, one does not see how, in Dilthey, the experience of resistance is going to lead out of the sphere of being of that which is immanent to consciousness. Actually, the relation between the experience of resistance and the being of that which is immanent to consciousness is the converse. The consciousness of a drive does not lead to the experience of resistance; neither does the consciousness of an obstructed drive. Rather, it is the primarily ecstatically experienced resistance that first occasions the act of reflection through which the impulsive drive can now become a matter of consciousness. Becoming a matter of consciousness (and the concomitant relation to a "self") is, in all the manifold levels and grades in which it occurs, always the result of our suffering the resistance offered by the world. Real being is, therefore, always given to us along with anything whatsoever which is immanent to consciousness. Thus, the experience of reality and the advent [*Werden*] of the being of that which is immanent to consciousness are of at least the same degree of originality. Dilthey makes a third connected error when he calls resistance an experience of the will. He clearly is thinking here not so much of the spontaneous, involuntary life of our impulsive drives as of the conscious, central will. Since the experience of reality is not based on the being of that which is immanent to consciousness, this thesis certainly cannot be true. Rather, the factor of reality is the resistance to our continually active, spontaneous, but at the same time completely involuntary, impulsive life. It is not, accordingly, resistance to our conscious willing. The latter is forever coming upon a completed reality, the character of which is already determined in some way. Therefore, willing, if by this term we understand (correctly) only positing and affirming or negating the value of projects, cannot be the act in which resistance is experienced, for willing and not willing (in this sense of the term) are acts which cannot be increased or intensified to any degree. Resistance can arise only when the willing of a project advances to the willing of a deed, to the intention and impulse to movement. In this case, however, the willing (in the sense specified) has already merged with an impulsive drive, namely, the one from which it has removed some obstruction. And precisely for this reason, it cannot be "spiritual" willing which experiences resistance, since, as we have shown elsewhere,[38] this willing always has a negative character. That is, insofar as it is connected with

38. [See "Probleme einer Soziologie des Wissens," *Die Wissensformen und die Gesellschaft,* p. 141.—TRANS.]

the sphere of activity, it always only obstructs present impulsive drives or removes obstructions from them.[39]

Finally, Dilthey connected the question of the experience of reality with the so-called problem of the reality of the external world in a manner which is much too onesided. The problem of reality arises in every possible sphere of being, not only in that of the external world. We have shown this in the cases of mental being and the being of the past. On the other hand, "being in the sphere of the external world" has no claim to reality at all. Space, which indeed constitutes the external world, certainly has no reality, since it can have no effect. Shadows, mirror-images, after-images, rainbows, a *Fata Morgana,* the colors on a surface, etc., are, to be sure, objects of the external world. This in no way makes them real. Furthermore, there is, even in the sphere of the internal world, a distinction between real and unreal, a distinction which Dilthey erroneously denies. The problem of the spheres of being is, as we have shown, autonomous and independent of the problem of reality. The foundational laws obtaining between these spheres are surely different from those Dilthey assumes in his treatise, as I have pointed out in detail in "Erkenntnis und Arbeit." The sphere of the possible experiences of the "Thou" and of "society" is certainly given prior to the sphere of the individual— leaving aside the general form of the multiplicity of the "self," which is the same in both spheres. Furthermore, the sphere of the external world is given prior to that of the internal world (compare Kant's "Refutation of Idealism").

Without becoming more deeply involved in these questions here, I should like to investigate a question not posed very precisely in my earlier treatise. This is the question of how the experience of reality is related to the givenness of space and time. Here, too, we can ask whether and in what sense the manifold of space and time is given before or after reality. Only after this question has been answered can we determine with greater exactness the correctness of arguments like these of Rehmke and Heidegger: "How could the one who wills experience resistance, without presupposing the external world?"

39. Also, the continuity of the experience of resistance is intelligible only as resistance to the drive-life, not as resistance to the central willing of the person. Only the drive-life is continuous; willing is an intermittent act.

(Rehmke), or, "The discovery of resistance, that is, of what resists our strivings, is ontologically possible only on the basis of the disclosedness of the world." [40]

1. *Reality in relation to space and time*

We are interested in understanding what foundational relation there is between the "reality of something" and spatiality and temporality.

"Spatiality" does not yet mean "space." Every space has a certain form, for example, three-dimensionality, uniformity or nonuniformity, etc. Spatiality, in contrast, is that which makes every space, whatever its form, into a *space*. By "spatiality" we understand only the fact that there is a *simultaneous apartness* [*gleichzeitiges Auseinandersein*] in general. [41] By "apartness" (which as such belongs to temporality as well), we mean that an identical nature does not collapse into one thing so long as a number of instances of it can be given. Spatiality, as well as space, are, in turn, to be sharply distinguished from *extension*. It has recently come to appear plausible that vision *alone* is always giving us extension directly and that the extension phenomenally given to us along with tactile contents passes from the optical datum into the tactile datum, always and exclusively by means of kinesthetic sensations. However, to conclude from this (as Wittmann does) that spatiality, too, is only an optical datum is completely mistaken. [42] Extension is either a property of an already objectified "physical body" and its surfaces or a modification of the contents of sensation themselves. Space, on the contrary, is in every case, as Kant observed, a *uniform object* and a form of order independent of things and sensations. Its properties are entirely different from those which belong to extension. We can indeed imagine a space being given *without* any extension, for example, a spatial ordering of unextended points. On the other hand, we can imagine a world of extended things in which there is no "space"

40. Heidegger, "Sein und Zeit," p. 210. [*Being and Time*, p. 253.—TRANS.]

41. [In "Idols," Scheler used the term *Aussereinander* to capture the same idea, namely, that items in space stand apart from one another, lie outside one another, or are independent of one another.—TRANS.]

42. [See J. Wittmann, "Raum, Zeit und Wirklichkeit," *Archiv für die gesamte Psychologie*, Vol. XLII (1924).—TRANS.]

of any sort, despite all the extension. If we think of a being whose senses embraced everything at hand (without any thresholds), a being which lacked any self-movement, then in his world there would indeed be a multiplicity of contiguous things, a world in which every thing would be limited by the being of another and every thing would possess an extension; but such a being would still have *no space*.

Thus, Kant's principle that spatiality is given prior to any sensory contents continues in force, even though Kant surely goes much too far when he does not distinguish spatiality from a certain form of space. The widespread opinion that the central experience [*Kernerlebnis*] of spatiality itself first comes about only after a so-called visual space, a tactile space, a kinesthetic space, an acoustical and a vibratory space, have been coordinated, is completely indefensible, as J. v. Kriss recently proved.[43] The identically common something in which the "coordination" is to take place is missing altogether. Furthermore, this opinion is contradicted by the fact that every object given in a visual content, before particular expectations are disappointed, is also treated as "graspable." The so-called sensory spaces generally are not phenomena we experience but artificial products of the laboratory. No one of these modally distinct sensory spaces furnishes the properties wnich certainly belong to the space of natural experience. Visual space, for instance, is not uniform but has the character of a Riemannian space, as is demonstrated when we look along converging railway tracks. The nonvisual spaces develop the central experience of simultaneous apartness no less than the visual, but they develop it in a *historical fashion*—which in no way means that what is given in them (in the manifold) is not itself given as simultaneous. However, it does mean that this simultaneous apartness unfolds phenomenally not in one but in a multiplicity of experiences which are temporally ordered. This is not the place to show in detail how each one of these so-called sensory spaces diverges from the space given in natural experience. No one of these spaces, much less their sum, coincides with the properties of natural space. In the absence of a central experience to provide the foundation, neither the unity of space nor the continuity, the homogeneity (that is, the displaceability of

43. [See J. von Kriss, *Über die materiellen Grundlagen der Bewusstseinserscheinungen* (Leipzig, 1923).—TRANS.]

figures without alteration), the three-dimensionality, the limit-lessness, the sequential character of spatial elements can be understood on the basis of sensory spaces which were in fact previously conceived separately. Spatiality, however, is prior to the sensory spaces for another reason; the central experience of space is already contained as originally in the formation of spontaneous, impulsive fantasy as in the manifolds accessible to us through the senses. Jaensch has rightly pointed out that the wide-reaching coincidence which exists between the space of fantasy and representation and perceptual space does not stem from the mature perceptual space exhibited in the data of sensation (data which are roughly in proportion to the sensory stimuli). Instead the coincidence arises from the fact that, at least in the optical sphere, representations and perceptions diverge from one another only after they emerge from the prior stage of "eidetic images of intuition." This makes it easier to understand the applicability of the theorems of geometry, which are obtained from the material of the fantasy space, to the objects of experience.[44] Kant, too, speaks of a "pure imagination" which enters into all our perceptions, whose existence "no psychologist" has up till now suspected. If spatiality is given prior to the data of sense, then the question of the nature of the central experience of spatiality becomes all the more pressing. Kant thought that this central experience consists in a "pure intuition." If this were the case, and if spatiality were equated with a particular space (Euclidean space), then we could not understand why all the givens in the different sensory spaces do not produce just this particular spatiality and the forms and structures possible within it. We could not, as Herbart has pointed out, understand why three notes do not form a triangle.

Kant's error seems to be that he wants to grasp the central experience of spatiality in general as a "perceptual formation" (as an intuition). The central experience is originally only a creature's experience of his ability to produce certain spontaneous movements. Spatiality is acquired through activity [*erspielt*] before it is represented and thought. We are not thinking here of the so-called kinesthetic sensations which result from the displacements of our bodily parts and organs. The central experience of spatiality underlies these no differ-

44. See my remarks on "fantasy" in "Erkenntnis und Arbeit," pp. 343–48.

ently than it does all other sensations. Only because these sensations are the very first which follow upon the self-movements we perform can we understand that they have to take over the mediating role in the coordination of visual and tactile data. A spatially ordered scheme of our whole "body" precedes the kinesthetic as well as the remaining organic sensations, and the latter change with changes in the whole of this schema. (In no way does this schema represent a simple addition of these sensations.) [45] The notion that kinesthetic sensations themselves furnish the primary space is controverted both by the fact that the distinction between the space of the body and environmental space is secondary to their being spaces and by the fact that when the child has come to draw this distinction he assigns a doubtful *datum* primarily to the environment, and not to his own body and its sphere. The child treats his feet, for example, *first* as objects of the surrounding world and only gradually notices that they fall at the limits of his body-schema.

The "movement" in question, when we asserted that the primary experience of spatiality is the experienced power of spontaneous movement, can be generally characterized as necessarily a *living movement*. However, this is not an empirical concept. Rather, only when we see this kind of movement can we distinguish a living creature from an inanimate thing. Self-movement first constitutes "the living creature." We define a living movement as one in which, throughout the experience of movement, the change of place of an identical something, which is ingredient in every movement, proves to be founded on the "tendency" [*Tendenz*] which is likewise ingredient in all movement. Even in inanimate movements, a change of place of one and the same thing and a "tendency" are always simultaneously present, but here the tendency appears based upon an already given change of place or on one which is still under way. It is, so to speak, always *blown into* the phenomenon from the *terminus ad quem* of movement, while in a living movement the tendency appears at the *terminus a quo* and the change of place presents itself as the "consequence based upon" the tendency (and its changes). This is the ultimate reason why in the inorganic sciences we should assume as many elementary "forces" as there are elementary laws which cannot be

45. On this point, see Paul Schilder, *Das Körperschema* (Berlin, 1923).

derived from anything else and why these assumptions always remain based on the confirmation of *laws*. Thus spatiality, viewed from its subjective side, is at first nothing more than the experienced power of being able to perform living movements. Consequently, it is not our view that the already performed movement gives us the central experience of spatiality, any more than the actual movement being performed right at the moment; rather, the experience of the power of spontaneous self-movement, just to the extent it is not put in play but remains *in potentia,* furnishes the most original *datum* of spatiality.

We cannot represent to ourselves any sort of spatiality in which the peculiar phenomenon of the "void" does not appear, the phenomenon of that intuitive *mē on,* that "lack" which proceeds from the factual datum itself. This phenomenon is, in any event, prelogical and certainly has nothing to do with the function of negative judgment. The phenomenon of the void is of the greatest interest. It arises, in the last analysis, from the experience that occurs when a driving hunger [*Triebhunger*] for spontaneous movement has not been satisfied or fulfilled. This hunger in the end conditions all perceptions [*Perzeptionen*] as well as representations and the spontaneous images of fantasy, which are independent of external perceptions. Thus, the phenomenon of the void, which is bound up with the power of self-movement (insofar as the latter is connected with this unsatisfied hunger), must be given as a stable background prior to all changing perceptions and even the material images of fantasy. The "emptiness" of the heart is, remarkably, the principal datum for all concepts of emptiness (empty time, empty space). The emptiness of the heart is, quite seriously, the source from which all emptiness springs. The empty path, the stationary empty path, so to speak, which our drives take as they reach out in every direction is constantly at hand. So, too, is the background of perceptions which is connected with this empty path. And it is only man's urgent impulse to move, varying in force and direction, which produces that rare marvel, the unheard-of fiction of man's natural world-view, that a particular kind of nonbeing (*mē on*) seems to him to precede every positively determined being as its foundation: empty space. In the natural world-view space appears as a stationary, unlimited void, truly prior to and independent of all things and movements; it appears as a *substantial* void. And this "form" seems to remain in existence, even if one imagines all things and their properties to be arbitrarily changed or even completely abolished. It seems to remain even if one discovers or assumes totally different laws of motion than those that in fact obtain. The natural world-view shows us things "in" space, that is, things which are represented *in* space like goldfish in their tank. It contains the strange paradox that it shows us the truly positive being of existent things as a mere "filling" of an antecedent underlying space, absolute, empty, and stationary—as if things were present only to "stuff out" [*auszustopfen*] this void at particular spots and to move themselves in it for a time like goldfish in a glass bowl.

In antiquity Democritus was the first to raise this strange phenomenon suggested by the natural world-view to the rank of a rigorous philosophical concept. While his predecessors, the Eleatics, taught that only the full (*pleon*) "is" and the empty (*kenon*) "is not," Democritus asserted that the empty, this non-being, also "is," and with these simple words he makes us keenly conscious of the paradox of the phenomenon of the void. He boldly assumes an infinite void as a being which precedes things and their causal connection. And since, on this assumption, it is quite improbable that the things present in this infinite empty space form a single interconnected causal nexus (or that their natures are connected as ground and consequent), Democritus is consistent in positing an infinite series of islands of matter in this infinite void. We men live only on one of these, and we can have knowledge only of that island in whose causal nexus we ourselves are included. The Atomists later called the intervals between these worlds *inter-mundia* and made them the dwelling of the gods. It is decisive here that space is not understood as something immanent to this *one* world or as an ordering of images; rather, the "world" itself is arranged in a previously *existent* space. In fact, Newton's idea was not essentially different when, in his theory of space, he made *spatium absolutum* the basis of his physics. Aristotle had already convincingly demonstrated the inner impossibility of this theory of space in his physics. He discovered with classical clarity the perplexing problems [*aporiai*] which result from this strange supposition. Must we not, he asks, assume two spaces, one packed inside the other, one which the body itself "fills up" and which it carries with it when it moves, and one which remains behind when the body moves—if motion is going to be possible at all in this *kenon*. Or, if only *one* space is assumed and the body moves itself (and carries *its* space along with it), must the body not tear something like a "hole" in space? Though people, J. Locke, for example, would later contest the possibility of movement *without* the assumption of an empty space, Aristotle contests the possibility of motion in the case where this assumption is made. We shall never be able to escape these and similar *aporiai* if we do not make absolutely clear the origin of this totally fictitious being, an empty space that precedes things. Let us try to do just that.

The primary experience of spatiality and (to anticipate here what we shall show separately later) the primary experience of temporality have their common roots in a living creature's experience of the power of self-movement or self-modification. If one analyzes this in more detail than we propose here, it can be shown that a still deeper phenomenon underlies the phenomena we call motion and alteration, a phenomenon we can label fluctuating change or variation [*Wechsel*] in a manifold to which apartness [*Auseinander*] belongs but in which there is still no sharp distinction between temporal succession [*Nacheinander*] and spatial "nextness" [*Nebeneinander*]. We can, in principle, interpret any fluctuating variation in this four-dimensional manifold as alteration or as movement. What decides whether we do the one or the other is exclusively the reversibility or irreversibility of the change. Variations do not yet contain an identification of the changing contents beyond what is immediately given at the moment. For example, the colors of a surface and that which is given on analogous levels in other sensory domains can "vary"; a surface, in contrast, "alters" only its colors or its hardness and softness. In other words, if a variation of two or more contents appears to us reversible so that after the change has taken place what was given at the start could be reproduced, then we are inclined to interpret the change as movement and not as alteration. Thus we can interpret the variation of lights and shadows on the ground under a tree moved by the wind and exposed to the sun, both as a temporal alteration of particular surfaces or as a movement, that is, a change of place of different "specks" of shadow and light. However, the antecedent manifold in which the fluctuating variation takes place is in any case equivalent to the atemporal and nonspatial "togetherness" of the multiplicities which we find in us in *one* moment of consciousness. This manifold involves what we wish to call "interpenetration" [*Ineinander*].[46] The word "in" has its origin in this manifold and is only subsequently applied metaphorically to certain relations of things in space and time.[47]

Now it is a fundamental fact that fluctuating variation, movement, and alteration are phenomena which precede in the order of givenness any unvarying, unalterable, and immovable being. Our ability to grasp the smallest movements in every sensory region, even when we can no longer grasp the stable, qualitative differences among the temporal and spatial intervals between the stretches of movement and alteration, is totally independent of the construction of our sense organs and functions. This ability presents an a priori, albeit biological only, for all sense-perceptions. For this reason we must never say that movement presupposes the antecedent givenness of space and time—at least not in the case of living movement, on which change of place and tendency are based. Thus we must obtain the origin of the manifold of space and time and its proper sense from these primary concepts: variation, movement, alteration. We should not think that we can compound the phenomenon of movement out of space and time.

The fiction of which we were just speaking, the fiction of an empty form given prior to things, arises first from the fact that when we apprehend a phenomenon of movement, our immediate and ecstatic expectation leads us to trace in advance a representation of a sphere which already contains the "possible" future place of the moving object. Since this representation is an "ecstatic" perception, that is, one not "related to the self," the place which the body takes up in this next moment appears to us like an "empty place" which it subsequently "occupies," just in the way I sit down on an "empty" chair. The concept of place, which is always the "place of something" and which must never be made absolute, is here made into something absolute. It was already there "in advance." Furthermore, the

46. [See Translator's Introduction, note 45. Items in consciousness do not stand apart from or outside of one another but "interpenetrate."— TRANS.]
47. [See Heidegger, *Being and Time*, pp. 79–80.—TRANS.]

law which can be called the universal law of all perceptions, even the most primitive, and which has recently been labeled the "law of figure and ground" (that is, the fact that in every perception, in a variety of ways which are independent of any arbitrary attention, one element stands out from the complex, leaps out, as it were, while the other has only a background character), has been made absolute, as if there were a single, stationary background in which all backgrounds coalesce into a unity. This one background is then raised to the rank of a thinglike being.

It seems to me that this law of figure and ground, despite the opposition which it has encountered, is based entirely on the relative urgency of the individual drives of the organism (which are the foundations of possible perception) and on the relative obtrusiveness of the individual impulses accompanying these drives. The perceptual complex based upon the more obtrusive impulse becomes in each case the "figure" while the other remains the "background." Thus these drives create an oscillating play between "taking note of" and "overlooking" what is given. This play is in no way limited only to the perception of an image; rather, it determines the composition of the image. Indeed, in the last analysis, it determines the development and formation of the different thresholds of sensibility and discrimination belonging to the individual modalities of sense. However, since all these processes take place preconsciously and condition only the composition of what is met with in consciousness, what is overlooked as the result of certain drives appears as the phenomenon of the "void." "Empty" is an expression which should in fact be used only relatively, as "empty of something." What remains "empty" is in the first place what our drives led us to "expect," although this expectation was not satisfied by a perception corresponding to the thrust of the drive. The fiction of an empty form now arises from the fact that the concept of the relatively "empty," which alone makes sense, is made absolute and this emptiness is then posited as given prior to things and their extensions.

One question still remains. If the central experience of space is only our experience of spontaneous movement *in potentia* and if it is this experience which gives ultimate unity to all sensory spaces and allows them to be coordinated with one another, and if all intuitive data are secondary with respect to this basic experience, how does it happen that this experience of the power of movement has this strange predominance over the actual movements we perform? It has become probable that primitives, children at a certain stage of development, and especially animals do not possess a homogeneous and free-floating spatial form detached from things and perceptible contents, such as is present in the natural world-view of the civilized adult. It seems to be a definite process of development which leads to this predominance of the experience of the power of movement over actual movement. In particular, that man alone can acquire this strange fiction should be connected with the basic properties of his constitution, which has only an indirect relation with everything we are inclined to call "reason." That predominance can only come about in a creature whose unsatisfied desire is always greater than his satisfied desire, that is, a creature whose life is constituted by a surplus of unsatisfied desires, who is constantly holding back a greater part of his vital motor-drives than he is releasing. Since this surplus of unsatisfied drive (and a corresponding spontaneous surplus of drive-based fantasy over perceptions dependent on external conditions) is a basic mark of man in relation to all other animals,[48] it does not seem to me too bold an hypothesis that this surplus of the "empty" over the "full," this priority of a stationary empty space over all spatial content, has its roots in this primary property of human nature. It seems to me that Spengler was in principle correct when he connected the reappearance of the Democritean theory of space at the start of the modern period and its centuries-long currency in science (especially the theory of an actual infinity of space) with the unlimited power-drive of modern, or as he says, "Faustian," man. In no other single aspect does man prove himself so much a repressor of drives and "nay-sayer" than in the fact that he objectifies the always deficiently filled emptiness of his heart into an infinitely empty being and allows this emptiness to precede things and their causal relation. That it is his own "nay," the emptiness of his own heart, which yawns before him seemingly from the outside and awakens

48. See my lecture "Die Sonderstellung des Menschen," printed in *Der Leuchter*, Vol. VIII (Darmstadt, 1927). This will appear shortly in a separate edition. [English translation by Hans Meyerhoff, *Man's Place in Nature* (Boston: Beacon Press, 1961).—TRANS.]

the dread which Pascal so frighteningly depicted, is a wisdom which reason was late in discovering. Once it was found, it was immediately buried again in oblivion by an automatic compulsion of the human constitution.

Thus, if we make the being of the spatial manifold relative to living beings, two things follow. The first is a thesis which follows from the philosophy of biology quite independently of the present question. This thesis states that life itself is a process in time and, indeed, as we shall soon see, in absolute time and is not something in space; that all the spatial forms of organisms and their unities, from the organ to the cells and their subunits, must be conceived as built up from the formative [*gestaltenden*] functions into which the life-process can be analyzed. Life "spatializes" *itself*. The word "life" is taken here without regard to the distinction between "mental" and "physical." Second, it follows from our conception of the primary experience of spatiality that all the laws which are discovered on the basis of this primary givenness of a space must also hold good of the objects of perception which are spatially ordered. On the other hand, it also follows from this that the particular form of the character of space in which space is assumed to be a physical milieu is in no way univocally defined by pure geometry or by the ways "simultaneous apartness" is shaped by geometrical constructions. Geometry in general must hold true of everything perceivable, because the driving impulses which are the basis of the most primitive givenness of space are also the conditions of all possible perceptions. To this extent we agree with Kant. However, whereas Kant took space to be a possible intuition belonging to consciousness, we let its givenness precede intuition and consciousness. Space is for us existentially relative to the animal in man (including the peculiarity that his unsatisfied drives exceed those he satisfies), but not relative to consciousness, intuition, and cognition. Consciousness and intuition "experience" space as coming from the outside, exactly as they experience sensory impressions.

Furthermore, it also seems certain that the properties of natural space, such as unity (in relation to the many modalities of sense and in relation, further, to the diversity of individuals), continuity, homogeneity, and three-dimensionality can be understood only on the basis of our basic intuition. We have already shown how this is so in the case of unity. The continuity of space stems exclusively from the only thing which is strictly continuous, the dynamic continuity of movement. The possibility of this is indeed space itself. The continuity of extension rests, in the last analysis, on the intensive movement whose possibility is space. The uniform three-dimensionality of natural space, which is not given in any modality of sense, stems in the end from the three possible directions of human self-movement in accordance with the primitively experienced contrasts: right-left, up-down, forward-backward. That space in the natural intuition is homogeneous is, on our view, analytically true, since the identity of the mobile over the course of its motion helps to constitute the phenomenon of movement. However, none of these properties would be intelligible if we wanted to derive the central experience of space from sensible givens or from a merely logical recasting of these givens. The properties mentioned are also properties of natural space and have nothing to do with the basic concepts defined in geometry. Even the unlimitedness of natural space, which no sensationalistic theory can make intelligible, stems from the experience of our ability to continue spontaneous movements in one and the same direction as long as we like.

It will now be our task to show how the experience of reality is related to the objectification of these primary spatial givens into a world-space.

If a center of impulse meets with resistance several times, the resistant X, Y, Z . . . , insofar as they are grasped in their relationship to one another, are represented in a space which affords scope to their possible effects upon and movements toward one another. We can also say that the schema of the "experience of what is roundabout" [*Herumerlebnis*], which was previously related to the individual (as his primary experience of spatiality), is now *objectified* [*vergegenständlicht*]; it thereby becomes independent of the existence and characteristics of the individual man. To this extent the experience of resistance or reality precedes the being of objective space, as well as the being of that space which is given in the natural outlook. The space of the surrounding world which is relative to the organism now becomes the world-space. Now, for the first time, man can locate his lived-body "in" the world-space, just as he can other corporeal things. It is necessarily bound up with this positing of a spatial manifold independent of man that every definition of the space of real things in natural science depends on the laws of the motion of extended things. Their extension itself is now no longer grasped as a mere property and characteristic of the appearances and images of bodies, but as a part of the one, strictly objective world-space which is only "filled in" by bodies. Just as the one subjectively given space is only the sum total of our possibilities of spontaneous movement, so "objective" space is only the sum total of the possibilities of movement and changes of position on the part of the bodies themselves.

What distinguishes our conception from Kant's is the following. We start from the phenomena of variation, movement, and alteration as the genuinely primary phenomena and first define spatiality in relation to these. Thus, these do not define a space with any definite form, as for instance the Euclidean, which would necessarily have to coincide with physical space. Only the possibility of applying any geometry obtained from the basic phenomenon of spatiality in general to the being of bodies is absolutely and a priori guaranteed. The choice of a form of space defined in a particular axiom system is prescribed or suggested exclusively by observations and measurements of the changes of position which take place between bodies or other natural phenomena. Thus the laws governing the actual behavior of the ultimate subjects of our physical statements first decide the choice of a geometry. The objects of experience do not have to accommodate themselves to any geometry of the space of imagination; the choice of a geometry has to be accommodated to the laws of observable movements. Finally, the answer to the question of whether this objectification of our capacity for movement signifies simply a unification of our possible experiences, or whether such a spatial ordering is to be ascribed to the things themselves [*den Sachen selbst*], depends exclusively on whether we do or do not assume a single supra-individual "life." The existential relativity of spatiality to life in general—and in no way to reason—must be maintained in any case. If a supra-individual life is assumed, then we have the right to suppose that the chosen physical space exists independently of the being of man. If this is not posited, then in no way do we have the right, and what we call space is a form of appearance whose existence is exclusively relative to men.[49]

The problems of reality and its givenness in relation to temporality are analogous. Temporality is an "apartness," as is spatiality, but it is an "apartness" of "becoming."[50] That is, the "apartness" of temporality is contained in the transition from some nature or essence as such to the existence of this nature, or further, from this nature to some other nature.[51] The central experience of temporality, like that of space, is originally given to us in a particular modality of our drive-based striving: in man's power, his experience of an ability as an animal to modify his qualitative conditions spontaneously, that is, "by himself." It is part of the primary phenomenon of life that it exhibits not only self-movement but also self-modification [Selbstveränderung]. A creature that did not modify itself would have no access to time. Time, like space, is not originally given to intuition or perception but is a modification of our active and practical behavior. To have or to want to do "first" one thing, "then" another, to have barely enough time to do it, to have "already taken care of it," this dynamically experienced ordering of projects, not objects, is the basic experience of temporality. It is from this experience that phrases which express the periodic modes of behavior of everyday life get their currency: e.g., "Now it is time to get up," "time to eat," "time to sleep," "time to work," "there is barely enough time" to get this or that piece of the job done, "just enough time" to do it.

Thus temporality is a form of activity before it is a form of intuition and long before it is conceptually defined. The practical temporal ordering of our undertakings goes back to the degrees of obtrusiveness and urgency of our drives and driving impulses. That which obtrudes itself possesses the character of the "first of all," in contrast to the less obtrusive, which comes "afterward." Since the drives and impulses are the precondi-

49. My *Philosophical Anthropology* [not published] will furnish a resolution of this question.

50. "Becoming" [*Werdesein*] is, in contrast to "what will be in the future" [*Seinwerden*], a type of *being;* it in no way presupposes time, as logical "becoming" shows, for example, a genetic definition.

51. [I give Scheler's text in full: "Sie ist ein Auseinandersein des Werdeseins, d.h., des Überganges von Sosein in Dasein, ferner von Sosein in Anderssein."—TRANS.]

tions of the occurrence of every possible perception, whether its content is imagined or belongs to actual perception, the primary experience of time precedes all possible perceptions or sensations. For this reason it can never stem from our external experience, any more than it can from that internal experience which we have through the reflexive observation of perceptions. Thus, temporality is a priori vis-à-vis both kinds of experience and its forms of lawfulness must be valid for anything objective which we perceive. Even things like breathing, the heartbeat, and other intra-organic processes do not form the origin of our experience of time but simply furnish a primary material which it shapes. Indeed, subjective *consciousness of time* first comes about through the person's reflection on the variation in his perceptions and through the obstruction and resistance he experiences when he tries to complete the tasks [*Triebaufgaben*] involved in self-modification. He gains a subjective consciousness of time by being thrown back by this obstruction upon the present and, further, upon what is given as "already having been."

Our most primitive experience of time thus concerns what later, after the discovery of the present and the past, is called the "future." This single-minded focus on the future is essential to the mode in which life exists. "Future" means everything which an animal can experience through its self-modification, or, in a wider sense, that which it can "still" manage, which it can "still" keep under control, that for which it can "still" care. *The future is the possibility of spontaneous self-becoming through spontaneous self-modification.* Temporality is "in the first place" an order in the dependence of projects on one another, not an order of the cognizable *course* of objective and factual events. Only an artificial abstention from spontaneous vital behavior leads to theoretical time as a form in which actual events take place. The *present,* however, is originally that *wherein* we are actually operating and working; the past is that *over which* we no longer have any power, *that which* our *powerlessness* runs up against. What we can "still" instigate or avert is at each moment "what is coming next"; what we can "no longer" control is what has just passed. Thus there are three modalities which our ability to act acquires, "doing something right now," "no longer being able to do it," and "still being able to do it," in which the three spheres of present, past, and future are originally given to us. The animal could scarcely have another experience of time than the dynamic ordering of those times of activity given by phrases like "sleeping time," "mating time," "time to" start building a nest, etc.

Even the experience of growing old and dying as a passage toward a state in which one cannot and can-no-longer live is already evident to man in the peculiar variations in the experienced time-structure of present, past, and future.[52] Even if we exclude all the possible experiences a man could have of other men's growing old and dying, together with all the experiences he would have through his organic feelings and states of a growing feebleness and growing inability to act in certain ways, the variations in his experienced time-structure *alone* could give him the insight that he is advancing toward a "no-longer-being-able-to-live," toward death. The dynamic experience of the future has at each moment a definite range [*Spielraum*] of power which is experienced along with it. In the process of growing old this range continually diminishes, while the other sphere, that of what "has unalterably been," continually grows and takes the form of an increasingly intensive, dynamic experience of the resistance offered by his "past" pressing against and weighing down his "present." The sphere of the present itself, however, from childhood until gray old age, is always becoming narrower and "more fleeting." It is a well-known fact, quite in keeping with this law of the variation of the structure of time, that the same length of objective time (e.g., a year) seems to elapse more and more quickly as one grows older. For this reason, growing old and death are not empirical concepts any more than the concept of life itself is. They are necessarily posited along with that basic law which must be seen as the essential law of life (as a psychophysically undifferentiated fact), namely, that every step in the process of self-modification *narrows* the range of possible self-modifications and their development. The growing experience of being determined [*Determinationserlebnis*] and the experience of the decreasing range of what one is "still able to do" in no way presuppose time as the object of intuition or thought; they are something

---

52. I have already discussed this idea in detail in a lecture on death, which I delivered in Göttingen in 1914. [See "Tod und Fortleben," Maria Scheler, ed., *Schriften aus dem Nachlass, Gesammelte Werke* X (Berlin: Der neue Geist Verlag, 1947).—TRANS.]

which an essential law connects with life and the living experience of life [*Erleben des Lebens*].

Just how much the experience of time is based on the dynamic interrelation of our drives and impulses is shown not only by the alterations of the time-structure we have mentioned but also by the fact that an undatable order of the contents of life *precedes* all the datable temporal orderings of perceptible events in external and inner life. For example, the effective operation of the unconscious is still temporal but it is not datable. An animal cannot have a datable temporal ordering of his experiences at all (for measurability presupposes datability). Analogously, what is given to the group in the form of myth, tales, and saga is undatable, although, naturally, the events which are seen and are therefore given names succeed one another in a certain order.

Just as in the case of space, here, too, it is only man who brings forth the strange phenomenon of an empty form of becoming [*Werdekönnens*], a form of empty time. Empty time goes on continually or is continually intuited, even when nothing definite happens—indeed, even if nothing at all varies [*wechselt*] or is altered. Empty time seems to *precede* all events (in their being or becoming); it seems to underlie these and to set up "duration" and "alteration" as the two completely equi-primordial modes in which contents are related to time. Newton's *tempus absolutum quod aequabiliter fluit* is only the conceptually rigorous version of this phenomenon of empty time which belongs to the natural viewpoint. Newton's absolute time must be "infinite," absolutely homogeneous (that is, it must neither retard nor accelerate events); it should continue to flow even though the world-process come to a stop for millions of years. Just as Democritus, the great investigator of the matter of which the world consists, had to imagine space as projecting into infinity, so, too, people had to imagine time as "going on" infinitely, even if they imagined all events in the world brought to nought. Naturally this phenomenon is a pure fiction. It is the result of the fact that man's unsatisfied drive, his hunger for self-modification, outweighs the satisfiable part of this hunger. As in the case of space, the mere possibility of self-modification achieves a curious predominance over actual self-modifications. Possibility does not here mean a thought or a logical possibility which we grasp in reflection; it signifies the dynamic experience of having what we become in our own power. As an automobile throws its cone of light ahead of itself into the night, so life itself throws its being-able-to-live ahead of itself, for as long as it lives and to the extent that it lives. This is the source of a fictional image of a single, immaterial process of becoming, whose elements are the fleeting moments and stretches of time themselves. This process takes its course even though nothing meaningful happens.

This fictional image alone is the source of the notion that "duration" is as much a primitive possibility for things as alteration and succession. The "duration" of things now appears as a strangely active resistance, as a self-assertion against the frantically racing stream of time. The possibility that things which are in some way embraced in this stream endure [*dauern*] and the possibility that they are changed now seem equiprimordial. This, too, is a pure fiction. Thomas Hobbes said, correctly, that a simple impression of a red speck, for example, were it given as a man's *unique* experience, would provide no reason for him to form the idea of time. Time is in fact completely bound up with the alteration and succession of events and would be completely annulled if they were. Duration is never anything else than the relative background of the unalterability of some one thing, whatever it may be, against which the increased alterability of some other thing stands out. It should not be concluded from this law that the alterable necessarily stands out in relief against the relatively durable, that there can be something absolutely durable. The concept of duration can in reality never be applied to anything other than something which changes less quickly, relatively speaking. The positive concept is that of alteration; the negative, that of the *relatively* unalterable or durable.

The fact that a number of characteristics are common to the phenomenon of empty time and of empty space, or sequential form—for example, continuity, homogeneity, unity, unlimitedness, and dimensionality—shows that space and time trace back to a partially identical primary experience. The continuity of space and time will never be guaranteed unless we derive both phenomena from variation, movement, and alteration. Continuity is guaranteed only by the identity of the subject moving "itself," for the movement and alteration of this is the source of these forms [namely, of space and time]. A static "intuition" would never be able to guarantee continuity, even if it were always independent of and prior to the *discrete* sensory sensations which are limited to definite minima. The homogeneity of space and time, if one derives them from movement and alteration, becomes an analytical proposition. The unity of the two forms, independently of their content, immediately follows from the unity of the life-center whence drives originate. Unlimitedness, which patently has nothing to do with infinity, results from the reflexive consciousness one has of being able to continue the process of self-movement and self-modification in oneself as long as one likes. An either-or of "finite" and "infinite" thereby falls away, as Kant has shown in his theory of the antinomies, since this alternative presupposes a *definite* magnitude.

At this point we must ask again how the objectification of the temporality experienced in this way comes about. The way it comes about is the exact analogue of what we have shown to be the case for space. The possibility of self-modification, the experienced *potentia,* the "ability" to modify oneself, and the passion for this which remains unsatisfied and "empty," are transferred to what is given in the surrounding world. Exactly as in the case of the possibility of movement, the possibility of modification as "possibility" seems intuitively to take precedence over the actual modifications of the forms in the environment, as if these modifications subsequently had merely to "fill out" *the* one antecedently given time. The fiction of an empty time is likewise transferred to things.

Here the decisive question arises. In this objectification, is the experience of reality prior to the distinction between the time of objective events and the subjective time of action and experience, or the time of consciousness (which depends on the latter); or is the objectification of time already present when the experience of reality sets in? This is only a slightly different form of the Kant-Hume problem. Do reality and causality first determine the objectively temporal order of appearances, so that the formula: *propter hoc, ergo post hoc* is true, or does the *propter* consist only in the "regular *post hoc*" of events in objective time? Naturally, the question is independent of the particular form which Kant gave it in his theory that the understanding legislates to nature. Leibniz, too (*Nouveaux Essais*), had concluded that the *propter* first guarantees the objective *post*. However, he did so in a purely ontological sense, without assuming the legislative role of the understanding and without taking the "Copernican" turn.

It is the experience of reality and of resistance to our striving for self-modification which forces this objectification of temporality as the possibility of the modification of real things. It is the experience of reality which gradually and at length teaches us to distinguish genuine perceptions from every kind of fantasy and thus to distinguish fantasy-time (e.g., the time of dreams) from that time in which the objects of our perceptions are situated. Since perceptions and fantasy-images themselves are always partly conditioned by drives and impulses, and since perception, moreover, is partly conditioned by the experienced resistance to these impulses, temporality in the objective sphere must precede all possible images and perceptions. Thus, objective time follows reality and real causal connections in the order of givenness but, at the same time, it precedes all the possible perceptible images of the world. For this reason and for this reason alone, the dynamic, causal connection of happenings as one of "ground and consequence" (that is, the resistance which things no longer exercise upon "me" but upon one another as relatively autonomous causal centers) is what makes possible an objective temporal determination according to "before" and "after." This is what allows us to distinguish the subjective and historical succession of our apprehension and cognition of the world from the succession and relative duration of objective events within the world.

The objectification of experienced temporality thus passes through the following preliminary stages: (1) The experience of reality is objectified. (2) Our experience of having an effect on things is objectified and made into an effective action of things on each other. (3) The possibility of self-modification is objectified into a form in which the possible modifications and alterations of things take place. The discovery of the present and the past, made when one confronts some inward obstacle, comes after the time of action which is primarily directed toward the future. The consciousness of time arises through reflection on the perceptions which vary with our drives and impulses. Then the experience of reality and its objectification become the basis of the distinction between the time of lived-experience and objective time. Finally, the temporal position of an event and its sequential relation to other events result from the causal relation of events.

The objectification of the individual's original experience of time advances through a series of stages, each of which brings in its train a peculiar concept of time. More and more characteristics of the time of lived-experience drop out of these concepts. The first to arise is the intersubjective "social time" of the whole group in which the individual in question lives. Everything drops out of social time that is individual and unique in the time of the individual's lived-experience. In particular, social time obviously reaches beyond the death of the individual into an indeterminate distance. Similarly, it goes back before the birth of the individual, flowing away into the "olden times" of the *historical* existence of the group which is primarily filled with content only in undatable myth. In this social time, of which there are as many varieties as there are groups associated together in a life-community, all the rhythms of what happens to the group and of the so-called "historical periods" run their course. These periods are given specific unity by the existence of successive chieftains, rulers, and their dynasties, and, further, through the associated destinies of the group. In this social and historical time there is in each case a "present of the We," a "past of the We," and a "future of the We." The individual's experience of time, which begins with his birth and ends with his death, appears to be "enclosed" within the temporal schema they form. A second stage of objectification is the time of organic life itself, which is primarily divided into the "seasons." At any rate, it still contains the stretches of present, past, and future, although independently of the time of the individual's experience and the time of the "We."

A *third* stage is *the* time commonly called *physical* time. What characterizes this more than anything else is the complete falling away of the dimensions past, present, and future which are obviously existentially relative to living things alone. Physical time is the first to be completely deprived of structure and rhythm. It alone is that *tempus quod aequabiliter fluit.* Further, physical time alone is strictly *relative* and in it every "before" and "after" of happenings must be established along a one-dimensional line on the basis of causal relations, no longer on the basis of a rhythm immanent to the events themselves.

Since we cannot compare the succession of events with the successive parts of time in such a way that we could establish in what "part of time" an event falls, all the temporal determinations of events are relative to one another. Any occurrence which seems to come close to uniform movement can be arbitrarily established as the standard of comparison; then we count the number of the units of this standard which are contained in other events. This time is always immediately measured by spatial determinations, by dividing the *path* of the chosen standard into certain segments. It is only this physical time which is, by the law of its essence, ineffective and thus strictly homogeneous as well. In vital processes, physiological as well as mental, another time always necessarily means a different nature or character [*ein anderes So-Sein*]. Duration is here assumed from the start to be something merely specious, while in the physical sphere one always tries to reduce all events to the conjunction, mixture, and unmixing of enduring units. Thus, while in vital time content and position can *never* be purely separated from one another (and so every happening is only a consequence of the whole preceding stream of life), in physical time *one and the same* event can, in principle, "recur." Finally, physical time is a time which has arisen because the spheres of the past and the future have been completely *erased*. Not so the "present." Physical time is rather a continual sequence of *nows* [*Jetztpunkten*] independent of any peculiarity of the creature whose "now" these points are. There can be "happenings" [*Geschehen*] in physical time, but no "history" [*Geschichte*]. It belongs to the nature of "history" that a past is at every moment still active and living, and that the contents of this past are variously brought into relief by the tasks belonging to the future. In physical time cause and effect are thus always touching one another in time and "follow" one another in the line of before and after. Since the arrangement of physical time depends wholly on the arrangement of events, when the same state of the world recurs, time itself runs back into itself. That there is something like time, that is, that the process of inanimate nature too has a certain direction, is first genuinely proved by the second law of thermodynamics. It is on account of this law that there are something like "traces" in the inanimate world which not only sanction inferences to preceding states but also symbolically point to these states.

Finally, we must ask how much importance the concept of *absolute time* has. Only a time in which temporal positions and locations, on the one hand, and temporal contents, on the other, are necessarily connected with one another, could be called absolute in contrast to physical-relative time. In this sense, the time of the individual's experience is absolute time in the strictest sense. Furthermore, the social-historical time of the "We" as well as vital time are absolute. For instance, the geologist measures the periods of time during which the various species arose not by means of the present periodic and recurrent life-processes but by the sudden mutations of species. If, therefore, the existence [*Sein*] of absolute time is not open to doubt, and if it is only physical time which lacks absoluteness, then in view of the examples of absolute time we have given, physical time completely lacks the unity of absolute time. There are as many absolute times as there are individuals, societies, and organic unities. Physical time, in contrast to these, is unique. However, it pays for this unity with its unbounded relativity, which is first completely disclosed in the theory of relativity. The question still remains: Is there also one, unique, absolute time, a time in which the dimensions of past, present, and future are preserved but are no longer relative to a particular living creature? Is there a unique time in which nature [*Soscin*] and temporal position are so linked to one another that a unique, absolutely irreversible process runs its course in it and "the same" being and happening consequently can never recur? [53]

Here we must take note of a very essential distinction between space and time. We can no longer pose this question for space. The supposition of an "absolute space" presupposes the fiction of an empty form of space and is preposterous. This is not at all true of time. I shall answer the question only hypothetically. We should assume that such an absolute time exists if a supra-individual Universal-Life exists which lives in all living forms, and if the world itself, at a level of existential relativity which is no longer relative to life, is an organic process which is first formed and completed in time. Then the world as a whole would also know an origin, would grow old and die. Since I do assume that such a Universal-Life exists, for

53. On this last point, see the confrontation with Martin Heidegger in the final chapter of this study [not published].

reasons which do not belong here, I also assume a unique absolute time for the whole of the universe.[54] On this view, the same events would recur only in artificially isolated systems. However, according to this conception of absolute time, there is no longer what the Greeks called a "cosmos." *The world does not "have" a history, but is a history.*

In any case, space and time are very different in regard to their existential relativity. Space, which in its own being is relative, is in addition existentially relative to life, in other words, to a thing having the nature [*Wesen*] of a living being. Temporality, on the contrary, is the form of the process of life itself (which has the ontological status of "becoming") [*als ontischen Werdeseins*]. Thus, it is not existentially relative "to" life, since it is the form of the process of life itself. To be sure, temporality, according to our theory, is still existentially relative to spirit, which stands ontologically higher than life and can still *see* the life-process itself and the form of its becoming [*seine Werdeform*].

2. *Reality and causality*

Finally, we must still say a word about the relation between the givenness of reality and the category of causality. We understand "what it is to be real" [*Realsein*], as distinguished from the factor of reality [*Realitäts moment*], in such a way that everything is real which is causally effective [*wirkfähig*]. For us, being-real [*Realsein*], reality, and causality belong essentially together. That which is not effective is also not real. In our view, the *unity* of the corporeal thing is prior to its sensory and other qualities, ontologically as well as in the givenness of the order of composition. A corporeal thing has such and such properties *because* it is this thing, that is, this unity of causality and resistance. It is not, conversely, this thing because such and such sensory properties enter into our image of it [*Bildeigenschaften*]. The unity of the corporeal thing is thus given prior to all its sensibly perceptible qualities and in no way exhibits merely the sum or the compositional order of these qualities—to say nothing of its being only the ordered sum of the possibilities of its perceptibility. It is impossible, on our showing,

54. [See "Erkenntnis und Arbeit," pp. 268–71, 361.—TRANS.]

for there to be a real and purely passive "matter," which would be the "subject" of causal activity, but could itself be without having any causal effects. This concept is absurd.

If we inquire into the origin of the idea of causality, the answer is that it is primarily given in our own spontaneous acting upon things, not insofar as we are spiritual beings but insofar as we are living beings. Everything that we call spirit [*Geist*] is originally only a sum of intentions which are completely incapable of having causal effects.[55] The origin of the concept of causality therefore cannot lie in the experienced relation which exists between our spiritual person and our action. The idea of causality thus in no way has its origin in the spiritual *fiat aut non fiat* of an act of will to which no degree of activity belongs, but simply accepts or rejects "what is held up before me." Rather, the causal concept has its origin in the operation of the living creature's vital center upon the environment. In my discovery that a project has been realized after a time by me and my action, I have the primary phenomenon in which the core of the category of cause, of "effective action," can be reflectively grasped. It is a matter of complete indifference how this realization comes about or through what intermediate steps the evidence arises that a great deal can come into existence [*Dasein*] "through me" which was before for me only an ideal [*Sosein*], a "project." The evidence that "this ideal has become real through me" is completely independent of the knowledge of how such a thing comes about or takes place. That it has taken place is as clear as day, while the "how" is obscure. This primary experience comes much earlier than any distinction which I make in me between lived-body, soul, corporeal body, and the like. It is also independent of any consciousness or experience of the self. An example of this "effective action" is given even in ecstatic behavior springing from drives, in which the driving impulse translates itself into realization without bearing any antecedent relation to the self.

Hume's objections to this theory of the origin of the concept

55. Even "spiritual" willing is merely an inactive "yea" and "nay" [*fiat aut non fiat*] to projects. It "motivates" driving impulses which are already on hand when it holds certain ideas before them or withdraws such ideas, without having the least "causal influence" on these impulses themselves. Since it can only indirectly obstruct or "free" drives and impulses by "presenting" or "withdrawing" these ideas, the will *always* determines our action *in a negative way.*

of cause rests on a faulty analysis of the facts. He objected, first, that even in action nothing more is present than a vivid idea and a series of sensations that follow it in time, sensations aroused by the movement of the body which follows upon the idea; and second, that we lack any experience or knowledge of the transition in which our will sets the limbs in motion. The original project of an act of will is not, in general, a "movement of the body." If I take my hat from the hatstand in order to put it on my head, my project is not the bodily turns and movements involved in this action, but solely the content to be realized, that "my hat be on my head." When, after this act of will has been performed, I confirm that the project has been realized and I also know that this realization came about "through me," then the whole state of affairs we have in mind is given. Furthermore, the experience of obstruction, for example in the case of sudden paralysis or other forms of *akinesia* [i.e., inability to move], proves that an experience of the transition from the impulse to move to the execution of the movement is given and experienced.[56] Thus what is given here is in no way simply a temporal succession of will, impulse, and movement. We can see immediately that the experienced driving impulse, freed from obstruction by the act of will when it affirms the project, translates itself into the movement performed. Even if we stand back from the experiences of consciousness and follow some purely objective vital movement of a plant or an animal, the change of place of the animal's bodily parts, a necessary ingredient in the movement, is given as produced "through" (and not only "after") a spontaneous impulse to move. If the primary experience of causality is given in such an example and if the category of cause is grasped in reflection upon experience, then it is precisely this category which is transferred to the mutual relations of the things in the environment.

The course of the development of the causal concept in the history of the human spirit also furnishes rigorous proof that the genuine origin of the idea of causality is to be seen here (as John Herschel and Maine de Biran have already seen).

56. In *Formalismus* [see pp. 145–48], I have analyzed the relevant phenomena in detail (e.g., the motor-intention which is independent of the present situation of the parts of the body, the impulses to move, the kinesthetic sensations which report the occurrence of a movement after the fact). Therefore I shall not go more deeply into this matter here.

The question "Why?" appears among primitives and children only when the customary and immediate connection of expectations about what will happen in the environment (which can be innate and instinctive) is broken. It occurs only when a phenomenon comes upon the scene decked out with the character of "novelty." This becomes intelligible when we reflect that the driving impulse which we originally experience in our own action is objectified and made into an activity of which things are the agent [*Subjekt*]. A further characteristic of the primitive's causal question is indicated by the form his question takes: "Who is responsible?" (the word *aitia* in Greek means "responsibility" and "cause" at the same time). The causal question originally has more to do with an unwished-for event of negative value than with one of positive value (e.g., "To whom is credit due for that?"). This clearly proves the *moral* origin of the causal concept. Closely linked with this is the fact that originally no distinction is made between what are later called natural law and ethical law (the law of the "ought"). Its origin is shown even more clearly by the fact, which we can illustrate with a thousand examples, that all causes are originally seen as personal and moral, while every natural event is seen as the result of the action of a "spirit" or a "demon," including those events whose empirical preconditions are very well known. For instance, the birth of a man, even after men knew the connection between the act of procreation and birth, was traced back to the possession of the wife by a demon.[57]

The causal concept became objective in the history of the spirit only very slowly and by gradual stages. In place of "Who is responsible?" the question increasingly became "What is responsible?" Consequently, we must say that the slow dismantling of moral explanations in favor of objective ones, the slow exculpation and removal of guilt in the conception of events in the world, is a basic tendency in the development of the human spirit. All mythical cosmogonies display at the start a preference for the historical mode of explanation over any explanation in terms of laws. It is a further basic law of the

---

57. Almost all of the features of the most primitive notion of causality mentioned here appear in L. Lévy-Bruhl, *La Mentalité primitive* (Paris, 1922). [English translation, *The Primitive Mentality* (Boston: Beacon Press, 1966).—TRANS.] See also my essay "Probleme einer Soziologie des Wissens." [*Die Wissensformen und die Gesellschaft*, pp. 65–68.—TRANS.]

unfolding of the causal concept that the objectification of this first stage does not pass directly over to the behavior of inorganic events or those grasped as inorganic. The transition to these is mediated by that organological causal conception of inanimate nature which is still present, e.g., in the *Physics* of Aristotle. The process of purifying the causal category of the concrete accompaniments of the primary experience, a process which continues until we reach the assumption of a reciprocal causal relation of things which is free of any goal, aim, or value, rests on the progressive removal of certain components of the original experience. The course of the causal concept is shown with total clarity in the phases of this development.

The causal idea which arose in this way owes its validity in the case of everything we perceive and can bring into our perceptual grasp to the fact that every possible perception takes place through the drives and impulses to move against and in opposition to the source of resistance (that is, the "real") underlying our perceptual "images." Everything which we perceive must, before we perceive it, in some way address and interest our vital drives. For this reason the objectification of the primary experience must always be possible even independently of all our contingent perceptual experiences. This means that, although the causal concept is created out of our living experience of activity, and although its origin has not the least to do with purely rational acts and principles and can in no way be viewed as a "rational" a priori of our experience, it is nonetheless necessarily applicable to everything which a living creature can experience and perceive. The immediate outcome of the objectification of the category of cause and its application to the world of objects is the principle that we can experience nothing which is not a link in one and the same causal nexus, within which even our own lived-body, objectified into one corporeal body among others, forms one link. We have seen that the temporal, like the spatial, unity of things and data presupposes this basic principle of universal reciprocal action. The application of this principle makes the objectification of space and time possible. Even the unity (= oneness) of space and time presupposes the unity of the dynamic nexus of action and is in no way its consequence.

The priority of our experience of causal action (an experience which we have in every one of our movements and actions *before* this movement brings about a reaction in our "sensations") is carried over to the causal relation between inanimate things in the environment. Hume thought that if one billiard ball strikes another and, as we say, "sets it in motion," the causal relation grasped here [*miterfasste*] between the ball A and the ball B is nothing more than a result of the frequent experiences we have had of the succession of similar phenomena of motion. Accordingly, we are led to assume that the ball B will change its place only because an idea is forced upon us by the so-called rules of association. If we take a case in which a percipient subject has previously perceived only a single instance of this occurrence, and where, second (because some unknown force, whatever it may be, causes it to remain in place), the ball B stands still and is not set in motion, then, Hume had to conclude, the concept of "causing an effect" would have to remain totally unknown to this subject. Only the regularity of the repeated occurrence of analogous events should, according to Hume, evoke the ideas of cause and effect. Hume's notion is certainly false. Even in the case mentioned, the subject would *experience* the "effect" of the ball A on B and, since he is "surprised" that the ball B does not assume the dynamic movement of the ball A which precedes its change of place, he would look for a special "reason" why the ball B stands still.

It is not my purpose here to pursue the particular formation of this central experience of the causal category in various regions. This formation depends entirely on the peculiarity of the various essential regions of being and the associated forms of law. The form of formal-mechanical law, which ties the occurrence of an effect to the spatial proximity of the cause, is only one form among many others. It presupposes that the strictly identical nature of the cause can recur identically in different places and at different times. We have already shown that this presupposition is in no way rationally a priori, any more than it is due to sense perception and induction from sense perception; in the last analysis it results from the fact that everything which can recur in the same form in the course of the world, and thus can be controlled by our actions and movements, enjoys a conspicuous advantage as far as possible perceptibility is concerned. If it were not a law that a living thing prefers the uniformity of the course of the world over the absence of uniformity in all its possible perceptions, then the formation of the empty forms of space and time could not take place. Nothing then could remain identical during the course of motion. It is the presupposition of formal-mechanical lawfulness which makes it possible for images to have certain "positions" in space and time; this makes it possible for position and content to get detached from one another in representation and to seem to be alterable independently of one another. This proves that relative space and relative time and the principle of formal-mechanical causality are only parts of one and the same structure of being which is all of a piece.

The entire formal-mechanical structure can in no way be applied to the constitution of the world independently of its existential relativity to living creatures, for the existence of this structure is completely relative to the sensory-motor system of living things. It is obvious that this structure lacks validity as well for the very life-process to which its existence is relative. Consequently, the form of the laws of life must deviate completely from this form of causal law.

However, it is even more obvious that the structure described has no validity for the spiritual acts of persons. This structure first arises out of the question "What would the course of nature be like if there were no subjects of vital movement and no living creatures generally, and if there were no free, spiritual persons who determine themselves in accordance with their own form of law?" It is only if we are not conscious of the artificial abstraction from the existential relativity of this structure to life and of life, in turn, to spirit, that the illusion is created that this structure is valid for the absolute reality of the world.[58]

58. See, on this point, "Erkenntnis und Arbeit."

Index